LIBERTY, EQUALITY, AND HUMBUG

LIBERTY, EQUALITY, AND HUMBUG

ORWELL'S POLITICAL IDEALS

DAVID DWAN

OXFORD

UNIVERSITY PRESS

OXFORD
UNIVERSITY PRESS

Great Clarendon Street, Oxford, OX2 6DP,
United Kingdom

Oxford University Press is a department of the University of Oxford.
It furthers the University's objective of excellence in research, scholarship,
and education by publishing worldwide. Oxford is a registered trade mark of
Oxford University Press in the UK and in certain other countries

First Edition published in 2018

Impression: 1

Published in the United States of America by Oxford University Press
198 Madison Avenue, New York, NY 10016, United States of America

British Library Cataloguing in Publication Data
Data available

Library of Congress Control Number: 2018938175

ISBN 978–0–19–873852–7

Printed and bound in
Great Britain by Clays Ltd, Elcograf S.p.A.

For Aida and Rahel

Acknowledgements

This book was written in three universities and drew on friendships made in each. I discussed my initial ideas for the book with Mark Burnett, Debbie Lisle, Andrew Pepper, Adrian Streete, Caroline Sumpter, Ramona Wray, and Ed Larrissy at Queen's University Belfast and am grateful for their encouragement and advice. At York, I gained enormously from conversations with John Bowen, Hugh Haughton, Adam Kelly, Michelle Kelly, and Clare Westall. I owe a particular debt to Emilie Morin, who believed in the book when I didn't and read my Introduction at short notice. Several people at Oxford have been generous with their time and talents: Matt Bevis, Alan Bogg, Andrew Dean, Roy Foster, Kate McLaughlin, Dana Mills, Conor Morrissey, and David Russell looked at chapters and suggested several improvements. I am particularly indebted to Marina MacKay, who whipped through a big chunk of the manuscript with characteristic insight and humour.

At Hertford, Charlotte Brewer and Emma Smith could not have been more supportive and I feel blessed to have them as colleagues. I also owe much to Stefan Collini, Tarik Kochi, Benjamin Kohlmann, and Phil Tinline for their input on key sections of the book. Theo Dombrowski read the full manuscript and subjected it to a demanding form of verbal hygiene. I am forever in his debt.

I am also beholden to the anonymous readers at OUP, to Aimee Wright for her help and encouragement, and to Jacqueline Norton, who embodies everything one could want from an editor. Thanks are due too to Charles Jarvis for research assistance and to Lucia Alden for help editing the manuscript. Parts of the book appeared earlier in *ELH* and *Philosophy and Literature* and I am grateful to the editors of both journals for allowing me to reuse some of this material here. Thanks also to Curtis Brown for permission to cite Auden.

The writing of this book would have been a lot less fun—and its argument a lot poorer—without the friendship of Chris Insole. The Dwans and the Edemariams have been unstinting in their support and I have drawn upon it repeatedly. My greatest debt is to Aida Edemariam, whose fierce sense of truth has improved the book no end. It is dedicated to her and to our daughter Rahel, who has brought more joy to the last six years than I can say.

Contents

Introduction

George Orwell is watching you and you're watching him. Britain pays its respects in the form of the Orwell Prize, the Orwell Lecture, and, more recently, Orwell Day—which in its inaugural year in 2013 generated an Orwell season on the BBC. A statue of Orwell now stands outside Broadcasting House in London (though it triggered hot debate about the appropriateness of the icon's dress) and he continues to tower over broadsheet journalism. Events from the invasion of Iraq to Britain's secession from the EU trigger the inevitable question in the newspapers: 'What would Orwell say?'

The same thought-experiment is, of course, regularly repeated in the British Houses of Parliament. Countless proposals—from the Special Powers Act of 1972 ('the embodiment of George Orwell's 1984'), to the Data Protection Bill of 1983 ('George Orwell's 1984 come to life'), to the Community Charges Bill of 1990 ('an Orwellian dream come true'), to the Gender Recognition Bill of 2004 ('an Orwellian nightmare'), to the Counter-Terrorism and Security Act of 2015 ('how Orwell would have shuddered')—have been subjected to the Orwell-test. In Westminster, it seems, it is always 1984. Some MPs have stressed the banality of this rhetoric, emphasizing its tendency to mislead through histrionic analogizing, but this has done little to check the cult of George either in Parliament or elsewhere. Orwell continues to play a key role in the political education of the young in Britain: *Nineteen Eighty-Four* tends to top teachers' list of books that 'all children should read before leaving secondary school' and it is likely to remain in this position for some time. Since the election of Donald Trump, it appears that *Nineteen Eighty-Four* is once again a best-seller in America, though ever since the beginnings of the Cold War, Orwell has had his cheerleaders in the US.

Orwell-worship in Britain and America has inevitably triggered a sizable counter-movement. Since the death of Orwell in 1950, a long line of critics—from Isaac Deutscher to Will Self—has queried his political and cultural achievements. He continues to be taken to task—as a snitch, as a reactionary, and as an intellectual mediocrity—but ultimately, the iconoclasts and the idolaters seem to be locked into a lovers' quarrel, each blast and counter-blast merely entrenching the thin moustachioed face in the imagination of the next generation.

So Orwell is part of the political vocabulary of our times, yet, partly because of this popularity, what he stands for remains opaque. It is a cliche about a cliche to suggest that the term 'Orwellian' means very little—though its very vagueness heightens its general nimbus of spookiness. In Richard Rorty's eyes, Orwell was a man who served 'human liberty'. However, liberty can mean any number of things and it certainly means different things in Orwell's writings. In an age of 'alternative facts', Orwell's investment in 'truth' seems particularly salient; nonetheless, he also stressed the political advantages of collective illusions. How these different views can be squared is not entirely straightforward, yet given Orwell's centrality to our civic culture, the interpretative task remains an important one. This book tries to account for Orwell's apparent inconsistencies by exploring the broader moral conflict at the centre of his work. I focus in particular on the ways in which the conflict plays itself out in Orwell's views on justice and its constituent ends. His various ideological leaps and pivots, I shall argue, are both interesting and instructive, because they highlight the extreme difficulty of getting justice right. Like many, I regard Orwell as a great political educator, but less for the solutions he proffered than for the problems he embodied and the questions he allows us to ask.

Of course, several fine treatments of Orwell's politics exist, but this study aims to do two distinctive things: a) to test the coherence and abiding value of his political opinions by subjecting them to a more philosophically oriented analysis than they have so far received, and b) to make sense of his views by situating them within wider traditions of political thought.

Orwell would probably have disapproved. The first aim flies in the face of his own strictures about philosophy (I'll say more on this in a moment). The second objective chafes against his sense of himself as a maverick. He was a man who was hostile to smelly orthodoxies and preferred to do all of his own thinking for himself. The lines he cited from a nineteenth-century evangelical hymn say much about his aspirations to independence:

> Dare to be a Daniel,
> Dare to stand alone;
> Dare to have a purpose firm,
> Dare to make it known.

Orwell dared to be a Daniel and inspired others to dare the same. But the fact that he advertised his autonomy through borrowed lines—written by the American Philip Bliss, who drew in turn on a broader tradition of religious dissent—may say something about its ambiguous nature. Orwell's desire to stand alone has often been taken at face value and it has fostered a strangely decontextualized view of his political beliefs. This makes his views more original than they are, but it also renders them less intelligible and often less controversial than they might otherwise be. So this book places Orwell alongside some of his contemporaries—R. H. Tawney (one of the few socialists he professed to like), Professor Harold Laski (with whom he enjoyed a much testier relationship), the philosopher and public intellectual Bertrand Russell (an under-appreciated influence), as well as Wells, Shaw, and the Auden gang—considering these voices, often in some detail, as a foil and frame for his work. The design of the book is to show how Orwell's views emerged as part of a shared conversation about the nature of justice and of the good (it says a lot about Orwell's moralized vision of politics that these ends often amounted to the same thing).

At various points in the book I try to extend the scope of this conversation by situating it within a wider history of political thought. Of course, Orwell is always liable to cut a curious figure within such a history. He may have wanted to make 'political writing into an art', but it is hard to say that he ever produced a distinctive corpus of political thought. In many respects, he seems to have bequeathed a rhetoric rather than a doctrine to posterity—a reusable set of phrases in which some are more equal than others, two plus two is generally five, speech is frequently newspeak, and brothers tend to be on the big side. Or he presides over an attitude rather than a coherent set of propositions—a pose of republican vigilance where truth is baldly told to power and even rudeness helps to keep society civil. The extent to which the attitude or the rhetoric is reducible to anything more than a set of platitudes—all power corrupts, eternal vigilance is the price of freedom, truth is good—is debatable. His political 'oeuvre' amounts to a series of polemical responses to specific events—Franco's coup in Spain, the abuse of power in Russia, Hitler's acts of conquest; they are not integrated efforts to produce a coherent system.

Yet Orwell's political thinking partly derives its strength from these contingencies, for they allowed him to stress-test the traditions and ideals upon which he draws (though, clearly, he was rarely in full control of the tests). We can map the challenges he presents for political philosophy without ascribing to him a rigour to which he never aspired. He was at best a 'political thinker' in Leo Strauss' sense of the term, not a 'political philosopher'. According to Strauss, the political thinker was an eminently practical person: he got his hands dirty, he delivered public speeches, he might even write stories and poems in an attempt to mobilize and persuade. The political thinker could argue vigorously, but his arguments were usually a means of vindicating pre-existing convictions or received myths. The political philosopher, on the other hand, was 'primarily interested in, or attached to, the truth'. This character's terrain was the treatise—the genre most suited to the task of replacing 'opinions about the political fundamentals by knowledge regarding them'. Not everyone would retain this Platonic confidence in the distinguishability of truth from opinion, particularly where politics was concerned. Yet it is easy to see how Orwell's brand of polemic might have made him a thinker rather than a philosopher in Strauss' books.

Orwell's own definition of politics says something about the way he practised it: behind all political activity, he argued, was a desire 'to push the world in a certain direction, to alter other people's idea of the kind of society that they should strive after'. Like others before him, he had no wish simply to describe the world; his aim was to change it. Though he would stress the political importance of objectivity, he would also cast politics as an irreducibly partisan exercise. When push came to shove, one had to take sides. Orwell claimed to be on the side of 'the oppressed'—no doubt a pretty plastic friend—and for a while at least his politics boiled down to a simple dictum: 'the oppressed are always right and the oppressors are always wrong'. He would soon declare this view mistaken, but he continued to admit that his politics derived from a strong 'feeling of partisanship'. Solidarity did not necessarily compromise objectivity, in Orwell's eyes, because he was convinced that 'some causes are objectively better than others'. Despite or because of this strong confidence in the objectivity of values, the serene neutrality of Strauss' philosopher was not something Orwell ever tried to cultivate.

Orwell was an aggressively practical operator, but I shall argue that the problems he encountered in politics had an irreducible conceptual element. The philosophical dimensions of these difficulties can easily be described without miscasting him as philosopher or political theorist. After all, he often stressed the futility and moral hazards of theory, and was a great believer in common sense—a faculty he defined as the 'acceptance of the obvious and contempt for quibbles and abstractions'. He had little time for misdirected depth. 'There is one way of avoiding thoughts', he insisted, 'and that is to think too deeply'. Philosophy, he seemed to feel, epitomized this imbecile rigour. So Bertrand Russell's *Human Knowledge: Its Scope and Limits* (1948)—by no means the most trying instance of the discipline—was enough to make him conclude 'that philosophy should be forbidden by law'. However, these declarations should not be taken entirely at face value (he had at least attempted to read Russell and would review and critique his political works). Indeed, Orwell's strictures against philosophy should probably be situated in a broader tradition of philosophy-bashing—an ancient and very British sport in which many philosophers themselves gamely partook. As Russell noted in *Philosophy and Politics* (1947)—another text that Orwell appears to have owned—the 'British are distinguished among the nations of modern Europe, on the one hand by the excellence of their philosophers, and on the other hand, by their contempt for philosophy'. 'In both respects', Russell quipped, 'they show their wisdom'.

Moreover, this wise contempt had a distinguished political history. It had been pressed into service, for instance, during the French Revolution—most successfully perhaps in Edmund Burke's *Reflections on the Revolution in France* (1790)—and would be revived in the 1920s and '30s. So Burke's condemnation of the 'philosophical fanatics' of France could be adapted to meet the new fanaticisms emerging from Russia, Italy, and Germany. The philosophical credentials of Bolshevism and fascism were certainly open to dispute—in Russell's eyes 'there is no philosophy of Fascism' (it was too irrational for that); such triumphant insanity, he believed, could only be the subject of 'a psycho-analysis'. Others, however, would accuse Bolshevik schoolmen and the fascist intelligentsia of trading their humanity for an abstract theory. 'To follow the syllogism alone', Stanley Baldwin reminded his English brethren, 'is a short cut to the bottomless pit'. Fortunately, for people like Baldwin, the Englishman's sturdy pragmatism 'preserves him from strange alien forms of political upheaval to which more logical or, if you like, more intellectual races have succumbed'.

Orwell also shied away from the syllogism and stressed the unsystematic character of the English: they had no need 'for an ordered system of thought or even for the use of logic'. It was a great comfort to him that they 'would never develop into a nation of philosophers'. Yet, as Russell pointed out, a scepticism about philosophy when pursued systematically enough begins to look a bit like a philosophy. Orwell may not have taken his contempt for the discipline to these lengths, but his mistrust of abstruse method gave a significant pattern to his politics and invested it with its rich vein of paradox. He spent a lot of time thinking about the dangers of thinking—or at least a certain style of it—and he deliberated at length over the value of remaining intuitive. Excess of intellectuality, he insisted, was a form of 'evasion'. In Orwell's eyes, our most basic moral responses did not require a theoretical defence. The common man—unfortunately, all too uncommon in Europe in the 1930s and '40s—simply knows that it isn't right 'to march into the houses of harmless little Jewish shopkeepers and set fire to their furniture'. He does not need the help of Strauss' philosopher to determine why this is the case; indeed, in these practical scenarios, the sophisticated intellectual is all too often a moral idiot. 'Any intellectual', Orwell opined, 'can make you out a splendid "case" for smashing the German Trade Unions and torturing the Jews'. But the common man—who in this fond yet patrician vision of things has 'no intellect, only instinct and tradition'—simply knows that these practices are wrong.

So for Orwell, then, our ordinary moral intuitions—so regularly appealed to in his journalism and his fiction—provide both the conditions and limits of political thought. They serve as its conditions because we would have no orientation in moral or political space without them. They also form its limits, because they mark the boundary-point of rational justification itself. If it is obscene to supply reasons for torturing Jews, it is equally repugnant to furnish reasons for *not* torturing them. Only a monster or an idiot—and Orwell's intellectual was usually both—would cavil about these matters. Faced with a clash between intuition and theory, Orwell suggests that it is the theory that should be abandoned. But intellectuals, he believed, usually took the opposite approach, forfeiting their moral feelings in the name of a monstrous consistency. This unhinged dedication to a system partly explained why 'nearly every modern intellectual has gone over to some or other form of totalitarianism'.

Orwell's sense of the moral limits of 'theory' marks, in fact, one of his more interesting contributions to political thought. It also helps to explain why much of this political thinking was pursued through the newspaper article, the essay, and the novel rather than in the form of a theoretical tract (how fiction or the novel might constitute a particular kind of political thinking will be addressed later). However, it does not take too much thought to see the limitations of his anti-theoretical animus. Intuitions, as Orwell suggests, provide us with some moral coordinates, but they frequently point in different and rival directions. Orwell's certainly did. He insisted, for instance, that socialism was 'elementary common sense' but entertained different intuitions about the content of socialism and about the value of 'common sense' itself (it could be 'shallow' and was often sadly insufficient). In such contexts, it would seem to be fairly intuitive to doubt intuition or to seek some wider coherence between warring outlooks through a process of deliberation. These efforts might imply that the impulse to systematize is itself fairly basic. Orwell conceded that the differences between the intellectual and the 'ordinary man' were not as great as people imagined. Yet he often talked up these differences and exaggerated the gap between 'common sense' and theory. When Orwell's own publisher, Victor Gollancz, challenged his 'intellectualist anti-intellectualism', he drew attention to the fact that Orwell's position was far from intuitive or theoretically innocent. Indeed, Orwell's own sense of himself in 1937 as a 'degenerate modern semi-intellectual' was already a semi-acknowledgement of this basic fact. His 'common-sense' socialism rested on long and intricate intellectual traditions in which Orwell himself was substantially immersed. Orwell's pamphlet collection alone—which contains over 2,700 items of political discussion from Trotsky to Harold Laski to G. D. H. Cole—gives some sense of this immersion.

This book draws out the theoretical entanglements of Orwell's ordinary-man's-wisdom. Even his anti-intellectualism, as I have suggested, was intellectually indebted, owing something to political traditions that were once deployed against Jacobinism, but were subsequently used against other exotic diseases. Orwell's defence of everyday moral intuitions was also a polemical intervention into national and international debates about the ethical foundations of socialism. In 'Their Morals and Ours' (1938), Trotsky maintained that there was 'nothing more flat, stale, self-satisfied and cynical than the moral rules of common sense'. Orwell's common sense, however, was aimed against the moral cynicism of people like Trotsky as well as the 'uncommon sense' of men like G. B. Shaw—a figure who, he believed, had invented 'metaphysical reasons for behaving like a scoundrel'. Shaw was one of those on the Left who had cast the morality of common sense aside in his support for Stalin—a 'disgusting murderer' in Orwell's eyes. Viewed in these intellectual contexts, Orwell's position looks a little less intuitive—and a little more interesting—than it might at first appear.

Orwell's plain-man's pose was not theoretically innocent; nor, however, was it always intellectually sophisticated. For example, he often wielded the word 'justice' as though it were a discursive magic wand. Socialism, he boldly declared, meant 'justice and liberty when the nonsense is stripped off'. Yet he seemed to have little sense that both justice and liberty might be the source of social problems as much as their solution. As Harold Laski pointed out in 1937, in a scathing review of *The Road to Wigan Pier*, people had different and rival conceptions of what is just. The issue was exemplified in contemporary Spain: here, according to Laski, people were cheerfully killing each other 'with the profound conviction that "justice" is on their side'. Orwell later admitted that the term 'justice' was one of those words with several irreconcilable meanings, though he never really took the time to clarify what he meant by the concept. Moreover, his own writing continued to enact different and contradictory ideas of what is just. This exposes the limits of his own 'common sense', but, as I hope to argue, it also expresses a more tragic set of conflicts at the heart of justice itself.

Justice, for Orwell, was many-headed. Conceived as an umbrella-concept (as I shall do here), it incorporated a number of different and sometimes rival ideals. This book treats five of these constitutive principles—liberty, equality, solidarity, truth, and happiness—exploring their individual facets and fraught connections across five chapters. These core values, I shall argue, provided the basic grammar of Orwell's politics: seldom justified, they provided the justification for almost everything else. They remained, however, essentially contestable concepts and their meaning and practical ramifications were repeatedly contested throughout Orwell's writing. He was not always in control or even aware of this ideological contest, but his writing, I shall argue, repeatedly casts its animating ideals in different lights, exposing their cracks and limitations.

Precisely because these five principles are both basic and contestable, they represent a better starting-point for grappling with Orwell's politics than the more involved set of 'isms that he and some of his followers have supplied—from the Tory anarchism that he allegedly embraced in his youth to the 'democratic Socialism' he openly espoused in later life. These umbrella terms have their uses—and will be used along the way—but they also beg important questions about fundamental values and give a false unity to a much more conflicted and provisional set of attitudes.

Orwell's attitudinal shifts are, of course, well known: his transformation from the disgruntled policeman who returned from Burma, to the ambivalent socialist who went to Wigan, to the radicalized figure who came back from Spain, to the war-time patriot who felt that England's victory would entail its social revolution, to the happy but politically chastened man who worked for *Tribune*, to the hermit of Jura who tended his garden and predicted a future of horrors. My aim is not to tell this story again, but to show how these phases of his career placed distinctive demands on his political ideals. The focus throughout is thematic, not chronological.

One of my opening claims is that Orwell's politics were self-consciously predicated on the blessed trinity of French revolutionary lore; what Orwell might have meant by 'liberty', 'equality', and 'fraternity' is the concern of the first three chapters of the book. Socialism, he insisted, was a simple application of this happy triad, though he increasingly worried that it had lost sight of its own moral foundations. He therefore longed for the restoration of 'the older conception of Socialism', which had always given pride of place to 'liberty', 'equality', and 'human brotherhood'. Alongside this sense of moral decline, Orwell also feared that 'the very concept of objective truth is fading out of the world'. The basis for this conviction and his reasons for regarding 'truth' as a political virtue will be explored in Chapter 4. As we shall see, Orwell gave serious thought to the cliche that the truth will set people free, but he was never persuaded that it would make them happy. Nor was he convinced that this really mattered. The final chapter of the book examines Orwell's very mixed views on happiness as a political ideal. He claimed, of course, that socialism had nothing to do with happiness, but he also declared that it had everything to do with it. The reasons for this oscillation will be explored in detail.

Since ancient times, happiness has often been cast as a type of harmony between different values that were judged to obtain within the individual and in the community. One of the implications of this book is that this happy balance eluded Orwell and may continue to elude the rest of us. For a start, the holy trinity—liberty, equality, and brotherhood—can often be found at each other's throats. Liberty might plausibly require equitable conditions (as Laski pointed out, 'great inequalities of wealth make impossible the attainment of freedom'), but the attempt to guarantee this equality through State intervention can easily undermine minimalist interpretations of freedom. Indeed, recourse to a centralized State can even contradict equality itself—at least if it is conceived as a radical equalization of power. Orwell presented a very muscular ideal of brotherhood as the inspiration for equality and liberty. However, fraternity had often been conceived as a corrective to the anti-social tendencies of both—a curb to a self-absorbed freedom or a peevish mistrust that might in fact stem from an egalitarian ethos. Brotherhood might keep freedom clubbable, yet it is easy to imagine how it might deprive it of life—a fact advertised in the arresting revolutionary slogan 'Fraternity or Death'.

Orwell tended to downplay these tensions in his own political universe, yet, as I shall argue, they play a major role in his writings. So while he repeatedly expressed a firm 'belief in human brotherhood', its actual practice— even on a rhetorical level—proved to be a much more fraught affair for him. The fraternity of porcupines seemed to suit Orwell best: distance between individuals was necessary, otherwise freedom would suffer. Indeed, freedom is often a deeply anti-social matter in Orwell, but precisely for this reason it is liable to undermine itself (I'll say more about this in Chapter 1). Most of Orwell's major work from *Down and Out in Paris and London* to *Nineteen Eighty-Four* provides a scathing indictment of inequality. Yet he also worried about the ways in which liberty might suffer in the name of equality. Or he was concerned that the attempt to address one type of inequality (say, economic) would trigger another (namely, political). He grew increasingly receptive to the view that the 'attempt to establish liberty and equality always ends up in the police state'—a fact arguably borne out by his last two novels, *Animal Farm* and *Nineteen Eighty-Four*. The overriding pessimism of his late work reflects a stunted form of idealism: it expresses his commitment to liberty, equality, and brotherhood (in this regard, he always remained an old socialist), but his writing records his increasing uncertainty about how these ideals might be institutionalized—a position that could often make him sound like the great Eeyore of the Left.

The aim of the book, therefore, is to examine the civil war in Orwell's republic of ends. If it dwells upon his contradictions, it does not set out to be a hostile analysis, not least because those inconsistencies appear to track real conflicts within justice itself. Of course, some might be inclined to attribute his contradictory performances to intellectual complacency or to aggressive opportunism—coherence being abandoned in the service of good copy or in the desire to squash an opponent. As Orwell himself admitted, a writer's motives are often ugly—driven as they are by vanity, ambition, and vengeance. Orwell was not immune to these grubbier ends, but as Raymond Williams maintained, he also 'expressed much more than himself' in his writings. Whatever psychological portrait we may wish to draw of him, his work has a lot to tell us about the grammar of key political concepts and the awkwardness of ideals. Orwell-worship today can distract us from these difficulties, but proper scrutiny of his work can also reacquaint us with the complexity of our own moral heritage. To those of us who continue to believe in ideals of liberty, equality, or solidarity, his writing mounts a profound challenge.

The possibility remains, of course, that these grand ideals will yield little more than 'humbug'—to use one of Orwell's pet phrases. Values so vague, one might argue, can have scant practical purchase and service at best a toothless moralism. The charge is a damning one and it is one to which Orwell was particularly vulnerable. After all, the moral outlook he brought to politics was often judged to have had its day. As the historian E. H. Carr put it in 1939:'What confronts us in international politics today [is] nothing less than the complete bankruptcy of the conception of morality which has dominated political and economic thought for a century and a half'. Indeed, the meaning and importance of morality as an institution had been disputed on the Left for generations. 'Virtue, morals, ethics', G. B. Shaw reported in his best superman-mode, 'are all a noxious product of private property'. The enemy of socialism, Shaw added, was 'the Good Man'. Orwell, on the other hand, clearly wanted to restore the good man to socialism and it put him on a collision course with people like Shaw.

Orwell was an indefatigable moralist—a firm believer in the objectivity, motivational power, and political significance of moral values. He had no desire for a republic of saints—after all, human beings 'want to be good, but not too good'—but he did wish to restore a notion of 'absolute right and wrong' to politics. Orwell seemed to recognize that this vocation was liable to strike some contemporaries as somewhat old-fashioned. 'I wasn't born for an age like this', one of his poetic personas proclaims, speculating that he would have been a happy vicar in an earlier epoch. Unfortunately, this unhappy conscience is trapped in an 'evil time'—his sense of 'evil' merely confirming his anachronistic vision. Orwell's embattled moralism is worth exploring, for it allows us to test one of the main premises of the book—i.e. that moral concepts *do* matter in politics—against some key debates of his time. More importantly, it will give us a better grasp of Orwell's political style, which was also, of course, a pugnacious style of writing.

Moralism

In his famous essay on Dickens (1940), Orwell set out a basic opposition that dictated the shape of much of his own political thinking. 'The moralist and the revolutionary', he claimed, 'are constantly undermining one another'. His sense of their differences was fairly simple: the moralist believed that social reform presupposed the moral transformation of individuals; the revolutionary assumed that genuine moral change could only happen when society in general had been radically altered.

It is worth noting that Orwell's quintessential revolutionary was Karl Marx—hardly an eccentric choice of candidate shortly after the end of what was soon labelled the 'Marxist decade'. Of course, the extent of Orwell's own knowledge of Marx is still a matter of considerable dispute, but it was difficult to operate as an intellectual—particularly when writing for left-wing publications such as *The Adelphi*, *The Left News*, *Tribune*, and *Partisan Review*—without some awareness of his ideas. 'Marx', he proclaimed in 1937, 'is a difficult author to read, but a crude version of his doctrine is believed in by millions and is in the consciousness of us all'. Or as Christopher Caudwell boldly avowed: 'all contemporary politics are of significance only in so far as they are with Marx or against him'. Some socialists felt uneasy about the dogmatic reverence to which the great man was subject. Echoing Marx's own repudiation of Marxism, Cole declared: 'An "orthodox" Marxist may be learned in the Marxian scriptures: the one thing he cannot be is a follower of Karl Marx'.

Orwell could never be accused of being an 'orthodox' follower—of Marx or indeed of anyone (even perhaps of himself). He named his poodle Marx, but this seems to have been an expression of contempt—for the philosopher, at any rate, if not for the dog. Orwell's seeming dislike of Marx partly reflects the frustration he expressed for all hair-splitters and abstract thinkers. He recoiled from the abstruse metaphysics of a dialectical method, dismissing—in his best common-sense pose—'the pea-and-thimble trick with those three mysterious entities, thesis, antithesis, and synthesis'. The 'superior smiles' and 'polysyllables' of 'Marxist prigs' clearly brought him out in hives. Not all poodles went by the name of Marx, but most Marxists appeared like poodles to him—pretentious versions of the 'gramophone' mind. He disparaged 'the dreary attitude of the typical Marxist towards literature', but it was the apparent amoralism of Marxism that distressed him the most. As he put it in 1940, 'an education in Marxism and similar creeds consists largely in destroying your moral sense'. This conviction, I wish to argue, is key to understanding Orwell's distinctive brand of socialism. Yet the power of Marx's attacks on 'moralising criticism' was something he found difficult to overlook and it produced interesting kinks in his politics and in his style of argument.

In the *Communist Manifesto*, Marx had provocatively dismissed morality as one of those 'bourgeois prejudices' that communism aimed to leave behind. The degree to which this was a dismissal of morality per se or simply a rejection of its bourgeois forms is difficult to determine. In the *German Ideology*, Marx certainly claimed to have 'shattered the basis of *all* morality'. The coherence of a total dismissal of morality is certainly open to dispute: after all, the statement that morality is 'bad' is liable to contradict itself. But not all normativity, perhaps, is 'moral' and many would defend the consistency of Marx's critique of morality, however value-driven it seemed to be. The ambiguity of Marx's own rhetoric made the issue difficult to resolve—and the mixed messages would survive in his followers. 'We do not believe in an eternal morality', Lenin announced. Yet in the same breath he endorsed a seemingly transhistorical criterion of ethics: that which 'serves the purpose of helping human society rise to a higher level and rid itself of the exploitation of labour'. Not wishing to get snared in the subtleties, Trotsky chose to stress Lenin's 'amoralism' and would go on to summarize the basic tenets of this steely outlook: 'that morality is a product of social development; that there is nothing immutable about it; that it serves social interests; that these interests are contradictory; that morality more than any other form of ideology has a class character'. Armed with these convictions, Trotsky aimed to go beyond bourgeois good and evil.

Some in England aspired to a similar transcendence. 'There is not much left of importance in bourgeois ethics', Christopher Caudwell coolly concluded from his grave in 1938 (*Studies in a Dying Culture* would appear a year after Caudwell was killed in Spain). But it was once more unclear whether it was ethics itself or simply its bourgeois forms which had ceased to be important. Caudwell certainly spoke in very general terms about 'morality', dismissing it—alongside religion, metaphysics, and democracy—as one of those 'secondary illusions' soon to be sloughed off. Not everyone on the Left could perfect this insouciance about ethics. R. H. Tawney, for instance, condemned the hackneyed diatribes against 'bourgeois morality' and insisted on the moral foundations of Marxism itself: Marx was 'as saturated with ethics as a Hebrew prophet'. But others worried that Marx's ambiguous assaults on 'morality' had set a very dark example. Writing in the shadow of Stalin's extermination of the Kulaks, the Moscow trials, and the Molotov-Ribbentrop pact, Victor Gollancz had very mixed feelings about Marx's legacy:

> The work of Karl Marx has had many good, and at least one very bad, result: for though moved to do it, as his followers are moved to do theirs, by moral

passion, he ended by appearing to banish from his examination of capitalism any moral considerations whatsoever.

Orwell was in two minds about the moral credentials of Marx. He sometimes cast him as the father of a morally committed politics that his successors would distort, but he also claimed that Marx had done away with moralism. As he put it in 1940: 'Marx exploded a hundred tons of dynamite beneath the moralist position and we are still living in the echo of that tremendous crash'.

Orwell was clearly awed by the explosion, but he remained a committed moralist nonetheless. Ethical concerns, he insisted, should take precedence over everything else: 'human society must be based on common decency, whatever the political and economic forms may be'. This investment in the priority of morals—over politics and economics—arguably inverted Marx's sense of social causation. Rarely pausing over doctrinal nuances, Orwell chided Marxism for writing off morality as mere 'superstructure' and for downplaying its causal significance.

Orwell's antipathy to Marxist methods should not be overstated: as he argued in 1944, 'Marxism may possibly be a mistaken theory, but it is a useful instrument for testing other systems of thought'. And he frequently deployed that instrument to decry the empty moralism of others. Dickens's social criticism, for instance, was taken to task for being 'almost exclusively moral'. Extended odes to charity, Orwell argued, overlooked the structural basis of social problems. Indeed, Dickens's 'whole message' seemed to amount to a toothless platitude: ' "If men would behave decently the world would be decent" '. Yet Orwell would famously go on to defend Dickens's circle of decency: 'it is not such a platitude as it sounds'.

Orwell's sense of decency could sound hopelessly frail, reflecting a naive confidence in the general scope of very specific and historically contingent convictions. As Laski pointed out to Orwell, people 'live too differently to think similarly' about moral affairs. Orwell seemed to concede to the relativity of ethics when he produced his own confessions of a guilty toff (a fashionable genre in the 1930s) in *The Road to Wigan Pier*. 'All my notions—notions of good and evil, of pleasant and unpleasant, of funny and serious, of ugly and beautiful—are essentially *middle-class* notions'. It is hard to determine what Orwell meant by an essentially middle-class notion: it is one thing to admit that one's beliefs were acquired as part of a group or even that they are characteristic of a group; it is another thing to say that they serve the interests of that group; it is another matter again to say that these notions have no meaning or validity outside of one's group. Orwell could certainly inveigh against 'bourgeois illusion' in ways that suggested that the illusoriness of such belief was a mere function of its bourgeois character. Yet, like Tawney, he refused to believe that virtues ceased to be virtues when practised by the middle classes. So while his comrades on the Left would insist that 'bourgeois culture is seriously ill', Orwell would often recoil from this type of cant. As he wearily complained: 'Everyone knows, or ought to know by this time, how it runs: the bourgeoisie are "dead"... bourgeois culture is bankrupt, bourgeois "values" are despicable, and so on and so forth'. Bourgeois-baiting was a bore.

Behind Orwell's criticisms of verbal class-warfare we repeatedly find a strong confidence in the existence of universal moral norms. Even his acknowledgement of moral variation confirmed his entrenched universalism. Take, for instance, his breezily tendentious remarks about proletarian virtue: 'It is universally agreed', he announced in 1944, 'that the working classes are far more moral than the upper classes'. So even the nasties could agree on what goodness was and who the good guys were. Here and elsewhere Orwell exaggerated the amount of moral consensus that was to be found in the world. Many of his stock phrases exude an aggressive presumption ('Everyone knows', 'anyone able to use his eyes knows', 'everyone who uses his brain knows', 'everyone who is not a fool knows'). He was clearly no relativist about knowledge or about the virtues it might reveal. He spoke in a general key for 'All people who are morally sound', 'all decent people', 'all sensitive people', 'Everyone, barring fools or scoundrels', insulting in advance those who might happen to hold different views. His 'common man' was a loaded dice—used to posit a moral consensus and to account for its absence (the common man was everywhere disenfranchised).

The bullishness of Orwell's rhetoric may betray some feeling that the universalism it so confidently advertises was, in fact, on the wane—a decline he sometimes attributed to the weakening of religion. Of course, it was far from clear that moral absolutes had ever depended on religious conviction (Orwell had himself insisted in a letter to Humphry House that 'common decency' did not depend on 'any transcendental belief'). Orwell's own sense of decency seemed to have survived the demise of God in his life, although there may have been an element of theatre in all this moral confidence (Anthony Powell certainly felt that there was a 'touch of make-believe, the air of acting a part' in his friend). A belief in universal moral values might as well be performed, if it could no longer be discovered. He was, after all, a great believer in the constitutive power of shared illusions—as he put it in

1941, 'a mask can alter the expression of a face'. His confident universalism may have been a mask, but it was certainly at odds with some of the dogmas of contemporary Marxism—Lenin's and Trotsky's much-repeated conviction that there were no 'supra-class morals'.

Not only did Orwell object to the relativism of contemporary Marxism, he also took issue with its moral psychology. 'If no man is ever motivated by anything except class interests', Orwell inquired, 'why does every man constantly pretend that he is motivated by something else?' Again, the mere pretence was practically binding and had more social influence than Marxists were prepared to allow. Here Orwell also contested some of the explanatory methods of Marxism: namely, its causal and functional explanations of moral belief. Marx had often engaged in a type of genetic criticism, casting certain class 'interests' as the cause or origin of specific ideas. He had also assumed that the genetic history of a specific belief went some way to undermining its pretentions to impartiality and universality. But Orwell found it difficult to accept that the specific origins of a belief precluded it from being just or true. Ironically, he made this point in defence of Marx. 'Marx's ultimate motives may well have been envy and spite, but this does not prove that his conclusions were false'. Here Orwell spoke of personal motives rather than class interests, but his point could also serve as a repudiation of Marx's form of genetic criticism.

When insisting on the irrelevance of Marx's motives, Orwell drew on a type of functional explanation that Marx had himself practised. The underlying assumption of this method was that the meaning of an idea or action depended primarily on its social function or pragmatic consequences. 'Actions have results, irrespective of their motives', Orwell declared, and he often took the view that 'objective' consequences should take precedence over 'subjective' intentions when interpreting the meaning of social phenomena. He repeatedly invoked this functional method to explain the actions—or lack of action—of pacifists. 'Objectively the pacifist is pro-Nazi', he declared in 1941, whatever his or her subjective views on the matter. But he later recoiled from this crude form of functionalism:

> We are told that it is only people's objective actions that matter, and their subjective feelings are of no importance. Thus, pacifists, by obstructing the war effort, are 'objectively' aiding the Nazis: and therefore the fact that they may be personally hostile to Fascism is irrelevant. I have been guilty of saying this myself more than once. The same argument is applied to Trotskyists. Trotskyists are often credited, at any rate by Communists, with being active and conscious

agents of Hitler; but when you point out the many and obvious reasons why this is unlikely to be true, the 'objectively' line of talk is brought forward again.

If Orwell had once prioritized 'results' over 'motives', he now rejected this position as both dishonest and naive. The phenomenology or inner life of moral actions could not be rudely cast aside, for the motives we bring to bear on our actions are irreducible constituents of their meaning. Moreover, he firmly believed that motivations served as the actual cause of actions and needed to be consulted not only to explain, but also to predict people's behaviour. 'If you disregard people's motives', he concluded, 'it becomes much harder to foresee their actions'. The moral cynicism of Marxism, he argued, undermined its power as a predictive science. Indeed, when it came to prophecy, Marxists were not much more successful than the followers of Nostradamus.

When charting the ideological commitments of Orwell's moral style, it is also important to note how his critique of functionalism mirrored his broader criticisms of moral consequentialism—namely, the view that the consequences of an action are a necessary and sufficient determinant of its value. As Stephen Spender put it in 1937: ' "The ends are judged by the means"—this phrase has become almost a slogan among idealists now'. A year later, Trotsky chose to defend this principle in characteristically pugnacious terms. Trotsky appreciated that consequential justifications could produce an infinite regress: at some point, the process of justifying some 'x' in the light of 'y' and that 'y' in relation to 'z' must stop with some end in itself. That end for Trotsky was 'the increase of the power of man over nature and . . . the abolition of the power of man over man'. The principle might seem a bit misty, but it allowed Trotsky to justify any number of things, from the use of lies to systematic murder. Trotsky was no sentimental humanist. 'As for us', he proudly admitted in 1920, 'we were never concerned with the Kantian-priestly and vegetarian-Quaker prattle about the "sacredness of human life" '. Language about the sanctity of human life, after all, was mere hypocrisy in a world where the majority of human beings were systematically exploited.

Orwell seemed to have shared Trotsky's distaste for Quakers and vegetarians, but he recoiled from his brand of consequentialism. There were, he suggested, moral limits to what one could do even in the fight against exploitation. In fact, as far as Orwell was concerned, 'the theory that the end justifies the means' already expressed an authoritarian mindset. Arthur Koestler had clearly made the case against this consequentialism in *Darkness at Noon* (1940). Here, for instance, the true brutality of the dictum that the end justifies the means ('all means, without exception') is visited upon a former advocate of that same principle, Comrade Rubashov (in Orwell's eyes a literary substitute for Trotsky or some 'relatively civilised figure among the Old Bolsheviks'). Despite Orwell's qualms about Koestler's pessimism, he regarded the novel as a 'masterpiece' and he would go on to condemn consequentialism in similar terms in his own fiction. Winston and Julia, for instance, seem to believe that virtually everything is permitted in the service of revolution:

> 'You are prepared to give your lives?'
> 'Yes.'
> 'You are prepared to commit murder?'
> 'Yes.'
> 'To commit acts of sabotage which may cause the death of hundreds of innocent people?'
> 'Yes.'
> 'To betray your country to foreign powers?'
> 'Yes.'
> 'You are prepared to cheat, to forge, to blackmail, to corrupt the minds of children, to distribute habit-forming drugs, to encourage prostitution, to disseminate venereal diseases—to do anything which is likely to cause demoralisation and weaken the power of the Party?'
> 'Yes.'
> 'If, for example, it would somehow serve our interests to throw sulphuric acid in a child's face—are you prepared to do that?'
> 'Yes.'

The conversation may not be the most plausible ever penned. Once it has been established that Winston and Julia are prepared to murder and send hundreds of innocents to their deaths, the questions about corrupting young minds, drug-dealing, and even prostitution might seem to be redundant, even prudish. There is some titillation too, perhaps, in the imagined forms of moral sacrifice—not least the arduous revolutionary labour of spreading venereal disease. The sadism, moreover, has its saccharine elements: in the all-too-literal acid test of political commitment the hackneyed figure of the child is pressed into service as the ultimate moral threshold. Yet the point seems clear: Winston and Julia are no set of Kantian-priests or vegetarian-Quakers; they believe that virtually all means are justified in the service of revolution. Like Rubashov, they are forced to experience the full implications of this logic at the end of the novel. In an ironic nod to consequentialism, Orwell's novel spells out the grim consequences of this credo.

Of course, it is easy to exaggerate Orwell's resistance to consequentialist forms of justification. He may have berated the 'amoralism' of Auden's phrase the 'necessary murder' in 'Spain 1937', but Orwell seemed to accept that some killing was necessary enough, particularly in the context of war. Orwell insisted on representing war-time killing as murder, but however morally disapproving the language, he argued that it was often the lesser of two evils. In 1941 he condemned the government's scruples about attacking neutrals (it was 'merely the sign of a subconscious desire to fail'). 'People don't have scruples', he announced, 'when they are fighting for a cause they believe in'. When contemplating a socialist revolution in England in the same year, he had no difficulty with the fact that 'it may be necessary to use violence'. Though he hoped this could be kept to a minimum, he could also sound pretty unmoved about the full extent of blood-letting ('I dare say the London gutters will have to run with blood. All right, let them, if it is necessary'). In 1944, however, we learn that 'all efforts to regenerate society *by violent means* lead to the cellars of the Ogpu'. He cast this as a ventriloquization of Koestler's views, but it may have also been a description of his own revised outlook.

Orwell's sense of the moral limits of political action was pretty mobile, but he had no doubt that there were such limits. As we have seen, this made him deeply sceptical of contemporary Marxism—a 'German theory interpreted by Russians and unsuccessfully transplanted to England', according to this stern policeman of cultural borders. But Orwell's defence of moral ideals would also put him in conflict with a not unrelated school of politics known as 'realism'. In Orwell's eyes, this cynical and even amoral doctrine had assumed a dark pre-eminence in the modern world, with disastrous ramifications for everyone. This realist moment constitutes another key context for understanding Orwell's political voice—in particular, its strange mixture of surly idealism and moral combativeness. He cast himself as realism's enemy, but, as we shall see, he also had a deep fascination for what he professed to despise.

Realism

'Realism' was a hot topic in the 1930s and '40s—although what it stood for was not always very clear. Orwell believed that it was reducible to the credo 'Might is Right', although this was a very crude shorthand indeed. Realism's origins were often traced back to Machiavelli—a derivation that tended to focus on the cynical advisor of princes rather than on the passionate defender of *virtù* that emerges from the *Discorsi*. Orwell called realism 'the game of Macchiavelli' [*sic.*], but he also attributed its modern reinvention to Otto von Bismarck. As Bismarck declared in his first speech as Prussian minister-president in 1862: 'the great questions of our time will not be decided by speeches and majority decisions...but by Blood and Iron'. For all its dismissiveness about speech-making, the rhetoric made a deep impression and was deemed by many in Europe to embody a new style of politics.

The style certainly took off. Bolsheviks prided themselves on being realists in Bismarck's sense and duly borrowed the metaphors of blood and iron to promote their ends. Lukács would praise Lenin's 'realism'; others would do the same for Stalin. Though often used as a pejorative term in Britain, realism had its liberal defenders. As Orwell noted, Chamberlain had defended the policy of appeasement on realist grounds. One notable appeaser was E. H. Carr, whose controversial work *The Twenty Years' Crisis* (1939) was soon viewed as one of the classics of political realism. Many of the beliefs that Carr attributed to realists were anathema to people like Orwell. So while Orwell wished to restore a moral objectivity to politics, Carr's realist assumed that all morality was relative, not universal. Orwell insisted that basic decency was a prerequisite for all other values, but the realist took a very different view: morality was the product of power, not its foundation or ultimate arbiter. It's not clear that Orwell read Carr directly, though he certainly encountered his ideas through Hayek's *The Road to Serfdom* (which he reviewed in April 1944). Moreover, by the end of the 1940s, he knew Carr well enough to include him in his notorious notebook of politically suspicious figures (though here Orwell chose to issue him with the waiver 'Appeaser only'). Orwell also took his measurements of realism from James Burnham—the ex-Trotskyite professor at NYU who became an international name in the 1940s. Orwell would review Burnham's *The Machiavellians* (1943) on two occasions, treating it as a disturbing ode to realism and to 'power politics'.

Since Burnham's book epitomized all that was wrong with contemporary political life for Orwell, it is worth sketching out some of its main claims. Machiavelli, in Burnham's eyes, was the first to supplant wishful thinking about politics for a proper science of power. In this disenchanted science, all rulers aim to consolidate and to increase their power through either force or fraud. As Burnham declared: 'No theory, no promises, no morality, no amount of good will, no religion will restrain power'. 'Only power can restrain power', he explained. Orwell largely ignored the ways in which this unsentimental vision was accompanied by a fairly earnest commitment to freedom. In Burnham's books, freedom was best secured not through moral exhortation and good will, but through the practical division of power. By making force contend against force, power would constrain itself, allowing freedom some chance of taking root. None of this freedom-talk impressed Orwell. Instead, he picked up on Burnham's desire—pursued with delighted *sang-froid*—to depose moralism in politics.

Burnham did not deny the political significance of 'moral ideas', but he often adopted a functional explanation of their meaning. The political effects of moral ideals were what mattered; moreover, their practical results were often at odds with their ostensible content. So while democracy might imply popular self-rule, this idea was invariably deployed by elites to consolidate power. In Orwell's disapproving summary of Burnham's basic position: 'All moral codes, all idealistic conceptions of politics [. . .] are simply lies conscious or unconscious, covering the naked struggle for power'.

Orwell was convinced, however, that this cynical vision was 'no more scientific than the idealistic theories that it aimed to debunk'. For one thing, it seemed to get human psychology wrong. By casting power as an end in itself, it overlooked the reasons why people usually sought power—namely for other ends. It also ignored the ways in which people believe and fight for their ideals. Orwell thus chose to emphasize the considerable resistance 'realists' had encountered across Europe:

> In our own day Mussolini, the conscious pupil of Machiavelli and Pareto, does not seem to have made a very brilliant success of things. And the Nazi regime, based on essentially Machiavellian principles, is being smashed to pieces by the forces which its own lack of scruple conjured up.

Realism, therefore, was self-undermining: 'the Machiavellian system', he argued, 'fails even by its own test of material success'. The self-defeating nature of power politics needed to be brought home to modern Machiavellians. 'If there is a way out of the moral pig-sty we are living in', he declared in 1943, 'the first step towards it is probably to grasp that "realism" does *not* pay'.

Yet Orwell wasn't always convinced that 'realism' doesn't pay. After all, by the end of the 1930s, it had already proved to be dangerously successful. 'Bully-worship', he observed in January 1939, 'has become a universal religion'. In fact, when Russell predicted that power politics would prove 'self-refuting', Orwell dismissed this at the time as wishful thinking. He insisted, moreover, that the tyranny envisioned by power politicians might well prove to be a stable form of government—a possibility he clearly explored further in *Nineteen Eighty-Four*. The novel also implies that it is entirely possible to pursue power for its own sake, even though he seemed to have doubted the psychological plausibility of this objective in his discussion of Burnham. The tyrannical O'Brien is certainly convinced that 'Power is not a means, it is an end'. Of course, the ability to treat power as an end in itself may be a lunatic's talent. Russell had declared power philosophies to be 'in a certain, precise sense insane' and O'Brien arguably epitomizes the point. With his ambitious aims of overruling all moral, epistemic, and physical laws—even the laws of gravity—he serves as a vivid illustration of the harm done to 'the sense of reality by the cultivation of what is now called "realism"'.

Orwell believed that realism got reality wrong on some fundamental psychological and social level, but he also worried that it would reconstitute those realities by winning collective assent. As Orwell had repeatedly argued, 'Myths which are believed in tend to become true'. In fact, it could sometimes seem as if Orwell had begun to believe in the myth of realism himself. 'There is no "law", there is only power', he announced in 1942, already giving voice to his inner O'Brien. He qualified his position by suggesting that the statement was not necessarily true; it was simply an outlook that 'all modern men do actually hold'. 'Those who pretend otherwise', he added, 'are either intellectual cowards, or power-worshippers under a thin disguise'. It is hard to know if Orwell saw himself as one of these modern men. Yet the pugnacity of his conclusions about the realism of moderns—which dismissed all dissenting views as intellectual cowardice or self-deception—suggests that he had acceded to power politics even in his basic methods of argument. The combination of thuggishness and high principle that he could communicate in his prose indicates that he was not averse to a bit of bully-worship himself.

Yet he continued to decry 'the folly of "realism"', while also worrying that its cynicism would be treated as cleverness. In the brutal world that it would produce, 'realism' could look like the most plausible account of political life. Or as Orwell declared, 'the mere fact that it throws ordinary decency aside will be accepted as part of its grown-upness and consequently of its efficacy'. Next to the disenchanted outlook of realism, a morally committed politics could seem naive or utopian. This certainly seemed to be the position adopted by Carr in *The Twenty Years' Crisis*: utopianism was an example of 'immature thought', while realism was considerably more grown-up—though he worried, too, that it could become unserviceably geriatric. Carr's sympathies clearly seemed to lay with realism, but, significantly, he insisted that a wise politics had need of both attitudes. Without a sense of realism, the utopian had no means of instantiating his ideals, but without ideals the realist lacked both motivation and purpose.

Orwell aspired to a very similar balance. In terms strikingly reminiscent of Carr, he argued that there were two sorts of political thinker: 'the Utopian with his head in the clouds and the realist with his feet in the mud', and he clearly wished to pursue some middle way above the trees. The aim was to cultivate an idealism without illusions. His objective, therefore, was 'to dis-associate Socialism from Utopianism'—or at least this was the stated aim in 1943. Politics was the art of the possible and needed to be constrained by the facts. Indeed, as far as Orwell was concerned, 'to wish for the impossible, even the impossible good, is inherently reactionary'.

Orwell took no small pride in his self-proclaimed 'power of facing unpleasant facts'—this is a key feature of his rhetorical style—and repeatedly rounded on other people's failure to confront them. The 'pious hope' of liberals, the 'fantasy world' of nationalists, the 'masturbation fantasy' of leftist intellectuals were all fair game—as was the 'wish-thinking' of realists them-selves. He clearly perceived himself as a realist in the non-technical sense of that word. The school of 'political realism', on the other hand, flew in the face of moral facts. As we have seen, however, Orwell worried that realism would reconstitute those facts, validating its own moral nihilism in the light of the brutality it helped to produce. Stalinism—which had infected 'the whole Socialist movement with Machiavellianism' in Orwell's eyes—epitomized this cynical circle. Indeed, faced with Stalin's brand of *Realpolitik*, Orwell would declare the utopians to be 'the true upholders of Socialist tradition'. He continued to speak critically of a 'woolly-minded Utopianism', but he had no time for those who would preach 'the doctrines of Machiavelli in the jargon of Lawrence and Wishart'.

So throughout the 1940s Orwell attempted to steer between the Scylla of utopianism and the Charybdis of realism, though the political naivety of 'Utopian dreamers' ultimately appeared more attractive to him than the moral cynicism of 'Marxist realism'. Marxists joined hands with Machia-vellians, Orwell believed, in assuming that all moral beliefs are disguised expressions of 'interest'. The Marxist's jaded '*cui bono?*' (who does it serve?) resembled 'the "realism" of the saloon-bar cynic who *always* assumes that the bishop is keeping a mistress and the trade-union leader is in the pay of the boss'. Against this type of moral cynicism, Orwell would defend the innocence of everyday moral beliefs. 'Either power politics must yield to common decency', he declared, 'or the world must go spiralling down into a nightmare of which we can already catch some dim glimpses'.

Orwellian decency could itself look fairly utopian in the face of the brutal effectiveness of *Machtpolitik* in the early '40s. But many on the Left in England would turn to this vague credo in their quarrels with fascism. In response to the question, 'What we are fighting for?', John Strachey in 1941 had a one-word answer: 'decency'. According to Strachey: 'This hopelessly inadequate, colourless, pathetic little word "decency" is the best we seem to be able to do to express our positive purpose'. During the early years of the war, Strachey would row alongside Orwell, as would Victor Gollancz. The three men famously collaborated in *The Betrayal of the Left* (1941)—a critique of communist policy and a strident attempt to reassert the ethical foundations of socialism. As Gollancz put it (rearticulating a position that Orwell had assumed since 1937): 'The most important thing about capitalism is that it is wicked, not that it will destroy itself through its own contradictions'. Of course, for some readers of *The Left News* this was 'idealism in its purist form'—that is to say, idealism in its worst form. It expressed a naive confidence in the power of moralizing criticism and falsely assumed that moral judgements were 'absolute' when they were simply relative.

Judged in this stark light, Orwell was clearly a born-again 'idealist' or what I have also called a 'moralist'. The only hope for the world, he insisted, was 'if the concept of right and wrong is restored to politics'. But, as we have seen, this moralistic socialism was far from uncontroversial in the 1930s and '40s. For figures like Trotsky, for instance, 'the appeal to abstract norms is not a disinterested philosophical mistake, but a necessary element in the mechanics of class deception'. Moral ideals, for the ex-Trotskyite Burnham, were also tools of deception. The Machiavellians had at least seen behind all moralizing cant and told 'the full truth about power'.

Of course, the utility of such truth-telling might itself be queried on 'Machiavellian' or instrumental grounds. Burnham liked to stress the political virtues of deceit, but he could become peculiarly shrill about the 'hypocrisy' of Anglo-Saxon politics. Orwell readily accepted that the British excelled at hypocrisy. However, he also believed that it was a fairly commendable vice; it was the homage vice paid to virtue in England. So despite his repeated commitment to truth, Orwell gave two cheers to humbug: it tacitly recognized, at least, some 'moral code'. He continued to criticize hypocrisy in England, but perhaps this was itself hypocritical—appearances about truth needed to be kept up. I will say more about this issue in Chapter 5, yet it is worth stressing here that there may have been a 'Machiavellian' dimension to Orwell's own moralism. 'If people *pretended* to be decent then the world would be decent' is not such a platitude as it sounds. It is hard to tell how much of Orwell's career was characterized by this virtuous pretence. While a mask may alter the expression of a face, pretending to be Orwell must have been tough work for Eric Blair: as I have argued, it involved a theatrical sense of moral purpose conducted alongside much fighting talk. Here was an idealist who could keep things real.

Citizen or writer?

Cyril Connolly captured something about his old friend in 1955: 'Orwell was a political animal. He reduced everything to politics...He could not blow his nose without moralising on the conditions in the handkerchief industry'. Orwell, as we have seen, was a moralist as much as he was anything else, but this could make him a peculiar—indeed unhappy—political animal. As Carr noted, the 'moral man' often turned his back on politics, because the entire practice failed to live up to his august ideals. Orwell never quite turned his back, but he repeatedly held his nose. Again and again, politics presents itself in his work as a disgusting enterprise—a 'monstrous harlequinade', a 'dirty, degrading business', a 'sordid' process, a 'mass of lies, evasions, folly, hatred and schizophrenia'. Orwell has come to epitomize the politically committed writer, but perhaps it is a measure of that commitment that he had a self-professed 'horror of politics'. The misgivings were a reflection of his exacting moral standards, but, as I wish to suggest here, they also derived from Orwell's sense of himself as an artist.

'I am a writer', Orwell declared in 1938, while also adding that the 'impulse of every writer is to "keep out of politics"'. He repeatedly questioned both the viability and desirability of keeping out, but he also nursed deep qualms about 'the invasion of literature by politics'. The very sense of such an invasion seemed to assume that in normal circumstances art should remain independent from political matters. Indeed, he was repeatedly drawn to the idea of an autonomous art—a position that partly explains his deep attraction to modernism—but he would also dismiss the 'illusion of pure aestheticism'. 'The opinion that art should have nothing to do with politics', he insisted in 1946, 'is itself a political attitude'. It is hard to know if this made a nonsense of a non-political art in Orwell's eyes, or whether it simply clarified the political conditions for an otherwise independent, aesthetic realm. As we shall see, he often presented liberal institutions as the necessary precondition of autonomous art. Yet he could also speak disparagingly about 'the illusions of Liberalism'. Moreover, the very notion of an autonomous art could seem like one of those illusions. Such vacillation reflected deep uncertainties about the nature and vocation of art, but it also recorded his difficulties in drawing a boundary line around politics.

After all, the meaning and location of politics could be hard to pin down for Orwell's generation. Spender suggested that in the 1930s 'everything became politics', and while he initially seemed sanguine—even enthusiastic— about this fact, he would soon protest against the 'political interpretation of everything'. 'The fallacy of thinking and acting entirely in terms of politics', he announced in 1945, 'is one of the greatest evils of our times'. Spender saw himself as a deeply engaged poet, yet even at his most committed, he argued that the 'final aim of civilized men must be an unpolitical age'. This improbable hope owed something, perhaps, to the general influence of Marx. The telos of Marx's own politics, it would appear, was an apolitical civilization—or at least one that had no need for States. Moreover, Marx could be fairly dis- missive of conventional politicking: it was a derivative or secondary sphere of action—a superstructural reflection of a more foundational, namely economic, set of relations. If parliamentary politics had any real function, it was to reflect and sustain existing relations of power. The former and soon- to-be-reborn parliamentarian, John Strachey, dismissed Parliament in 1936 as 'the mouthpiece of the capitalists as a class', while Laski concluded that under a capitalist democracy 'the main purpose of the rulers is to protect the owners of property'. Yet it was Laski who also condemned Marxism in 1943 for stressing the 'impotence of all politics'.

Marxism might have fostered public cynicism about politics, in Laski's eyes, but it also seemed to have extended people's sense of the political, allowing all aspects of economic and social life—even the institutions of art—to be incorporated into a comprehensive critique of power. Orwell certainly possessed this capacious idea of politics. 'All issues are political issues', he declared, in 1945—a conviction that may help to explain his alleged hand-wringing about handkerchiefs.

Orwell's politicization of everything owed as much to his moralism as it did to his socialism (if politics is conflated with ethics, it is liable to loom very large indeed), but it was also bound up with contemporary political developments—not least of all the expanding role of the State across the 1930s and '40s. It was 'an age of State control'—or so Orwell maintained. In the long shadow of the State, everything could feel political, which is why freedom in Orwell is often cast as a freedom from politics and the State altogether (I'll say more about this in Chapter 1). This libertarian fantasy never comes off in his work—partly because the State is everywhere—but the very articulation of the dream illustrates a deeply ambivalent view of politics. The ambivalence may point to Orwell's anarchist sympathies, but it also reveals a more conventional liberal element in his thought. Within a particular strand of liberalism, after all, freedom implies an absence of interference—a condition that can only be fully enjoyed where there are protected non-political spaces.

There may be something paradoxical about the idea of a protected non-political space, for its very protection would appear to depend upon politics. But this was a paradox that Orwell was certainly prepared to incur in the context of art. The existence of an autonomous aesthetic sphere, he suggested, necessitated a certain kind of politics, namely liberalism. This was an ostensibly self-limiting form of politics in which power restricted itself in order to make way for freedom. As he declared in 1940, the writer qua writer was essentially 'a liberal'. The writer was a liberal not only because he believed in protected non-political spaces (art being one such sphere), but also because he believed in personal autonomy. As we shall see in Chapter 1, Orwell often wondered if the idea of the autonomous individual was an illusion, but it was also an illusion that he found difficult to shake off, not least because he regarded it as a precondition for literature. Unfortunately, 'the literature of liberalism' (at this point almost a tautology in Orwell's journalism) was on the wane, because the autonomous individual was in the process of being 'stamped out of existence'—or so he declared in 1940. 'As for the writer', Orwell concluded, 'he is sitting on a melting iceberg; he is merely an anachronism, a hangover from the bourgeois age'.

Orwell did not always survey the 'destruction of liberalism' in this spirit of weary fatalism. In 1948, for instance, he called upon writers and artists to fight to keep 'the spirit of Liberalism alive', but how this was to be done was not entirely clear. After all, to call for a political art was arguably to destroy the non-political spaces that liberals aimed to preserve. Indeed, many commentators in the '30s objected to a politicized art for broadly 'liberal' reasons. Writing in *Scrutiny* in September 1939, the political philosopher Michael Oakeshott observed that in times of crisis (the outbreak of the Second

World War was one such moment), there was a special temptation to regard politics as supreme and to force the artist into a political role. However, in Oakeshott's eyes, this temptation should be avoided. In his defence of art's independence from politics, the political philosopher revealed a remarkably disenchanted view of political action:

> The things that political activity can achieve are often valuable, but I do not believe that they are ever the most valuable things in the communal life of a society. A limitation of view, which appears so clear and practical, but which amounts to little more than a mental fog, is inseparable from political activity. A mind fixed and callous to all subtle distinctions, emotional and intellectual habits becomes bogus from repetition and lack of examination, unreal loyalties, delusive aims, false significances are what political action involves. And this is so, not because the politically active are under the necessity of persuading the mentally obtuse before their activity can succeed; the spiritual callousness involved in political action belongs to its character, and follows from the nature of what can be achieved politically. Political action involves mental vulgarity, not merely because it entails the concurrence and support of those who are mentally vulgar, but because of the false simplification of human life implied in even the best of its purposes.

Oakeshott did not deny that art had a social vocation—it did—but this function needed to be disaggregated from the business of politics.

Though they ultimately took different positions on the question of political art, Oakeshott's jaundiced conception of politics was entirely shared by Orwell. A 'reduced state of consciousness' was a political virtue, Orwell contended, because it facilitated the type of conformity that made collective action possible. Modern political discourse both exemplified and conditioned this vitiation of thought: it involved a set of 'prefabricated phrases bolted together like the pieces of a child's Meccano set'. Political writing, he concluded, was generally bad writing.

Partly for this reason, Orwell had profound misgivings about the artist's involvement in politics. As he put it in 1948, 'the acceptance of *any* political discipline seems to be incompatible with literary integrity'. Much hangs on what he meant by the word 'discipline', but he was often inclined to believe that organized political action involved a forfeiture of intellectual freedom. It was hard to be a Daniel when prosecuting a common cause. 'To yield subjectively, not merely to a party machine, but even to a group ideology', he announced, 'is to destroy yourself as a writer'. He felt the evidence of such destruction was observable everywhere. Indeed, the whole literary history of the 1930s served 'to justify the opinion that a writer does well to keep out of politics'.

And yet there was no keeping out of politics—or so he repeatedly insisted. Orwell was fairly comfortable defending the autonomy of the artist, or the idea of art as a protected social space free from direct political coercion—these, after all, were entirely consonant with a liberal defence of free speech and freedom of the person. Yet he had considerable difficulty even conceiving of the idea of a fully autonomous art-work. In 1940 he provided a scoffing summary about how autonomy had been pursued by the mandarins of taste: 'Literature was supposed to consist solely in the manipulation of words. To judge a book by its subject-matter was the unforgivable sin, and even to be aware of its subject-matter was looked on as a lapse of taste'. And he made fun of this purism by recycling a joke:

> About 1928, in one of the three genuinely funny jokes that *Punch* has produced since the Great War, an intolerable youth is pictured informing his aunt that he intends to 'write'. 'And what are you going to write about, dear?' asks the aunt. 'My dear aunt,' says the youth crushingly, 'one doesn't write *about* anything, one just *writes*.'

Orwell clearly worried that the representational and even intentional content of art would be relinquished in the pursuit of aesthetic purity. Here 'art-for-art's-saking extended practically to a worship of the meaningless'. For literature to be meaningful, it had to be 'about' something, but in so far as it had this quality of aboutness, it was difficult for it to remain autonomous in Orwell's eyes. He never really countenanced the possibility that art could be about itself. In so far as it had a content, it made claims about the world—it had, as he put it, a 'purpose' or 'message'—and these claims were always coloured by moral and political judgements.

His conviction that 'no book is ever truly neutral' produced aggressive disavowals of art's independence. As he proclaimed in 1936: 'Few people have the guts to say outright that art and propaganda are the same thing'. Orwell clearly had the guts, facing down anyone who might take issue with such coarse claims. In 1940 he reasserted that all art is propaganda, though he was careful to insist that not all propaganda is art. He thus left some space for aesthetic criteria to count in their own right (after all, even Trotsky had argued that 'artistic creation has its laws—even when it consciously serves a social movement'). Orwell's plan for his own art, therefore, was 'to fuse political purpose and artistic purpose into one whole' and the success of this venture has been debated by critics ever since.

While Orwell wanted to give the aesthetic its due, it wasn't entirely clear what he meant by an 'artistic purpose'. The phrase had a faintly self-contradictory ring, given his occasional tendency to associate art with a radical purposelessness. In 'Why I Write', for instance, he repeatedly associated aesthetic practice with a 'non-utilitarian' endeavour, with 'useless information' (though the word 'information' may have had a too workmanlike smell) and with commitments 'that a full-time politician would consider irrelevant'. This was hardly an uncommon view of art—'if any social function can be ascribed to art at all', Theodor Adorno proclaimed, 'it is to have no function'— and, as we shall see in Chapter 5, Orwell would defend this noble uselessness in an inexhaustibly instrumental world.

Yet Orwell arguably reneged on this uselessness by investing his works with a 'political purpose'. The balance he hoped to strike between the demands of art and politics might easily read like a philistine's ambition. Be that as it may, Orwell was convinced that the strategy benefited his art: 'Looking back through my work', he confided, 'I see that it is invariably where I lacked a *political* purpose that I wrote lifeless books'. He may have presented all writers as tacit liberals, but in 1946 he proclaimed that every line he had written for the past ten years was done for 'democratic Socialism'. How this dedication to a cause squared with his assertion in 1948 that collective ideologies were detrimental to a writer is difficult to determine. Presumably, he regarded his own socialism as too independent-minded to court the hazards of group-think.

So Orwell defended the idea of a political art, but how exactly was art supposed to function politically? The very defence of the writer-citizen might seem to reflect an exaggerated sense of art's social import. Though Orwell pointed out that a song like the Marseillaise was much more politically effective than a treatise on dialectical materialism, he also took pains to note that 'nothing advocated by well-meaning literary men ever happens'.

This defeatism certainly flew in the face of some of the wilder claims that were made for art in the 1930s, although Auden's heady picture of 'poets exploding like bombs' would soon give way to a more disenchanted vision. In 1939 Auden was convinced that 'poetry makes nothing happen'— although even here Auden seemed to express a residual commitment to art's constitutive power: it allows the nothings of the imagination to *happen* as emotionally lived events. Looking back on the literary activism of the 1930s,

Louis MacNeice would disparage its blend of self-importance and impotence. 'The armchair reformist sits between two dangers', he contended, 'wishful thinking and self-indulgent gloom'. Both the gloom and the wishful thinking are observable features of Orwell's work, but he made valiant attempts to get off the armchair. He attempted—with mixed results—to understand poverty from the inside by living on the streets in Paris and London; he resided in working-class Wigan—at some discomfort to his middle-class self; and, of course, he took a bullet in the neck fighting for republican Spain. He appreciated the inadequacy of many of these gestures—the class problem, he admitted, would not be solved by hanging out with tramps—but they also expressed an egalitarian ambition, attempting to incorporate disadvantaged or excluded others into the moral remit of literature.

Orwell's writing makes a good case for what Henry James once called the 'civic use of the imagination'. Indeed, artists and philosophers continue to claim that the arts perform a vital political role in this regard: by allowing us to imagine the lives of others, they produce the conditions for an enlarged altruism and a more 'compassionate citizenship'. Admittedly, the cultivation of the sympathetic imagination may yield little more than an imaginary sympathy; as moralists have pointed out, the arts may flatter our *amour propre* as sensitive souls, while distracting us from real suffering. Orwell, as we shall see, was aware of the dangers of a purely bookish compassion, yet he continued to regard literature as a vehicle for a very lived form of solidarity. However, his writing also raises interesting questions about solidarity's limits. As the frequent abstractness of his appeals to 'brotherhood' makes clear, the principle itself can become vanishingly broad; indeed, a love of everyone may imply fellowship with no one. Moreover, a politics of universal brotherhood can overlook the basic condition of politics: namely, the existence of conflict. Orwell, of course, rarely shirked conflict—a fact communicated in pugnacious, sometimes brutal prose. E. M. Forster's advice for his generation, 'Be soft even if you stand to get squashed', was certainly not Orwell's credo. His remarks about homosexuals, feminists, vegetarians, sandal-wearers, and fruit-juice drinkers reveal a talent for offence—in fact, he even wondered if 'a touch of bigotry is the condition of literary vitality'—but they indicate that solidarity is sometimes a fairly constricted principle in his work.

So Orwell's writing puts its own idealism on trial. Through both his journalism and his fiction we witness the dignity and motivational power of certain ideals—liberty, equality, solidarity, truth, and happiness—but we also see these abstractions put to the test. Thus, *The Road to Wigan Pier* expresses the need for solidarity between social classes, but it also embodies (even in its basic style of address) the practical and conceptual difficulties of this type of fellowship. *Homage to Catalonia* and *Animal Farm* capture the inspirational nature of equality as well as its ambiguity—differences of meaning that sometimes play themselves out in violent conflict. *Keep the Aspidistra Flying*, *Coming Up for Air*, and *Nineteen Eighty-Four*, stage different and rival interpretations of what it means to be free. This interrogation of political concepts is not necessarily deliberate, assuming it ever makes sense to speak of deliberateness in the context of art. As MacNeice once put it: 'Poets do not know (exactly) what they are doing, for if they did, there would be no need to do it'. I'm not sure Orwell always knew what he was doing in art or indeed in politics. The moral confidence of his journalistic voice often betrays a deep uncertainty about the function of the aesthetic or the nature of the good. Indeed, he may have been drawn to art—and particularly the novel—as a home for his uncertainties, allowing them to take refuge in its formal ambiguities, plurality of voices, and cunning silences.

It has been suggested, of course, that Orwell's art would be better if it were more ambiguous and a little less certain. Nonetheless, for all its brittle edges, his writing illustrates how literature can serve as a distinctive mode of political thinking. This view has not always had its backers. In the 1980s Judith Shklar asked with disarming frankness whether political theory should care about texts like *Nineteen Eighty-Four*. Shklar's answer was that it should: such literature tells useful 'stories about how ideas are incarnated in experience'. Yet political theorists have only fitfully cared about Orwell's writing. The reasons for this are obvious enough: he was not, as I have indicated, a particularly systematic thinker. But this lack of a system is one of the more interesting things about his work—not least in the way it expresses doubts about 'theory' itself. Indeed, according to Shklar, literature can compensate for theory's worst faults—that is, its tendency 'to talk in a vacuum and about nothing at all, to heap words upon words that have no bearing on anything or anyone who has ever lived and spoken in the actual world'. This, of course, is a caricature of theory and as Orwell's claims about 'art-for-art's-saking' demonstrate, it is not entirely clear that literature escapes the problem of excessive abstraction or social irrelevance.

In her apology for literature, Shklar may have exaggerated its representational powers or its proximity to the real: it may be no closer to the world than any other discourse is. Nonetheless, it does ask specific kinds of questions that are a mere function of its form. The basic use of narrative, for instance, can help us to see the situational complexity of abstract political norms. For instance, though *Animal Farm* begs several questions about equality, it also illustrates its many-headedness by giving it plural incarnations across the plot. Characterization in *Animal Farm*—bald as it often is—raises questions about the psychological viability of certain ideals like equality (I'll say more about this in Chapter 3). Moreover, the basic phenomenology of reading the tale may lead us to wonder about the various feelings that sustain or undermine egalitarian principles. Elsewhere in this book I will consider the political significance of sentiments like love, pity, and disgust—feelings that are described and sometimes aroused by Orwell's writing. Reading such work can produce self-reflexive feelings that are also complex political thoughts.

Of course, it is easy to exaggerate art's cognitive or truth-revealing powers. Not all poets are liars, but Orwell's polemical writing (this includes his novels) easily recalls Platonic misgivings about rhetoric: it is a discourse that aims to persuade rather than to educate us about right and wrong, producing 'conviction without understanding'. This is the effect that has sometimes been attributed to works like *Animal Farm* or *Nineteen Eighty-Four*—not entirely without foundation. So this book treats Orwell's rhetoric as a distinctive form of political thought, but it also highlights moments where his texts might attempt to hoodwink the understanding rather than to enlighten it. The power of Orwell's writing, I argue, can only be fully appreciated by a refined sense of the conceptual difficulties it simultaneously represents and attempts to repress. Orwell liked to keep truth simple in what he perceived to be a post-truth era—an aim advertised in the studied plainness of his prose. But there was nothing simple about his style—however it may have aspired to a second innocence—or about the beliefs it serviced. Through the cracked windowpane of his art we can see both the majesty and difficulty of political ideals.

I

Liberty

Freedom was Orwell's great hurrah-concept. His journalism repeatedly extols and arguably embodies its various forms—'freedom of the intellect', 'freedom of speech', 'freedom of the press', etc. He would also fight for the concept on very practical fronts, most notably as vice-chairman of the *Freedom Defence Committee* (an organization he joined in 1945 with the aim of defending 'the essential liberty of individuals and organisations'). All of Orwell's fiction involves some form of liberty-quest. So Dorothy makes an ambiguous bid for autonomy in *A Clergyman's Daughter*—she literally sleep-walks into independence. Though she sometimes wonders if subjection to a tradition is better than 'rootless freedom', the basic structure of the novel (essentially a *Bildungsroman*) privileges the project of becoming free. The hero of *Burmese Days* is aggressively committed to a certain ideal of liberty: he craves freedom of thought and expression in circumstances where these are virtually 'unthinkable'. In *Keep the Aspidistra Flying*, Gordon Comstock also hopes to escape his servile circumstances: his aim is 'to breathe free air, free from the money-stink' that issues from the modern world. George Bowling in *Coming Up for Air* feels that he is one of those poor bastards 'who's *never* free except when he's fast asleep'. He duly sets out to reclaim some freedom for his waking hours. The beasts of *Animal Farm* rebel in the name of freedom ('they had been slaves and now they were free, and that made all the difference'). The hero of *Nineteen Eighty-Four* also decides to revolt in the name of liberty: 'To die hating them, that was freedom'.

Yet all of these bids for freedom end in failure. The image of the glue-pot that concludes *A Clergyman's Daughter* is symbolic of how many of Orwell's characters end up: stuck—or too tranquilized by the 'penetrating smell of the glue-pot' to fully appreciate their lack of freedom. Poor Boxer, of course, will end up as glue. These grim outcomes may be an indictment of modern life (as Orwell announced in 1937, 'We are living in a world in which nobody is free'), but they also raise questions about his confidence in freedom itself. Orwell's account of Swift—a man dedicated to 'despising authority, while disbelieving in liberty'—easily rebounded on himself. Freedom is the ever-retreating telos of his fiction, giving everything its narrative shape as well as its presiding sense of disappointment. Celebrated as freedom's champion, Orwell's relationship to the concept was, in fact, a deeply troubled one: it is both the grand ideal and great delusion of his life's work. The aim of this chapter is to explore the reasons for this volatility and the light this casts on what remains the most banal and most precious of our political concepts.

The banality of freedom was certainly an observable feature of the 1930s. Looking back on the decade in 1940, Malcolm Muggeridge was struck by the ubiquity of the concept: 'it was as though there had been a Freedom ballot—millions voting that they were in favour of being free'. But the freedom voted for was dizzyingly plural:

> How varied was our freedom—stockbrokers freely buying and selling shares, lawyers freely obtaining briefs and clergymen freely obtaining benefices, each individual freely struggling to feed and clothe and house himself as best he might. This so varied freedom was in peril, and needed to be defended. 'Lend to defend the right to be free', posters pleaded; 'Your resolution, your courage, will defend our freedom'.
>
> Calamity unspeakable if our freedom were allowed to perish; calamity unspeakable if dearly prized and hardly won liberties were lost... In the darkness of change, men tried to formulate their freedom in order to defend it; in the darkness of change, they watched their world disintegrating under their eyes, and knew not whether they were happy or regretful that it should thus pass away—Oh, let it pass! or, Oh, let it stay!
>
> In so confused a state of mind, the Thirties drew to an end—looking for freedom that it might be defended.

So freedom was everywhere and nowhere in Muggeridge's '30s. Or, as Stephen Spender pointed out in 1937, 'freedom is so fundamental to the modern mind that every political battle is carried on its name'. The ambiguity of the concept might account for its widespread use (while also exacerbating the ambiguities), but it could also lead to a loss of faith in the ideal.

As E. M. Forster noted sadly in 1935, 'many people do not believe in freedom now'. The slogan, 'we spit on freedom', had done the rounds in Berlin in the '30s, while back in the '20s, Mussolini had pledged to 'trample on the more or less decomposed body of the Goddess of Liberty'. Hitler certainly mocked liberal concepts of freedom and announced that the ability to suspend personal liberty in the name of a higher end was the epitome of human development. Yet he too wished to rebuild the 'Tempel der Freiheit' (access to the temple, of course, being severely restricted to the right sort of folk). For all his criticism of bourgeois liberty, Stalin would also cast himself as freedom's darling. Strachey conceded that this liberty-loving side of Uncle Joe was not well known in the West, but he insisted that freedom was the ultimate goal of Stalin's project. In 1939 Leonard Woolf was still presenting Stalin as a Marxist Pericles whose commitment to freedom was absolute. With so many friends, freedom did not need enemies. Many decried the liberties taken with liberty, but the vagueness of the concept made its true meaning difficult to police. As Hayek complained in 1944, '"Freedom" and "liberty" are now words so worn with use and abuse that one must hesitate to employ them'. But even Hayek would not hesitate for long.

In 1945 Orwell included freedom in his category of virtually meaningless words, yet he still made copious use of the term. An enthusiast of liberty, Orwell proclaimed to want 'freedom for the other fellow' as much as for himself. This solicitude for others suggests that he was committed to the principle of equal freedom—a commitment that might even suggest that equality, rather than freedom, remained the more fundamental good in Orwell's eyes. Or it simply revealed that both were codependent values for Orwell as they were for many on the Left. After all, it was impossible to feel free, Orwell claimed, when one lived in fear of one's political, social, or economic superiors, for fear could be a terrible curb or determinant of one's actions. As he repeatedly argued in the '30s and '40s, 'terror of the boss', 'terror of the sack', and 'the haunting terror of unemployment' kept people in conditions of unfreedom. Here freedom implied non-domination—a situation where 'no one owned anyone else as his master'. Mastered by others, however, the worker lacked a proper sense of agency: 'He does not act, he is acted upon'. Orwell thus believed that the conditions for non-domination could only be achieved under some system of socialism: 'pure freedom', he maintained, 'will only exist in a classless society'.

The ideas of equal freedom and non-domination also informed Orwell's criticisms of colonialism. 'I am all in favour of European freedom', he declared in 1945, 'but I feel happier when it is coupled with freedom elsewhere'. The French and English Empires—'with their six hundred million disenfranchised human beings'—violated the principle of equal freedom for all. In 'Shooting an Elephant', Orwell famously claimed that masters became slaves in their own bid for mastery: 'when the white man turns tyrant it is his own freedom that he destroys'. This paradox of power had, of course, been noted many times before. As Rousseau put it, '*Quiconque est maître ne peut être libre*', while Hegel famously maintained that the master cannot consolidate his freedom in the world when he refused to recognize the same property in others. But Orwell's grasp of master–slave dialectics owed more to Burma than it did to Hegel. In his role as imperial policeman— or the literary version of himself that he summoned up afterwards—he was under the distinct impression that he was subject to those he mastered: 'Here was I, the white man with his gun, standing in front of the unarmed native crowd—seemingly the leading actor of the piece; but in reality I was only an absurd puppet pushed to and fro by the will of those yellow faces behind'. Those yellow faces: Orwell's rhetoric participates in the colonial superiority it indicts, but it also captures well the ironies of domination. Clearly, Orwell struggled to recognize the full autonomy of the colonial subjects he wanted to see liberated—indeed, he allegedly declared to Christopher Hollis that 'Libbaty's a kind of thing / Thet don't agree with niggers'. But he had certainly an alert sense of how colonialism connived against his own freedom. Like his creation John Flory, he had no desire to be 'a cog in the wheels of despotism'.

Orwell wanted freedom for the other fellow, but, crucially, he also wanted freedom from the other fellow. He set great store in privacy both as a social institution and as a metaphysical ideal—a secret citadel within the self that secures one's independence from others—and it could make him conceive of freedom as an absence of interference from other people. Indeed, for all of his odes to brotherhood, Orwell sometimes saw the relationship between the individual and the community in strikingly oppositional terms. In 1941, for instance, he spoke of 'the struggle that always goes on between the individual and the community'. Communal life may always involve conflict, but Orwell's highly polarized account of the antagonism—the eternal face-off between the individual and a univocal community—might seem to rest on a dubious anthropology of the individual as a fundamentally asocial, even anti-social entity. Yet he also rejected this atomistic vision of things, even doubting in the process the category of the individual. As he put it in 1940: 'Man is not an individual'. The experience of war—with its deep feelings of all-in-it-togetherness—would help to convince him that the ego is 'only a cell' in a broader social organism. However, in *Nineteen Eighty-Four* this turns out to be a tyrant's language: as the terrible O'Brien points out to Winston, 'the individual is only a cell'—a philosophy that allows him to ride roughshod over Winston's freedom.

Orwell's last novel expresses a train of thought that had been in development for some time. As he argued in 1941: 'We live in an age in which the autonomous individual is ceasing to exist—or perhaps one ought to say, in which the individual is ceasing to have the illusion of being autonomous'. The statement is, of course, a remarkable fudge. Much hangs on what Orwell meant by autonomy, but he seemed to lament the disappearance of a coveted ideal while simultaneously declaring it to be a myth. As we have already seen, he invested heavily in the self-constituting power of shared illusions, but his remarks express a strange scepticism about what would appear to be one of his core values. The doubt may extend less to the idea of freedom as such than to a particular conception of it, for different and rival freedoms fight for supremacy in Orwell's work. Yet his difficulty deciding between these different freedoms often seems to have eroded his confidence in the general concept.

Varieties of freedom

Orwell liked to criticize other people's freedom-talk: it yielded 'a vague bumbling, in which the liberty which is supposedly being defended is never clearly defined'. Yet, as Laski and Gollancz complained in 1937, he never provided a strict definition of the word himself. Having observed 'liberty explained away by sleek little professors', he may have decided that it was counterproductive to attempt strict definitions—though this hardly squares with his demands for them. He also refused to get embroiled in the metaphysical niceties of freedom: all the arguments, he declared, were on the side of determinism, but everyone retained an 'instinctive knowledge' of the freedom of the will. It never seemed to bother him that to be ruled by instinct was the antithesis of freedom in some people's eyes. Whatever his instincts may have told him, Orwell's rhetorical practice bears out his own contention that freedom was one of those words with 'several different meanings which cannot be reconciled with one another'.

His attempts to distinguish between different freedoms—economic, moral, and political—testify to this incorrigible plurality. He sometimes abstracted 'economic liberty' from what he judged to be a more important set of freedoms, although at other moments he wondered if this liberty was not so trivial after all. On some occasions, he worried that 'moral liberty'—ironically reduced to the right to talk about sex in print—had been dangerously prioritized over 'political liberty'. And yet he sympathized with those who regarded political liberty as a fraud. His books, moreover, give a certain amount of airtime to a form of metaphysical freedom that has very little to do with politics. In *Down and Out in Paris and London*, for instance, the pavement artist, Bozo, believes that political and economic realities—which so often connive against people's liberty in Orwell—do nothing to constrict him. For Bozo, the question of freedom is relatively simple: 'You just got to say to yourself, "I'm a free man in *here*"—he tapped his forehead—and you're all right'. Bozo is arguably a modern-day Epictetus: freedom is what we might loosely call inner freedom and no matter the external circumstances, the mind remains its own sovereign. So when Bozo is sent to Wandsworth prison for begging, Orwell suspects that prison is unlikely to worry him very much. His inner freedom will see him through.

This metaphysical freedom has its attractions, but it is also a distinctly apolitical conception of liberty: it depends on no particular political arrangement or on any broader socio-economic conditions for its existence. Yet at other points in Orwell's writing even inner freedom depends on economic and political factors. Like Bozo, the hero of *Nineteen Eighty-Four* sets considerable store in a form of inner liberty—those 'few cubic centimetres inside your skull'. However, these few centimetres of freedom are ultimately denied Winston. Even Bozo, perhaps, would have struggled to retain his equanimity in Room 101; certainly, by the time Winston emerges from his torture chamber, his belief that 'They can't get inside you' has been sorely tested. The circumstances outlined in Orwell's last novel may be extreme, but they ultimately suggest that even 'inner' freedom seems to depend on political factors—a point to which I will return. Of course, the self's dependence on external conditions might lead some to question the possibility of freedom in any form. This is a very drastic form of doubt, but it is a scepticism that often seems to accompany a disappointed dream of liberty in Orwell's writing.

In *Keep the Aspidistra Flying*, for instance, Gordon Comstock veers between a naive confidence in his own freedom (one that allows him to opt out of economic and social norms) and a repetitious insistence on his total servitude. He wants to escape the money world, convinced that it is the source of all unfreedom. On the other hand, he believes that 'all is money' and that funds are a prerequisite for any type of agency in a modern context. As Comstock concludes: 'Your money goes and your freedom with it'. So, for much of the novel he lives in a state of extreme bad faith: too much of a moaner to accept his unfreedom, too committed to moaning to exercise any freedom he may possess. Comstock would rather read Humphry Ward than Karl Marx, yet his economic determinism is more extreme than the most vulgar Marxist of the 1930s. So while Bozo might enjoy a freedom of mind that is independent of all external circumstances, Comstock is convinced that even this liberty is money-dependent. 'The first effect of poverty', he opines, 'is that it kills thought'. Inner freedom depends on economic conditions, which leads Comstock to doubt the possibility of its authentic existence. He puts his unfreedom into verse—'*The lord of all, the money-god ... rules us blood and hand and brain*'—the clanging iambs providing a phonic reminder of necessity's obdurate laws. If the lines are substandard, we can only blame the money-god.

Comstock gives up on freedom in the end ('He would sell his soul so utterly that he would forget that it had ever been his'). While this might seem to be a paradoxical assertion of agency, he also casts his surrender in fatalistic terms: 'he was merely repeating the destiny of every human being'. Comstock's life trajectory is at best an ironic endorsement of Engels' claim that freedom is the acknowledgement of necessity—a much-repeated thesis in the 1930s. The hero denies himself this freedom for much of the novel by pretending he can escape the system; however, by succumbing to necessity, he ultimately acquires this notional liberty—alongside a wife, a job, and an aspidistra. The sense of irony he brings to this submission may be a last protest against his fate—an attempt to preserve some inner freedom (namely, the freedom to sneer) in the face of grim necessity—but it does little to dislodge the fact that his project of radical independence has turned out to be a dismal failure. Drawing on Engels' credo, Christopher Caudwell argued that a true 'understanding of ... iron determinism brings freedom'; yet Comstock's repetitious reflections on destiny's iron laws might suggest otherwise.

Keep the Aspidistra Flying has obvious autobiographical echoes (the portrait of a cranky writer jobbing in a bookshop did not emerge from a vacuum), but Orwell seemed to stick with freedom in his own case—at least if his activities for the *Freedom Defence Committee* mean anything. But what kind of freedom did Orwell want to defend in this context? One of the key debates in the 1920s and '30s was whether freedom was a 'negative' or 'positive' concept. Orwell took no direct part in the discussion, but an awareness of its basic terms may sensitize us to the different shades of freedom in his work. Indeed, the shades can be plotted on a spectrum, moving from a negative pole—in which freedom involves a simple absence of restraint—to a more 'positive' position in which freedom implies a particular practice or a set of determinate ends, such as the practice of self-mastery or the pursuit of reason (neither of which looked like particularly straightforward operations in a very Freudian age). Orwell, I shall argue, took up a number of positions across this spectrum—a fact that partly accounts for both the richness and extreme instability of freedom in his work.

He was not alone in his inconstancy. Indeed, one way of charting Orwell's vacillation is to situate it in the context of other people's more clearly signalled problems with freedom—most notably, Harold Laski's. A professor at the London School of Economics from 1926, an executive member of the Fabian society for much of the '30s, a co-founder of the Left Book Club, and an indefatigable public intellectual, Laski was one of the key theorists of freedom on the Left in Britain. He took Orwell to task for his sloppy uses of the concept in *The Road to Wigan Pier*, yet Laski was no advert for precision himself. Indeed, his efforts to define freedom across the '20s, '30s, and '40s throw a more charitable light on Orwell's vagueness. So in 1925 Laski was adamant that liberty was 'a positive thing' ('It does not merely mean absence of restraint'). But less than five years later he had changed his mind: it was 'a purely negative condition'. In fact, the definition of freedom he now endorsed contained both positive and negative elements. Liberty, he declared, 'is essentially an absence of restraint', while immediately adding the caveat that it 'implies a power to expand'. So the definition pointed to an absence and to a positive power. These various shifts and turns may testify to Laski's belief that descriptions of freedom were historically relative—if so, history seemed to move quite fast for Laski. He would change his mind again on the matter in 1943, exhorting Britons to move 'from the plane of negative to the plane of positive freedom'.

Laski's flip-flopping about freedom reflected an understandable uneasiness with different ends of the liberty spectrum. Negative accounts, Laski suggested, were often unserviceably abstract: an absence of restraints may provide opportunities for action, but such opportunity was meaningless without certain powers. As he put it: 'Men may well be free and yet remain unable to realize the purpose of freedom'. Yet to say that freedom has a particular purpose or that it entails a positive set of activities might seem excessively prescriptive. Laski was deeply worried about the authoritarian potential of 'positive' accounts—an approach that might stipulate certain kinds of practice or behaviour as basic constituents of freedom. He was haunted by Rousseau's paradox—that one can be forced to be free—and it made him insist, in seeming contradistinction to the drift of much of his own thought, that liberty was essentially a 'negative' matter. Indeed, as Orwell suggested, Laski entertained an 'old-fashioned version of liberty'—namely, a negative one—that was ostensibly at odds with his 'positive' sense of the State.

Orwell could have said the same about himself: while he sponsored the radical redistribution of wealth through a socialist State, he also dreaded 'the nightmare of State interference'. The nightmare was the flipside of a libertarian dream in which freedom is a purely negative condition: it implies an absence of restraint and Orwell had a fairly capacious sense of what counted as a restraint. The shortcomings of this libertarian ideal are repeatedly expressed (if never fully acknowledged) across his work: in several contexts, the licence he associated with freedom often comes across as neither possible nor desirable. This leads him to entertain a more 'positive' conception of freedom—say, as rational self-rule—but the decision to make 'reason' a condition of freedom is not without its dangers. For instance, O'Brien masquerades as reason's guardian, helping his victims to become 'sane'—and thus properly free agents—by inflicting upon them unfathomable tortures. Here 'FREEDOM IS SLAVERY'—a grotesque inversion that might seem to indict 'positive' schemes of freedom. But negative freedom could produce its own set of paradoxes in Orwell and it is to this issue that I now turn.

Negative freedom

When defending freedom in the '40s, Orwell liked to draw on Milton's famous line: 'By the known rules of ancient liberty'. The phrase carried with it a certain air of paradox: the idea that liberty was composed of rules would certainly seem contradictory to some fundamentalists of freedom. The liberty that George Bowling craves, for instance, is built upon a reminiscence of his anarchic youth—a sentiment that is 'all bound up with breaking rules'. Orwell may not have wished to break rules—though he admitted that he put much of himself into George Bowling—but he sometimes suggested that freedom implied an absence of them.

Orwell tended to assume, in other words, that freedom was essentially a negative concept. Judged from this pole of the liberty spectrum, even the rule of law can seem like a restriction of freedom. This may have come as no surprise to Freudians, but it remained a contentious issue within key strands of political thought. John Locke, after all, had claimed that it was absurd to regard law as a restraint on liberty ('that ill deserves the Name of Confinement', he insisted, 'which hedges us in only from Bogs and Precipes'). But not everyone saw things this way. While acknowledging the necessity of law, Hobbes nonetheless felt that freedom was optimised when it was silent. Bentham took up a similar position. 'All coercive laws', he argued, 'are, as far as they go, abrogative of liberty' (though the word 'coercive' here would also seem to beg the question). Orwell's views of freedom were arguably affiliated to this liberal tradition, yet the sense that freedom implied an absence of restraint could also bring him into more anarchic waters.

In *The Road to Wigan Pier*, Orwell admitted he had been attracted to anarchism in his younger days, believing at one point that all government and all punishments were 'evil'. Left to their own devices, individuals would prosper in peace. He soon learned to see this as 'sentimental nonsense': people's freedom would always need defending from the encroachments of others. Hence, the necessity of law. Not all of Orwell's characters seem happy with this fact. In *Down and Out in Paris and London*, for instance, Charlie—the fond abuser of women—makes his disgruntlement clear: 'if it were not for that accursed law that robs us of our liberty, I would have murdered her at that moment'. The attitude of Orwell's narrator in *Down and Out in Paris* is hard to make out: he regards people like Charlie with a fascinated disgust, but it is possible too that he admires his pluck. In *The Road to Wigan Pier*, however, Orwell made it vividly clear that coercive laws—harshly administered—were 'always necessary to protect peaceful people from violence'.

Orwell made his peace with rules, admitting that no liberty could be 'absolute', but the concession itself might suggest that he still conceived of freedom in negative terms. This is borne out in some of his subsequent reflections on anarchism. As he argued in 1946, the problem was not that anarchism was too permissive; in fact, it was not permissive enough. Within the idea of a lawless utopia, he explained, there was often a 'totalitarian' tendency:

> In a Society in which there is no law, and in theory no compulsion, the only arbiter of behaviour is public opinion. But public opinion, because of the tremendous urge to conformity in gregarious animals, is less tolerant than any system of law.

Arguably, it is Orwell's own sense of freedom that is intolerant here. His commitment to independence is so extreme that it seems to overrule humanity's more clubbable sentiments: if gregarious animals wish to conform, are they any less free for doing so?

Orwell seems to downgrade the desire for others in the name of a highly negative—yet deeply coercive—model of independence (even negative freedom, it seems, can lead to paradox). It dictates a radical absence of interference from others. Law, he feels, is a form of interference and thus a curb to one's freedom, but at least it sometimes falls silent. Public opinion and societal norms, on the other hand, never cease their din, making their coercive potential limitless. As Orwell explained:

> When human beings are governed by 'thou shalt not', the individual can practise a certain amount of eccentricity: when they are supposedly governed by 'love' or 'reason', he is under continuous pressure to make him behave and think in exactly the same way as everyone else.

The kingdom of love, for Orwell, is always a potential gulag, while the republic of reason promises to be equally joyless. Orwell's attitude to the rule of reason was considerably more complicated than his critique of a rationalist utopia suggests. But if his account of Swift's Houyhnhnms is anything to go by, he also tended to think that a fundamentalist commitment to reason culminates in tyranny. As he insists, there can be 'no freedom and no development' in a rationalist wonderland. His emphasis on 'development' gestures perhaps to a 'positive' or teleological model of freedom (the freedom of self-realization), but it also entails a negative dimension, namely the absence of external restrictions on the self. His sense of restriction, moreover, is extraordinarily catholic: it includes not only coercive laws, but also social norms and even the basic precepts of reason itself.

This negative ideal of freedom did not sit well with contemporaries like Christopher Caudwell. As Caudwell put it, 'all the "constraints", "obligations", "inhibitions", and "duties" of society are the very means by which freedom is obtained by men'. But the modern individual experiences its conditions of freedom as mere impediments to it—or so Caudwell believed. Caudwell traced this erroneous conception of freedom back to Rousseau's picture of a natural independence that preceded all social incorporation. This fantasy of pre-social freedom, he believed, accompanied 'all bourgeois thought'. Pledged to a vision of humans as radically independent creatures, the bourgeois was always likely to experience social life as a deprivation of liberty. These criticisms of an asocial or anti-social freedom were a fairly standard refrain on the Left in the 1930s. Yet Caudwell's criticisms of the 'pastoral heaven' that services the bourgeois myth of independence alert us to the libertarian dimensions of Orwell's own pastoralism.

Orwell never openly espoused the notion of pure, bucolic independence and he had no confidence that the 'noble savage' had ever existed. Nonetheless, nature repeatedly presents itself in his work as a space of freedom in which one wins a delightful immunity from others. This retreat is not absolutely anti-social—since it is often embarked upon with a lover—but it is not far off. Indeed, he sometimes cast the individualist as a solitary who prefers the quiet of nature to the din of towns.

Yet trips to the countryside tend to produce a very disappointed form of Rousseauism in Orwell's writing. Gordon Comstock's ramble in the hills with his lover Rosemary brings him a temporary 'feeling of freedom', but the feeling is spoiled by the realization that even in the country there is no escape from the money-god. This sense of unfreedom finds its consummation in Comstock's huffy realization that he will not be allowed to have unprotected sex in the open air. Money, it seems, is the ultimate prophylactic: the risk of pregnancy is also a financial risk and such costs can't be incurred. Comstock experiences this as an assault on his freedom: 'Money again! Even in the most secret action of your life you don't escape it; you've still got to spoil everything with filthy cold-blooded precautions for money's sake'. It says a lot about Comstock's obsessiveness that the issue is essentially economic (after all, capitalism isn't always the reason for one's inability to get laid) and a terrible insult to his own liberty. It doesn't seem to have much to do with Rosemary's claims to freedom or her rights over her own body. In any event, his Rousseauian moment quickly curdles and his desire grows cold: 'In a wet field on a Sunday afternoon—and in mid-winter at that! Impossible! It had seemed so right, so natural only a minute ago; now it seemed merely squalid and ugly'.

The fantasy of bucolic freedom is also entertained and brutally dashed in *Coming Up for Air*. George Bowling returns to Binfield House—the pastoral idyll of his youth—only to find it has been transformed into a 'lunatic asylum'. This is an apt metaphor for where Rousseauian idylls are liable to end up: the desire for an asylum from the world is a lunatic's dream. 'There's no escape', Bowling dejectedly concludes. In *Nineteen Eighty-Four*, Julia and Winston find some escape in the woods. They even manage to have sex. The bird that alights upon their solitude is almost a symbol of freedom—with no mate or rival in sight, he sings 'to please himself'. Yet this little oasis of liberty proves to be tragically short-lived. Though repeatedly yearned for, nature is an unsustainable source of freedom in Orwell. Thus, Orwell's novels seem to endorse Caudwell's assertion that the old pastoral myth of a primordial freedom is an empty dream. Yet the fantasy of the Golden Country—memorably aired in *Nineteen Eighty-Four*—can fan a fantastic hope of independence from all social bonds. Like Rousseau's state of nature, the Golden Country may have no existence in fact, but the utopian ideal feeds the impression that freedom is absent—not only from Oceania, but from all organized life.

The dream of freedom in Orwell does not necessarily entail a bucolic setting, but it frequently involves a desire to escape the dominant social order. A powerful hater of cranks, Orwell was also a celebrant of eccentrics—those who have 'fallen into solitary, half-mad grooves of life and given up trying to be normal or decent'). Unfortunately, eccentricity is itself parasitic on social norms—it's hard to identify what's odd without some idea of what's normal. Nonetheless, Orwell sometimes seems to entertain the improbable hope that one might be able to opt out of social codes altogether or that one might enjoy a strong sense of fellowship without the fun-spoiling mediation of moral and social norms. In *Down and Out in Paris and London*, for instance, he celebrates an underworld of freedom, where people find liberation from the normal trappings of social life. As Orwell explains: 'Poverty frees them from ordinary standards of behaviour, just as money frees people from work'. Here one is down, but at least one is out. It is hard to tell if Orwell's impoverished comrades savour their penury as a basis for liberty, or whether this freedom can only be enjoyed from without—mainly by the middle-class social tourist who is on holiday from his norms. Gordon Comstock has grand designs of joining the 'great sluttish underworld where failure and success have no meaning' and 'shame, effort, decency do not exist'. But the chances are that this is another 'Rousseauism'—a fantasy of radical independence that says a lot about Comstock's libertarian ideals. As we have seen, the dashing of the dream of freedom will lead to fatalism.

Doing as one likes

So Orwell was deeply attracted to a negative ideal of freedom, but this orientation could also be described in more positive terms: it implied a liberty to do as one likes. This construction of freedom was, of course, repeatedly subjected to criticism. When Milton defended the 'known rules of liberty', for instance, it was in opposition to such abandon ('Licence they mean when they cry libertie'). Thinkers from Matthew Arnold to

Harold Laski would continue to present doing as one likes as a flawed ideal of freedom, although not everyone was so disapproving. According to Christopher Caudwell, for instance: 'Any definition of liberty is humbug that does not mean this: liberty to do what one wants'. Orwell's commitment to this kind of license is arguably advertised in the title of his *Tribune* column: 'As I Please'. The attraction of doing as one pleases is certainly a leitmotif of his fiction, although the elusiveness of such pleasure is also a key theme. George Bowling complains, for example, that no one gets to pursue their heart's desire, going to considerable lengths in his syntax to make this an indictment of his times: 'in this life we lead—I don't mean human life in general, I mean life in this particular age and this particular country—we don't do the things we want to do'. Bowling thus sets out to do the things he wants to do—namely, to go fishing in the old stalking grounds of his youth. The bid for freedom fails, but the idea that liberty involves doing what one wants still lingers in the air.

But doing what one wants is a tricky and dangerous business in Orwell and, as I shall argue, this significantly complicates his ideal of liberty. The issue is not simply that our desires may prove harmful to others—consider an entirely emancipated Charlie free to rape and murder at leisure—but it is also the case that our desires may prove harmful to ourselves. Indeed, a standard refrain of rationalism is that the rule of desire is a particular form of thraldom, for it makes one subject to passions that inhere in the self, but are neither chosen nor grounded by reason. As Rousseau put it in one of his more rationalist moments, 'the impulsion of mere appetite is slavery, and obedience to the law one has prescribed to oneself is freedom'. Orwell, of course, never openly indicted desire in this way—in fact, feelings often tend to be a more trustworthy source of motivation in Orwell than arguments or theories. Moreover, emotion tends to be more expressive than reason of who one really is. Reason, by its very nature, is a public resource—its aspirations to universality necessarily entail that anyone can in principle follow its methods and arrive at its conclusions—but Orwell often presents feelings as irreducibly private. So Winston has fond memories of his mother, whose 'feelings were her own, and could not be altered from outside'. He hopes to keep his 'inner heart inviolate', convinced that it is the true locus of his freedom.

However, the absence of a boundary line between inner and outer determination is one of the key problems of *Nineteen Eighty-Four* and indeed much of Orwell's work. Emotions are rigged from the 'outside' on a systematic

basis. Few, for instance, can withstand the energies unleashed by the
State-sponsored hate orgies. 'The horrible thing about the Two Minutes
Hate', we are told, 'was not that one was obliged to act a part, but that it
was impossible to avoid joining in'. *Nineteen Eighty-Four* is a fairly extreme
form of fantasy, but Orwell repeatedly worried about the manipulation of
desire in modern life. Nowadays, he complained, emotions can be turned
'on and off like a tap' and everyone is vulnerable to 'newspaper and radio
hypnosis'. Modern advertising, for Gordon Comstock, is a form of mass
deception, sustaining an economy of false wants. George Bowling may wish
to do as he wants, but he has a talent for talking people 'into buying things
they don't want'. In fact, synthetic desires and authentic needs become
difficult if not impossible to decipher. The very idea of doing as one wants
therefore begs important questions and ceases to be a meaningful account
of freedom.

The case against doing as one likes reaches its apogee in the portrait of
the proles in *Nineteen Eighty-Four*. The account is built upon a fairly condes-
cending set of assumptions: the proles cannot even address questions about
their own liberty (asked if there was 'more freedom now' than in former
times, an old prole responds with addled memories of plebs and gentlemen).
It is clear that they lack every conceivable form of political power or what
some might call 'political liberty'—not that they particularly care. For on
another basic level they remain blissfully free: no attempt is made to indoc-
trinate them with Party ideology, their ancestral codes are not interfered
with, their religious practices are tolerated, and even the police tend to leave
them alone. The proles thus enjoy the liberty of non-interference. Or, conceived more 'positively', they are largely free to do what they want. On
several levels, of course, this freedom is an illusion: the proles are constantly
interfered with not least because their desires are repeatedly manipulated
from outside. Even pornography is administered, while other distractions—
like the lottery—produce an imbecile contentment that ensures obedience
('It was their delight, their folly, their anodyne, their intellectual stimulant').
The freedom to pursue vapid desire doesn't come across as the worthiest
kind of enterprise in the novel.

The problem with prole freedom might again seem to derive from the
simple fact that desire is not, in fact, free and is controlled by external agents.
But Orwell's extravagant account of an all-encompassing State (involving
improbable institutions such as 'Pornosec') tends to obscure his more
fundamental point: that even desires, which are not subject to the control of

others, are a potential source of unfreedom. According to Leonard Hobhouse, one of the great liberal thinkers of the early twentieth century: 'a man may be set free from all external restraint only to find himself the slave of a passion'. No matter who runs the lottery, the emotions it unleashes are potentially imprisoning, fuelling as they do irrational expectations of future largesse. Here, doing what one likes is an insufficient index of freedom; what is required is a thicker sense of autonomy or what Orwell's contemporaries called 'self-mastery'. As Hobhouse explained, 'I am "free"... if my self as a whole is master in its own house, lord, or, better, leader of all its constituent emotions, interests, impulses'. Here the lord of the manor is some form of reason, allowing the self to manage its own desires according to some rationally defensible set of principles.

All this may have seemed like a very quaint ambition in the age of Freud. After all, the 'discovery' of the unconscious could make the very idea of 'self-mastery' look like a delusion: 'Perhaps we are not really "directing ourselves" at all', the young Kingsley Martin (later to become editor of the *New Statesman*) proposed. Of course, it was possible to argue that psycho-analysis ultimately aspired to a type of self-mastery, enabling the self to become lord of its own house by confronting and ultimately controlling its warring constituents. The 'neurotic is unfree'—or so Caudwell maintained— a helpless plaything of his disordered passions and fantasies. Though Freud may have helped to put one's psychic house in order, he also suggested that what often passes for self-mastery is simply repression. Thus, in the great heyday of Freud, the self's subordination to its own inner bully—the superego—could seem like a very questionable form of freedom. The brittle-ness of self-mastery as an ideal is evident throughout Orwell. Throughout his writing, after all, repressed impulses often find expression in homicidal yearning ('I thought that the greatest joy in the world would be to drive a bayonet into a Buddhist priest's guts', the narrator of 'Shooting an Elephant' confides) or in fantasies of rape. Consider the fond Charlie again or the more respectable Winston—a figure who exposes his own unconscious drives in the Two Minutes Hate:

> Vivid, beautiful hallucinations flashed through his mind. He would flog her to death with a rubber truncheon. He would tie her naked to a stake and shoot her full of arrows like Saint Sebastian. He would ravish her and cut her throat at the moment of climax.

This is not an advert for doing as one likes and points to the importance of self-mastery. But the rage and violence is also a product of repressed desire

('He hated her because she was young and pretty and sexless, because he wanted to go to bed with her and would never do so'). It was common fare in the 1930s to extend this repressed frame of mind to society as a whole: power sustained itself through its taboo on pleasure and desire. For all of Orwell's misgivings about Freud, *Nineteen Eighty-Four* provides a lurid extension of this repressive hypothesis. The Party has ambitious plans of abolishing the orgasm, and redirects its citizens' libidinal energies into a hysterical love of country or a virulent xenophobia. Things would be alright, perhaps, if everyone was allowed to do as they liked, but no one is afforded this type of licence in Oceania. And yet the hate-fests and rape fantasies also advertise the virtues of continence.

So Orwell expressed very mixed feelings about the ability to do what one likes. Total licence is not enough—at least as an account of freedom. This is presumably why proletarian freedom is equated with the liberty of beasts: as the Party slogan goes, 'Proles and animals are free'. The proles, it is assumed, are not fully rational agents—a position that is implicitly endorsed by Winston himself. He sometimes regards their stupidity as a boon ('By lack of understanding they remained sane'), but it means they also fail to practise the type of rational self-determination that Winston associates with freedom. The proles are trapped in a bind: '*Until they become conscious they will never rebel, and until they have rebelled they cannot become conscious*'. Winston's paradox of the proles communicates a superb condescension, yet it rests on a strong belief that freedom entails the exercise of reason. Ignorance is not strength and stops us from being true agents.

But this conception of freedom is not without its risks: as we can see, it potentially discredits the agency of others, overruling their freedom in the name of a higher or more rational version of it. The paradox of Rousseau now looms into view. After all, O'Brien forces people to be free, torturing their bodies and reconstituting their minds in the service of a highly dubious model of reason. As he grimly announced to Winston, 'It is not easy to become sane'. With his white coat, elaborate chair, and seemingly limitless access to Winston's unconscious, O'Brien is a grotesque kind of analyst and the 'sanity' he offers is a parody of the type of self-mastery a therapist might promote. Here, of course, freedom becomes slavery. The historian of ideas Isaiah Berlin was convinced that positive schemes of liberty—in which freedom is identified with a specific attribute or practice like reason—are always liable to produce this form of paradox and he lauded Orwell for powerfully making the case against them. Yet the case was less clear-cut than Berlin was inclined to think. Winston also seems to think that rationality is a key constituent of a free life (this is clear from his portraits of the proles) and associates ignorance with unfreedom.

I shall return to the question of rationality in Chapter 4, but one can say with some certainty at this point that Orwell communicates mixed feelings about reason because he entertains radically divergent ideas about freedom. On the extreme end of the spectrum, liberty implied an absence of rules. In this context, even the rules of reason can feel coercive and intrinsically conformist. This is clearly the conclusion he derives from his study of Swift's Houyhnhnms: 'the "Reason" by which they are governed is really a desire for death'—a relinquishment of the labour of selfhood. This is an extremely crude caricature of rationalism, but it clearly reveals Orwell's deep concerns about a republic of reason.

But elsewhere in Orwell reason is a condition of individuality, not its antithesis. In this context, death—often a metaphor for impaired agency or a lack of freedom in Orwell—is associated with those who refuse to deliberate. Perambulating around London, George Bowling feels he is surrounded by the living dead—zombies who are deeply unfree. Perhaps he has been reading too much T. S. Eliot, but he clearly associates mental lassitude with a kind of death. 'We say that a man's dead when his heart stops', Bowling muses, but he believes this is a bit arbitrary: 'a man really dies when his brain stops, when he loses the power to take in a new idea'. The emphasis here is on novel thinking rather than independent thinking per se, but it is clear that he views these practices as intimately related. So while Orwell denigrated reason in the name of eccentricity in his analysis of Swift, he also does the reverse elsewhere, presenting rationality as the basis for individual difference. As we are told in *Nineteen Eighty-Four*, 'Orthodoxy means not thinking—not needing to think. Orthodoxy is unconsciousness'. Critical reason, it seems, is a necessary constituent of a properly free life.

Security or freedom?

Orwell's view of freedom was, as we have seen, an extremely mobile one. But no matter where he stood on the liberty spectrum, his fiction suggests that the modern world is sadly deficient in the actual resource. 'You'd no sense of acting of your own free will', Bowling complains. No one was independent, no one got to do as he or she wanted, no one was one's own master. As Bowling puts it, 'there's some devil in us that drives us to and fro on everlasting idiocies'—the theme of inner possession serving as a metaphor for heteronymy. For Bowling, the inner devil often seems to be fear. 'Fear! We swim in it. It's our element', Bowling declares. Comstock notes the same omnipresent terror: every little clerk carries 'fear of the sack like a maggot in his heart'. For Orwell, it was 'an epoch of fear' and fear, as Laski argued, 'has always been the main enemy of freedom'. Tawney would claim the same in 1944:

> Of all emotions the most degrading and the least compatible with freedom is fear. The brutal fact is that, as far as the mass of mankind are concerned, it was by fear, rather than by hope, that the economic system was in the past kept running—fear of unemployment, fear of losing a house, fear of losing savings, fear of being compelled to take children from school, fear of what one's wife would say when these agreeable events all happened together.

Orwell's Bowling is also a hassled patriarch beset by the same insecurities. He lives in 'a line of semi-detached torture-chambers where the poor little five-to-ten-pound-a-weekers quake and shiver, every one of them with the boss twisting his tail and the wife riding him like the nightmare and the kids sucking his blood like leeches'.

Fear, one might argue, conflicts with both negative and positive ideas of freedom: it is an impediment that resides within the self, making it impossible to do what we truly want or to feel as if we are masters of ourselves. Indeed, the existence of fear implies that others are our masters. Bowling duly complains of a culture of abjection where it is difficult to look people in the eye ('One back-answer and you get the sack'), where everyone has turned into 'yes-men and bum-suckers'. Bowling recoils from the servile mores of modern service culture—typified by the emasculated lump of a lad in his local grocery store ('"Yes, sir! Very true, sir! Pleasant weather for the time of year, sir? What can I have the pleasure of getting you today, sir?", practically asking you to kick his bum'). In another chain store he considers the terrified response of a shop assistant to her boss—'The girl flinched like a dog that sees the whip'—and concludes that the boss probably lives in a similar terror. Fearful himself, Bowling longs for an earlier and more peaceable age, where people had a 'feeling of security, even when they weren't secure'. Such benign false consciousness no longer seems possible.

Throughout the '20s and '30s in Britain, the importance of security was repeatedly stressed while its absence was deplored—as Tawney put it, 'the need for security is fundamental, and almost the gravest indictment of our civilization is that the mass of mankind are without it'. The State's role, it was argued, was not only to provide the security of the person from foreign and domestic threats, but also some economic security. Laski acknowledged that security should not be confused with liberty, but he insisted that the latter was pointless without it: 'Those who know the normal life of the poor, its perpetual fear of the morrow, its haunting sense of impending disaster...will realise well enough that without economic security, liberty is not worth having'. For Laski, Cole, and Russell, the argument for security was one of the most powerful cases for socialism. Indeed, according to Orwell, Britain's journey leftwards was driven above all by the desire for 'more security'.

Not everyone approved of the journey—least of all the Austrian émigré and political thinker Friedrich Hayek. As Hayek famously argued in *The Road to Serfdom* (a book that received a surprisingly tolerant reception from Orwell when he reviewed it for the *Observer* in April 1944), security might be celebrated in the name of freedom, but it was in many respects freedom's antithesis. It pained Hayek to witness people like Laski advocating the kind of arguments that had induced 'the German people to sacrifice their liberty'. Hayek acknowledged that some security is essential to liberty, but when an overambitious idea of it was pursued, then it constituted one of freedom's gravest threats. The idea that centralized control of the economy could be combined with other liberal freedoms was, from Hayek's perspective, a dangerous illusion: since so much of human life had an economic basis or set of entailments, managing the economy would effectively require the management of everything. Totalitarianism would be the ultimate result. In the face of this dark prospect, Hayek found himself reiterating Franklin's dire warning: 'Those who give up essential liberty to purchase a little temporary safety deserve neither liberty nor safety'.

In his review of *The Road to Serfdom*, Orwell admitted there was 'a great deal of truth' in the negative elements of Hayek's thesis. Of course, he could never accept that free market capitalism was the best guarantor of individual freedom: this economic system had already produced its own form of 'tyranny'. Besides, capitalism was 'dead'—or so he had told himself and anyone prepared to listen in 1941. So Orwell, therefore, was no member of team Hayek. Nonetheless, *The Road to Serfdom* seemed to reanimate questions in his mind about the relative merits of security and freedom. He had already observed in 1940—well before Hayek produced his celebrated polemic—that 'Hitler's success within Germany itself shows that many prefer security to liberty'. And as the 1940s wore on, he worried that the English had opted for the same set of preferences.

'Is liberty any use without economic security?' This was the question Orwell posed to his BBC listeners in 1942, but he never produced a definitive response to the question himself. Admittedly, it was difficult to answer during the war. In war-time conditions, after all, it was common practice to prioritize collective security over individual liberties. Before the outbreak of hostilities in September 1939, Orwell had worried about the 'fascising processes which war-preparation entails'. But, as Emma Robinson has shown, he was fairly reconciled to the suspension of civil liberties—from preventative arrest to the use of internment—during the conflict itself. War necessarily implied 'a general diminution of liberty'. He also accepted the need to curtail economic liberties, choosing to see it as a form of 'War Socialism'. Indeed, the war convinced him that centralized control of the economy was the way of the future. He was not alone in this conviction. Debate about the relative merits of what was loosely called 'planning' would come to dominate the 1940s. Viewed by many in England (Laski, Cole, and the Webbs, for instance) as a key means of providing economic security for all, it was predictably disparaged by Hayek and others as the high road to serfdom.

Orwell acknowledged that he had become a socialist out of disgust for poverty rather than a 'theoretical admiration for a planned society'. Yet he also declared that a planned economy was better than 'a planless one'—namely, the capitalist 'free-for-all in which the worst man wins'. Moreover, the war helped to persuade him that a planned economy was inevitable. As he put it in 1941: 'The forces making for centralised control and planned production and consumption are overwhelming. It is the way the world is going'. Hayek roundly condemned this type of inevitability-thesis—claiming it allowed dubious ideological positions to masquerade as historical necessities—but Orwell would simply reiterate the view that a planned economy was inevitable: 'the drift towards collectivism is bound to continue if popular opinion has any say in the matter'. Here and elsewhere he bowed to popular opinion, while expressing superb confidence in his own abilities to track the people's will. 'Hayek's able defence of capitalism', he argued, 'is wasted labour, since hardly anyone wishes for the return of old-style capitalism'. Noting Hayek's worries about the diminution of freedom in the name of security, Orwell made the striking prediction: 'Faced with the choice between serfdom and economic insecurity the masses everywhere would probably choose outright serfdom, at least if it were called by some other name'. For such an avowed freedom-lover, he sounded remarkably sanguine about the choice.

Indeed, throughout the 1940s, Orwell repeatedly associated security with serfdom, while also suggesting that serfdom might not turn out to be so bad. And he took refuge in the view that this gilded servitude was the people's choice. As he put it in 1946: 'it is not much use telling people that compulsory education, compulsory social insurance, control of investments, and direction of labour add up to slavery, since even if it is true, the great mass of the people would rather have slavery than the alternative'. Not all slavery enslaved, and not all liberty was liberating—at least in Orwell's eyes. For instance, he was quite happy to consign 'economic liberty' to the dustbin of history, convinced once again that this was the popular choice. 'I don't believe economic liberty has much appeal any longer', he observed in April 1941. He was confident, however, that other freedoms would thrive in spite of 'the totalitarianisation of our economy'.

But just over a month later, he adopted a very different tone. He now gave full voice to repressed concerns that numerous liberties may be bound up with economic freedom and may perish with it:

> When one mentions totalitarianism one thinks immediately of Germany, Russia, Italy, but I think one must face the risk that this phenomenon is going to be worldwide. It is obvious that the period of free capitalism is coming to an end and that one country after another is adopting a centralised economy that one can call Socialism or State Capitalism according as one prefers. With that the economic liberty of the individual, and to a great extent his liberty to do what he likes, to choose his own work, to move to and fro across the surface of the earth, comes to an end. Now, till recently the implications of this weren't foreseen. It was never fully realised that the disappearance of economic liberty would have any effect on intellectual liberty. Socialism was usually thought of as a sort of moralised Liberalism. The state would take charge of your economic life and set you free from the fear of poverty, unemployment and so forth, but it would have no need to interfere with your private intellectual life. Art could flourish just as it had done in the liberal-capitalist age, only a little more so, because the artist would not any longer be under economic compulsions.
>
> Now, on the existing evidence, one must admit that these ideas have been falsified. Totalitarianism has abolished freedom of thought to an extent unheard of in any previous age.

Even Hayek would have struggled to match this level of alarm in the 1940s. In this bonfire of freedoms—including freedom of contract, freedom of movement, and even freedom of thought—very little would survive.

Orwell's own brand of 'moralised liberalism' was increasingly directed at authoritarian forms of socialism. If socialism implied centralized ownership of property and a planned economy, then he was happy to concede that all industrialized countries 'will be "Socialist" before long'. This was to anticipate Hayek's claim that 'we are all socialists now'. He would also pre-empt Hayek in arguing that Nazism '*was* a kind of socialism', albeit of a non-democratic kind. According to Orwell, both Nazi Germany and Communist Russia had clearly demonstrated that 'the contradictions of capitalism can be got rid of non-democratically and without any increase in individual liberty'. The Soviet Union, in particular, had made it clear that 'Economic insecurity can be abolished at the price of handing society over to a new race of oligarchs'. He berated Laski for skirting over this fact. Laski, in turn, attacked Orwell's identification of Bolshevism and Nazism as a 'monstrous error'.

Orwell tried to reassure himself that the English would be able 'to centralise their economy without destroying freedom in doing so'. He took succour in England's traditions of liberty and tolerance, but he also conceded that these habits were perishable. Indeed, as the 1940s wore on, Orwell would sound increasingly bleak about the prospects for freedom in Europe. Internal to these concerns was a strong distinction between security and liberty and a fear that the former had been disastrously prioritized over the latter. As he put it in April 1946: 'Today the whole world is moving towards a tightly planned society in which personal liberty is being abolished and social equality unrealised'. Again, he attempted to remain fairly quiescent in the face of the popular will: 'This is what the masses want, for to them security is more important than anything else'. But despite his respect for the popular will, he had clear misgivings about the direction taken. His repressed concerns would find full vent in *Nineteen Eighty-Four*—a dark portrait of eternal serfdom. The novel is also an elegy for *ownlife*—or what is defined in the novel as 'individualism'. It is to this many-headed 'ism that I now turn.

The defence of ownlife

In 1945 Orwell complained that the word 'individualism' had become an empty term of abuse. Oscar Wilde had famously backed socialism on individualistic grounds (it would spare him the indignity of living for others), while later currents of socialism denounced capitalism on the grounds that it 'destroys freedom and individuality in the workers'. Nonetheless, many socialists tended to regard individualism with some suspicion: it involved a negative and deeply anti-social view of freedom. Tawney made the case in *The Acquisitive Society*: 'individualism begins by asserting the right of men to make of their own lives what they can, and ends up by condoning the subjection of the majority of men to the few whom good fortune, or special opportunity, or privilege have enabled most successfully to use their rights'. Many more took up the cudgels: 'if liberty is essentially an individualistic and negative factor in life', the socialist academic Delisle Burns proclaimed in 1928, 'the sooner we abolish liberty the better'. In the 1930s Christopher Caudwell adopted a predictable line: the bourgeois 'pursuit of liberty and individualism had led men into the mire'. Spender issued a similar report: 'the European individualist is, in fact, a sick soul'.

Not everyone joined in the abuse. 'I ... deplore the contemporary reaction against individualism and towards what I may call groupism', Huxley declared in 1929. E. M. Forster was an equally unrepentant 'individualist'. In Hayek's eyes, individualism had been reduced to a caricature by its critics, and had been falsely associated with 'egotism and selfishness'. Individualism, he insisted, had nothing to do with a lack of regard for others; it simply assumed that individuals rather than communities were ends-in-themselves, and should be entitled to be their own end-setters. As Hayek put it: 'It is this recognition of the individual as the ultimate judge of his ends, the belief that as far as possible his own views ought to govern his actions, that forms the essence of the individualist position'. Orwell often professed to be happy for individuals to be overruled in determining their own economic ends—as we have seen, 'economic liberty' was something he was prepared to relinquish— but he would also want individuals to be their own end-setters. The problem for Orwell was that the vast majority of people could not set their own goals in a capitalist system. Workers found themselves outmanoeuvred by life and ended up 'gazing at their destiny with the same sort of dumb amazement as an animal in a trap'.

Orwell was a great advocate of individual autonomy, but partly for this reason he communicated mixed messages about 'individualism'. For instance, he had little time for 'an individualistic society in which property rights are absolute and money-making is the chief incentive'. He welcomed the fact that the old English myth of 'sturdy individualism' was no longer swallowed by the masses. In 1945 he was happily reconciled to the fact that individualism was a 'sinking ship'. However, at other points he chose to celebrate the revival of 'individualism'—a credo he associated with intellectual independence and creativity. The contradictory messages stemmed in part from the basic ambiguity of the term: as Max Weber pointed out in 1905, 'the expression "individualism" comprises the most heterogeneous ideas imaginable'. But partly because of the word's tremendous vagueness, Orwell grew tired of left-wing 'tirades against "individualism"' or 'petit-bourgeois individualism': it was a frothy, yet damaging cant that risked eroding respect for fundamental freedoms. His own mixed signals about individualism may be largely semantic—he meant different things in his use of the word—but, as I wish to suggest, they also reflected a more substantive set of problems.

In the eyes of its critics, individualism rested on a dubious metaphysics of the self—an individual who was complete and sufficient to itself prior to its entry into society. The perfect man, according to this scheme, was an existential Crusoe—or so Delisle Burns claimed in 1928. From this asocial starting-point, 'fantastically misrepresenting the basic facts of all experience, it was possible to reach the conclusions of individualism that the less government the better, and that all regulation was interference'. Hayek always denied that individualism entailed a belief in 'isolated or self-contained individuals', but its critics would continue to argue that it was a credo predicated on the myth of the asocial individual. The idea of the solitary self was attacked, for instance, by the likes of J. A. Hobson, Leonard Hobhouse, and Harold Laski. 'None of us is a Crusoe', Laski insisted, and he condemned 'an individualistic scheme of social organisation which refused to freedom that social context...from which alone it can derive a creative meaning'. Caudwell, as we have seen, was an excoriating critic of this anti-social fantasy. The human being, he insisted, is 'unfree alone'. Only through cooperation with one's fellows could true freedom be found.

Orwell may have been attracted to the myth of radical independence, but he also dismissed this asocial vision. The communitarian elements of his politics were heightened by the experience of war. As he put it in 1941, 'War brings it home to the individual that he is *not* altogether an individual'. It might seem a mistake to derive one's sense of life's fundamentals from such extreme situations, but Orwell seemed to think that there was something clarifying about these life-or-death moments: people 'only become aware that they are not individuals in the very moment when they are facing bullets'. In these contexts, it was demonstrably the case that human beings were prepared to sacrifice themselves for a cause bigger than themselves— namely, for the 'sake of fragmentary communities—nation, race, creed, class'. He stressed the value of self-sacrifice not only as a patriot, but also as a socialist. In a review of one of Jack Lindsay's pamphlets in 1944, for instance, Orwell endorsed the seemingly paradoxical thesis that the human being 'is most truly individual when he surrenders his individuality to the struggle for the classless society'.

This idea of emancipating service to a bigger cause was fairly standard fare on the Left in the '30s and '40s. In 1932 Auden suggested that communism was often embraced as a cure for alienation: 'its increasing attraction for the bourgeois lies in its demand for self-surrender for those individuals who, isolated, feel themselves emotionally at sea'. One of the most striking advocates for self-surrender was John Middleton Murry—Orwell's friend and editor at the *Adelphi*. In Murry's eyes, Marx had comprehensively shown 'not merely that the "individual" is an illusion, but that his sole concrete reality is that of a cell of a social organism, governed by unconscious laws'. At the centre of Marxism, therefore, 'lies a grim effort at "depersonalisation" '—a process Murry explained with the help of Christian mysticism. Marxism was simply 'the modern and *real* form' of a Christian ideal of self-purgation. As Jesus had declared: 'He that will lose his life, the same shall save it', and those who were prepared to lose their lives for Marxism had, in fact, everything to gain. Murry had little time for those who might query the costs:

> 'What! Give up everything?' Yes, give up everything. 'All I possess?' Yes, all you possess. 'But my freedom—surely not that?' Yes, your freedom—that above all else. 'But how can I surrender my freedom: I *am* free?' No. You are not free. Your freedom is bondage—to the desire to do what *you* will; you are the slave of interest and self. Freedom is to be free for ever from that bondage, that slavery. That freedom you will gain; that other 'freedom'—that bondage to the self—Communism will take away. 'But this demand is fearful. Such a thing has never been asked of human men before'. Yes, it has been asked. God and Jesus once demanded it; now it is Man who demands. 'But you want me to destroy myself'. That is required. That you should annihilate your self. Destroy your self, or be destroyed! Choose!

This grim either/or confirmed what Murry was only too happy to concede: that he was a politico-religious fanatic ('We mystics, we fanatics! Yes, that is true . . . out of our final loss of all illusion, arises mysticism, arises fanaticism'). Longing for a communist *unio mystica*, he had little regard for 'the supreme bourgeois value, the fine flower of bourgeois culture, the ethical end of bourgeois society . . . the "individual" '.

It is hard to know if Orwell had his friend Murry in mind when he penned his famous portrait of a tyrant—a figure who also identifies freedom with bondage and conceives of the individual as a mere 'cell'. Like Murry, Orwell's O'Brien also preaches a form of self-dissolution: 'The individual only has power in so far as he ceases to be an individual...if he can make complete, utter submission, if he can escape from his identity, if he can merge himself in the Party so that he *is* the Party, then he is all-powerful and immortal'. When Winston finally wins the ultimate 'victory over himself' and learns to love Big Brother, both the moment of surrender and his former resistance are described in a mystical register that Murry also affected: 'O stubborn, self-willed exile from the loving breast!'

In *Nineteen Eighty-Four*, Orwell may have been parodying his Marxist-Christian friend, but he also may have been deriding himself. After all, it was not just Murry who conceived of the individual as a mere cell or conflated self-realization with self-surrender. Nonetheless, throughout the 1940s, Orwell grew increasingly impatient with 'pious platitudes to the effect that "true individuality is only attained through identification with the community"'. *Nineteen Eighty-Four* seems to mount a full-scale critique of a positive conception of freedom in which the telos of the individual is located in a higher-order personality—'the mind of the Party, which is collective and immortal'. Not all forms of positive freedom are necessarily indicted here, but Orwell clearly suggests that metaphysical ideas of a corporate self allow slavery to be sold as freedom.

The Last Man in Europe gives expression to widely shared concerns about the status of the individual in the modern era. 'Our epoch', Eugene Lyons declared in 1937, 'is gangrened by a contempt for the protoplasm of society: the individual human being', and in his last novel Orwell attempts to outline where such contempt would lead. The novel also gives a particular application to Acton's claim that 'All liberty consists *in radice* in the preservation of an inner sphere exempt from State power' (a remark casually cited by Orwell in 1946). That 'inner sphere' in *Nineteen Eighty-Four* resides in the person. The assertion, 'Nothing was your own except the few cubic centimetres inside your skull', may say something grim about Oceania, but it also gestures towards a broader metaphysical truth for Orwell: at some fundamental level, he suggests, the self remains radically private from others.

Of course, such privacy could produce alienation. Orwell would speak, for instance, of 'the star-like isolation in which human beings live'—a solitude so complete that it led to 'the practical impossibility of understanding others or being understood'. Privacy may be a prison, but it is also a space of freedom in Orwell's works. Winston, for instance, is a strong believer in 'the inner heart, whose workings were mysterious even to yourself'. People may be inaccessible even to themselves, but this also provided them with some refuge from others. This metaphysical privacy had always remained deeply attractive to certain kinds of libertarian socialist. As Laski insisted, to be human was to be radically separate from others:

> Man is a one among many obstinately refusing reduction to unity. His separateness, his isolation, are indefeasible; indeed, they are so ultimate that they are the basis out of which his civic obligations are builded [*sic*]. He cannot abandon the consequences of his isolation which are, broadly speaking, that his experience is private and the will built out of that experience personal to himself.

Given these ontological commitments, it is understandable why Orwell would regard Laski as 'an individualist' by disposition. So was Orwell himself. But as his last novel acknowledges, the individualism he advocates is highly vulnerable. The ontological privacy that Winston defends is easily obliterated.

In *Nineteen Eighty-Four*, Orwell may simply have wished to reiterate what he had already argued in 1944:'The fallacy is to believe that under a dictatorial government you can be free *inside*'. But the context-dependency of 'inner freedom' may trigger doubts about its basic existence. Or, at the very least, it may lead one to suspect that the private individual is itself a social creation. After all, in the same year that Orwell published *Nineteen Eighty-Four*, Michael Oakeshott insisted that 'the "private individual"... is an institution, a social, indeed for the most part a legal, creation, whose desires, emotions, ideas, intelligence, are social in their constitution'. Removed from its social environment, this existential artefact would cease to exist. This was not to repudiate the notion of a private 'individual', but it did put pressure on the radical privacy and independence that sustained certain myths of individualism. As Orwell's last novel seems to concede, there are no metaphysical Crusoes and ownlife is never fully one's own.

So *Nineteen Eighty-Four* expresses Orwell's growing concern that the autonomous individual was at risk of extinction, but it also voices his suspicion that this much-esteemed entity is, in fact, an illusion. By conceding to the illusory nature of the private individual, Orwell may simply have been emphasizing its artificial qualities. As Oakeshott suggested, the private self may be little more than an institution—a fragile construction held in place by other devices like the rule of law and by a broadly 'liberal' government.

Nineteen Eighty-Four suggests that these structures require defence if that artefact is to survive. But he also seemed to recognize that the defence of these liberal institutions may be hampered by the very individualism they had helped to foster. It is to this ostensible paradox that I now turn.

Individualism: vice and virtue

Privacy, as Charrington admits, is 'a very valuable thing'. Orwell seemed to have meant different things by privacy—it could imply an inner space behind the breastplate or within the skull; it could also stand for an external but relatively asocial space to be found in 'nature' or in the confines of one's home; or it could refer to a very social domain that remained distinct from the State. But it also stood for a particular kind of value—a negative ideal of freedom in which people's right to be left alone is acknowledged and cherished. Orwell was convinced that this negative ideal of freedom was deeply revered in England:

> The liberty of the individual is still believed in, almost as in the nineteenth century. But this has nothing to do with economic liberty, the right to exploit others for profit. It is the liberty to have a home of your own, to do what you like in your spare time, to choose your own amusements instead of having them chosen for you from above.

Here Orwell celebrated the right to be left alone and to be one's own end-setter. His claim that this freedom had nothing to do with 'economic liberty' may seem somewhat tendentious—particularly since it seems to presuppose a home of one's own. This form of ownership equips people with the conditions for the negative form of freedom he reveres, providing them with a protected space where they are not interfered with by others. Of course, such a space can only be achieved by interfering with the freedom of others (denying their right to camp on your lawn, sleep in your bed, use your toothbrush, etc.). It was arguably for this very reason that Orwell declared private property to be an 'obstructive nuisance' in 1940.

But whatever its economic preconditions, Orwell was deeply attached to the 'privateness of English life'. It yielded, he believed, a deep form of solidarity that had nothing to do with the State—a culture that was 'communal' but not 'official' to be found in the pub, the football match, the back garden, the fireside, and over a cup of tea. Moreover, the broad respect for privacy had produced a hobby-horsical nation—a community of enthusiasts who pursued their own private obsessions unchecked. As Orwell put it: 'We are a nation of flower-lovers, but also a nation of stamp-collectors, pigeon-fanciers, amateur carpenters, coupon-snippers, darts-players, crossword-puzzle fans'. There was nothing, perhaps, particularly heroic or civic-minded about these forms of enterprise, but they suggest that the English had opted for what Constant called 'the liberty of moderns' over 'the liberty of the ancients'. Freedom for the ancients required active participation in politics—or so Constant argued—but moderns sought a different liberty: the freedom to be left alone to pursue their own ends. Constant may not have had stamp-collecting, coupon-snipping or darts-playing in mind, but he maintained that there were other worthy ends outside of politics. Indeed, it violated the grammar of freedom for moderns to suggest that this fundamental value must serve some predetermined end.

So the freedom of moderns necessarily implied some independence from politics—a point that would be conceded by many of Orwell's contemporaries. Aristotle may have defined the human being as a political animal, but Laski insisted it was 'a grave error to assume that men in general are, at least actively and continuously, political creatures'. The main setting for people's lives, he insisted, 'is a private context'. Even if one wanted to lay claim to the freedom of the ancients, the vast scale and specialized nature of modern political units made it difficult for the ordinary individual to assume a big political role. For this reason, Leonard Hobhouse sometimes played down the significance of political liberty for moderns: 'Political liberty, so often spoken of as a guarantee to the individual of his other rights, in reality secures very little to the individual as such, precisely because it has to be shared with so many'. The modern citizen, as Auden famously intimated, was largely unknown, while politics itself, he suggested, was often a tedious affair. Even at heightened moments of republican zeal, Auden found time to complain of 'the expending of powers / On the flat ephemeral pamphlet and the boring meeting', his disillusion sounding a lot more convincing than his vision of civic-minded poets exploding like bombs.

Orwell could find politics just as dispiriting. The election campaign depicted in A Clergyman's Daughter, for instance, is a grubby affair. The slogans produced by electoral candidates—'Who'll save Britain from the Reds? BLIFIL-GORDON! Who'll put the Beer back into your Pot? BLIFIL-GORDON! Blifil-Gordon for ever!'—lack a certain gravitas. Warburton's assessment of the situation is fairly damning: 'Look at it! Just look at it! Look at those fawning hags, and that half-witted oaf grinning at us like a monkey that sees a bag of nuts. Did you ever see such a disgusting spectacle?' This is the liberty of the ancients staged as a grotesque farce:

> Half the ladies of the town seemed to be hurrying forth, with lapdogs or shopping baskets on their arms, to cluster about the car like Bacchantes about the car of the vine-god...There were eager feminine cries of 'Good luck, Mr Blifil-Gordon! *Dear* Mr. Blifil-Gordon! We *do* hope you'll get in, Mr. Blifil-Gordon!'

The sexist cliches—organized around the incontinence of women—loudly make the point that modern elections have a subrational character and are no theatre for the virtues. Here lapdogs carry lapdogs. And the obtrusive shopping baskets underline the point that modern politics is a shabby form of commerce. The bitterness of such polemic may partly derive from the fact that it is an account of a Conservative rally, but socialist campaigners often fare no better in Orwell's fiction.

Consider the famously disparaging account of a Left Book Club meeting in *Coming Up for Air*. George Bowling is not the kind of bloke who usually engages in this kind of stuff, but his worries about the onset of war have produced a spasm of civic interest. So he attends a talk against fascism. The very setting for the meeting—'You know the kind of place. Pitch-pine walls, corrugated iron roof and enough draughts to make you keep your overcoat on'—is unpromising. Few people turn up—the 'usual crowd of fifteen or sixteen people'—and the meeting starts late in the misguided hope that others will appear. 'Why the hell are we doing this?', Bowling asks; 'Why is it that people will turn out on a winter night for this kind of thing?' The seeming pointlessness of such activism may simply emphasize its moral valour for the reader, but it is clear that Bowling mistrusts all forms of civic zeal. The busy attentiveness of the women of the front row, the high ceremony of the 'born chairman', and the main speaker himself—'A rather mean little man, with a white face and a bald head, standing on a platform, shooting out slogans'—all provoke derision.

The speaker is no *zōōn politkon* who seeks to affirm his own rational essence through participation in public affairs; he is one of those 'stream-lined men who thinks in slogans and talks in bullets'. In the reported snatches of his speech, the metaphorical bullets assume a typographical form: 'Democracy.... Fascism.... Democracy.... Fascism'. These decontextualized fragments may say something about Bowling's powers as a listener, but

they are also an indictment of the speaker's methods: sound bites masquerade as arguments, while abstractions so vague allow seeming antinomies to
function as synonyms. Of course, the seemingly interchangeable character
of 'democracy' and 'fascism' may also say something about Orwell's politics
in the late 1930s. Both credos, he contended, functioned as little more than
apologies for capitalism—a position that partly accounts for his initial pacifist stance in the face of a 'capitalist' war.

Bowling finds anti-fascism a 'queer trade': it is self-undermining in its
virulence and replicates the violence it pretends to indict. In the end, he
believes he can see inside the speaker and into the heart of his malign
dream. The man, it seems, wants to philosophize with a spanner:

> Smash! Right in the middle! The bones cave in like an eggshell and what was a
> face a minute ago is just a great big blob of strawberry jam. Smash! There goes
> another! That's what's in his mind, waking and sleeping, and the more he
> thinks of it the more he likes it.

This, of course, is a fantasy of a fantasy and it reveals a jarringly cynical conception of political commitment. Bowling believes that there is something
psychotic in the speaker's absolute identification with a cause. It involves a
commitment so complete that it concedes to a total absence of independent
selfhood ('If you cut him open all you'd find inside would be Democracy-
Fascism-Democracy'). Bowling, after all, is a supreme individualist—a
figure sceptical of authority, suspicious of group-think, and deeply solicitous
of his own freedom, which he often casts as a license to do as he wants.
For many classical republicans, politics was the science that best protected
and best expressed one's autonomy; for Bowling, however, it is an irrational
space, host to a frightening kind of collective unfreedom. Freedom, for
Bowling, seems to imply a freedom from politics—a type of withdrawal
which he hopes to find in the lonely pond of Binfield House.

But *Coming Up for Air* also suggests that there may be something self-
undermining about this quest for freedom. Individualism, after all, was often
regarded as an ethos that was at odds with its own ends. According to
Tocqueville, for instance, it was both a political vice and cognitive failure
which stemmed from a dangerous inability to appreciate the connection
between public and private liberties. So when citizens removed themselves
from public affairs to concentrate on their own private ends, power, he
suggested, was relinquished to administrative elites who begin to enjoy a
dangerous type of license. Thus, individualism potentially culminated in

tyranny, leading to the destruction of the very liberties that have been so thoughtlessly pursued. This dark prospect is certainly courted in *Coming Up for Air*. The focus may be on external threats to personal freedom—Hitler, Stalin, and all the rubber-truncheon boys who wait by England's shores— but the suggestion is that these dangers are heightened by the complacent individualism that prevails in the land.

Initially, Bowling seems to embody this complacency: faced with the prospect of fascism in England, he tries to convince himself that it 'won't make the slightest difference' to chaps like himself. Private life will continue much as it was. But he finds it difficult to believe his own wishful thinking and gradually becomes obsessed with the many spectres haunting Europe. Sitting in bed at night, he is aware of the fact that the political destiny of Europe has become 'more important than the rent and the kids' school bills and the work I'd have to do tomorrow'. He tries to dismiss these preoccu-pations as 'just plain foolishness', but he cannot put his worries to rest. Bowling has slowly come to appreciate the connection between public and private liberties, but this link seems to be lost on many of his peers. He is appalled by the quietism of bookish men such as Old Porteous—a figure who fails to see that 'Hitler matters'.

Travelling through London's suburbs, Bowling is moved by the vulner-ability of its oblivious citizens:

> Miles and miles of ugly houses, with people living dull decent lives inside them. And beyond it London stretching on and on, streets, squares, back-alleys, tenements, blocks of flats, pubs, fried-fish shops, picture-houses, on and on for twenty miles, and all the eight million people with their little private lives which they don't want to have altered. The bombs aren't made that could smash it out of existence. And the chaos of it! The privateness of all those lives! John Smith cutting out the football coupons, Bill Williams swapping stories in the barber's, Mrs Jones coming home with the supper beer. Eight million of them! Surely they'll manage somehow, bombs or no bombs, to keep on with the life that they've been used to?

Bowling dismisses the idea that these people and their practices will survive— 'It doesn't matter how many of them there are, they're all for it'—and it produces a pained set of meditations on the value of privacy.

Bowling has a deep affection for the privateness of all those English lives—a privacy that seems all the more attractive in a totalitarian age where the distinction between public and private realms no longer seems to obtain. But he also suggests that those lives will be undone by that selfsame privacy: immersed in their own private worlds, people do little to rally to their own defence. As Bowling puts it: 'They can't defend themselves against what's coming to them, because they can't see it, even when it's under their noses'. Orwell repeatedly rued this self-induced blindness. As he put it in 1948: 'The British people accept freedom as a matter of course, and tend to forget that its price is "eternal vigilance" '. The citizens of *Coming Up for Air* are subject to an eternal paranoia, but they also feel strangely secure. Indeed, the very sentiment that Bowling believes to have been lost—a 'feeling of security, even when they weren't secure'—is, in fact, disastrously operative. 'They think that England will never change', Bowling complains, 'and that England's the whole world'. Such confidence indicates that security is a paradoxical good and is liable to be squandered when it is most enjoyed.

Bowling recognizes England's peril, but feels helpless to do anything about it. 'All the decent people', he suggests, 'are paralysed'. The sense of paralysis that pervades *Coming Up for Air* may say something about Orwell's pacifist standpoint in 1939—his reluctance to get embroiled in the 'Fascism–democracy dogfight', despite his deep loathing for Hitler. The inertia may also reveal something about Orwell's own conflicted individualism—his deep regard for the freedom to be left alone and his clear recognition that this sort of freedom is liable to undermine itself. In order to defend liberty, it may be necessary to engage in the dirty business of politics, but as figures like Bowling suggest, politics is also a space that seems to undermine freedom, producing a terrible conformism in the name of collective action. Bowling has no intention of relinquishing his private life in order to become a human gramophone. He is, therefore, caught between a rock and a hard place.

Conclusion

'Freedom may be an illusion', Orwell wrote in 1940, 'but you could not, in England, induce large numbers of young men to march up and down proclaiming "We spit upon Freedom" '. For Orwell that fact was vitally important, but he also worried that it was not enough. The problem might be getting English people to march up and down for anything. Orwell was in two minds about the complacency of his compatriots: 'I don't know whether this semi-anaesthesia in which the British people contrive to live is a sign of decadence, as many observers believe, or whether on the other hand it is a kind of instinctive wisdom'. The apathy of the English may have helped to secure them from the bad energy of fascism, but it could also make them peculiarly vulnerable to the foes of freedom. The same could be said of the very English emphasis on 'privacy'. 'The most hateful of all names in an English ear', Orwell opined, 'is Nosey Parker'. If so, Orwell could sound very English: Nosey Parkers from Mrs Semprill in *A Clergyman's Daughter* to Big Brother in *Nineteen Eighty-Four* tend to be particularly loathsome. But as the telescreens and the spies suggest, privacy is a very vulnerable good.

In *The Lion and the Unicorn*, Orwell declared that the English belief in a 'purely private liberty is a lost cause'. Liberty was being supplanted by security and like 'all other modern peoples the English are in process of being numbered, labelled, conscripted, "co-ordinated"' by an increasingly meddlesome State. This interference generates a deep sense of entrapment in people like George Bowling. At the end of *Coming Up for Air*, he dreams he is being pursued by a vast army of meddlers intent on the destruction of his individuality:

> And all the soul-savers and Nosey Parkers, the people whom you've never seen but who rule your destiny all the same, the Home Secretary, Scotland Yard, the Temperance League, the Bank of England, Lord Beaverbrook, Hitler and Stalin on a tandem bicycle, the bench of Bishops, Mussolini, the Pope—they were all of them after me. I could almost hear them shouting:
> 'There's a chap who thinks he's going to escape! There's a chap who says he won't be streamlined! ... After him! Stop him!'

Bowling, I have argued, is an aggressive individualist and Orwell appears to give two cheers to this liberty-loving attitude in *Coming Up for Air*. But he also suggests that there is something self-undermining about the freedom that individualists so doggedly pursue. A narrow preoccupation with one's own personal liberties jeopardizes those very liberties. The public or political conditions of freedom are neglected and power is concentrated in the hands of those 'you've never seen but who rule your destiny all the same'. Bowling is a harsh critic of this type of cultivated ignorance—'Like turkeys in November... Not a notion of what's coming to them'—but his deep cynicism about politics suggests there is nothing to be done. As Bowling declares: 'Fight against it if you like, or look the other way and pretend not to notice, or grab your spanner and rush out to do a bit of face-smashing along with the others. But there's no way out. It's just something that's got to happen'. Bowling is just another turkey, even if he is aware of the approach of Christmas.

Bowling's sense of paralysis may be a function of his conflicted individualism, but it may also say something about the nature of citizenship in the modern world. As I have argued, it was hard to be a Pericles in modern times: the large size and centralized nature of modern States denied individuals a proper forum for their virtues; in a more global setting citizens could feel even more impotent. The ordinary man, Orwell complained, is a passive creature: 'Within a narrow circle (home life, and perhaps the trade union or local politics) he feels himself master of his fate, but against major events he is as helpless as against the elements. So far from endeavouring to influence the future, he simply lies down and lets things happen to him'. Orwell was not alone in ruing this passivity. 'If democratic government is to survive', Laski asserted, 'it must discover means of restoring the individual his personal initiative and responsibility'. Like Laski, Orwell suggested that a policy of decentralization and local government might help to rejuvenate citizenship. Yet for all of his own activism, he also communicated mixed messages about political responsibility. Underlying this ambivalence, I have argued, was a firm commitment to independence—a value he often feared would be compromised by collective action. Even anarchism was 'simply another 'ism' and couldn't avoid the fact that 'all movements involving large groups of people tend to be alike in their intellectual atmosphere'—namely, deeply conformist. Informing his sense of independence was a highly negative ideal of freedom involving the right to be left alone. Of course, this ideal is always liable to erode itself in Orwell, but it was a dream of freedom to which he repeatedly returned. How such a dream managed to coexist with his commitment to equality is an issue to which I now turn.

2

Equality

'The whole English-speaking world', Orwell declared in 1941, 'is haunted by the idea of human equality'. He was convinced that the principle had never been properly realized, but he remained hopeful nevertheless: 'the *idea* is there, and it is capable of becoming a reality'. Orwell insisted that human beings had now produced the practical means for the equalization of social conditions across the globe: 'Human equality is technically possible whatever the psychological difficulties may be'. The psychological difficulties may have been considerable, but the issues were also conceptual and semantic: people meant many things in their use of the concept. Orwell acknowledged that equality was a many-headed ideal, although true to his moralism he also declared that the word was used 'dishonestly' by his contemporaries. The dishonesty almost seems to be enshrined as a principle in *Animal Farm*—'All animals are equal but some animals are more equal than others'. The paradox of the pigs neatly encapsulates the moral inconsistency of a specific regime, but it also raises questions about the coherence of equality as a general concept. Are some forms of equality unequal in the light of others? This was a question that Orwell generally opted to ignore rather than to address, but it had a very practical bearing on his political life. Few writers made a better case for the nobility of equality as an ideal, but few embodied its inner tensions more painfully than Orwell himself. This chapter explores the structure of these difficulties.

Orwell was a champion of equality, but what did this necessarily entail? After all, many of his socialist peers found it difficult to subscribe in an unqualified way to the factual claim that all humans are equal. As William Morris announced: 'Socialists no more than other people believe that persons are naturally equal'. For Morris, the commitment to equality derived from a basic equivalence of need: so when it came to some fundamental issues—like the need for food, security, and opportunities for self-expression—we have generally similar requirements. For people like Tawney, on the other hand, equality derived from the metaphysical assumption that all individuals were of equal worth. 'Equality', he explained, 'does not mean that all men are equally clever or equally virtuous any more than they are equally tall or equally fat. It means that all men, merely because they are men, are of equal value'. Because of this moral equality, individuals were 'equally entitled as human beings to consideration and to respect'.

Yet respect and consideration mean different things to different people and can often seem to be in short supply in Orwell's writing. Take his concerns about the proliferation of 'the gangster and the pansy' in modern civilization or his various reflections on ethnic difference—the Jew in *Down and Out in Paris and London* 'muzzle down in the plate...guiltily wolfing bacon' or the violent fantasies that another of his kind incites ('it would have been a pleasure to flatten the Jew's nose'). He condemned 'Race-prejudice' as a type of neurosis, but he effortlessly concluded in 1942 that 'the majority of Indians *are* inferior to Europeans'. Nor is equality of respect or consideration always on show in his remarks about women. He acknowledged that women 'are the equals of men in everything except physical strength', but female subgroups often fare quite badly in his writing. Consider 'the dreary tribe of high-minded women' in *The Road to Wigan Pier*; 'those malignant respectable women who keep lodging-houses' in *Keep the Aspidistra Flying*; or the 'stringy old women who reminded one of boiling-fowls' in *Down and Out in Paris and London*. Even alarm clocks express 'a nagging, feminine clamour' in Orwell. His socialism may have been founded on equality; yet he rued 'the personal inferiority of many individual Socialists'.

These comments certainly raise questions about the practical purchase of Orwell's egalitarian rhetoric. In fact, in texts like *The Road to Wigan Pier*, he tended to present 'justice' rather than equality as the fundamental aim of socialism. The reasons for this may have been purely strategic. As Hobhouse noted in 1922: 'Justice is a name to which every knee will bow. Equality is a word which many fear and detest'. Overall, however, it is fairly clear that Orwell backs equality as a key constituent of justice: indeed, this is fundamental to his sense of himself as a socialist. As he put it in 1941: 'Socialism aims, ultimately, at a world-state of free and equal human beings. It takes the equality of human rights for granted'. Here Orwell circulated a fairly conventional understanding of socialism: as several of his contemporaries claimed, a 'passion for equality is the one thing that links all socialists'. Yet Orwell also believed that equality was an increasingly embattled principle in socialist circles. He cast this as a betrayal of Marx's legacy, even though the concept of equality was not something that Marx wholeheartedly endorsed.

In fact, Marx's qualms about equality are worth stressing, for they underline both the depth and vulnerability of Orwell's own commitment to the principle. Egalitarian ideals had served a creditable historical purpose in Marx's eyes and he retained a reference to 'equal rights' in the programme for the Workers' International. But in his *Critique of the Gotha Programme* (1875) he also claimed that the notion of 'equal right' was an exhausted and even reactionary ideal. By overlooking the particular circumstances of individuals, rights perpetuated inequalities in the name of justice. According to Marx, the very idea of right entails the application of an equal standard; yet the application of such a standard to different individuals had deeply invidious results. So the seemingly fair-minded claim that one had the right to rewards proportionate to one's labour was a right to inequality: those who are stronger or more adept than others would gain considerable advantages over time. In effect, some would be more equal than others. 'To avoid all these defects', Marx concluded, 'rights would have to be unequal, rather than equal'. Thus, the concept of equal right is deeply at odds with itself.

If Marx sometimes conflated equality with sameness, he plausibly suggested that it was hard to find a specific expression of equality that did not erode the principle on some other level. For utilitarians and democrats alike, equality was embodied in the formula 'everybody to count as one, nobody for more than one', but literal-minded applications of this rule could ultimately lead to highly inegalitarian outcomes. Indeed, the age-old fear that majorities under a democracy would not treat minorities fairly or 'equally' was not an irrational concern in the 1930s. According to Bertrand Russell, 'the rule of majority has the merit that, at worst, it is a minority that is coerced', but this was small comfort if you were a minority. Moreover, the equal right to vote had certainly sanctioned the maintenance of huge asymmetries of wealth. This was one of the key criticisms of 'capitalist democracy' in the 1930s. Here the formal equality of rights between the wage earner and the property owner often served as 'the decorous drapery for a practical relationship of mastery and subordination'. So some forms of equality are less equal than others, although it is extremely difficult to say which should come out tops. To put the issue to the vote is already to decide upon a particular conception of equality and a controversial one at that. And any other proposed procedures for resolving disagreements about equality are liable to prove question-begging. Orwell's hero, Winston Smith, believes that 'Where there is equality there can be sanity', but the sanity of proposing equality as a solution to social problems is at least open to question.

It was certainly questioned by Marx and Engels, and their criticisms of equality were not lost on socialists in the 1920s and '30s. In 1931, for instance, Stalin drew on Marx's *Critique of the Gotha Programme* to declare that 'equalitarianism has nothing to do with Marxist Socialism'. A literal-minded commitment to equality, he maintained, owed its origins to a 'peasant type of mentality'—an atavistic outlook he had made considerable strides to vanquish. Stalin's defenders, the Webbs, also condemned a naive egalitarianism: when it came to questions of the distribution of goods and honours, the slogan of communism 'has always been one of inequality'. In *Assignment in Utopia* (1937), the American journalist Eugene Lyons provided a bitter account of the 'abandonment of equality—in income, living standards, social privileges, etc.—as a socialist objective'. Trotsky's *The Revolution Betrayed* would also make the same charge. As Orwell put it in 1938, 'it is now the fashion to deny that Socialism has anything to do with equality'. 'In every country in the world', he complained, 'a huge tribe of party-hacks and sleek little professors are busy "proving" that Socialism means no more than a planned state-capitalism with the grab-motive left intact'. But he remained confident that the common man had not lost sight of the ethical basis of socialism. As he put it in 1938: 'The thing that attracts ordinary men to Socialism and makes them willing to risk their skins for it, the "mystique" of Socialism, is the idea of equality; to the vast majority of people Socialism means a classless society, or it means nothing at all'.

Equality, of course, was not the only political virtue for Orwell. He would criticize others—H. G. Wells, for instance—for making a fetish of equality at the expense of other political values. Orwell clearly recognized that liberty and equality could clash, although, as we shall see, he provided mixed messages about which value should take priority. He was also concerned that under socialism one form of inequality could supplant another. The economist Evan Durbin spelled out the problem in 1940: 'Economic equality can be fully achieved, and social justice remain as far away as ever because one kind of injustice has replaced another—because one kind of privilege (political) has been substituted for another (economic)'. Orwell found it all too easy 'to imagine a world-society, economically collectivist—that is, with the profit principle eliminated—but with all political, military, and educational power in the hands of a small caste of rulers and their bravos'.

The aim was to avoid this inegalitarian outcome—a dark 'world of rabbits ruled by stoats'—but as the 1940s progressed, Orwell wondered if the hegemony of stoats or, indeed, the tyranny of pigs was well-nigh universal.

Homage to equality

Equality can sometimes seem like an improbable ideal. However, Orwell claimed to have seen something like it in practice. In Spain in December 1936 and early 1937, he had, as he put it, 'breathed the air of equality'. On his arrival in Barcelona, he was awed by what he witnessed. Here the working class 'was in the saddle' and social life had been transformed:

> In outward appearance it was a town in which the wealthy classes had practically ceased to exist. Except for a small number of women and foreigners there were no 'well-dressed' people at all. Practically everyone wore rough working-class clothes, or blue overalls or some variant of the militia uniform.

Orwell appears to have wildly exaggerated the mass observance of a new dress code (at least if contemporary newsreels are anything to go by), but the very idea of such uniformity might seem troubling to some. Even Orwell admitted to an instinctive dislike of some of Spain's egalitarian mores. In fact, some of Orwell's comrades in Spain found him an unrepentant snob. Frank Frankford disliked the 'supercilious bastard' from the start and found his commitment suspect ('He didn't like the workers... There was no depth to his socialism at all'). And yet Orwell declared himself to be deeply moved by the practice of equality in Spain. The apparent removal of inequalities of condition allowed for a certain equality of status: 'Servile and even ceremonial forms of speech had temporarily disappeared. Nobody said "*Señor*" or "*Don*" or even "*Usted*"; everyone called everyone else "*Comrade*" '. Orwell records the angry surprise of an army officer when he was referred to as '*Señor*' by an ignorant recruit: 'What! *Señor*! Who is that calling me *Señor*? Are we not all comrades?' Thus, even the militia system was run on egalitarian lines. As Orwell explained, the 'essential point of the system was social equality between officers and men. Everyone from general to private drew the same pay, ate the same food, wore the same clothes, and mingled on terms of complete equality'.

Orwell initially wondered about the viability of this system of rule, and for good reason. Military discipline did not exist; troops were often clueless about the methods and objectives of the war; many were incapable of standing in line and 'if a man disliked an order he would step out of the ranks and argue with the officer'. He later insisted that dissent could be overcome not by punishments, but by appealing to dissenters in the name of 'comrade-ship'. This put a considerable burden on the idea of solidarity and reflected Orwell's difficulties in challenging a stubborn cliche of political thought: that military effectiveness presupposed a hierarchical system of rule. Orwell attempted to argue that democratic armies were structured around fellow-ship, not fear, and were consequently more efficient, but it was clearly a hard sell. As he put it in 1944, 'even in revolutionary armies the tendency is always away from egalitarianism'.

Yet Spain was the closest Orwell had come to a concrete instantiation of socialist ideals. On the Aragón front, traditional class distinctions seemed to have lost their purchase and many 'of the normal motives of civilised life—snobbishness, money-grubbing, fear of the boss, etc.—had simply ceased to exist'. 'In theory', he concluded, 'it was perfect equality and even in practice it was not far from it'.

However, as I have suggested, these egalitarian practices were not problem-free. Equality and efficiency did not necessarily travel hand in hand—at least when running an army. Moreover, the relations between equality and liberty could appear equally fraught. In Barcelona, for instance, it was clear that equality imposed considerable constraints on the liberty of some, even if it proved emancipating for others. Orwell's ambiguous assurances that the 'wealthy classes had ceased to exist' or his casual observations that priests were 'driven out or killed'—a phenomenon that had appalled Auden, but which Orwell clearly took in his stride—were symptomatic of the problem.

Spain also exposed tensions within the concept of equality itself. The fierce disputes between socialist and anarchist groups in Barcelona were a product of disorganization, poor communication, and mistrust as much as principle. They owed much too, or so Orwell insisted, to the malevolence of external agents such as the USSR. But the factionalism also expressed competing interpretations of equality or—what could often appear to be the same thing—rival views of how it should be put into practice. The government in Barcelona defended its democratic mandate to rule; its critics on the radical Left—including the anarchist P.O.U.M—dismissed democracy in its current form as a hollow or even reactionary practice. Looking back on his account of these feuds, Orwell admitted to giving 'a more sympa-thetic account of the P.O.U.M "line"' than he had actually felt at the time.

In *Homage to Catalonia*, however, he certainly gave that line strong backing, sympathetically rehearsing the view that 'Bourgeois "democracy" is only another name for capitalism, and so is Fascism'. He gave remarkably short shrift to the argument that the Spanish Civil War was 'a war for democracy'. As he baldly declared: 'No one in his senses supposed that there was any hope of democracy, even as we understand it in England or France, in a country so divided and exhausted as Spain would be when the war was over. It would have to be a dictatorship, and it was clear that the chance of a working-class dictatorship had passed'. So *adios* to political equality then.

Orwell later admitted that the Spanish Republic had been much more tolerant and democratic than he had imagined ('In Government Spain both the forms and the spirit of democracy have survived to an extent that no one would have foreseen'), yet after his return from Spain he continued to make the claim that 'Fascism and so-called democracy are Tweedledum and Tweedledee'. Following the outbreak of the Second World War, he made another ideological pivot: 'The intellectuals who are at present pointing out that democracy and fascism are the same thing', he declared in 1940, 'depress me horribly'. The view that democracy and fascism were identical twins was now dismissed as a Stalinist mantra. Yet it had been his own mantra since his departure from Spain.

The vacillation partly derived from Orwell's commitment to two different conceptions of equality—economic and political—each of which would chase the other's tail throughout his political life. A commitment to both equalities was enshrined in 'democratic Socialism'—the credo that Orwell claimed in 1946 to have sponsored for most of his writing life—but the 'ism itself provided little direction as to which equality should take priority. To insist on having both simultaneously was all very well, but it overlooked some of the key political choices of the 1930s and '40s.

Equality as democracy

Orwell, we have seen, embraced 'democratic socialism' as his credo, but the phrase itself could sound either like a tautology or a contradiction in terms. After all, socialists repeatedly proclaimed that they were advocating 'a much broader deeper and more highly developed form of democracy' than was currently available. If this made 'democratic socialism' sound like a very egalitarian form of egalitarianism, it could also make the credo appear deeply at odds with itself—at least if it made the democratic procedures of capitalist States the legitimizing basis for socialist reforms. In 1938 Orwell had no intention of being 'led up the garden path in the name of Capitalist democracy'. During the Second World War, however, he was prepared to travel some way up that path, insisting that democracy in Britain was not entirely negated by its capitalist setting. He still hoped, of course, that a socialist revolution would introduce a 'genuine democracy' to Britain. But much of this was a very circular form of hope, because he also wanted this revolution to be 'democratic'. What a 'democratic' revolution would actually entail was far from obvious. Few revolutions, after all, had been decided by plebiscite. Indeed, he conceded in 1941 that there was 'no certainty that the rule of a privileged class can ever be broken by purely democratic means'.

Orwell had never been very precise about what should be understood by a 'democratic means'. After all, socialists like G. D. H. Cole condemned those who 'would mistake a system of parliamentary elections on a popular franchise for the quintessence of democracy'. These 'doctrinaire democrats', he insisted, were 'the worst enemies the socialist movement suffers from'. Orwell was not one of these doctrinaires. He admitted, for instance, that 'democracy' was a vague word and that any number of regimes had claimed to be its champion. In 1936, for instance, Stalin had proclaimed to have instituted the 'only thoroughly democratic Constitution in the world', while in the 1940s Franco peddled his brand of fascism as 'organic popular democracy'. In these contexts, the word 'democracy' could sound like a fairly empty hurrah.

Nor was Orwell particularly impressed by democracy's conventional forms: a general election, for example, was not 'a pleasant or edifying spectacle'—a point loudly made, as we have seen, in *A Clergyman's Daughter*. He was often troubled by the fact that 'in a democracy people are called on to vote upon things which in practice they know nothing about'. Similar concerns about the people's nous would appear in *Animal Farm*. The prospects for deliberative democracy on the farm are never good, given a sizeable portion of its constituents—sheep and ducks in particular—cannot really deliberate. We learn that all animals 'understood how to vote, but could never think of any resolutions of their own'—a fact which allows Snowball and Napoleon to be 'by far the most active in the debates'. I will return to *Animal Farm* shortly, but an initial assessment of its democratic procedures suggests that Hobbes was right: democracy is always on some level an 'aristocracy of orators'. However, it was the power of newspaper magnates that generally prevailed in England, and Orwell maintained that the orators—at least in parliament—were increasingly irrelevant. MPs were 'simply ghosts gibbering in some corner while the real events happen elsewhere'. Indeed, like many of his contemporaries, he felt he was witnessing 'the twilight of Parliamentary democracy'. He later insisted that the Commons had acquitted itself well during the war and served as a useful megaphone—'a kind of uncensored supplement to the radio'—but it remained 'relatively unimportant' as a legislative instrument. He was prepared to defend these beleaguered institutions ('British Democracy is *not* altogether a sham'); yet he also insisted that 'If democracy means popular rule, it is absurd to call Britain democratic'.

So Orwell tended to distinguish between two concepts of democracy: a literal definition 'in which power is in the hands of the common people', and a secondary or weaker ideal in which democratic values are identified with broadly 'liberal' principles. According to this second definition, a democracy is 'a form of society in which there is considerable respect for the individual, a reasonable amount of freedom of thought, speech and political organization, and what one might call a certain decency in the conduct of the government'. It was only in the light of this description that Britain could claim to be a democratic country—or so Orwell argued. One can easily make the case that it is the principle of freedom rather than equality that is privileged in this second and weaker account of democratic values. Or if equality does survive, it does so as a broad principle of equal protection under the law. The principle of economic equality—or indeed equal power—has clearly receded from view.

To what extent, therefore, should this fairly thin model of democracy— tolerant, decent, liberal, but potentially riven with economic inequality— operate as the precondition or, indeed, limit of socialism? On this point, Tawney was fairly clear:

> It is not certain, though it is probable, that Socialism can in England be achieved by the methods proper to democracy. It is certain that it cannot be achieved by any other; nor, even if it could, should the supreme goods of civil and political liberty, in whose absence no Socialism worthy of the name can breathe, be part of the price.

When it came to the 'proper' democratic methods, Tawney seemed to have in mind conventional criteria for assessing popular consent—namely elections—as well as established civil liberties. It may well seem that liberty rather than equality stands as the core principle here—a position that certainly squares with Tawney's stated views. Equality and liberty were not, he insisted, the Cain and Abel of politics (and their antagonism was often widely exaggerated), yet faced with a clash between these principles, he was clear that 'liberty is rightly preferred to equality'.

It is possible to argue that Orwell shared the same ethical priorities (liberty first, equality second), but it is also demonstrable that he flipped his position at several junctures. 'Liberty, according to some', he noted in a noticeably non-committal vein, 'is incompatible with equality'. He then went on to observe: 'But at least it is certain that the present drift *is* towards greater social equality, and that is what the great mass of the English people desire'. From this relatively irenic description it is difficult to determine what Orwell's actual priorities were. But he often cast himself as a democrat in quite a literal sense—a figure who respected the popular will, while entertaining a wild—even undemocratic—confidence in his abilities to interpret the content of that will. 'But what then do people want?' His answer in 1942: 'more social equality'. In 1946, however, the people's oracle had a different message: 'The masses everywhere want security much more than they want equality'. While Orwell, as we have seen, was deeply concerned that security would supplant liberty, he was also prepared to bow to the people's view: 'This is what the masses want, for to them security is more important than anything else'. Thus, the popular will—however impression-istically or capriciously invoked—could overrule Orwell's weaker sense of democracy—namely, a society committed to broadly liberal values.

Democracy, therefore, was a word to conjure with in the 1930s and '40s. As I have argued, Orwell's 'democratic socialism' included a ragbag of equalities—moral, legal, political, and economic—without ever fully stipulat-ing which should take priority. He may have endorsed political equality in the form of democracy, but he also argued that 'economic inequality makes democracy impossible'. He was highly critical of Huxley's vague hopes that a political revolution towards a centralized economy might be achieved democratically (Huxley failed 'to explain with any precision how we are to set about this'). However, his own thinking on this score did not represent a major advance in precision. He insisted that a revolution was required to make a real democracy possible, yet, as we have seen, he also wanted a revo-lution to be democratic. Orwell's prediction that the 'will of the majority will prevail' under such a revolution—with only a 'treacherous minority' offering resistance—clearly exaggerated the moral and political consensus that was to be found in Britain. As the 1940s wore on, Orwell seemed to lose confidence in the possibility or even desirability of revolution. *Animal Farm* is arguably an expression of this disenchantment. The tale is a powerful account of equality's betrayal, but as I now wish to argue, it is also an intriguing interrogation of the ideal itself.

An egalitarian parable?

Orwell's copy of Godwin's writings contains the following highlighted sentence: 'Fables may use the imagination, but can never stand in the place of reason and judgment as the principles of human conduct'. Orwell may well have agreed with Godwin, but *Animal Farm* is, in fact, a vivid instance of political reasoning. The tale is an example of what Auden called 'parable-art', but what, we might justifiably ask, is its coded wisdom about? Critical discussion of the tale has understandably focused on its immediate polemical function: its damning indictment of Russian communism. As he wrote to Leonard Moore in 1947: 'A.F. is intended as a satire on dictatorship in general, but *of course* the Russian Revolution is the chief target. It is humbug to pretend anything else'. The tale is not uncritical of Trotsky, but it seems to adopt his view that 'the October Revolution proceeded under the banner of equality', while also sharing his contention that Stalinism represents 'monstrous inequality'. Indeed, Orwell referred to *Animal Farm* as his 'little anti-Stalin book'. And in his depiction of the great Berkshire boar, Napoleon, he seemed to recycle Trotsky's claim that Stalinism was 'a variation of Bonapartism'.

Yet the parodic force of *Animal Farm* also functions on a more general level. As Orwell explained in November 1946: 'I intended it primarily as a satire on the Russian revolution. But I did mean it to have a wider application'. Orwell's professed intentions may not provide the ultimate key to the tale's meaning—indeed, I shall argue that the story often means more than Orwell ostensibly intends. However, it is clear that *Animal Farm* has a breadth of reference that is an irreducible feature of its form. Orwell famously called *Animal Farm* a 'Fairy Story' rather than 'a fable'—ironically talking up, it might seem, its improbable aspects. But if the fable and the fairy tale were utterly distinct genres for people like Chesterton ('There can be no good fable with human beings in it. There can be no good fairy tale without them'), Orwell's narrative seems to make short work of these distinctions. A fairy story without fairies, but involving human and non-human animals, the tale has much in common with Aesop's fable of 'The Wolves and the Dogs' (where wolves incite dogs to escape from their bondage to humans, only to devour them after they have emancipated themselves). Orwell clearly exploits the aura of universality that clings to the fabular form: by presenting things as a farmyard fable, he manages to give historical particulars a peculiarly extended life.

This generality gives the novella a special 'kind of permanence' in the eyes of some, although it is also what makes the tale so ideologically problematic. Viewed as a timeless parable, the story potentially rehearses the same general law of revolution that Orwell had once voiced in his diaries:

> A revolution starts off with wide diffusion of the ideas of liberty, equality, etc. Then comes the growth of an oligarchy which is as much interested in holding onto its privileges as any other governing class. Such an oligarchy must necessarily be hostile to revolutions elsewhere, which inevitably re-awaken the ideas of liberty and equality.

Animal Farm stops well short of an emancipatory reawakening, but this only heightens the gloom that emanates from its circular account of revolution. Indeed, the basic plot of the novella seems to ratify the donkey's pessimistic prediction: 'life would go on as it had always gone on—that is, badly'.

Orwell frequently presented pessimism as a reactionary outlook that was wedded to a dogmatic assumption that radical change is impossible. However, he also proclaimed that pessimism was the only 'ism that had ever been vindicated by history. *Animal Farm* does little to challenge time's bleak judgement. This was the 'reactionary bromide' that Northrop Frye detected in Orwell's story: its sad conviction that human character—and by extension political reality—never changes. One of the defining features of the fable form for Chesterton was the static quality of its characterization—the 'wolf will always be wolfish; the fox will always be foxy'. Orwell's characters are not always so reducible to type: Mollie and Clover are quite different and not all of the pigs are swine—at least in a moral sense. Yet the incorrigible stupidity of sheep—or the terrible servility of ducks—seems to put severe limits on what revolution or democratic deliberation can achieve. According to Orwell, 'one revolution after another... has simply led to a change of masters, because no serious effort has been made to eliminate the power instinct'. But his own novella seems to suggest that the instinct is always liable to remain intact, while asymmetries in power will remain as constant as the differences of ability they track.

So the generality of *Animal Farm* makes it an obnoxious piece of propaganda in the eyes of some—one that appears to convert the contingent failings of Bolshevism into a transhistorical morality tale about the intrinsic shortcomings of communism per se or, as Frye maintained, the impossibility of root-and-branch change. It may not have been part of Orwell's polemical intention to deliver this sweeping rebuke, but it is certainly how the novella has functioned for many cold warriors (a position bolstered, perhaps, by Orwell's own conviction in 1947 that the vital political question of the day was 'for Russia—against Russia, for America—against America'). However, the story can be read as a criticism of any number of political ideologies— communism, liberalism, democracy—partly because it is organized around a concept that is usually fundamental to each: namely, equality. There would be no story without this fundamental concept, yet, as I shall argue, the story puts the concept under considerable pressure.

The questions the novella asks about equality are in many respects basic to its structure and often appear to arise behind Orwell's back. As William Empson pointed out to Orwell, he had used 'a form that inherently means more than the author means, when it is handled sufficiently well'. Empson was by no means dismissive of authorial intentions (it would be an absurd 'self-castration', he claimed, to prohibit attempts to recover them), but he also recognized that in literature as in life we often say more than we mean, and vice versa. Orwell never set out to put equality on trial—or so it would seem—but his story, nonetheless, subjects this noble concept to certain stress tests.

The tests derive in part from the story's fabular form. So whatever Orwell's views on animal welfare, his decision to use animals as protagon- ists immediately triggers questions about the proper scope of equality: should it incorporate, for instance, non-human beings? Orwell's ultimate concern may lie exclusively with humans, but the huge differences between, say, naturally clever pigs and incorrigibly stupid sheep put banal assurances about human equality under critical pressure, forcing us to re-examine what the inspirational assertion, 'All men are created equal', might ultim- ately mean. As in most fables, characterization in *Animal Farm* is fairly diagrammatic (characters in fables, Chesterton insisted, must function 'like abstractions in algebra'). Yet the invocation of traits such as intelligence, dishonesty, and vanity may make us wonder about the virtues that might need to be in place if equality is to be practised and maintained. As I shall argue, the tale certainly suggests that equality cannot be guaranteed by purely formal procedures or rules. Finally, the plot of *Animal Farm*—not least because it is often modelled on historical events—contains a series of concrete scenarios (say, when the animals choose leaders, formulate laws, and distribute goods) that stress the situational complexity of any application of egalitarian principles.

Here different contexts reveal different conceptions of equality that put the basic coherence of the general concept in some doubt. Thus, the famous paradox of the pigs has real horns: some forms of equality are potentially unequal in the light of others. This difficulty is both suppressed and constituted by the egalitarian cant of the modern world. Indeed, the pigs' brilliant nonsense suggests that equality is so basic to our language of legitimization (so much so that 'more equal' implies 'more deserving') that we may have forgotten what it means. *Animal Farm* can certainly help us reflect on what the concept might mean. In the following discussion, I shall explore the different permutations of equality that appear in the tale, examining how it functions as a moral ideal, as a legal principle, and as a distributive norm. In doing so, I shall try to emphasize the peculiar doubleness of *Animal Farm* as a moral fable. So the story suggests that there is something very basic or morally primitive about equality as a concept—this is what is so apposite about the tale's ostensibly simple form. Yet the fable also contains a sceptical energy that troubles the intuitions upon which it draws.

Equality as a moral fact

So equality makes its appearance in *Animal Farm* as both a statement of fact and as a value. 'All animals are equal', we are told—a description of how things are and a rule or 'commandment' about how things ought to be. The descriptive statement and the rule are seemingly complementary, but they can also pull against each other. The demand that animals should be treated equally seems to imply that they are not at present equal, which raises questions about the factual claim that ostensibly grounds the norm. Indeed, it is not immediately obvious what equality construed as a fact actually means outside of the banal confidence that animals are animals. On any more determinate set of criteria, a factual assertion of equality amongst animals seems to be blatantly false. It is obvious, for instance, that pigs are cleverer than sheep or ducks. Boxer is stronger than all and if he is more stupid than pigs ('he was not of first-rate intelligence'), he is also, it would seem, more virtuous. For these reasons, he 'was the admiration of everybody'—there is no equality of esteem here, just as there is no equality of intelligence, strength, motivation, virtue, or any other identifiable good on 'Animal Farm'.

This may make the factual assertion of equality between animals difficult to decipher. Indeed, even the definition of an animal is not straightforward in the new republic, and so the scope of equality is unclear. In the end, the animals rely on a simple friend–enemy distinction to designate the object of egalitarian concern—an arbitrary arrangement and the result, perhaps, of transferring the concept of class warfare to human–animal relations. But the essential principle of Animalism—'Four legs good, two legs bad'—is unsettling to some. When the birds of the farm query this maxim, Snowball tries to provide reassurance: '"A bird's wing comrades," he said, "is an organ of propulsion and not of manipulation. It should therefore be regarded as a leg. The distinguishing mark of Man is the *hand*, the instrument with which he does all his mischief"'. This is a joke about legal and political casuistry, but it also raises a more genuine issue of determining the precincts of moral obligation. To whom or to what is equality owed? The difficulties with using elections to decide this issue are quickly exposed. The animals agree by an overwhelming majority that 'rats are comrades', but the exclusion of the rats (and other wild animals) from this vote might already seem to beg the question against them.

More generally, the anthropomorphism of Orwell's fable appears to rebound upon itself and raises questions about traditional distinctions between animals and humans. The line drawn by the animals (two legs vs four legs) is wholly arbitrary and parodies the moral parochialism of human beings. The parody, of course, may be entirely inadvertent: much has been made of Orwell's love of animals—from his attachment to Muriel, his goat, to Marx, his dog—but it is also well known that he loathed vegetarians and related do-gooders (the 'food-crank is by definition a person willing to cut himself off from human society in hopes of adding five years onto the life of his carcase'). Nevertheless, Boxer is a poor advertisement for the knackers' yard and even the pigs may make us think of the moral price of bacon. The claim that the lives of animals are 'miserable, laborious and short'—thanks in large part to humans—resonates through and beyond the text. Indeed, the problem of animal welfare is implicit in Orwell's own account of the book's origins:

the actual details of the story did not come to me for some time until one day (I was then living in a small village) I saw a little boy, perhaps ten years old, driving a huge cart-horse along a narrow path, whipping it whenever it tried to turn. It struck me that if only such animals became aware of their strength we should have no power over them, and that men exploit animals in much the same way as the rich exploit the proletariat.

Some philosophers have interpreted the novella's slogan—'All animals are equal'—on a literal level and have gone on to compare human-centric views of morality (or speciesism) as equivalent to racism and sexism. But Orwell rarely seemed to regard things this way: as critics have argued, Orwell's 'humanism is fundamentally speciesist' and tends to assume that humans have moral priority over animals. The moral thrust of 'Marrakech,' for instance, seems to be that something is seriously awry when one feels more pity for an ailing donkey than for human beings. He may have felt that a concern for animals was built into a 'human' view of the world, but— outside of *Animal Farm*—he did not use the language of equality to make sense of these obligations. Indeed, the animal is repeatedly invoked in his work as a sign of the low and the abject (I'll say more about this in Chapter 3). In *Nineteen Eighty-Four,* for instance, we learn that 'the Party taught the proles were natural inferiors who must be kept in subjection, like animals'; the statement appears to query the treatment of proles, not necessarily the sub-jugation of animals, although once again, concern about the mistreatment of all sentient creatures may be the unintended effect of such analogizing.

Species-centred as Orwell's outlook may have been, he repeatedly con-demned those who would deny that 'human beings are all one species of animal'. The entire rhetorical strategy of *Animal Farm*—which compares the plight of the working class to those of farmed beasts—may connive against this sense of a unified species, although it is certainly consistent with some of his other portraits of the poor and the working classes. In fact, Orwell's tough-talking narrators sometimes struggle to regard others as members of the same species. The narrator of 'Marrakech', for instance, has real difficul-ties identifying with the city's inhabitants: 'Are they really the same flesh as yourself? Do they even have names? Or are they merely a kind of undiffer-entiated brown stuff, about as individual as bees or coral insects?' Yet Orwell liked to suggest that there was a basic equality to be derived from the mere fact of being human—so much so that the phrase 'human equality' becomes a near tautology in his writing.

And yet the nature of this equality was never made fully clear. Human physiology, perhaps, might indicate some basic equality of need. As Orwell sometimes liked to argue, a 'human being is primarily a bag for putting food into', and on some fundamental fronts he seemed to assume we are all fairly similar. So we tend to need food, shelter, and security as a basic function of what we are (though the difficulty of measuring 'need' will be explored downstream). Hobbes, moreover, had famously attested to a natural equality on the basis that all humans were equally vulnerable to injury. This sense of vulnerability was brilliantly captured by Auden during the Sino-Japanese War and it testified, he believed, to the fundamental equality of human beings. As he put it, 'the hospitals alone remind us / Of the equality of man'. Orwell's egalitarianism may have stemmed from a similar sense of human frailty (we shall explore his preoccupation with the suffering body at some length in Chapter 3), but he also seemed to subscribe to a more metaphysical thesis that human beings—despite their many differences—are of equal worth. Unlike Tawney, he had no obvious religious bent, but he explicitly endorsed 'the "Jewish" or "Judæo-Christian" idea of equality'—namely the belief that all human souls are equal before God.

Orwell often suggested that a presumption of equal worth was built into a 'human' outlook on others. He roundly mocked evaluative uses of the term 'human' in *Keep the Aspidistra Flying* (where it appears as an empty and pretentious assignation of value) and he would go on to dismiss it as a meaningless epithet in 1946. But this had little bearing on his own practice. Orwell's rhetoric, after all, was all too human. He advocated, for instance, a 'fully human life', discriminated between policies that would make people 'more human or less human', and distinguished between 'a human and an inhuman world'. He also praised somewhat unctuously the 'deeply human atmosphere' of working-class homes. Evidently, the word 'human' possessed a dizzying semantic range in his oeuvre. In some settings, it seemed to have little to do with equality: he praised feudalism, for instance, for being more 'human' than capitalism. Yet in other contexts it clearly had an egalitarian dimension. In Spain, for instance, he proclaimed that 'Human beings were trying to behave as human beings'—under socialism, in other words, humans were behaving as equals, treating each other with equal respect and concern. And yet he worried that socialism itself 'appeals chiefly to unsatisfactory or even inhuman types'.

Orwell's brand of humanism might seem as vague as it was winsome. No values concerning humans, one might argue, can be derived from the simple fact of their being human, though it's hard to see why the movement from 'what is' to 'what should be' necessarily involves a logical error. Some on the Left, moreover, found it both empty and self-deceiving to ask humans to behave as humans. Marx had famously mocked the abstraction of much human-talk: all classes melt away before the solemn concept of 'humanity', and Orwell was clearly sympathetic to this line of criticism. 'A humanitarian is always a hypocrite', he declared in 1942—a pious pontificator whose abstract moralism easily cohabited with the structural inequalities it professed to indict. Like many in the 1930s, he also wondered if a basic belief in a stable human essence were not a conservative outlook; pessimists who insisted on the 'immutability of "human nature"' were merely turning their back on radical political change. Orwell, in contrast, believed that 'human society, and therefore human nature, can change'. Here he insisted that the acquisitive instincts—often invoked as a psychological argument against socialism—might be 'bred out in a couple of generations'. Yet in other contexts he worried about this same malleability. As he declared in January 1939, it was 'just as possible to produce a breed of men who do not wish for liberty as to produce a breed of hornless cows'. He could have said the same about equality also.

Orwell's humanism may have been vague, platitudinous, and more historically contingent than he was always willing to concede; nonetheless, his idea of treating people from a 'human' point of view was not completely empty. It implied a sense of respect and concern for the other as a moral agent equal to oneself. It was arguably best summed up by Orwell's concept of decency—on one level a hopelessly 'bourgeois' notion, but on another level a noble ideal that attempted to see others as ends in themselves. This might sound like a very vague ambition, yet contemporary history provided several examples of where the decent or 'human' view was not adopted. Orwell frequently itemized instances of exploitation where it was assumed that 'the exploited *are not human beings*'. Nazism was the most spectacular example of this sectarian outlook (here 'Jews and Poles aren't human beings'). Indeed, it was the idea of human equality, above all, 'that Hitler came into the world to destroy'. 'The driving force behind the Nazi movement', he insisted, 'is the belief in human *inequality*'. Here the idea of a common humanity is either relinquished or drastically circumscribed. Under Nazism, as he put it, 'only Nordic man is fully human'.

Throughout the 1940s, Orwell appealed to a more inclusive model of the human. Indeed, he chastised Sartre—unfairly—for fostering the impression that there is 'no such thing as a human being, there are only different categories of men'. Yet *Animal Farm* communicates mixed messages on this score: all may unite as animals, but they also operate as different species of animal. Readers may feel that Orwell distorts and exaggerates differences of ability and character between humans by aligning them with distinct types of animals. Indeed, it can be easily argued that Orwell begs the question against equality by making the distribution of virtues so asymmetrical and biologically basic on 'Animal Farm' (I'll say more about this later).

Orwell's point may simply be that equality does not entail identity and that the differences between animals do not preclude the need to treat them equally. After all, Hayek once made the laconic claim that 'only because men are in fact unequal can we treat them equally'. Hayek was again emphasizing how the injunction to treat people equally may pull against the impression that they are in fact already equal. He clearly had difficulties subscribing to the bald fact. Equality, for Hayek, did not imply an identity of capacities, interests, or social roles, but rather general norms of equal treatment. This was achieved 'by the formal equality of the rules applying in the same manner to all'. But, as I now wish to argue, *Animal Farm* has very interesting things to say about the limits of rules as guarantors of equality.

Equality as universality

In Hesiod's *Works and Days*, it is intimated that the distinguishing mark of the human is a sense of justice. As Hesiod declares to his brother Perses, this is what differentiates humans from beasts:

> The son of Kronos has laid down the law for humans.
> Fish and beasts and birds of prey feed on
> Each other, since there's no justice among them.
> But to men he gave justice, and that works out
> All to the good.

Animal Farm affirms this species-distinguishing justice through its ironic inversion: animals possess a sense of what's right but humans, it would seem, don't. The sign that pigs have crossed a moral Rubicon is that they ultimately become indistinguishable from humans ('The creatures outside looked from pig to man, and from man to pig, and from pig to man again: but already it was impossible to say which was which').

But if the tale emphasizes the importance of justice as the distinguishing mark of the human, it also suggests that equality is its key constituent. As John McMurray argued in 1933, 'equality is the basis of justice and law', and *Animal Farm* often encourages us to think the same. The Seventh

Commandment—'*All animals are equal*'—is in a sense the law of laws, outlining as it does both the motive and the form of justice. The motive of the law comes from the fact that animals are moral equals, and this equality is embedded in the form of the law, namely its universal character. Thus, the law is equally inclusive of everyone. But Orwell immediately raises questions about the sufficiency of these laws: only some animals get to formulate the law, only the clever can remember it, and 'the stupider animals such as the sheep, hens and ducks were unable to learn the Seven Commandments by heart'—itself not a very good measure of legal understanding. This unequal grasp of the law exposes the inadequacy of the formal equality the law enshrines. It certainly helps the pigs to break the rules or to modify them for their corrupt purposes. Thus, the law itself becomes the instrument of arbitrary power.

So in *Animal Farm* Orwell seems to record his doubts about the sufficiency of law as a guarantor of equality. He always found it difficult to believe that law was a mere superstructural expression of relations of power, but he felt that there were deep inequities in the application of justice. 'Everyone knows', he declared in 1941, 'that there is one law for the rich and another for the poor'. He disparaged the English for conflating the law, which was often 'stupid and cruel', with morality; at the same time, he admired their 'respect for constitutionalism and legality'. Above all, he applauded an English confidence in the impartiality of the law: everyone believed 'that the law can be, ought to be, and, on the whole, will be impartially administered'. In *Animal Farm*, however, the pigs both exploit and negate this shared belief in the impartiality of justice. In their trotters, the law becomes an instrument of oppression.

Yet if readers are to understand the iniquity of the pigs, they must also assume that justice should be impartial or equal. Moreover, for justice to be equal, it must be universal: a rule for one is a rule for all. It is striking how little needs to be said about this within *Animal Farm*. Indeed, the often spare and seemingly non-committal features of the narrative voice merely emphasize the commitments readers bring to the text on this issue. Admittedly, the narrator helpfully notices 'injustices' (like the shirking of work by some or the stealing of goods by others), and these observations are arguably implicit normative judgements; yet explicit inferences about the injustice of these acts and the reasons for deeming them so are generally avoided. Here readers must enact their own commitment to the principle of universality and the equality it presupposes: they easily intuit, for instance, that the pigs, the cat, and the vain mare all act unfairly when they exempt themselves from the universal scope of the moral law. These creatures repeatedly treat themselves as exceptions in ways that break the Seventh Commandment and regard their own ends as unequal compared to the ends of others.

As I suggested earlier, the very form of Orwell's fable gets us to think in a general key, and the story, as a whole, helps us to recognize that an ability to think generally—or in universal terms—is a prerequisite for treating people equally. As Tawney put it in his great study of equality: 'The test of a principle is that it can be generalized, so that the advantages of applying it are not particular, but universal'. Indeed, parts of Orwell's novella can be read as a Kantian morality tale that shows how a sense of universality shapes our sense of justice. Let us run with this rather counter-intuitive reading for a while, because it will help us to expose the kind of moral intuitions we do in fact bring to the text. This moral tact is not easily reducible to rules and it can seem tactless to attempt to construct them. It may be another violation of tact to regard *Animal Farm* as a Kantian parable, yet the obvious limitations of such an approach also expose an interesting set of limits: that equality (and morality) per se is not reducible to rules. Nor is it exhausted by ideas of universality, however basic this may be to our sense of justice.

So in order to enshrine a type of equality that was compatible with freedom, Kant asked us to submit our actions to certain tests. He encouraged us to imagine a rule for an action, which everyone could freely follow and choose to apply, and in a further step he asked us to imagine the universal observation of that rule. If this could be done without self-contradiction, then the action was permissible. Of course, none of Orwell's animals set themselves these arcane exercises; yet the paradox of the pigs brilliantly emphasizes how far equality-as-universality is fundamental to our sense of moral coherence. Their attempts to justify their behaviour lead to self-contradiction: their iniquity cannot be coherently formulated into a universal law for it breaches the most fundamental feature of all justice—the formal equality of law itself. Indeed, on the basis of this paradox, it might be tempting to think that all iniquitous actions on 'Animal Farm' would yield contradictions when universalized, thus violating—however indirectly—the precept that all animals should be treated as equals.

But such an approach is troubled by basic issues of plot. While the actions of some animals may seem contradictory, only propositions—not actions— yield genuine contradictions. If pressed, we might try to construct maxims for certain moral deeds we observe in the tale in order to see where their universalization would lead; yet actions are not self-interpreting and lend themselves to different descriptions or maxims. Even if the idle Mollie accompanied her behaviour with the helpful statement—'it is right that I sit on my haunches while others work'—the universalization of this claim is not logically incoherent. And yet some Kantian animal might say that it points to a practical contradiction: if idleness became the universal norm, the practice 'work' would disappear on 'Animal Farm'. Here Mollie's maxim would not even make sense. Her idleness can only be properly enjoyed if it is the rule of other people to work. This means that Mollie effectively wills two contradictory things: that work is a binding rule and that it is not binding. Mollie's double standard violates the form of the law, for it cannot be coherently universalized, and it breaches the motive of the law—her own needs take priority over the equal consideration of others. Her idleness, therefore, transgresses the equality that is fundamental to 'Animal Farm'.

The same holds true of the pigs. They repeatedly lie in ways that seem deeply unfair on an intuitive level, but these intuitions can be sharpened into something more philosophically explicit. Once again, the double standard of the pigs reveals a practical contradiction: the very concept of lies is parasitic on the practice of truth-telling. If lying were universal, the practice of truth would break down and even the notion of lying would not make sense. Thus, the universalization of a maxim in favour of lies would be incoherent both in its conception and as a form of volition: in order for lies to work, the pigs must will that animals are ruled by truth and not ruled by truth. In this arbitrary commitment to truth, they prioritize their own ends over those of others and thus practise a form of inequality.

All this makes things sound like a very Kantian fairy tale in which justice as universalizability holds a special role. But the ingenious proposals of Orwell's pigs also put this conception of justice under pressure. The strong links between equality, universality, and fairness may explain why some rules on the farm, like the prohibition against killing, may initially seem right to readers: the rule guarantees an equal right to life and can be universalized without contradiction. However, its opposite—a rule sanctioning killing—initially seems to survive the test of universalization. Life in a state of universal war may be nasty, brutish, and short, but it is not unthinkable—some have imagined it in detail. In any event, a rule that precluded all killing might easily be regarded as too strong. Shaw would have certainly thought so: the killing of 'scoundrels and good-for-noughts', he believed, 'is quite reasonable and very necessary'. Not everyone might share this tough-minded vision; nonetheless, the idea of justifiable killing—in self-defence or in the resistance of tyranny—was a widely accepted view in Orwell's England. So we might doubt the virtue of the pigs, while essentially agreeing with the content of their modified rule—'No animal shall kill any other animal *without cause*'.

Naturally, some readers may wonder about the justice of this modified rule, but it brilliantly captures the limits of universalizability as a criterion of justice, for the principle is either too strong in what it prohibits or too weak in what it allows. The dangerous supplement of the pigs (*'without cause'*) suggests that a host of rules can be universalized if they are made sufficiently indeterminate, and can even license exceptions to themselves. Such rules expose the limits of what rules can achieve. They also demonstrate that universality does not exhaust the idea of justice or equality. Indeed, many of the rules on the farm—*'No animal shall wear clothes'*, *'No animal shall sleep in a bed'*, or *'No animal shall drink alcohol'*—can be universalized without self-contradiction. But so too can their opposites. The institution of private property, which the animals ostensibly bring to an end, is easily universalizable, but it is not regarded by them as just.

When Kant asked us to imagine what the universalization of a rule would look like, he showed how acts of imagination are fundamental to moral understanding. But Orwell imagined a series of moral scenarios that easily expose the limits of the Kantian imagination and the type of justice it envisages. However necessary, the universalizable feature of a law is an insufficient indication of its justice on Orwell's farm. Moreover, substantive issues of equality cannot be settled by this principle alone. This pertains especially to the idea of distributive justice—an idea that is central to 'Animal Farm'. But here again, Orwell imagines a number of scenarios that put some classical theories of distributing social goods under pressure—capitalism seems to be dismissed from the very outset of *Animal Farm*, but throughout the tale some of Marx's proposals also come under pressure.

Equality and distributive justice

In his preface to the Ukrainian edition of the novella, Orwell indicated that he had attempted 'to analyse Marx's theory from the animals' point of view'. It is not clear what exact theory Orwell had in mind, nor is it even evident that he had a comprehensive grasp of Marxist doctrine. Old Major is sometimes viewed as a porcine Marx, but it is doubtful that the real Marx would have given unqualified support to the pig's teachings. 'All animals are equal', Old Major maintains, but Marx, as we have seen, criticized equality for being vague in conception and often incoherent in its application. In his *Critique of the Gotha Programme*, Marx condemned the idea of equal right as a distributive principle, but here he also endorsed an alternative theory of what is called distributive justice, even though Marx recoiled from the idealistic odour of terms such as 'fair distribution'. Here he reiterated Louis Blanc's famous phrase: 'From each according to his abilities, to each according to his needs!' The same principle was endorsed by both Lenin and Stalin, and would do the rounds in leftist circles in Europe throughout the 1930s.

In 1936 John Strachey presented the abilities–needs principle as a useful alternative to 'equality' as a distributive programme; however, it might easily be regarded as a specific application of egalitarian values. The principle, after all, guarantees equal respect and consideration for all, while accommodating the differences between individuals and their circumstances. For as Tawney argued in 1931: 'equality of provision is not identity of provision. It is to be achieved, not by treating different needs in the same way, but by devoting equal care to ensuring that they are met in the different ways most appropriate to them'. The abilities–needs principle clearly obtains on 'Animal Farm'—hardly a surprise, given that Stalin had declared it to be one of the key distributive principles of the USSR. So we repeatedly hear that the animals are 'all equal, each working according to his capacity, the strong protecting the weak'. The contribution of the hens and the ducks at harvest time is modest (they save five bushels of corn by gathering up stray grains), but it is proportionate to their abilities. In theory, at least, each animal is rewarded according to its needs.

Orwell does much to highlight the moral substance and efficiency of this distributive system: it initially yields 'the biggest harvest that the farm had ever seen' and the animals find themselves 'happy as they had never conceived it possible to be'. But he also raises some of the standard objections to the practice of grounding distribution on relative need. While this may seem to be an efficient and fair system in theory, the actual content of these needs is not self-evident. The pigs, for instance, can invoke the language of necessity for corrupt ends—'Milk and apples (this has been proved by Science, comrades) contain substances absolutely necessary to the well-being of a pig'. Readers may easily dismiss this special pleading, but the incident shows that our needs are not self-evident. In any event, the principle of need would tell us little about how to distribute a broad range of goods such as social or political honours or items such as ribbons, alcohol, or sugar. These goods may be superfluous to need, but they raise key problems about the criteria for fair distribution on 'Animal Farm'.

The corrupting effect of luxury is, of course, an ancient theme of political thought and Orwell was alert to the ways in which opulence can aggravate desire, enervate citizens, spawn inequality, and erode the social bond. During the Second World War, he gave his backing to the laws against luxury: 'since certain luxuries—high powered cars, for instance, fur coats, yachts, country houses and what-not—obviously can't be distributed to everybody, then it is better that nobody should have them'. Though *Nineteen Eighty-Four* might seem to communicate some misgivings about rationing, Orwell also endorsed curbs to 'luxury feeding'. Orwell's animals similarly institute a series of sumptuary laws not only to ensure social equality, but also to restrict appetites to needs. So, '*No animal shall wear clothes*'; '*No animal shall drink alcohol*', etc. Old Major also prohibits trade with other farms: values mediated by exchange should not supplant those predicated on need.

This autarchic experiment is soon abandoned in an effort to secure raw materials for the windmill—a key component of the electrification programme. This is an obvious reference to Soviet trade agreements that had been in operation since 1921, but it also foregrounds the difficulties of aligning production with brute need. In 1937 Orwell had already depicted electricity as a corrupting luxury that supplanted real necessities: here he was struck by the 'queer spectacle of modern electrical science showering miracles upon people with empty bellies'. This account of skewed priorities leads to the following reflection: 'Whole sections of the working class who have been plundered of all they really need are being compensated, in part, by cheap luxuries which mitigate the surface of life'. Orwell's campaign against electricity may have seemed somewhat Luddite even to contemporaries, but it certainly indicates that what we 'really need' is a highly contestable issue.

Distribution according to need also fails to accommodate notions such as 'desert'—a key point of debate on the Left in the 1930s. The system on 'Animal Farm' is certainly vulnerable to abuse by free riders such as Mollie and the incorrigible cat ('It was soon noticed that when there was work to be done the cat could never be found. She would vanish for hours on end, and then reappear at meal-times, or in the evening after work was over, as though nothing had happened'). The animals seem to accept this abuse stoically enough—much more generously than some of Orwell's contemporaries.

In Shaw's books, the idler 'was the common enemy of mankind' and he had radical proposals for dealing with such figures. As he explained to Graham Wallas, 'we must get rid of the notion than any choice can be tolerated in the obligation to work'. 'Direct unhesitating compulsion', he insisted, 'should be a matter of course'. Mollie would be unlikely to thrive on one of Shaw's farms—or indeed, one of Stalin's. After all, St Paul's tough love—'He who does not work, neither shall he eat'—had long been established as 'the prime, basic and root principle of socialism' in the USSR.

Orwell's animals are in contrast a rather forgiving bunch: if work or desert is not a criterion of reward on the farm (at least initially), neither is it one of censure. Nonetheless, Mollie's laziness and the cat's truancy raise painful questions about incentives under socialism. For it is clear that work is not its own reward on 'Animal Farm'. Orwell made much of the joys of work (I'll say more about this in Chapter 5), but he also conceded that it was difficult to escape the fact 'that certain jobs which are vitally necessary are never done except under some kind of compulsion'. This problem, he claimed, had been almost entirely overlooked by socialists. But this was clearly untrue: the problem of incentives had been a point of considerable debate throughout the 1930s. As John Strachey put it in 1936: 'Any economic system which is to get the best out of such beings as we are to-day must know how to provide incentives appropriate of different men and women, and of the same men and women at different times'. He hoped that work would become its own end under socialism, but he also suggested that it should be supplemented by 'socialist competition' and a benign shame culture—'a system of public praising for good work, and public blaming for bad work'.

To what extent does Orwell rely on incentives in *Animal Farm*, given that work is sometimes cast as a bore? The fable never seems to entertain Marx's suggestion that work would become a direct pleasure and expressive need— 'not merely a means of life, but life's prime want'—in the communism of the future. On 'Animal Farm' it is 'an acute positive pleasure' to consume the product of one's labour, but work is still a drudge. The electrification programme is ultimately a bid to reduce 'sordid' labour and Snowball hopes that technology will one day make it seem like an anachronism: 'fantastic machines... would do their work for them while they grazed at their ease in the fields or improved their minds with conversation'. But in the meantime, work still feels like a chore.

It thus appears that neither equality nor solidarity has sufficient motivational force on 'Animal Farm'; other incentives are required. This problem is implicitly acknowledged in the honours system on the farm. After the 'Battle of the Cowshed', Snowball and Boxer are awarded the title 'Animal Hero, First Class', while the decoration 'Animal Hero, Second Class' is conferred posthumously on the dead sheep (even in glory, the sheep always remain an inferior type of beast on 'Animal Farm'). Orwell is obviously parodying the Soviet awards system—the Order of the Red Banner given to Trotsky for his defence of Petrograd or the numerous honours given to Stakhanov—but these new titles raise general questions about the relationship between equality and merit.

Egalitarians had often defended the idea of merit-based distinctions. Rousseau, for instance, promoted two types of equality: one which indifferently distributes advantages to all, and another which is based on merit. The State, he maintained, has need of both systems. 'Animal Farm' also employs these two forms of equality, although it is not clear if each system marks the corruption of the other. Orwell clearly indicates that the honours system is open to abuse. Napoleon confers several titles upon himself ('Animal Hero, First Class' and 'Animal Hero, Second Class') and soon other distinctions are introduced: other animals must stand aside for pigs on public paths, and pigs get to wear ribbons on Sundays. These distinctions have ostensibly nothing to do with merit, although the corruption of the merit system should not obscure the fact that 'need' is not the only distributive norm on 'Animal Farm'; nor, perhaps, should it be. As Tawney forcefully argued in the '30s: 'No one thinks it inequitable, that, when a reasonable provision has been made for all, exceptional responsibilities should be compensated by exceptional rewards, as a recognition of the service performed and an inducement to perform it'.

If 'Animal Farm' makes distinctions on the basis of merit, it also discriminates between abilities. The request for input from all that is proportionate to the capacities of each may seem like a fair and efficient form of social organization, but, as *Animal Farm* indicates, it also has some worrisome downsides. For instance, it yields an almost Platonic—and deeply elitist—set of social arrangements on the farm. Plato had recommended the distribution of social roles according to natural aptitude ('each individual should follow, out of the occupations available in the city, the one for which his natural character best fitted him') and had consequently defended a strict division of labour in his ideal republic. Thus, if you are naturally disposed to shoe-making, you should stick to making shoes—indeed, 'doing one's own job, and not trying to do other people's jobs for them, is justice' in Plato's eyes.

The creatures on 'Animal Farm' also have natural traits and talents, which equip them for certain occupations. But since leadership is one such role, the political outcomes of a strict division of labour are fraught. The pigs, it seems, constitute a natural aristocracy: 'With their superior knowledge it was natural that they should assume the leadership'.

It is difficult to tell if the perceived naturalness of this decision is endorsed or merely reported by Orwell's narrator. T. S. Eliot certainly believed that the pigs were 'best qualified to run the farm—in fact there couldn't have been an Animal Farm without them'; all they needed to do was to supplement their superior intelligence with a superior virtue. Orwell's pigs certainly raise tough questions about the relationship between competence and equality. So do his brainless sheep. Nonetheless, by making intellectual competence a fixed and innate trait in certain animal species, Orwell arguably downplays the ways in which goods like intelligence are socially constituted and expressed differently across different practices. As Tony Crosland argued a decade after the publication of *Animal Farm*, 'superior intelligence' is often a product of parental status and beneficial upbringing. Its fair distribution in society is already an important moral and political question.

Goods such as intelligence dictate a basic division of labour on 'Animal Farm'. The pigs make much of the fact that they are 'brainworkers' (incidentally, a type of labourer that was repeatedly lauded by Shaw and the Webbs), and assume leadership for themselves. However, intelligence may be the product of the division of labour as much as it is its legitimizing condition. Adam Smith, for instance, extolled the division of labour as the engine of progress, but he also worried that it stupefied workers, making them unfit for 'rational conversation'. Since this stupidity is socially constituted, the distribution of intelligence already raises questions of social justice—a point repeatedly emphasized by Marx in his criticisms of the division of labour. Marx acknowledged that both the specification and delegation of function 'develop spontaneously or "naturally" by virtue of natural predisposition', but he also insisted that it shaped the personality of man, usually for the worse (it 'turns man as far as possible into an abstract being, a machine tool, etc., and transforms him into a spiritual and physical monster'). Presumably, this is why he suggests that the division of labour must be transcended before the distributive principle of communism—'from each according to his abilities'—can fairly apply, although his earlier account of this transcendence (where one hunts in the morning, fishes in the afternoon, rears cattle in the evening, and criticizes after dinner) reads like an extravagant hope rather than a plausible prediction.

Nevertheless, Marx's criticisms of the division of labour help to emphasize the complacency of Goldstein's account of modern social development in *Nineteen Eighty-Four*: it 'was still true that men were not equal in their native talents and that functions had to be specialized in ways that favoured some individuals against others; but there was no longer any real need for class distinctions or for large differences of wealth'. The specialization and delegation of function—as James Burnham pointed out—often served to recast rather than obliterate distinctions of class and allowed for the indirect monopolization of wealth by concentrating power in the hands of managerial elites. Burnham's account of a 'new structure of class rule' over which a tyranny of managers presides was a histrionic restatement of established concerns about the oligarchical cast of modern social structures. Orwell criticized the fatalism of Burnham's thesis, but he was clearly influenced by its bleak diagnosis, as the managerial tyrannies of *Animal Farm* and *Nineteen Eighty-Four* clearly attest.

Orwell exaggerated the natural character of certain abilities or traits in *Animal Farm* and thus repressed the political significance of the inequalities they sanction. But his account of the entrenched character of these differences in ability and function merely serves to dispel romantic hopes that the specialized character of modern social organization can simply be sloughed off in the communism of the future. At the same time, Orwell also manages to question the meritocratic prejudices of modern times. Shaw may have extolled socialism as 'the paradise of the able'; yet the decision to make ability or competence the sole criterion for distributing social roles is to risk undermining equality, however it may purport to advance other conceptions of this good (open competition presented as equal opportunity). The pigs embody the dangers of fetishizing 'superior brains' and they help to bear out Trotsky's case that privileging the 'intellectual at the expense of the physical... is a source of injustice'.

Animal Farm powerfully illustrates that the first clause on communism's banner—'from each according to his abilities'—is not necessarily benign. As a distributive principle, it leads to huge asymmetries of power and status and these inequalities are not held in check by the second principle ('each according to his needs'). As we have seen, the distribution of goods on the basis of needs has a clear moral force, but the content and limits of these needs are not self-evident (as the apple-monopolizing, milk-thieving pigs demonstrate). The principle of need is clearly insufficient when it comes to a range of simple goods such as ribbons and social roles such as political leadership. Here modern societies usually invoke an abilities-principle or a concept of merit based on actual or presumed competence. But, as Orwell shows, the fetishization of competence sanctions huge imbalances of power in public life and seriously jeopardizes equality of respect. Of course, for some, respect is also a meritocratic concept and to insist upon its equalization is to lose sight of the fact that it should be earned. But a world that operated in this way would be a fairly unforgiving place and even Orwell had difficulties imagining it. On his farm, even free riders are shown tolerance and respect by others, although how 'equal' this respect is or should be remains a vexed question.

Conclusion

'Socialism', Orwell declared in *The Road to Wigan Pier*, 'is such elementary common sense that I am sometimes amazed that it has not established itself already'. Orwell never dropped his conviction that socialism was a simple matter of executing justice and the nature of that justice seemed to him largely self-evident:

> The world is a raft sailing through space with, potentially, plenty of provisions for everybody; the idea that we must all co-operate and see to it that everyone does his fair share of the work and gets his fair share of the provisions, seems so blatantly obvious that one would say that no one could possibly fail to accept it unless he had some corrupt motive for clinging to the present system.

Here and elsewhere Orwell nursed a naive sense of certitude. He rightly stressed the importance of common-sense attitudes and everyday intuitions in moral life, but he became a dogmatist when he presented these as sufficient. There are, of course, plenty of corrupt motives for clinging to the present arrangement, but even its strongest critics would realize that conceptions of what is fair or otherwise are not 'blatantly obvious'. The idea of fairness is contestable and this contestability has to be built into any reasonable interpretation of the principle.

In *Animal Farm*, Orwell managed to capture this complexity through a simple fable. According to Chesterton, fables are built upon the 'firm foundations of common sense'—which may explain Orwell's attraction to this form. *Animal Farm* certainly shows that there is something very basic or commonsensical about equality as a concept; yet the notion isn't easily translatable into precepts, rules or political institutions. All animals are nominally equal on 'Animal Farm', but what this really means or should entail is an extremely taxing issue. We soon learn that equality is an umbrella term for different and sometimes contradictory conceptions of fairness. Democracy is not a solution to this problem because it is expressive of it. Indeed, the tale puts Orwell's own proposals for a *democratic* revolution under considerable pressure. As I have indicated, the prospects for democracy on 'Animal Farm' are never bright, given that a sizeable number of animals cannot reason or debate. Indeed, Orwell's account of docile ducks and stupid sheep does little to dislodge Schumpeter's contention that the typical citizen becomes 'a primitive' in the political sphere. The portrait of democracy in *Animal Farm* may be excessively cynical, and may reflect the same patrician disdain for the masses that Orwell condemned in others. On the other hand, the tale clearly records Orwell's deep suspicions of intellectual elites. As he explained in 1940: 'I have never had the slightest fear of a dictatorship of the proletariat, if this could happen...But I admit to having a perfect horror of a dictatorship of theorists'. This fear is expressed throughout *Animal Farm*: the dictatorship of the pigs is yet another version of 'the dictatorship of the prigs' that he had condemned since 1937.

Orwell's outlook on equality was increasingly a despairing one. Indeed, in *Nineteen Eighty-Four*, Goldstein proclaims that 'no advance in wealth, no softening of manners, no reform or revolution has ever brought human equality a millimetre nearer'. Of course, it is not entirely clear if Goldstein's thesis is also Orwell's, but his last two novels clearly paint a fairly gloomy picture for egalitarian ideals. He was right to present inequality as a moral failure, but the issue was not simply reducible to human malevolence or to the pig that resides within us all. As I have suggested, the problem of instituting justice also has a conceptual element. Orwell's own parable suggests that equality is not the spurned solution to all our difficulties; it is a fundamental difficulty in its own right. Of course, the same might be said about 'brotherhood'—another of Orwell's key concepts. On 'Animal Farm', the conviction that 'all animals are equal' flows naturally from the belief that 'we are all brothers'. But, as I shall now argue, there is often a distressing gap between these two propositions in Orwell's writing.

3

Solidarity

Orwell's account of the Spanish Civil War opens with a striking image of an Italian militiaman:

He was a tough-looking youth of twenty-five or -six, with reddish-yellow hair and powerful shoulders. His peaked leather cap was pulled fiercely over one eye. He was standing in profile to me, his chin on his breast, gazing with a puzzled frown at a map which one of the officers had open on the table. Something in his face deeply moved me. It was the face of a man who would commit murder and throw away his life for a friend... There were both candour and ferocity in it; also the pathetic reverence that illiterate people have for their supposed superiors. Obviously he could not make head or tail of the map; obviously he regarded map-reading as a stupendous intellectual feat. I hardly know why, but I have seldom seen anyone—any man, I mean—to whom I have taken such an immediate liking... Queer the affection you can feel for a stranger! It was as though his spirit and mine had momentarily succeeded in bridging the gulf of language and tradition and meeting in utter intimacy. I hoped he liked me as well as I liked him.

Here Orwell pays homage to the notion of solidarity, or what he preferred to call human brotherhood. In his recollections of the militiaman, Orwell provides a very gendered sense of fellowship—an issue to which I will return—but the episode clearly communicates a strong belief in the possibility of international solidarity. For a brief moment, Orwell seemingly transcends the divisions of class, nationality, and language that so often constrain our encounters with others. 'Queer the affection you can feel for a stranger'—the shift from the first-person pronoun to an inclusive 'you' extends the act of solidarity to the reader, inviting us to identify similarly with strangers. It is a powerful opening vignette, for it vividly enacts the moral basis of the fight against fascism: the international friendship it enshrines clearly rebuts the racist and xenophobic aspects of much fascist attitudinizing. Moreover, in so far as this fellowship rests on a sense of equality between individuals, the moment with the militiaman is also a form of resistance: for it is precisely this idea of 'human equality'—or so Orwell believes—that fascism sets out to demolish.

'Equality', William Morris insisted, 'only means fraternity', and Orwell's moment with the militiaman may bear this out. Yet some egalitarians might balk at this fraternal scene. The portrait of the militiaman reveals a deep liking, but it is not clear that affection translates into equality of respect. After all, respect is not much in evidence in the blunt anatomizing of the man's stupidity. The insistence on its self-evidence ('Obviously he could not make head or tail of the map; obviously he regarded map-reading as a stupendous intellectual feat') says as much about the dogmatism of the narrative voice as the mental deficiencies of its subject. This type of tough talk often accompanies acts of sympathetic identification in Orwell—keen, as he seems to be, to convey an impression of critical distance within an emotive moment, disarming the charge of sentimentality before it can ever be advanced. Nonetheless, Orwell's brand of brotherly love raises questions about solidarity as a general value. His exasperated pity for the militiaman's servile state—the man's 'pathetic reverence' for his conceived superiors— may be informed by a belief in equality, but it is also expressive of the social hierarchies to which Orwell objects. Indeed, the passage lends some endorsement to Huxley's claim that 'the brotherhood of men does not imply their equality'.

If Orwell's solidarity can fall short on egalitarian grounds, it also has an uneasy relationship with justice. After all, Orwell supplies the militiaman with a morally ambiguous face: it is 'the face of a man who would commit murder and throw away his life for a friend'. The self-sacrificing nature of the ardour may feel impressive, but its homicidal tendencies are, perhaps, less winning. As we have seen, Orwell objected to the feckless insouciance of Auden's phrase 'the necessary murder'. Yet his smitten response to the murderous loyalties of an Italian stranger may communicate the same easy 'amoralism' that he disdained in the poet. The terms 'murder' or 'murderous' may read like a form of moral hyperbole in the context of war, but the militiaman in all his 'candour and ferocity' certainly raises questions about the general relationship between solidarity and our sense of what's right. However generous, solidarity is often a dangerously partisan feeling, easily overriding the impartial outlook we might expect from justice. Orwell continued to defend this type of partisanship—'The essence of being human', he declared, '[is] that one *is* sometimes willing to commit sins for the sake of loyalty'—but his portrait of the militiaman certainly indicates that solidarity is not without its moral hazards.

Orwell often complained, after all, that our various solidarities were all too partial. 'Sympathy for one group', he declared in 1947, 'almost invariably entails callousness towards another'. This was best observed, he suggested, in modern sporting events—orgies of hatred and euphemized violence. Here is Orwell on the deplorable attractions of sport:

> People want to see one side on top and the other side humiliated [...] Serious sport has nothing to do with fair play. It is bound up with hatred, jealousy, boastfulness, disregard of all rules and sadistic pleasure in witnessing violence: in other words it is war minus the shooting.

Contemporary sporting events, he suggested, were a local manifestation of the nationalistic outlook—that is, 'the lunatic modern habit of identifying oneself with large power units and seeing everything in terms of competitive prestige'. Orwell, as we shall see, had a complicated relationship to nationalism: unlike some on the Left, he was willing to call himself a patriot; yet he also believed that nationalism was the 'great modern disease'. It was a disease, moreover, that had ravaged the peace of Europe throughout the 1930s.

The nationalist and racist bloodletting of the 1930s and '40s would make universal solidarity look deeply attractive. Orwell often appeared to champion this inclusive ethos: fascism—a highly inflamed expression of nationalism— would not be defeated until we 'reinstate the belief in human brotherhood'. And yet the partiality that is arguably constitutive of brotherhood would also seem to militate against its limitless extension—a point that Orwell would make against Gandhi, a figure whose declared goal was 'friendship with the world'. Orwell demurred from this global chumminess: to be a friend to all, he insisted, is to be a friend to no one. Here the very idea of universal solidarity looks like a contradiction in terms. Not only is it contradictory, it is potentially destructive, for it risks encouraging us to opt out of our local attachments and political loyalties in the name of an impossible ideal such as 'humanity'. Orwell always insisted that humanity is 'not an abstraction', yet he recognized that in the modern world it often took second place to love of country.

Looking back on the Spanish Civil War, Orwell dwelt on the distinctive cant of those times—'phrases like "international proletarian solidarity", pathetically repeated by ignorant men who believed them to mean something'. He may have continued to admire those ignorant believers, but his own belief in global brotherhood would weaken over time. How strong it had been in the first place is hard to determine. One of the striking things about his encounter with the militiaman is its self-consciously ephemeral character ('I...knew that to retain my first impression of him I must not see him again'). Arguably, the intensity of the encounter was entirely dependent upon its superficiality. Nonetheless, he would return to this intimate moment both in poetry and in prose. In 1942 he imagines the militiaman dead, but also gives him a certain kind of immortality: 'the thing that I saw in your face / No power can disinherit'.

However, the things that we have seen in the militiaman's face raise troubling questions about solidarity as a general ideal. These issues include a) its compatibility with other values—for example, equality, justice, and freedom, b) its internal coherence, as it sometimes re-enlists the social divisions it seeks to transcend through a patronizing compassion or presumptuous solicitude, c) its problematic scope, given its seemingly partisan nature, and d) its practicality in a modern social setting. In the sections ahead, I shall explore these problems in detail, showing how they contribute to the particular heft of Orwell's writing—its angular sympathies and superbly uneven tone.

According to Bertrand Russell, 'no idea is so practical as the brotherhood of man', but Orwell's writing—so sensitive as it is to the bad smell of others—puts this confidence to the test. Orwell's unclubbable features may have been a quirk of personality or they may have stemmed from a certain conception of intellectual duty—'Group loyalties are necessary', he proclaimed in 1948, 'and yet they are poisonous to literature'. But his qualms also had a political root. Orwell was too ardent an enthusiast of freedom—or a certain version of it—to feel fully at ease with thick conceptions of fellowship. Big Brother is the most lurid manifestation of fraternity's coercive face, but as we shall see, Orwell often balked at the prescriptive bonhomie of even the mildest forms of socialism—the 'Boy Scout atmosphere of bare knees and community singing' that characterized the Auden group, for instance. Indeed, Auden's observation about Bertrand Russell might easily have been applied to Orwell himself: 'It is curious that Mr Russell should be drawn to Communism, because he does not give the impression of liking community life very much'. Brotherhood may have been a core principle for Orwell but it was also experienced as an ordeal. The nature of this discomfort is worth taking seriously because it provides an interesting set of psychological tests for solidarity as a general principle.

Brotherhood in context

'Nearly everyone, whatever his actual conduct might be, responds emotionally to the idea of human brotherhood'—or so Orwell believed. He seldom
paused to consider the emotions that it may have triggered in his sisters.
'Brotherhood' may be a metaphor that is theoretically inclusive of everyone,
but it is often a very manly matter in Orwell. In a 1942 rendition of his
beloved militiaman, the soldier's 'battered face' is 'Purer than any woman's'—
an evaluation that may seem as ethical as it is aesthetic. In fact, women often
connive against solidarity in Orwell's writing. In *The Road to Wigan Pier*, for
instance, Orwell suggests that 'almost every middle-class wife' would urge
their husbands to blackleg in strike. He fudges the slur, making betrayal a
symptom of class as much as gender; still, a large swathe of women lure men
away from their loyalties to others. Guardians and representatives of the private sphere, women militate against a more capacious philanthropy. In *Keep
the Aspidistra Flying*, the very scent of a woman is 'a powerful wordless propaganda against all altruism and all justice'. Comstock's misogyny is taken to task
in the novel; nonetheless, women tend to make poor brothers in Orwell's
oeuvre. Elizabeth's solidarity is aggressively circumscribed in *Burmese Days*
(she cannot bear the idea of 'being kin to creatures with black faces'). In
Down and Out in Paris and London, Orwell is struck by the way women fail
to sympathize with the poor: 'When a badly dressed man passes them they
shudder away from him with a quite frank movement of disgust, as though
we were a dead cat'. Men in Orwell are seldom so fastidious.

If Orwell was blind to and complicit with the gendered qualities of
brotherhood, he was more ready to acknowledge its Christian origins. Call
no man your father, Matthew advises, for there is only one Father in Heaven;
'and all ye are brethren'. In 1940, however, Orwell believed that this vision
of brotherhood could be successfully abstracted from its religious context:

> Brotherhood implies a common father. Therefore it is often argued that men can
> never develop the sense of a community unless they believe in God. The answer
> is that in a half-conscious way most of them have developed it already. Man is
> not an individual, he is only a cell in an everlasting body, and he is dimly aware
> of it. There is no other way of explaining why it is that men will die in battle. It
> is nonsense to say that they only do it because they are driven. If whole armies
> had to be coerced, no war could ever be fought. Men die in battle—not gladly,
> of course, but at any rate voluntarily... All that this really means is that they are

aware of some organism greater than themselves, stretching into the future and
the past, within which they feel themselves to be immortal.

The 'organism' with which men usually identify, Orwell maintained, is the
nation-state; however, he suggested that with a little tweaking this could be
transformed into humanity itself—a brave hope in March 1940.

Orwell's use of the battlefield as evidence for brotherhood might suggest
that solidarity is always dependent on some friend–enemy distinction,
however disguised this may be. But Christianity preached love of one's
enemies ('I say unto you, love your enemies, bless them that curse you, do
good to them that hate you'). This was not the easiest advice to follow in
war-time Europe and Orwell clearly worried about its implications. He was
keen to dismiss the idea that loving one's enemies entailed total pacifism:
'Actually you can only love your enemies', he declared in 1941, 'if you are
willing to kill them in certain circumstances'. Being loved by Orwell may
have been quite a frightening business. Orwell's attempts to secularize the
Christian ideal of brotherhood certainly have a rather disturbing side. The
ideal of an immortal community, for instance, leads to a troubling euphemi-
zation of death. His subordination of the individual to the community—
'Man is not an individual, he is only a cell'—may be understandable in the
context of war, but it has distinctly illiberal implications. As we have seen, it
is O'Brien who advances this type of argument in *Nineteen Eighty-Four*,
enlisting the same biological analogy of cell and organism ('Can you not
understand, Winston, that the individual is only a cell? The weariness of the
cell is the vigour of the organism. Do you die when you cut your fingernails?').
When Winston finally relinquishes his independence to Big Brother—
'O stubborn, self-willed exile from the loving breast'—the dangers of a
politicized return to the Godhead become clear.

Brotherhood can have its nasty sides and it's hardly a surprise that many
had already dismissed it as a panacea for social ills. For instance, the Victorian
moralist James Fitzjames Stephens had little time for 'the religion of fraternity' and its cosy talk of the great human family. 'I have far too much respect
for real relations', he announced, 'to give these endearing names to all sorts
of people of whom I know and for whom, practically speaking, I care nothing at all'. 'Yes all men are brethren', the Chartist Ernest Jones once admitted, 'but some are Abels and some are Cains'. Jones's contemporary Karl
Marx announced that there were many people he would decline to esteem
as brothers. Indeed, Marx often mocked 'fraternity' as a deeply inadequate

principle in a structurally antagonistic world: it offered a purely 'sentimental reconciliation of contradictory class interests'.

Orwell's Old Major is often viewed as a Marxist boar, but the Major's dictum—'we are all brothers'—has, in fact, little in common with Marx's stated views. Marx, after all, abandoned the inclusive motto of the League of the Just ('All men are brothers') for his revolutionary programme, opting for a far more circumscribed form of solidarity: 'Working men of all countries, unite!' The irreducibly antagonistic structure of society, he suggested, could not be transcended through moralistic appeals to fellowship. Solidarity was inescapably partisan or class-specific. So there was little to be said for the 'universal brotherhood swindle'.

Keen, however, to have it both ways, Marx did seem to believe that amongst communist workmen 'the brotherhood of man is not a mere phrase with them, but a fact of life'. So the false universality that characterized bourgeois notions of fraternity did not apply to proletarian appeals to brotherhood. This was because the proletariat constituted a 'universal class'—a class that cannot emancipate itself without 'emancipating all other spheres of society'. Its historical task, therefore, was to abolish all classes and thus to do away with domination in general. Of course, one might justifiably wonder about the magic formula that makes the proletariat such a privileged benefactor of everyone. Nor is it entirely clear why the end of classes constitutes the end of domination as such. Orwell's *Animal Farm* and *Nineteen Eighty-Four* can be read as sceptical responses to this type of prophecy—or at least they suggest that new classes or dominant groups (like Burnham's new class of 'managers') are likely to emerge in the wake of those described by Marx.

Nonetheless, Marx's disenchanted views of universal brotherhood raise serious questions about Orwell's ambitions. They also expose the fragility of Orwell's attempts to present brotherhood as both the outcome and the condition of social reform. He insisted, after all, that true solidarity is impossible in a class-conflicted world ('There can be no co-operation between classes whose real interests are opposed'), but he was also convinced that solidarity is an essential prerequisite for the removal of social antagonisms ('I am implying that different classes must be persuaded to act together'). On first glance, these beliefs would appear to pull against each other, though Orwell had his own suggestions for how they might be reconciled. However, texts like *The Road to Wigan Pier* and *Down and Out in Paris and London* epitomized the enormity of the task: on the one hand, these works are self-conscious exercises in cross-class solidarity, but the fellowship to which they aspire would seem to be ruled by the structures of domination that the texts so relentlessly depict.

For all his discussion of 'the class-difficulty', Orwell never provided a considered definition of class. He insisted it was not simply decidable by income (a position he wrongly attributed to Marxism) or by profession—indeed by economic criteria as such—and needed to incorporate gradations of social prestige that could operate relatively independently of wealth. Or he would distinguish between 'economic' and 'social' definitions of class: 'Economically, no doubt, there are only two classes, the rich and the poor, but socially there is a whole hierarchy of classes'. The distinction between 'rich' and 'poor' was an extremely coarse economic rubric (and Marx would understandably reject it in his account of class struggle), yet Orwell seemed to think that it allowed ostensibly independent groups to find a common cause ('poverty is poverty, whether the tool you work with is a pick-axe or a fountain pen'). Thus, however different, smallholders, coal miners, typists, factory hands, and schoolmasters must combine, for it is always possible to combine 'so long as it is on the basis of common interests'. Of course, no solidarity of interest could be produced between the capitalist and the worker—the 'cat cannot co-operate with the mouse'—but he was convinced that 'the interests of all exploited people are the same'.

But what constituted exploitation in this context was never fully explained. Moreover, Orwell's own writing consistently troubles firm distinctions between exploiters and the exploited. Everyone in England, after all, is to some extent an 'exploiter' ('We all live by robbing Asiatic coolies'). English workers may be oppressed, but according to Orwell's racialized account of global trade, 'the white worker exploits the coloured worker', partly by benefiting from the cheap goods they provide. Here the 'coloured worker cannot be blamed for feeling no solidarity with his white comrades', because the differences between the living standards of each are so vast. This might simply heighten the case for the international brotherhood of the proletariat, but Orwell repeatedly emphasizes the difficulties that arise in establishing a sense of common interest between workers. All may be in prison, but not everyone chooses cooperation as the best means out of their dilemma.

Indeed, one of the strengths of Orwell's writing is its attentiveness to the psychological factors that militate against class solidarity—let alone global brotherhood. In *Down and Out in Paris and London*, for instance, he spends considerable time documenting the hostilities engendered by overwork and poor conditions (' "Get me down that saucepan, idiot!" the cook would cry... "Get it down yourself, you old whore," I would answer'). This is not *fraternité* at its best and brightest, though Orwell shrewdly charts the very real pressures—the cramped spaces, the stifling heat, the hectoring bosses—that put the concept under strain. Orwell also shows how the division of labour in places like a hotel generates an 'elaborate caste system' amongst workers ('staff... had their prestige graded as accurately as that of soldiers, and a cook or waiter was as much above a *plongeur* as a captain above a private'). In this economy of prestige, it was often difficult to experience or to identify a 'common interest'. Even those low down on the social scale have no necessary commitment to abolishing that scale. Consider, for instance, the psychology of waiters—figures besotted by the snobbery to which they are daily exposed. Invoking once again the brotherly pronoun 'you', Orwell paints a vivid scene:

> Sometimes when you sit in a restaurant, still stuffing yourself half an hour after closing time, you feel that the tired waiter at your side must surely be despising you. But he is not. He is not thinking as he looks at you, 'What an overfed lout'; he is thinking, 'One day, when I have saved enough money, I shall be able to imitate that man.'

Orwell's advice to his readers is 'never be sorry for a waiter': incapable of egalitarian brotherhood, they are undeserving of any demonstration of it.

As Orwell makes clear, poverty offers strong incentives to collective action, but it also creates conditions that militate against cooperation. 'If *plongeurs* thought at all', he reports, 'they would long ago have formed a union and gone on strike for better treatment'. Unfortunately, these workers have little time to consider their abject condition: 'they do not think, because they have no leisure for it; their life has made slaves of them'. In these circumstances, a politically effective form of cooperation is difficult to envisage.

The issue of 'proletarian solidarity', therefore, is an obdurate problem throughout Orwell's work, although he disliked the phrase and recoiled from its Marxist smell. His texts tend to confirm Marx's opinion that a shared set of interests does not beget a genuine 'community' of interest. For a proper sense of community to occur, a collective ethos and political organization are required amongst workers—or so Marx contended. Only then can common concerns become genuine 'class interests'. In Orwell, however, 'class consciousness'—another pompous expression, according to this commissar of plain-speaking—is difficult if not impossible to locate. He may have condemned Arthur Koestler for arriving at a pessimistic dead end: 'Without education of the masses, no social progress; without social progress, no education of the masses'. But it is hard to distinguish this from the double bind we have already explored in *Nineteen Eighty-Four*: '*Until they become conscious they will never rebel, and until after they have rebelled they cannot become conscious*'. Indeed, the mental deficit here—namely, consciousness—is disturbingly broad and suggests that there's little hope for the proles.

Marx had explicitly parted company with those who stated that the working class 'is incapable of emancipating itself by its own efforts', and must place itself in the hands of the educated and philanthropic bourgeois. The proletariat, he insisted, must be the agent of its own emancipation. And yet many of Orwell's contemporaries were drawn to Marx's account of an intellectual vanguard in *The Communist Manifesto*. Here members of a doomed bourgeois class would find common cause with the proletariat and steer history to its proper end:

> Finally, in times when the class struggle nears the decisive hour, the process of dissolution going on within the ruling class, in fact within the whole range of old society, assumes such a violent, glaring character, that a small section of the ruling class cuts itself adrift, and joins the revolutionary class, the class that holds the future in its hands. Just as, therefore, at an earlier period, a section of the nobility went over to the bourgeoisie, so now a portion of the bourgeoisie goes over to the proletariat, and in particular, a portion of the bourgeois ideologists, who have raised themselves to the level of comprehending theoretically the historical movement as a whole.

Presumably, this is how Marx made sense of his own solidarity with the proletariat—a solidarity that would otherwise seem to conflict with his bourgeois origins and 'objective' class interests. It was also the means by which many middle-class intellectuals in the 1930s rationalized their own identification with the working class.

Yet Orwell loathed the presumption of such brotherhood. Time and time again, he lambasted the arrogance of intellectuals—particularly 'the cocksure Marx-quoting type'—who might claim a superior understanding of 'historical necessity'. These socialist sages conflated a revolution from below with 'a set of reforms which "we" the clever ones impose upon "them", the Lower Orders'. All too often, the fraternity practised by genteel do-gooders was an exercise in moral vanity—as self-glorifying as it was self-deceived. Orwell's disparagement of middle-class socialists and related busybodies ('Are *these* mingy little beasts... the champions of the working class?') says a lot about the limits of his own capacity for brotherhood, but he understandably worries about the paternalism that inheres in the fraternal gesture: 'With loving though slightly patronising smiles we set out to greet our proletarian brothers, and behold! our proletarian brothers—in so far as we understand them—are not asking for our greetings, they are asking us to commit suicide'.

But left-wing moralists forget that the bonhomie they invoke in the name of a classless society is also made impossible by class divisions. 'Whichever way you turn', Orwell insists, 'class-difference confronts you like a wall of stone'. 'Or rather it is not so much like a stone wall as the plate-glass pane of an aquarium; it is so easy to pretend that it isn't there, and so impossible to get through it'. Those who think that they can penetrate the glass through moral effort alone are deeply self-deceived. Class distinctions, he insists, cannot 'be shouted out of existence with a few scoutmasterish bellows of good will'. This presumption is 'alluring', but it is also 'pernicious rubbish'. Yet for all his criticisms of an overreaching moralism, Orwell often suggested that fraternity was a moral property that could be enlarged through the diligent cultivation of the will. The class-wall might be vaulted through moral enterprise and effort. He acknowledges, of course, the difficulty of the task, but he has utter confidence that it can be done: 'it is no use clapping a proletarian on the back and telling him that he is as good a man as I am; if I want real contact with him, I have got to make an effort'.

And Orwell certainly made efforts. *Down and Out in Paris and London* and *The Road to Wigan Pier* are ostentatious experiments in solidarity. As Orwell put it, 'I wanted to submerge myself, to get right down among the oppressed, to be one of them and on their side against their tyrants'. He rarely feels this submergence is achieved—the hand of class intercedes everywhere—but occasionally he feels he has made true contact. In these moments of connection (usually involving the great leveller: tea), he believes he has achieved 'utter equality with working-class people'. Yet the very assertion of equality invites suspicions about its real existence, raising doubts about what should never have been in question—namely, equality. Similarly, a worrying condescension inheres in the very desire to join 'the lowest of the low'. Orwell criticized paternalism in others, but he was observably vulnerable to this outlook himself.

The snobbishness at the heart of his solidarity was best expressed in 1942 in a set of reflections on the proletariat's fight for justice: 'The struggle of the working class is like the growth of a plant. The plant is blind and stupid, but it knows enough to keep pushing upwards towards the light'. Moreover, the naive voluntarism he denounced in other people's solidarity also applied to his own. Many critics of *The Road to Wigan Pier* condemned its over-reliance on rhetorical exhortation and moral censure, insisting that it overlooked the structural or material basis of the problems it deplored. According to Victor Gollancz, Orwell had produced an '*emotional* Socialism'—a poor relation of the scientific socialism Gollancz saw himself as advocating. There was, perhaps, an emotive basis to Orwell's dream of brotherhood, but this is not to say that all emotions are blind and have no role to play in politics. Central to Orwell's sense of solidarity, for instance, is the notion of compassion—a sentiment that was and continues to be credited with extraordinary moral and political significance. But, as Orwell's writing demonstrates, compassion is also a highly volatile feeling that often threatens to merge into something akin to its opposite—namely, a visceral sense of disgust. It is to this issue that I now turn.

The politics of compassion

Looking back on the Spanish Civil War, Orwell gave a vivid report of an incident that occurred one morning on the battle lines outside Huesca. Orwell and a small party of comrades had left their trench before dawn to snipe at the enemy, but had become marooned in no man's land when first light appeared:

> We were still trying to nerve ourselves to make a dash for it when there was an uproar and a blowing of whistles in the Fascist trench. Some of our aeroplanes were coming over. At this moment a man, presumably carrying a message to an officer, jumped out of the trench and ran along the top of the parapet in full view. He was half-dressed and was holding up his trousers with both hands as he ran. I refrained from shooting at him. It is true that I am a poor shot and unlikely to hit a running man at a hundred yards, and also that I was thinking chiefly about getting back to our trench while the Fascists had their attention fixed on the aeroplanes. Still, I did not shoot partly because of that detail about the trousers. I had come here to shoot at 'Fascists'; but a man who his holding up his trousers, isn't a 'Fascist', he is visibly a fellow creature, similar to yourself, and you don't feel like shooting at him.

Having sketched the scene at some length, Orwell is fairly dismissive of its significance ('What does this incident demonstrate? Nothing very much'). Such incidents, we are told, occur all the time in all wars. But this can be read as a very Orwellian form of understatement: the insistence on the banal ubiquity of these events merely asserts the universal sway of the moral psychology it describes.

So the anecdote implies that there is something pretty basic and widely shared about the feeling of compassion. First, the story seems to bear out what many philosophers and psychologists allege: that we tend to identify with particulars, often at the expense of broader abstractions such as fascism or anti-fascism. Second, the tale indicates that we are often moved by the body's vulnerabilities: 'half-dressed', the man literally exposes his nature; 'holding up his trousers with both hands', he is as susceptible to humiliation as he is to death—indeed, he seems more worried about his honour than his safety. But bodily vulnerability is something we all share: a man holding up his trousers is 'visibly a fellow creature, similar to yourself' and the recognition of this fact breeds a certain compassion. In a familiar rhetorical move, Orwell shifts pronouns within the same sentence to include the reader in this sense of shared humanity ('I had come here to shoot...you don't feel like shooting him'). Subject positions become blurred in the practice of pity.

Orwell's emphasis on the ubiquity of pity or compassion is hardly original. According to its most famous apologist, Rousseau, pity was the source of almost all the social virtues; a basic sense of humanity was merely pity applied to the species in general. Moreover, the ground of compassion, for Rousseau, is our shared susceptibility to suffering. 'If our common needs unite us by interest', he maintained, 'our common miseries unite us by affection'. Our solidarity with others derives less from an identification with their pleasures than a keen sense of their pains, for it is in the act of suffering that we best observe the fundamental similarities in our natures. Or so, at least, Rousseau contends: 'it is our common miseries which turn our hearts to humanity'. Pity, for Rousseau, is our one natural virtue and Orwell seems to view this feeling as fairly basic to most of us (presumably, this is why he can thread his compassion for trouserless fascists through a generalized 'you'). He also suggests—again in a very Rousseauian vein—that compassion is often best preserved amongst the poor and the least sophisticated. The only person to object to the State's war propaganda in *Nineteen Eighty-Four*, for instance, is a lowly prole (she proclaims 'it ain't right' to display sadistic images of murder to children).

But to what extent are these compassionate feelings *political* virtues? As Harold Laski argued in 1943: 'Pity has no programme, because it is always an inadequate substitute for justice. It ignores relations and institutions in order to devote itself to the claims of persons'. Pity in Orwell is arguably an apolitical or anti-political good. His pity for the half-clad fascist, for instance, trumps the basic distinction between friends and enemies—the constitutive principle of politics in some people's books. So the scene might suggest that compassion is at odds with political duty. Is it not an obligation to kill fascists in a just war against them?

More salient, perhaps, in this context is Orwell's declared compassion for Hitler. Orwell clearly specialized in provocative confessions, but his thoughts about Hitler pack a particular punch: 'I should like to put on record that I have never been able to dislike Hitler [...] The fact is that there is something deeply appealing about him'. Here, of course, Orwell exploits a condescension that often conditions pity (an issue to which I will return). There is, he feels, a quality in Hitler's demeanour—his 'pathetic, doglike face, the face of a man suffering under intolerable wrongs'—that generates extreme compassion. Orwell implies that there is something about suffering that triggers sympathy in observers, no matter who the identity of the sufferer— the choice of Hitler as object vividly illustrates the point. Yet such inclusive compassion can generate its own form of paradox: is it morally contradictory, one might ask, to sympathize with the agony of someone who has inflicted so much suffering upon others? As Rousseau once put it, 'pity for the wicked is a very great cruelty to men'.

Orwell made his comments about Hitler in a review of *Mein Kampf* published in March 1940. Fuller revelations about Hitler's iniquities lay ahead, but by 1940, his moral record had already provoked widespread revulsion (Orwell owned several pamphlets outlining Nazi atrocities). So his declaration that Hitler fights an unwinnable war with destiny which, nonetheless, he 'somehow deserves to [win]' can seem morally perverse—it certainly contains a very questionable concept of desert. Orwell presumably felt there was something to be gained in not emulating the type of hatred that Hitler practised and so his sympathy for the man may constitute a principled form of resistance to the brutality that Nazism represents. 'To destroy Fascism', the communist Harry Pollitt announced, 'we must learn to hate', but Orwell endorsed a different approach. Indeed, one of the virtues of the campaign against Hitler, he suggested in 1944, was that 'there had been very little hatred' (unlike the conflict of 1914–18, when 'the British people were whipped up into a hideous frenzy'). 'Hatred', Orwell concluded, 'is an impossible basis for policy': it is too capricious to constitute a stable basis for moral judgement and it lacks the impartiality we have come to expect from justice.

But perhaps compassion, too, is as partial and volatile as the hatred it resists. Presumably it was for this reason that even Rousseau felt that pity should be made subordinate to justice in political life. Significantly, Orwell also seems to separate the demands of justice from those of sympathetic feeling. Given the opportunity, he declares that he would certainly kill Hitler—presumably out of justice—no matter what the heart's counsel.

But there are tougher cases, as Eric Blair had already discovered as a policeman in Burma—an experience which gave him an 'indescribable loathing' of systems of justice both at home and abroad. 'Say what you will, our criminal law (far more humane, by the way, in India than in England) is a horrible thing'. Of course, the justice of such justice may be in question, but it is clear that the execution of the law conflicts with the rudiments of compassion: justice, Orwell opines, 'needs very insensitive people to administer it'. He goes on to depict what administers of the peace must pass over:

> The wretched prisoners squatting in the reeking cages of the lock-ups, the grey cowed faces of the long-term convicts, the scarred buttocks of the men who had been flogged with bamboos, the women and children howling when their menfolk were led away under arrest—things like these are beyond bearing when you are in any way directly responsible for them.

This is a very generalized list of human suffering (all victims appear in the plural), yet extensive use of the definite article strives to make things viscerally particular. Moreover, the olfactory and visual particulars ('the reeking cages...the grey cowed faces...the scarred buttocks') might seem to outweigh the more abstract claims of justice. Such suffering leads Orwell to the radical conclusion that all punishment does more harm than good. Indeed, in this transport of compassion, Orwell concludes that all government is evil.

Orwell, as we have already noted, ultimately dismissed his anarchistic theories as 'sentimental nonsense'. Yet his subsequent conclusion—'In any state of society where crime can be profitable you have got to have a harsh criminal law and administer it ruthlessly'—can sound like an overcorrection. Orwell's migration between extremes reflects a deep uncertainty about the proper role of compassion in political deliberation: should it constrain justice or be constrained by it?

The relationship between pity and justice is particularly complex in his early literary sketch 'A Hanging' (published in the *Adelphi* in 1931). Once again, it is the fragile body that serves as the source of solidarity between strangers:

> It is curious, but till that moment I had never realised what it means to destroy a healthy, conscious man. When I saw the prisoner step aside to avoid the puddle, I saw the mystery, the unspeakable wrongness, of cutting a life short when

it is in full tide. This man was not dying, he was alive just as we were alive. All the organs of his body were working—bowels digesting food, skin renewing itself, nails growing, tissues forming—all toiling away in solemn foolery. His nails would still be growing when he stood on the drop, when he was falling through the air with a tenth-of-a-second to live. His eyes saw the yellow gravel and the grey walls, and his brain still remembered, foresaw, reasoned—reasoned even about puddles. He and we were a party of men walking together, seeing, hearing, feeling, understanding the same world; and in two minutes, with a sudden snap, one of us would be gone—one mind less, one world less.

The vulnerability or 'solemn foolery' of the body generates an outraged sympathy in Orwell's observer. Embodiment, documented again in visceral detail (bowels, skin, nails), is the fact that we all have in common and it produces a keen sense of fellowship in Orwell's narrator: 'He and we were a party of men walking together seeing, hearing, feeling, understanding the same world'. Through the act of compassion, the victim becomes 'one of us'. The shift in focalization allows the narrator to see what the victim sees and to think what he thinks about. This sense of solidarity produces a visceral sense of the 'unspeakable wrongness' of capital punishment. Here pity is an important supplement to or even an expression of justice.

Yet 'A Hanging' also reveals the extreme complexity of pity as a moral sentiment. For while it may lead us to identify with the suffering of others, it is also an irksome feeling: 'We looked at the lashed, hooded man on the drop, and listened to his cries—each cry another second of life; the same thought was in all our minds: oh, kill him quickly, get it over, stop that abominable noise'. There is a sense of solidarity here enshrined in the first-person pronoun, but it is not a particularly tender feeling, unless, of course, the impatience for the man's death is merciful. As Judith Shklar once observed, 'pity is a painful emotion, and relieving the suffering of others is a relief'. But presumably, another way of finding relief is to put an end to pity itself. It is difficult to decipher what psychological strategy is pursued in 'A Hanging'—arguably both—but it is clear that the man's death is viscerally welcomed ('An enormous relief had come upon us now that the job was done').

Compassion in 'A Hanging' may be an other-regarding feeling, but it also appears to be bound up with intense feelings of self-preservation. The tale intimates that the suffering of others is, perhaps, a humiliation to ourselves, for it confirms our own fragile state: we too may suffer and will eventually perish. Even the dog in 'A Hanging' grows timorous in the face of death—confirmation, perhaps, of Rousseau's belief that even beasts feel compassion. Rousseau also cast pity as the great moderator of *amour propre* or self-love;

however, it would also appear to be moderated by it. Orwell's tale suggests that we draw on such love to understand the pain of others, evaluating their upset on the basis of our own repugnance to suffering. But the same aversion also limits our compassion. So when the prisoner is finally hanged, the collective response is not simply one of relief, but of unmitigated joy:'One felt an impulse to sing, to break into a run, to snigger'. If the imminence of another's demise had activated a type of fear—and a heightened sense of one's own vulnerability—death can now be laughed at from a distance. Men exchange tales of botched executions, flattering the principle of self-love by emphasizing their relative safety.

Indeed, the need for mutual reassurance in the face of death triggers intense feelings of solidarity in 'A Hanging'. The spirit of camaraderie at the end of the tale overwhelms all divisions, between rank, race, and nation:

> I found that I was laughing quite loudly. Everyone was laughing. Even the superintendent grinned in a tolerant way. 'You'd better all come out and have a drink', he said quite genially. 'I've got a bottle of whisky in the car. We could do with it'.
>
> We went through the big double gates of the prison, into the road. 'Pulling at his legs!' exclaimed a Burmese magistrate suddenly, and burst into a loud chuckling. We all began laughing again. At that moment Francis's anecdote seemed extraordinarily funny. We all had a drink together, native and European alike, quite amicably. The dead man was a hundred yards away.

Solidarity can have its callous sides. The final image of the dead man puts all the hilarity in context: he is the repressed object and the guarantor of this amity. The boundaries of compassion in this story have radically retreated—and solidarity itself emerges as a very mixed virtue.

From pity to disgust

'A Hanging', as we have seen, is an impressively self-referential tale—figures trade stories about executions in a story about an execution—and it raises uncomfortable questions about the social or psychological purpose of such storytelling. Watching people watching a killing, readers come face to face with their own voyeurism or are at least invited to evaluate their own responses in the light of those displayed in the tale. Our responses may be compassionate, but as Rousseau intimated, there is, perhaps, a callousness built into compassion itself: 'Pity is sweet because, in putting ourselves in the place of the one who suffers, we nevertheless feel the pleasure of not suffering as he does'. And yet pity is not necessarily sweet. As Orwell's tale demonstrates, it tends to be irritating, which is why we often want it to cease. Presumably, this is why Orwell suggested that it was fatal for the poor to look hungry: 'it makes people want to kick you'. In fact, stories like 'A Hanging' reveal how quickly compassion tilts into sadism until we become voyeurs of other people's pain. As such, the tale queries its own moral function: the story may report an injustice—an 'unspeakable wrongness'—but it arguably perpetuates another wrong by indulging in a kind of pornography of suffering.

Since classical times, moralists have presented literature as a school of sentiment, one wherein pity or a broader compassion is both expressed and nurtured. Arguably, it takes imagination to sympathize with others—'no one becomes sensitive', Rousseau proclaimed, 'until his imagination is animated, and begins to transport him out of himself'—and literature ostensibly helps us to imagine the experiences of others. This was certainly how George Eliot understood the moral contribution of art: 'If Art does not enlarge men's sympathies, it does nothing morally'. This kind of sentimental education is still regarded as fundamental to modern societies, providing a key basis of 'compassionate citizenship'. Moreover, if solidarity is a liberal virtue—as Richard Rorty maintained—it was fostered, he suggested, by imaginative acts in which we learn 'to see strange people as fellow sufferers'. He commended Orwell, in particular, for sensitizing us to other people's pain.

It is easy to see how Orwell's writing might live up to this billing. The torture scenes of *Nineteen Eighty-Four*, for instance, help us to appreciate that cruelty may be the worst sort of evil. Moreover, works such as *Down and Out in Paris and London* or *The Road to Wigan Pier* test and extend moral horizons, incorporating disadvantaged others into the ambit of the readers' care. But if literature—or more specifically Orwell's writing—makes us imaginatively compassionate, it also risks fostering a purely imaginary compassion. Again, it was the great apologist of pity Rousseau who put this case most forcefully. In his famous indictment of the theatre—which also reads as a castigation of his own literary endeavours—Rousseau emphasized how the arts divert our moral energies from their proper object. In the theatre, for instance, people learn to 'forget their friends, neighbours and relations in order to concern themselves with fables, in order to cry for the misfortunes of the dead, or to laugh at the expense of the living'. The arts breed a form of pseudo-sympathy that is very different to real concern. In the theatre, our hearts bleed for fantasies—and we applaud our own sensitivity when they do—but, according to Rousseau, we often remain inured to real suffering. The theatre trains us to become moral voyeurs—passive spectators of suffering rather than committed agents who act to redress significant wrongs.

As 'A Hanging' indicates, Orwell was at least alert to the dangers of moral voyeurism and pseudo-compassion. He also recognized that poverty, like death, can be titillating to contemplate from a distance: 'since it is so remote, we rather enjoy harrowing ourselves with the thought of its unpleasantness'. But this enjoyment, Orwell suggests, leads to inertia. In his youth, literary depictions of the working classes triggered paroxysms of concern for their plight, but this, he admitted, was very different to real care: 'At a distance, and through the medium of books', he admitted, 'I could agonise over their sufferings, but I still hated them and despised them when I came anywhere near them'. So Orwell criticized a fictitious concern that books both express and feed. Yet awareness of the problem is no immunity from it: the possibility remains that Orwell's own works indulge the vices they indict. He is, of course, very keen to abandon the voyeur's passivity—*Down and Out in Paris and London* or *The Road to Wigan Pier* have only been written because something has been done: the poor have been actively sought out; Wigan has been visited and inhabited—at some discomfort to the writer. Nor does he covet the voyeur's detachment, but nurses deep fantasies of incorporation ('I even wanted to become one of them'). If these hopes don't quite materialize, the reasons, as we have seen, are partly structural—the curse of class is everywhere.

As a consequence, however, Orwell spends a lot of time outside the 'aquarium' looking in, observing the lower classes with an anthropological detachment or with a sightseer's fascination. Moreover, his books allow readers to engage in the same social tourism—'It is altogether curious, your first contact with poverty'—the possessive pronoun again assuming that the economic circumstances between author and reader are comparable, while those of the book's subjects are very different. After all, Orwell's exclamation—'is it ever possible to be really intimate with the working class?'—would be a puzzling question to address to one of its constituents. Orwell's poverty-tours reflect a strong compassion, but they also reveal the political difficulties that lurk behind such sentiment. Pity often enforces the differences it seeks to overcome. Take the famous image of a working woman spotted from a passing train: 'She had a round pale face, the usual exhausted face of the slum girl who is twenty-five and looks forty, thanks to miscarriages and drudgery;

and it wore, for the second in which I saw it, the most desolate, hopeless expression I have ever seen'. These are sad lines, made sadder still, perhaps, by the way the particularities of the girl's face quickly dissolve into their type ('the usual face of the slum girl').

The view from the passing train is perhaps deliberately superficial—Orwell's diaries suggest the encounter took place on foot. Nonetheless, the claim that suffering is the same for 'them' as it is for 'us' arguably enforces the distinctions it aims to subvert. We are told that the girl's face is not the face of 'an ignorant suffering animal', but the face of a self-conscious being who understands her plight. But it is not clear why any human face requires such special pleading. 'Most Lancashire women who read this book', Harry Pollitt observed, 'would like to dust Orwell's pants for his insults'. Elsewhere, in *The Road to Wigan Pier*, the animality of the poor is more fully advanced (we find them 'creeping round and round, just like black beetles, in an endless muddle of slovened jobs and mean grievances').

Indeed, compassion in Orwell often accedes to a visceral disgust. Such disgust, as many have noticed, is predominantly olfactory. Note, for instance, his notorious suspicion that '*the lower classes smell*'. He initially presented this as a social fantasy of his youth—casting it as a measure of just how extreme prejudice could be—although he would go on to suggest that there was some social reality to this perception: 'Of course, as a whole, they are dirtier than the upper classes'. Such dirtiness, he claimed in 1945, was one of those 'easily observed facts which it would be merely dishonest to deny'.

Orwell's sociology of smell is comically crude, but it sustains a provocative thesis about the biological limits of solidarity. Bad smell constitutes 'an impassable barrier' beyond which our sympathies cannot stray:

> no feeling of like or dislike is quite so fundamental as a *physical* feeling. Race hatred, religious hatred, differences of education, of temperament, of intellect, even differences of moral code, can be got over; but physical repulsion cannot. You can have an affection for a murderer or a sodomite, but you cannot have an affection for a man whose breath stinks—habitually stinks, I mean. However well you may wish him, however much you may admire his mind and character, if his breath stinks he is horrible and in your heart of hearts you will hate him.

If the body is the ground and object of solidarity, for Orwell it is also its limit. He quoted Somerset Maugham to support the point: 'In the West we are divided from our fellows by our sense of smell'. Much of Orwell's own writing seems to bear this out.

So the limits of solidarity are set by the nose, although the ears, too, are stern border guards. Sleeping in a dosshouse on the Waterloo Road, for instance, Orwell is appalled by the coughing of an old man: 'It was an unspeakably repellent sound; a foul bubbling and retching, as though the man's bowels were being churned up within him'. The gerunds vividly enact the churning noise, while the subsequent sight of the man adds a visual dimension to visceral distaste: 'Once when he struck a match I saw that he was a very old man, with a grey, sunken face like that of a corpse, and he was wearing his trousers wrapped round his head as a nightcap, a thing which for some reason disgusted me very much'. Perhaps there is compassion or pity here, but it is also suffused with disgust—a politically dangerous sentiment for some commentators. According to Martha Nussbaum, for instance, compassion is a key virtue, but disgust is its enemy. Disgust may serve some primary function, steering us away from immediate dangers, but extended into a general appraisal of persons or groups it is a deeply divisive force. It blocks 'equal respect', emphasizing the base animality of others.

Orwell, it seems, was often disgusted by the human animal. 'Man is not a Yahoo, but he is rather like a Yahoo and needs to be reminded of it from time to time'. There may be something inclusive, even egalitarian, in this misanthropy but, as Orwell argued, disgust could also be used to erode the belief in human dignity. This is well understood by the terrible O'Brien: 'What are you? A bag of filth. Now turn round and look into that mirror again. Do you see the thing facing you? That is the last man. If you are human, that is humanity'. In *Down and Out in Paris and London*, Orwell recognizes how disgust erodes equal respect. He is keen, for instance, to challenge a socially sanctioned repugnance for beggars, and to suggest that they are 'ordinary human beings' (though a few, he concedes, are 'impudent social parasites').

But, as we have seen, Orwell often accedes to prejudices he condemns in others, recoiling from the dirt and stench of the insect-like poor. Perhaps not all disgust in Orwell is politically regressive. He, at least, seems to hope that disgust for the abject can be transferred to the conditions that have produced it. So if poverty is 'spiritual halitosis', as Gordon Comstock opines, then it is a duty for all to end this bad smell. But disgust can also remain a deeply segregating emotion, expressing the class hierarchies that the author simultaneously decries. If disgust is solidarity-destroying, philosophers have contended that it is best defeated by love. But Orwell, as we shall see, has certain problems with love—at least as a political emotion.

The politics of love

Love was big in the 1930s. Moreover, its civic significance was repeatedly extolled. The task, it seems, was 'To build the city where / The will of love is done'. While love had often been viewed as a strictly private or interpersonal affair, this privacy was condemned in some leftist circles as a damaging ghettoization of the sentiments. Love needed to go public. For instance, Auden nursed ambitious plans for 'universal love' in the '30s, while Spender sang from the same hymn sheet: no reasonable person can 'doubt that the universalization of human love is a desirable end'. Here Freud seemed to join hands with Jesus in a merry left-wing dance: the aim was to love the self a little better and to love one's neighbour as one's self. The 1930s love-boat also contained a much-manhandled Marx. As John Middleton Murry explained, 'Marxism is the economics of imagination'—a science that was ultimately reducible to 'love'.

It is worth pointing out that Marx had repeatedly rejected such love-talk, seeing it as a sentimental distraction from the intractable realities of class conflict. According to Engels, the cant of love produced an 'orgy of reconciliation' in which everything remains unchanged. Yet many reformers in England—from William Morris to various proponents of Christian Socialism—continued to promote an ethos of neighbourly love. 'Socialism', Keir Hardie announced, 'is the reign of human love in room of hate'—a position that many on the Left in the '30s took to their hearts. Of course, love had a significant battle to fight. As Christopher Caudwell argued, capitalism had banished affection from social relations by reducing everything to the cash nexus. The repression of love in social life meant that such passion invariably reappeared in 'a compensatory and pathological form as neurosis, hate, perversion and unrest'. Indeed, with people like Hitler on the rampage, love could seem in bad shape. But for many on the Left, this merely emphasized the urgency of the task. As Auden famously put it in 1939: 'We must love one another or die'.

Yet in September 1939 it wasn't immediately obvious how love would stop the Panzers—and even Auden would regret the glibness of this particular love-summons. Indeed, the gospel of love triggered a sceptical response from many quarters throughout the 1930s and '40s. E. M. Forster had initially presented himself as one of love's apostles: democracy received two cheers from Forster in 1938, but only 'Love the Beloved Republic' got three. However, four years later, Forster was a lot less convinced about love's republican credentials: 'Love is a great force in private life; it is indeed the greatest of all things; but love in public affairs does not work'. In this context, Forster championed the more modest concept of tolerance. Tolerance, he admitted, was a boring virtue—no one ever wrote an ode or raised a statue in its name— but it did more to keep the peace than vague sentimentalities about love.

Orwell, I wish to argue, was also one of love's doubters. In 1948, for instance, he declared that a community structured by an ethos of love would be much more intolerant and intrusive than a State that was governed by laws. Most laws were purely negative and involved a simple 'thou shalt not'—but the dictates of love, he suggested, would demand a much more active and onerous form of loyalty. Love was not enough for Orwell, or rather it was too much. His difficulties with love may have been in part dispositional, but they had a long tradition of political argument on their side. Modern States, Hegel argued, should be ruled not by feelings, but by laws, for only the latter could be rationally examined, universally shared, and freely assented to. Or, as the curmudgeonly Victorian James Fitzjames Stephens proclaimed in 1873: 'It is not love that one wants from the great mass of mankind, but respect and justice'. Love, on the other hand, 'is frequently an insulting intrusion'—an outlook that the prickly Orwell would also come to share.

The intrusiveness of love, for Stephens, derived from the fact that it aims for the good of the beloved. This aim may sound benign, but since there is no unanimity about what goodness is, such benevolence in a public context is often deeply presumptuous. Indeed, in the absence of an explicit consensus about values, love can be an extremely coercive force. Orwell made this point in his essay on Swift—where the republic of love is potentially 'totalitarian'—and again in *Nineteen Eighty-Four*. The Oceanic State seeks to monopolize love: as O'Brien puts it, 'There will be no love, except the love of Big Brother'—and its politicization of the emotions is deeply despotic. In Oceania, external obedience is not enough; a more comprehensive form of obedience is required. Indeed, the demand for the citizen's love involves the entire reconstitution of the person. Winston has to be remade in order to love Big Brother.

The 'Ministry of Love' is, of course, a deeply ironic title because Oceania's administrators appear to give the sentiment little credence. As O'Brien explains: 'The old civilizations claimed that they were founded on love or justice. Ours is founded upon hatred'. Thus, the rather *simpliste* mindset that

Franz Borkenau attributed to Nazis ('Nazi psychology...boils down to simple concentrated hate') and extended to Bolsheviks is given a home in the future and made into a deliberate method of rule. As Orwell noted in his review of Borkenau's *The Totalitarian Enemy*: 'Hatred can be turned in any direction at a moment's notice, like a plumber's blow-flame'. In *Nineteen Eighty-Four*, hate is also 'switched from one object to another like the flame of a blowlamp'.

Given the political enlistment of hatred in *Nineteen Eighty-Four*, it can easily appear that Orwell sponsors something like its opposite—a politics of love. After all, the love affair between Winston and Julia is central to the novel and their lovemaking is famously cast as a political act: 'It was a blow struck against the Party'. But it's not much of a blow. The plot of *Nineteen Eighty-Four* certainly does little to confirm love's revolutionary power. Winston and Julia betray each other in the end and the bored lovelessness of their last encounter gives the novel one of its sadder hues. The tale seems to back the rather cynical position that the self-regarding emotions will always take priority over regard for another—a fact captured in Winston's urgent request: 'Do it to Julia!...I don't care what you do to her. Tear her face off, strip her to the bones. Not me! Julia! Not me!' One thing that Julia and Winston manage to agree upon in the end is that 'All you care about is yourself'.

If this seems too simple a conclusion to wrest from the novel as a whole, the book clearly indicates that basic human emotions require certain social and political conditions if they are to thrive: love cannot flourish under torture or in extreme duress. This suggests that love has a political basis, yet the final line of *Nineteen Eighty-Four*—'He loved Big Brother'—also emphasizes the dangers of politicizing the affections. If Winston's sentimental re-education stresses the importance of restrictions to the State's powers, it also constrains the ways in which love might be enlisted as a form of resistance. Since the private character of intimacy is one of its key attractions in the novel—'privacy, love and friendship' usually travel hand in hand—attempts to convert such affection into a political or public force risk distorting its very nature. Love may require certain political conditions if it is to thrive, but it can't serve as a basis for politics without imperilling itself. Auden hoped that love would work its 'public spirit' through our everyday 'private stuff', but Orwell clearly emphasizes the dangers of making love go public.

Orwell's disagreement with Auden on the question of civic love—often expressed through a thuggish homophobia—reveals interesting limits to his sense of brotherhood. As I have suggested, Auden's ethics of love owed much to Christian morality and to a kind of Sunday School socialism. But it also looked back—sometimes quite explicitly—to the example of the Greeks. In Aristotle, a certain type of *philia*, or friendship and love, was more important than justice, for friendship already entailed a desire for justice for one's friends, while justice alone was an insufficient virtue. Auden would also endorse a type of love 'that is to be judged by its social and political value', while George Roberts would commend the 'Greek conception of good citizenship' that was to be found in his verse and Spender's.

But as Auden's 'The Unknown Citizen' makes clear, an ancient ideal of civic friendship is difficult to foster in modern polities of enormous scale. Indeed, partly for that reason, friendship was often cast as an apolitical, even anti-political affair in the modern world. Consider, for instance, Forster's famous credo:'if I had to choose between betraying my country and betraying my friend, I hope I should have the guts to betray my country'. Drawn to coteries and cliques, Auden would often view friendship as a private matter, sometimes opting for 'the *polis* of our friends' over any obvious identification with the State. But he would also decry the corrupt privacy of modern relationships. In 1934, for instance, he was convinced that the idea of 'personal love is a neurotic symptom, only inflaming our loneliness'. 'Equal with colleagues in a ring', the speaker of 'A Summer Night' enjoys the comfort of friendship, but seems to deplore its ring-fenced character. Such exclusiveness allows Auden to re-energize cliches concerning the 'tyrannies of love'—there is something genuinely oppressive in a love that is so partial and selective.

Auden would thus attempt to extend personal intimacy into something bigger and better. In 'Spain 1937', for instance, he hoped to transform 'Our hours of friendship into a people's army'. Indeed, much of his work in the '30s is a hymn to political friendship—'Comrades to whom our thoughts return / Brothers to whom our bowels yearn'. But not everyone possessed these yearning bowels. As MacNeice tartly observed: 'Comradeship is the communist substitute for bourgeois romance; in its extreme form... it leads to an idealisation of homosexuality'. Orwell rarely idealized homosexuality— and brutally distinguished himself from the 'Nancy poets'—but he could sometimes celebrate the idea of comradeship in fairly rhapsodic terms. Recall once again his intimate moment with the militiaman ('I hardly know why, but I have seldom seen anyone—any man, I mean—to whom I have taken such an immediate liking'). Yet such moments are relatively rare in Orwell—a fact that reveals a lot about Orwell, but it also tells us something about the psychological and practical limits of love in the modern world.

For all his paeans to political friendship, Orwell found its practice quite difficult. His notorious remarks on humanitarian reformers—'all that dreary tribe of high-minded women and sandal-wearers and bearded fruit-juice drinkers who come flocking towards the smell of "progress" like bluebottles to a dead cat'—don't radiate strong feelings of affection or even tolerance. He rallied to the defence of socialism, but he famously recoiled from his fellow socialists:

> One day this summer I was riding through Letchworth when the bus stopped and two dreadful-looking old men got onto it. They were both about sixty, both very short, pink and chubby, and both hatless. One of them was obscenely bald, the other had long grey hair bobbed in the Lloyd George style. They were dressed in pistachio-coloured shirts and khaki shorts into which their huge bottoms were crammed so tightly that you could study every dimple. Their appearance created a mild stir of horror on the bus. The man next to me, a commercial traveller I should say, glanced at me, at them, and back again at me, and murmured 'Socialists', as who should say, 'Red Indians'. He was probably right—the ILP were holding their summer school at Letchworth.

As we have seen, the vulnerable body, with its susceptibility to pain and humiliation, is often the object of compassion, but it can also yield a visceral disgust—at least in the fastidious student of bottoms.

In his inexhaustible contempt for 'cranks', Orwell sought to advertise his solidarity with the 'ordinary decent person'. But this serviceable abstraction was arguably a means of justifying his own crankiness: his deep resistance to all fellow-travelling. According to Sean O'Casey (not the most cuddly sort of figure himself), Orwell's entire personality radiated the instruction: 'Keep Off!' Orwell may have felt like Theodor Adorno did: That 'Even solidarity, the most honourable mode of socialism, is sick'. Faced with 'the rib-digging camaraderie of our time', Adorno preached the good solitude: 'For the intellectual, inviolable isolation is now the only way of showing some measure of solidarity'. Perhaps this is the solidarity Orwell sought on Jura (I'll say more about his island retreat in Chapter 5), but in the meantime, he could find brotherhood a chore. Even the word 'comrade' seemed to bring him out in hives:

> How many a waverer has halted on the brink, gone perhaps to some public meeting and watched self-conscious Socialists dutifully addressing one another as 'Comrade', and then slid away, disillusioned, into the nearest four-ale bar!

And his instinct is sound; for where is the sense of sticking onto yourself a ridiculous label which even after long practice can hardly be mentioned without a gulp of shame?

The revulsion is consistent with his hatred of sham, yet its extremity is harder to fathom: why the scalding sense of ridiculousness or the spasms of shame? Orwell may have felt that the language of comradeship needed to be accompanied by deeds if it was to carry any conviction. He was convinced, for instance, that in Spain 'the word "comrade" stood for comradeship and not, as in most countries, for humbug'. Yet his hypersensitivity to humbug might seem to militate against most professions of public friendship— the performative and ritualized aspects of the discourse attest to the public character of such bonds. An appeal to authenticity in these contexts would seem to be misplaced.

Orwell may have been an extreme case, but he certainly raised doubts about the viability and desirability of making solidarity a direct end of political action. Modern States had often nursed this ambition. The wealth of festivals during the French Revolution, for instance, was a notable exercise in solidarity-making. The Soviet festivals of May Day and Victory Day had the same object, while Hitler threw several parties for the German State. Britain, too, got in on the act. The Festival of Britain may have taken place a year after Orwell's death, but planning for the event had begun well within his lifetime. It's hard to know if Orwell had the Festival in mind when he outlined the preparations for Hate Week in *Nineteen Eighty-Four*. Nonetheless, the novel clearly excoriates State-sponsored solidarity programmes just as Zamyatin and Huxley had done before him. The emotional tone of Orwell's 'Two Minutes Hate' is a little different from Huxley's Solidarity Services ('Orgy-Porgy, Ford and Fun, / Kiss the Girls and make them One'), but the object is the same—to cultivate a deep unanimity in the interests of power. In the 'Two Minutes Hate', even the independent-minded Winston cannot 'help sharing in the general delirium'. The brotherhood commanded by Big Brother confirms the perspicuity of Michelet's reflections: 'if fraternity is ... made mandatory, it is no longer fraternal'.

In *Nineteen Eighty-Four*, the State's bid for a monopoly on love leads to a destruction of all other solidarities. Gone, it seems, are private friendships. Gone too is the trust and intimacy of familial bonds. Winston duly yearns for a time 'when the members of a family stood by one another without needing to know the reason'. Indeed, Orwell saw the family as a vital source and object of love, but it was also an irreducibly partial concern that set limits on how public or all-inclusive love could be. Orwell was not an uncritical defender of family—George Bowling is a disenchanted *pater familias*, estranged from his wife and his 'Unnatural little bastards'. But Orwell also regarded the family as a crucial moral space and worried about its decline. As Middleton Murry put it in 1944, 'the family is the most fundamental community of all', and Orwell also regarded it as the key home for the affections. It was a commitment duly noted by his friends: 'He once said to me, a propos of nothing,' Richard Rees reported, "I hope you love your family?" ' As Rees suggests, it was a quaint kind of question that could sound particularly naive in certain left-wing quarters.

Since the nineteenth century, socialists had repeatedly challenged conventional ideals of the family. According to Engels, the bourgeois family was a deeply inequitable social structure grounded on the 'overt or covert domestic slavery of the woman', but when it came to families, there were clear limits to Orwell's egalitarianism. He may have criticized patriarchy and domestic tyranny in *A Clergyman's Daughter*, but he often seemed to be fairly at peace with it elsewhere. Indeed, his glorification of the working-class home partly derives from his conviction that it had retained its patriarchal structure: here 'it is the man who is the master and not, as in a middle-class home, the woman or the baby'. In *Nineteen Eighty-Four*, of course, it is the babies or at least the children that are in charge. Orwell's account of politicized brats ('"You're a traitor!" yelled the boy. "You're a thought-criminal! You're a Eurasian spy!" ') is a clear reference to the Hitler Youth and the Communist Youth League, but it shows how children have become agents of the State. 'Nearly all children nowadays were horrible', Winston concludes. Orwell's account of life chez Parson is an impassioned defence of parental authority and a parody of a Wellsian world (as Wells once put it, 'the old sentiment is that the parent owned the child, the new is that the children own the parent'). It is also a plea for the traditional idea of the family as a private institution independent of the State.

Marx and his successors had powerfully questioned this privacy: organized around the fact of private property, the bourgeois family was merely a form of collectivized egotism, aggressively competing with other groups in the search for private gain. Wells put the case most starkly in 1906:

> Socialism, in fact, is the State family. The old family of the private individual must vanish before it, just as the old water works, or the old gas company. They are incompatible with it. Socialism assails the triumphant egotism of the family to-day, just as Christianity did in its earlier and more vital centuries.

Similar arguments were voiced in the 1930s. According to Alick West—who would translate Engels' *On the Origin of the Family* in 1940—the bourgeois family must go.

Orwell, however, would plead with his fellow socialists not 'to destroy the family', casting it as 'the sole refuge from the State' in the modern world. *Nineteen Eighty-Four* clearly charts the destruction of this last refuge. Here the State strikes paradoxical attitudes: 'It systematically undermines the solidarity of the family, and it calls its leader by a name which is a direct appeal to the sentiment of family loyalty'. The fraternity of Big Brother marks the thorough perversion of family love and a terrible conflation of public and private solidarities.

This perversion was often viewed as the hallmark of fascism. As Auden argued in 1939, the appeal of fascism 'lies in its pretence that the State is one Big family'. In Auden's view, this was a transparent attempt to 'hoodwink the man-in-the-street into thinking that political relations are personal'. Auden had arguably done some hoodwinking himself in his efforts to convert personal affections into a public force. The universalization of love would undo its tyrannies—or so Auden had hoped. Orwell, as I have suggested, was deeply sceptical of this all-inclusive amity, recoiling from its intrusiveness and bad presumption. He also worried about its self-undermining qualities. 'To an ordinary human being', he declared, 'love means nothing if it does not mean loving some people more than others'. This partiality was basic to moral life and it explained why one backed one's own family and friends over unfamiliar others. It also indicated why one tended to identify with one's own countrymen rather than with humanity in general. Indeed, for all his suspicion of familial metaphors, and his attendant desire to keep private and public concerns separate, Orwell was inclined to believe that England 'is a family'. This family, he admitted, was a dysfunctional one, but Orwell was also one of its more committed members. So while he had significant doubts about love as a public force, he certainly gave his backing to a certain kind of *amor patria*. It is to Orwell's uncompromising love of country that I now turn.

National solidarity

As we have seen, *Homage to Catalonia* begins with a warm celebration of international friendship. Yet the book ends on a very different note with

Orwell's return home. Amidst the comfortable certainties of the south of England, Orwell finds it difficult 'to believe that anything is happening anywhere'. Thus, earthquakes in Japan, famines in China, revolutions in Mexico, and presumably war in Spain mean little here. So long as the old certainties still obtain, there is no cause for concern: 'the milk will be on the doorstep tomorrow morning, the *New Statesman* will come out on Friday'. Orwell has a clear fondness for these humdrum rhythms and the peace they presuppose, but after Spain—and arguably even before it—he seemed to feel that the country faced a terrible reckoning:

> Down here it was still the England I had known in my childhood: the rail-way-cuttings smothered in wild flowers, the deep meadows where the great shining horses browse and meditate, the slow-moving streams bordered by willows, the green bosoms of the elms, the larkspurs in the cottage gardens; and then the huge peaceful wilderness of outer London, the barges on the miry river, the familiar streets, the posters telling of cricket matches and Royal weddings, the men in bowler hats, the pigeons in Trafalgar Square, the red buses, the blue policemen—all sleeping the deep, deep sleep of England, from which I sometimes fear that we shall never wake till we are jerked out of it by the roar of bombs.

The long, winding list of definite articles and fond impressions enact a kind of dazed languor, which the dash destroys with the announcement of bombs. Orwell reiterated the same warning in *Coming Up for Air*: despite the irrepressible confidence of some, a political apocalypse was coming.

So, like many intellectuals on the Left in the 1930s, Orwell decried the political innocence of England—its failure to see that 'Hitler matters' or that European problems were also an English responsibility. How England was supposed to live up to its responsibilities, given Orwell's own refusal in 1938 and '39 to sanction another war, is hard to fathom. Yet he would continue to insist that most of the seminal events of the 1930s had passed most of the English by: 'Abyssinia, Spain, China, Austria, Czechoslovakia—the long series of crimes and aggressions had simply slid past their consciousness or were dimly noted as quarrels occurring among foreigners and "not our business"'. English complacency, he believed, was fed by traditional feelings of superiority (the belief that 'one Englishman was the equal to three foreigners'), and a consequent inability to take foreign threats seriously. It also owed something to Britons' sense of themselves as 'sturdy islanders' wholly removed from the continent.

Workers of the world had been asked to unite, but Orwell detected few signs of this happening in England. In *The Road to Wigan Pier*, for instance, he was struck by workers' total disengagement from European politics:

> I happened to be in Yorkshire when Hitler re-occupied the Rhineland. Hitler, Locarno, Fascism and the threat of war aroused hardly a flicker of interest locally, but the decision of the Football Association to stop publishing their fixtures in advance (this was an attempt to quell the Football Pools) flung all Yorkshire into a storm of fury.

This was to mount a fairly conventional complaint about the narcotic effects of gambling and entertainment industries in general—but whatever the causes of political indifference, it could make the idea of global brotherhood look like a distant dream. As Orwell declared in 1941, 'international working-class solidarity…doesn't exist any longer'. He reiterated the point a year later: 'Time after time, in country after country, the organised working-class movements have been crushed by open, illegal violence, and their comrades abroad, linked to them in theoretical solidarity, have simply looked on and done nothing'. In 1944 he was emphatic: 'the international class-conscious proletariat is a myth'. Proletarian brotherhood often took second place to racial prejudice ('between white and coloured workers there is not even lip-service to solidarity') or to national chauvinism. Indeed, the Second World War reflected and sustained the dangerous power of nationalism: 'the world is atomised', Orwell concluded, 'and no form of internationalism has any power or even much appeal'.

The reasons for this moral provincialism had been a point of discussion for centuries. There were spatial limits, it was often argued, to human sympathies. As David Hume contended: 'we sympathise, more with persons contiguous to us, than with persons remote from us: With our acquaintances, than with strangers: With our countrymen, than with foreigners'. Orwell's struggles to care about earthquakes in Japan or famines in China—however staged for rhetorical effect—seem to bear witness to these affective constraints. Hume proposed that we should attempt to extend the circle of our care in order to arrive at a more enlarged and equitable sense of the good. Nonetheless, he would also defend moral myopia as a basic and necessary feature of human agency: 'It is wisely ordained by nature, that private connexions should commonly prevail over universal views and considerations; otherwise our affections and actions would be dissipated and lost, for want of a particular object'. Adam Smith took a similar line: human beings had a set of concrete tasks—to care for themselves, for their families, for their friends, and after that, perhaps, for their country. A more sublime set of moral concerns should never be allowed to undermine these primary relationships.

Orwell never wished to set boundaries to his sympathies. Indeed, he deplored the way 'everyone is utterly heartless towards people who are outside the immediate range of his own interests'. Much of his writing (from his accounts of Burma, to his exploration of Wigan, to his memoirs of Spain) is an attempt to extend the moral horizons of his readers. Yet, as we have seen, he would also defend the deep partiality of the affections—a psychological tendency that might also help to account for the emotional draw of nationalism. Orwell had a fairly plastic understanding of nationalism—it did not just imply allegiance to a distinct people or geographical entity, but stood for virtually any emotional identification with a specific group or cause (hence, it could be identified with 'Communism' and even 'Catholicism'). However inclusive, it was an 'ism that he regarded with considerable ambivalence. It was an 'evil religion' and a cognitive disorder ('One prod to the nerve of nationalism and the intellectual decencies can vanish'), but he also recognized that it was a powerful form of solidarity that had triumphed across the earth ('in one form or other almost everyone is a nationalist').

Orwell gave structure to his ambivalence by distinguishing between an essentially benign patriotism and the ugly fact of nationalism. Patriotism was a highly partisan feeling—it implied 'devotion to a particular place and a particular way of life, which one believes to be the best in the world'—but despite this strong prejudice, patriots had no desire to foist their way of life on others. In its basic operation, patriotism is 'defensive, both militarily and culturally'. Nationalism, on the other hand, was an essentially aggressive ethos—it was defined by a naked desire for power and a consequent love of conquest. The distinction between these two loyalties might seem rather fragile: many invasions—Hitler's attack on the USSR, for instance—have been cast as 'defensive'. Moreover, the principle of non-interference hardly exhausts the question about the morality of patriotism and might even count against it (though a pacifist for much of the '30s, Orwell implied that there was something culpable about British isolationism during the decade). Be that as it may, the power of patriotism as a motivational force needed to be acknowledged; it couldn't be explained away as an irrational form of partisanship. 'Patriotism', he famously opined, 'is usually stronger than class-hatred, and always stronger than any kind of internationalism'.

Orwell's subsequent career reflected his generous accommodation of this alleged fact. As a socialist, he retained a theoretical commitment to 'liberty, equality and internationalism'—or so he announced in 1947. Moreover, when confronted by other people's nationalism—Mulk Raj Anand's, for instance—he liked to sound a cosmopolitan note: as he put it in 1942, 'the only answer to nationalism is international Socialism'. But he had never been particularly clear

about the institutional entailments of this cosmopolitan solidarity. During
the Second World War, he spoke irreverently about the 'squashy League
of Nations universe that... people had imagined' and he grew increasingly
impatient with the 'usual rigmarole of a World State'. Moreover, he was openly
critical of those who would seek to undermine patriotism in the name of
some vague international dispensation. England, he complained, 'is perhaps
the only great country whose intellectuals are ashamed of their own nationality'. While defending national pride, his own internationalism could be
angrily tossed aside: 'No real revolutionary', he bluntly opined, 'has ever
been an internationalist'.

Throughout the war, Orwell would argue for a socialist revolution in
England while remaining a firm patriot ('By revolution', he insisted, 'we
become more ourselves, not less'). His famous account of his country as an
ill-managed family captures the mixture of criticism and affection that
informed his patriotism:

> England is not the jewelled isle of Shakespeare's much-quoted passage, nor is
> it the inferno depicted by Dr. Goebbels. More than either it resembles a family,
> a rather stuffy Victorian family, with not many black sheep in it but with all its
> cupboards bursting with skeletons. It has rich relations who have to be kow-
> towed to and poor relations who are horribly sat upon, and there is a deep
> conspiracy of silence about the source of the family income. It is a family in
> which the young are generally thwarted and most of the power is in the hands
> of irresponsible uncles and bedridden aunts. Still, it is a family. It has its private
> language and its common memories, and at the approach of an enemy it closes
> its ranks. A family with the wrong members in control—that, perhaps, is as
> near as one can come to describing England in a phrase.

For all of the acknowledged squabbles and skeletons, this is a cosy kind of
Englishness—a cosiness betrayed by the strain put on the familial metaphor
as it totters through sentence after sentence.

Of course, it was a fairly common move to model civic relations on familial
ties and the analogy certainly needs to be put in a larger context if its ideological stakes are to be fully appreciated. Back in 1790, Edmund Burke had
already claimed that it was à characteristic of the English to conceive of
their relations as a form of 'family settlement'. As in most families, the rights
and duties of its constituents did not need to be established through a theory
or set down as a type of contract, but were bequeathed to them through the
generations in a form of tacit understanding. So the family was a moral bond
that was not the product of deliberation or choice. The French, for Burke,

revealed their fundamentalism about freedom in their contempt for family: it was non-elective and therefore unjust. Moreover, it was all too partial: the circumscribed nature of familial bonds was at odds with the principle of universal benevolence. Rousseau—'a lover of mankind, but a hater of his kindred' (he had famously committed his children to a foundling hospital)—was, for Burke, the perfect embodiment of this perverted charity. 'The bear', Burke noted, 'loves, licks and forms her young; but bears are not philosophers'. Luckily, the English, for Burke, were not a nation of philosophers—and had not alienated themselves from their natural sentiments. So the metaphor of the family could be used to question the voluntarist presumption and cosmopolitan ambition of a certain kind of political language.

Given the wide ideological oceans separating Orwell and Burke—particularly on the relative merits of democracy and political equality—it is striking to note the extent of their convergence on the question of Englishness: it was an intuitive, quasi-familial bond that required little intellectual grounding. As we have already seen, Orwell was adamant that the 'English will never develop into a nation of philosophers' and he nursed a very Burkean mistrust of the role of the theorist in public life. Such figures were liable to trade in their everyday moral intuitions for an abstract scheme and to turn their backs on their homeland in the pursuit of a more capacious justice. Jacobinism was the name of this specious benevolence for Burke, while Orwell linked it with Russian communism—'the patriotism of the deracinated'. Englishness—with its common memories and shared moral codes—was a bulwark against these diseased 'isms.

Such patriotism was in numerous senses a partial concern and was thus viewed by Orwell as a type of family love. Many of Orwell's readers have shrunk from this fond talk. The depiction of the State as a family would appear to exaggerate the 'emotional unity' of modern political units. And while Orwell may have sympathized with those who are 'horribly sat upon' in the family, the familial metaphor itself might seem to play down the true extent of class antagonisms. For Auden, as we have noted, it was a distinctly fascist move to regard the State as one large family ('The totalitarian state is a family image'). And Orwell's own Big Brother clearly emphasizes the dangers of big families.

When Orwell cast the English as one big family, he may have been thinking of the 'nation' more than the State—he at least tended to stress English practices that were 'not official' or exceeded State control ('The genuinely popular culture of England is something that goes on beneath the surface, unofficially and more or less frowned on by the authorities'). Indeed, he tried to suggest that a hostility to centralized power (despite Orwell's own call for centralized planning and nationalized production) was central to the concept of Englishness itself. Hence, the supreme value of privacy in English life (see Chapter 1). He also aligned Englishness with a number of political virtues—most notably a 'respect for constitutionalism and legality' as well as a tradition of tolerance and compromise. 'The gentleness of the English civilization', Orwell opined, 'is perhaps its most marked character-istic'. To those who knew about Amritsar or the activities of the Black and Tans in Ireland, these portraits of Englishness may be hard to credit. Of course, Orwell's own writing here may have been simply enacting another element of Englishness—most notably the country's 'world-famed hypoc-risy'. As I have already suggested, Orwell could sometimes give two cheers to hypocrisy: it was the homage vice paid to virtue in England. A country where people pretend to be decent is favourable to a place where there is no need for pretence because all ideas of moral constraint have been relin-quished. But how this benign illusionism squares with Orwell's famous commitment to truth is something that I now wish to examine.

4

Truth

'There is still such a thing as truth and falsehood', Orwell insisted late in life, but he worried that the distinction itself now counted for very little. Throughout the 1930s and '40s, Orwell argued that a relativism—even a nihilism—about truth was becoming institutionalized in the West. As he noted in 1942, 'the very concept of objective truth is fading out of the world'. Truth no longer served as either the goal or the horizon of intellectual debate; it was simply the metaphor used to exalt one's prejudices and to crush one's opponent. In this polemical context, 'truth...becomes untruth when your enemy utters it'. 'The most intelligent people', he observed in 1944, 'seem capable of holding schizophrenic beliefs, of disregarding plain facts, of evading serious questions with debating-society repartees, or swallowing baseless rumours and of looking on indifferently while history is falsified'. Politics, he concluded, was 'a mass of lies, evasions, folly, hatred and schizophrenia'. Orwell, of course, was not the only one to worry about a world without truth. In 1940 R. G. Collingwood complained that Europe had succumbed to an 'epidemic disease: a kind of epidemic withering of belief in the importance of truth and in the obligation to think and act in a systematic and methodical way'. Friedrich Hayek was also dismayed by the 'loss of even the sense of meaning of truth'. But it is Orwell's worries—so graphically set out in *Nineteen Eighty-Four*—that have been remembered best. Here two and two famously make five and the political consequences of such arithmetic are dark indeed.

Nineteen Eighty-Four may be set in the future, but Orwell had worried about the demise of truth since at least the Spanish Civil War. The 'orgies of lying' that had issued from all sides during the conflict made him fear 'that the most elementary respect for truthfulness is breaking down'. As he put it in 1938, 'our civilisation is going down into a sort of mist of lies where it will be impossible ever to find out the truth about anything'. His tone during the Second World War was a little more hopeful. The propaganda did not seem so brazenly false as it had been in previous conflicts—'I believe this is the most truthful war that has been fought in modern times'—but he nonetheless feared that the war had made it virtually impossible to verify facts. 'What were the rights and wrongs of the Warsaw rising of August 1944? Is it true about the German gas ovens in Poland? Who was really to blame for the Bengal Famine?' The truth to these questions was available in principle, but the raw facts were being buried under multiple and highly partial interpretations. 'The general uncertainty as to what is really happening', he added, 'makes it easier to cling to lunatic beliefs'. Since nothing can be exhaustively proved or disproved in such a climate, the most self-evident truths, he argued, can be impudently denied. The world, he felt, had entered the 'age of lies'.

Orwell liked to present himself as a lonely knight of truth in an age of universal deceit: 'I hold the outmoded opinion', he declared in 1938, 'that in the long run it does not pay to tell lies'. The ferocity of his sense of truth was also acknowledged by his friends. A respect for the facts was one of his defining qualities, according to Spender—a figure who had experienced first-hand how brutal Orwell's love of the 'brute truth' could be. Auden praised his 'astonishing fair-mindedness'—an estimate that was itself impressively fair-minded, given that Orwell had dismissed the young poet in 1937 as a 'gutless Kipling'. Orwell's honesty, in Koestler's estimate, was 'almost inhuman'. Philosophical friends such as Bertrand Russell also endorsed Orwell's 'impeccable love of truth'. The portrait of a tireless truth-seeker would be championed too by literary critics: according to Lionel Trilling, 'He told the truth, and told it in an exemplary way'. Of course, many have queried the veracity or *literal* truth of Orwell's colourful reportage in *Down and Out in Paris and London* and *The Road to Wigan Pier*, while others—like Kingsley Amis—recoiled from 'the dishonesty and hysteria that mar some of his best work'. In the 1980s Frank Kermode emphasized the extreme plasticity of Orwell's sense of truth. A key piece of evidence, for Kermode, was one of Orwell's war-time letters to the *Partisan Review* in which he falsely alleged that the authorities had torn down the railings of working-class areas for scrap, while leaving the assets of wealthier districts untouched. When his wife pointed out that this assertion was demonstrably false, he declared it to be '*essentially* true'.

His work for the BBC during the war years may have involved the same commitment to essential truth, but it also produced some interesting compromises. As he confided to his diary in 1942, 'I am regularly alleging in my newsletters that the Japanese are plotting to attack Russia. I don't believe this to be so'. Yet he continued to see himself as one of truth's guardians at the BBC ('I have kept our propaganda slightly less disgusting than it might otherwise have been'). Significantly, his conception of what propaganda amounted to was highly unstable. He argued that the truth is invariably the best propaganda, but he also committed himself to the paradoxical claim that all propaganda is lies, even when one is telling the truth. His sense that truth is converted into lies when it serves a political purpose may reveal an exorbitant ideal of impartiality. Yet for all his high-mindedness, he had, as we have seen, little difficulty in telling lies for political ends. As he explained it to himself in his diary, the act of lying did not matter, 'so long as one knows what one is doing, and why'. This was not the most demanding test for determining the righteousness of deceit. Moreover, it enlisted the same consequentialism that he denounced in other contexts. 'Within my own framework I have tried to be truthful', he wrote to Dwight Macdonald in 1943. Aspects of his career, however, certainly raised questions about the general framework.

So Orwell was not averse to a little lying, yet he never seemed to doubt that there was such a thing as truth. Indeed, some investment in truth, he believed, was usually built into the very idea of a lie. In the age of total deceit, however, this commitment could no longer be taken for granted. But he refused to nurse false hopes: it was a sentimental illusion, he insisted, 'that truth will prevail and persecution defeats itself'. *Nineteen Eighty-Four* gives a boot in the face to this kind of optimism, although it also mounts an urgent defence for truth by predicting the disastrous fallout from its demise. In the '30s Edward Upward argued that 'a modern fantasy cannot tell the truth', but soon after the publication of *Nineteen Eighty-Four*, Orwell's fantastic tale was being read as an accurate assessment of where the world was heading. Surveying political affairs in 1953, Bertrand Russell could find 'Symptoms of Orwell's 1984' everywhere, particularly in the widespread use of 'double-talk' and 'double-think'. Orwell continues to be viewed as a prophet in an age of alternative facts or post-truth politics. Given his status as truth's defender, I wish to explore the case he made for this ideal. 'The truth is very simple', he liked to proclaim, but he also mocked those who assumed this position. His hero, Winston Smith, insists on the importance of truth—it is, he thinks, the foundation of his freedom—but he often struggles to identify what truth is. I shall treat the reasons for this struggle in detail, but I want to begin by examining why the problem of truth became such a burning political question for Orwell and his generation.

The problem in context

Orwell regarded truth as one of the foundational values of politics, but not all of his contemporaries were so convinced. 'Realists' like James Burnham, for instance, were at best ambivalent about the political value of truth. Burnham certainly drew on the concept of truth in his conviction that politics could be reduced to an 'objective science'. Nonetheless, the science ultimately revealed that politics as a practice had little to do with truth or truthfulness. Its object was power and power was often more effectively vouchsafed by the use of force, fraud, and lies.

Throughout Orwell's lifetime, Hobbes' remark—'*sed Authoritas, non Veritas facit Legem*'—was sometimes shorn from its context and championed as the final word on the relationship between authority and truth. Ignazio Silone, for instance, gave ironic praise to Hobbes''excellent maxim' in *The School for Dictators* (reviewed by Orwell in 1939). Carl Schmitt had earlier invoked the dictum as a justification for his own authoritarian views: at best, truth was the product, not the legitimizing condition of power. Liberals—as Schmitt recognized—could also find succour in Hobbes. The 'first and Fundamentall Law of Nature', Hobbes had argued, was '*to seek Peace and follow it*', and this remained the overarching principle of political association for many of his successors. But in this peace-loving schema, truth remained a contingent good and in certain conditions it was a positive harm.

Hobbes, for one, was well placed to appreciate that fundamentalist seekers of truth had no necessary commitment to peace. The dangers of such truth-seeking were all too evident to later political commentators such as Edmund Burke. The hotheads of revolutionary France, he believed, based their politics 'not on convenience but truth' and were happy to destroy the peace and security of Europe in the process. Similar claims were made about Bolshevism in the twentieth century. According to Bertrand Russell, modern Russia exemplified the dangers of organizing politics around a metaphysical 'truth' (namely dialectical materialism). Since truth was universal, applying 'everywhere and always', its political pursuit could have a dangerously imperialistic form. Thus, 'people whose politics are supposed to be a consequence of their metaphysics grow absolute and unsweeping'. Six years after Orwell's death, Michael Oakeshott again made the case: the good in politics consisted of 'the enjoyment of orderly and peaceable behaviour, not in the search for truth'.

Peace was not the ultimate goal of politics for Orwell, although that is not to say that truth was. As we have seen, he was committed to a range of values—liberty, equality, solidarity, etc.—which were sometimes codependent and sometimes at odds with each other. But whatever balance was to be struck between these principles, they bore no obvious relation to the idea of truth. And it is very easy to see how they might clash. Even Plato (for whom 'truth heads the list of all things good') endorsed falsehood in the name of social cohesion. The prince must be 'a great feigner and dissembler', Machiavelli contended, and will always find 'plenty of people who will let themselves be deceived'. As we have seen, modern-day Machiavellians like Burnham liked to tell tough truths about the necessity of lies: 'The political life of the masses and the cohesion of society demand the acceptance of myths'. This, of course, raised problems for scientifically-minded rulers and those schooled in the ways of the fox:

> A scientific attitude toward society does not permit belief in the truth of the myths. But the leaders must profess, indeed foster, belief in the myths, or the fabric of society will crack and then be overthrown. In short, the leaders, if they themselves are scientific, must lie. It is hard to lie all the time in public but to keep privately an objective regard for the truth. Not only is it hard; it is often ineffective, for lies are often not convincing when told with a divided heart. The tendency is for the deceivers to become self-deceived, to believe their own myths. When this happens they are no longer scientific. Sincerity is bought at the price of truth.

Orwell berated Burnham for his cynicism, but, as we have seen, he too could tolerate deceit—or what Auden called 'the fairly-noble unifying lie'. Some beliefs—like the English confidence in the impartiality of law—were, he believed, false, but they were 'powerful illusions', which made public life possible. While he praised the English commitment to 'objective truth' during the war, this phenomenon and Orwell's statement about it may have been little more than a virtuous sham. Hypocrisy, after all, was a useful vice in England: a fraudulent commitment to justice was better than no commitment to it at all. The psychological viability of signing up to myths that one also deemed false might certainly be questioned (his subsequent theory of 'doublethink' is clearly an attempt to provide an answer). But whatever mental gymnastics it required, Orwell took considerable comfort from the fact that England had never reached a stage of depravity where 'humbug can be dropped'.

Orwell was not perhaps a very sincere defender of hypocrisy, because in other settings he judged it to be 'disgusting'. Moreover, he sometimes worried that democracies were more disposed to this vice than dictatorships. This was an ancient theme of political thought—since the days of Thucydides, democracies were cast as houses of subterfuge where one 'must lie to be believed'—and in the 1940s Burnham would make this case *ad nauseam*. Since, for Burnham, the very concept of popular self-rule was a 'myth', he was fairly at peace with different elements of democratic theatre. But Orwell's commitment to sincerity made him look on democracy with some disgust:

> When one looks at the all-prevailing schizophrenia of democratic societies, the lies that have to be told for vote-catching purposes, the silence about major issues, the distortions of the press, it is tempting to believe that in totalitarian countries there is less humbug, more facing of the facts. There, at least, the ruling groups are not dependent on popular favour and can utter the truth crudely and brutally. Goering could say 'Guns before butter,' while his democratic opposite numbers had to wrap the same sentiment up in hundreds of hypocritical words.

But Orwell did not flatter authoritarianism for very long: for all their pretensions to directness, the German and Russian regimes were equally awash with lies. In fact, he spent much of the '30s and '40s cataloguing Soviet deceit—'The fog of lies and misinformation that surrounds such subjects as the Ukraine famine, the Spanish civil war, Russian policy in Poland and so forth'. He was also well apprised of Nazi forms of misinformation. He argued, moreover, that Hitler's belief in his own bombast had seriously undermined the German war effort. Indeed, if German public opinion had been properly consulted, Hitler would never have been allowed to embark on his insane invasion of Russia:'The great strength of democracy, its power of criticism, was ignored'. So democracy, it seemed, received a cheer for truth-telling—or at least for rational oversight—but totalitarianism in the end got none.

As Orwell famously contended, totalitarian governments not only circulated lies, they attacked the very 'concept of objective truth'. This was not an unusual position to assume in 1944. The Nazis had been repeatedly cast as murderers of truth; in Strachey's eyes, for instance, they were 'the most thorough enemies of the truth which the world has ever seen'. Orwell, moreover, had been deeply struck by Russell's suggestion that 'power-philosophies' were insane, turning their back, as they seemed to do, on the very concept of objective truth. Yet it says a lot about Orwell that he never really countenanced the possibility that defenders of 'objective truth' could be equally tyrannical or deranged. After all, in 1945 Karl Popper traced the pedigree of modern totalitarianism back to Plato's absolutist views on truth, while in the same year, E. H. Carr suggested that Lenin abjured toleration in the name of 'absolute truth'. Russell, as we have seen, also cast Bolsheviks as dangerous zealots of truth.

Orwell's totalitarians, however, were generally opposed to objective truth—a position that may have been enhanced by his reading of Hermann Rauschning's dubious 'conversations' with Hitler (in 1941, Orwell declared Rauschning one of the 'best' writers of political polemic). While Hitler may have declared himself on the side of 'eternal truth' in *Mein Kampf*, Rauschning's Hitler proclaims that 'There is no such thing as truth, either in the moral or in the scientific sense'. Accompanying this was a purely pragmatic endorsement of science: 'Science is a social phenomenon, and like every other social phenomenon is limited by the benefit or injury it confers on the community'. In 1942 Orwell ascribed a very similar doctrine to Nazism. 'Nazi theory', he explained, 'specifically denies that such a thing as "the truth" exists'. 'There is, for instance, no such thing as "science". There is only "German science", "Jewish science" etc'. Nazism, in other words, was a type of relativism—an epistemology that quickly led to a 'nightmare world' in which truth is anything that the powerful say is the case. There were several steps missing in this argument—although texts like *Nineteen Eighty-Four* certainly add some rhetorical muscle to the claims against relativism. In general, Orwell spent little time refuting relativism as an epistemic theory, assuming, perhaps, that it was patently self-refuting: it adopted a universal viewpoint to deny the possibility of any such outlook. Relativists were thus exponents of the 'schizophrenic' outlook he despised.

Nazism, he believed, was particularly self-contradictory: 'It declares itself infallible, and at the same time it attacks the very concept of objective truth'. Yet, in some respects, the Nazi's terrible absolutism seemed to be compatible with his alleged relativism. For the Nazi, at least in Orwell's account of him, truth was not universal, but was specific to a particular community, race, party, or geographical domain. Within this restricted space, however, the idea of truth could remain as monolithic and uncompromising as it had been under a more universal schema—or so Orwell seemed to suggest.

All who lived within a particular regime of truth were bound by its rules. Orwell's most alarming—and contentious—claim was that political leaders could control the rules of an epistemic space. Relativism thus endowed governors with a demanding notion of truth, while precluding the possibility of any independent norm for adjudicating this concept. In *Nineteen Eighty-Four*, for instance, the Party sets the epistemic standards and there is no 'external standard' to which one can appeal.

He increasingly believed that this epistemic imprisonment was a real feature of the modern world. Throughout the Second World War, thinkers such as E. H. Carr and Hayek had worried about the increasing 'nationalisation of thought'—a surrender of the intellectual's independence to the State, coinciding with the State's secession from international legal and moral norms. Orwell complained of a similar process ('Everything in our age conspires to turn the writer, and every other kind of artist as well, into a minor official'). He would also deplore 'the atomisation of the world'—reflected and sustained by nationalism—and rued the intellectual ramifications of this balkanization. 'Indifference to objective truth', he explained, 'is encouraged by the sealing-off of one part of the world from another'. Cultural autarchy, he suggested, makes 'delusions easier to preserve' and truth harder to access ('To an astonishing extent it is impossible to discover what is happening outside one's own immediate circle'). It is no surprise that his fictional Oceania is entirely insulated from commerce with other States ('We can shut them out of existence'). Here thought can neither assess nor transcend its own limits, for 'Oceania is the world'. The result of such insularity, it seems, is collective paranoia and ignorance.

Red lies?

Since his days in Spain, Orwell had come to regard modern communism as a dangerous progenitor of lies. He was hardly alone in this conviction. As Eugene Lyons—a United Press correspondent in Moscow—put it in 1937: 'The international movement is soaked through and through with a fetid machiavellism that lies to its own adherents and to the rest of the world'. This was not a particularly difficult case to argue after the grim farce of the Moscow show trials. Even victims of the trials like Trotsky—prosecuted *in absentia* in 1936 for conspiracy and terrorism—would defend the revolutionary necessity of deceit ('"lies and worse" are an inseparable part of the class struggle'). Indeed, Trotsky proclaimed that the very concept of truth and falsehood was 'born from social contradictions'. What Trotsky meant by this was anybody's guess, but he suggested that the distinction between truth and lies did not matter very much until social 'contradictions' were eliminated (i.e. world communism had won). So an eschatological vision of a final and absolute truth could sanction any number of lies in the meantime.

Truth, according to Eugene Lyons, was at best plural under Bolshevism: 'The whole movement is committed to a theory of multiple truths, each diluted and doctored for the palate and stomach of the recipient, beginning with a "true" truth for the uppermost layer of leaders and graduated down to downright lies for the masses'. Communist attitudes to truth, he suggested, were best expressed by advertisements encouraging the completion of the Five Year Plan in four years: $2 + 2 = 5$. The bold slogan—in all its 'perverse optimism' and 'defiance of logic'—summed up 'the tragic absurdity of the Soviet scene'. Orwell was clearly struck by the symbolic power of such arithmetic; months after reviewing Lyons's book he proposed (in a review of Russell's *Power*) that it 'is quite possible that we are descending into an age in which two and two will make five'. He obviously fleshed out these fears in *Nineteen Eighty-Four*, basing his account of the eclipse of truth on a broad range of sources, from Russell's popular works to Burnham's fascinated tales of power. As we have seen, Burnham liked to suggest that politics as a practice had very little to do with truth or indeed with reason ('logical or rational action plays a relatively minor part in political and social change'). Yet as the 1940s progressed, Burnham seemed to change his tune about truth, becoming an impassioned defender of objectivity. Everywhere under communism, he claimed, this principle was in retreat:

Our culture has . . . always held in one or another mode the ideal of an objective truth as the guide and goal, beyond the limits of our passions and interests, of our inquiries. In Christian theology this standard of truth appears as the archetypal ideas in the Divine Mind, the eternal laws of the universe decreed by the Omnipotent God. Throughout the secular tradition of post-Renaissance science, an analogous standard of truth is implicit in the humility before the independent factual evidence that pervades scientific method. For communist doctrine and communist practice, truth, as merely another weapon in the class struggle, becomes a political tool. The Party can (as it has) declare the theory of relativity or the Mendelian laws of heredity false, because 'counter-revolutionary', as readily as it doctors statistics or rewrites history or invents a new childhood for Stalin. What communists call 'mechanical logic'—that is, the rules of objective inference and proof, the rules that permit us to test for truth and falsity—is replaced by 'dialectical logic'. The law of dialectical logic is simply that whatever serves the interests of communist power is true.

Orwell criticized the more histrionic features of Burnham's anti-communism—he was a man who 'thinks always in terms of monsters and cataclysms'—but he praised his defence of 'old-style democracy'. While the political geography of *Nineteen Eighty-Four* is often traced to Burnham's *Managerial Revolution* (1940), the novel also appears to share his apocalyptic worries about truth. We certainly find the same references to the retirement of eternal laws, the denial of fact, the politicization of science, the rewriting of history, and the sanctioning of nonsense through 'dialectical logic' or what Orwell preferred to call 'doublethink'. Of course, the similitude may simply rest on the fact that life under Stalin contained all of these abuses and they were apparent to anyone with some basic discernment.

Nineteen Eighty-Four—from the 'black-moustachio'd face' to the purges and public trials to the demonization of Goldstein to the three-year plans to the mind-bending mathematics—is a transparent critique of Stalinism, but in order to grasp the politics of truth in the novel, it is important to consider how it takes issue with some of the broader epistemological tenets of Marxism. Marx, after all, had famously declared to have 'abolished all "eternal truths"' in 1848. This Janus-faced claim could be read as a rejection of objective truth, or as an attack on 'bourgeois' pretentions to objectivity. Marx's second thesis on Feuerbach was equally ambiguous: 'The question whether objective truth belongs to human thinking is not a question of theory but a practical question. Man must prove the truth, i.e., the reality and power, the this-worldliness of his thinking in practice'. For some interpreters in the '30s, this was a pragmatic definition of truth that had little in common with a classical account involving some relationship between beliefs and an independent reality to which they refer. Thus, it was sometimes argued that the veracity of a judgement, for Marx, depended on the practical utility of its acceptance or rejection, not on some fit between the judgement and what really was the case. As Edward Upward put it in 1937: 'An idea, a theory about the world is true in so far as it works in practice'. This pragmatic conception of truth was certainly attributed to Bolshevism—in Koestler's *Darkness at Noon*, for instance, truth under communism 'is what is useful to humanity, falsehood what is harmful'.

But it is far from certain that this was ever Marx's confirmed position. It is one thing to present practical usefulness as a *definition* of truth; it is another matter to present this as a simple *criterion* of truth. The first option implies that truth means nothing other than what is useful and the route towards a certain kind of relativism becomes fairly clear. The second interpretation is less extreme and simply implies that the utility of a belief provides some evidence of its truth—a standpoint, as we shall see, which Orwell himself often adopted. Here faith may be retained in a reality that is independent of our beliefs and in truth as some kind of correspondence or fit between a belief and a reality that is external to it. The practical usefulness of an opinion simply serves to indicate that this 'fit' has occurred.

Yet some of Marx's interpreters would reject this form of realism as essentially un-Marxist. In the 1930s, for instance, Georg Lukács denounced the rigid distinction between 'thought and existence', paving the way for a tradition of interpretation of Marxism as a committed form of anti-realism (a position which rejects the idea that there are mind-independent facts, objects, or properties). Perhaps it is significant, therefore, that O'Brien in *Nineteen Eighty-Four* is a full-blown metaphysical idealist: 'Reality exists in the human mind, and nowhere else'. Idealism was often lampooned in England as 'a system for extremists', deeply at odds with English traditions of science and common sense. In Bertrand Russell's eyes, for instance, 'the Nazis upheld German Idealism' and Orwell's account of the grotesque idealist O'Brien may have been influenced by this general sense of intellectual genealogy. Yet it is hard to trace O'Brien's conviction that 'reality is not external' back to someone like Marx. Some of Marx's neo-Hegelian pronouncements may have had an idealist aura ('thinghood is itself only an illusion'), but across most of his work he comes across as a fairly hard-headed realist. The world, in other words, was distinct from the mind and the stuff of the world existed independently of the human agent ('the objects of his instincts exist outside him as *objects* independent of him'). Moreover, this basic realism often went hand in hand with a classical theory of truth as a type of correspondence between beliefs and a mind-independent reality.

Marx, of course, had little interest in 'scholastic' questions, making it difficult—if not impossible—to declare what his ultimate views on truth were. Engels, on the other hand, was more receptive to metaphysical enquiry, though his pronouncements on truth were characteristically eclectic. Like Marx, he presented practical utility as a criterion of truth and confidently declared that our everyday use of objects provides 'an infallible test' of the correctness of our perceptions of them. So, 'if we succeed in accomplishing our aim...then that is positive proof that our perceptions of [the object] and of its qualities, *so far*, agree with reality outside ourselves'. Here Engels clearly remained a metaphysical realist and was convinced that there is a reality independent of mind that is accessed through experience. Truth, moreover, involved a certain correspondence between this independent realm and our representations of it: all ideas were 'reflections—true or distorted—of reality'.

Nevertheless, Engels also chose to make a distinction between absolute truth and our forms of justification (or knowledge), which were relative to historical circumstances. This allowed him to preserve a demanding conception of truth, while remaining sceptical about its accessibility (although he grew impatient with sceptics who used an over-rigorous conception of truth—'immutable, final and ultimate truth'—to query existing knowledge). Some facts, of course, seemed to be transparent to us all: Paris is in France and, as Winston Smith would also insist, 'twice two makes four'. But beyond this there was little definitive knowledge. Even the truth-status of mathematics was ultimately dubious. In the *Dialectics of Nature*, Engels even argued— in slapdash fashion—that in some mathematical systems '2 multiplied by 2 does not equal 4'. Thus, for Engels, mathematical knowledge was at best relative and provisional ('The virgin state of absolute validity and irrefutable proof of everything mathematical was gone forever'). In the physical sciences, 'final and ultimate truths' were rare and in the moral sciences they were rarer still. Those who hunt for truth in these contexts 'will bring home but little, apart from platitudes'. Given this, Engels concluded that scientists should ultimately 'avoid such dogmatically moral expressions as error and truth'.

Subsequent Marxists would criticize Engels' mixed messages about truth (a concept he seemed wedded to but also wished to avoid), while others would amplify his scepticism about scientific certainties. According to the Bolshevik philosopher Alexander Bogdanov, 'Marxism contains a denial of the unconditional objectivity of any truth whatsoever, the denial of all eternal truths'. This remark may have been based on Marx's own pronouncements in the *Communist Manifesto*, but it drew an angry response from Lenin—a long-time rival of Bogdanov's—who in 1908 took it upon himself to reassert the genuine epistemological tenets of Marxism. For Lenin, the work of Ernst Mach and lesser men such as Bogdanov had eroded belief in the existence of matter—which was tantamount, he believed, to denying the existence of an external world. Thus, the virtues of common-sense realism needed to be defended:

> The 'naïve realism' of any healthy person who has not been an inmate of a lunatic asylum or a pupil of the idealist philosophers consists in the view that things, the environment, the world, exist *independently* of our sensation, of

our consciousness, of our *self* and of man in general...Our sensation, our consciousness, is only *an image* of the external world, and it is obvious that an image cannot exist without the thing imaged, and that the latter exists independently of that which images it. Materialism *deliberately* makes the 'naïve' belief of mankind the foundation of knowledge.

The epistemology was hardly subtle, but its realism was sincere. Orwell presented a realist outlook as an essentially 'liberal habit of mind', but it is worth remembering that it was also orthodox Leninism.

It would also remain Stalin's official epistemology. According to Stalin, 'Marxist materialist philosophy holds that matter, nature, being, is an object-ive reality existing outside and independent of our mind'. Matter was 'primary' and 'mind' was entirely 'secondary' or derivative. Reality, he assured Party members, was 'fully knowable' and science provided us with 'objective truth'. But, like Engels, Stalin would also claim that knowledge was historic-ally constituted and therefore relative to a particular social formation. This would seem to make absolute truth rather difficult to access.

Fortunately, history saved us from total relativism through its own dialect-ical nature—a logic that was both derived from history and served as its explanation. The category through which history became fully transparent to itself was the proletariat—Marx's universal class. According to Lenin and Stalin, the Party was the framework through which the proletariat became intelligible to itself. Thus, in effect, the Party served as the ultimate criterion and arbiter of truth. Trotsky spelled out the matter boldly at the Thirteenth Party Congress in 1924: 'The Party in the last analysis is always right, because the party is the only historical instrument given to the proletariat to resolve its fundamental tasks...I know that it is impossible to be right against the party. One can be right only with the party and through the party, for history has not created any other way of determining what is right'. This position clearly finds expression in *Nineteen Eighty-Four*. Here we learn that 'Whatever the Party holds to be truth, *is* truth'. Since the Party in the Soviet Union became increasingly accountable to Stalin in the 1930s and '40s, things tended to be true when Joe said they were (irrespective of his broader prognostications about realism and objectivity). As Orwell summed it up in 1942: 'If the Leader says of such and such event, "It never happened"—well, it never happened. If he says that two and two are five—well, two and two are five'. But Winston Smith cannot accept these sums—at least for the vast majority of *Nineteen Eighty-Four*—and it is to his fraught defence of truth that I now turn.

Criteria of truth

Winston defends a fairly simple claim: 'There was truth and there was untruth'. It may be contradictory to deny this, but as *Nineteen Eighty-Four* demonstrates, those who have no truck with truth will not be browbeaten by contradictions. Winston supports the idea of truth, but, significantly, it is never made clear in the novel what truth really is. Of course, on many levels this is unnecessary: the novel may simply rely on the reader's confidence that truth exists and can be known. And yet Winston's problems defending and defining truth can also destabilize such confidence.

Winston holds certain things to be true—he insists, for instance, that he exists, that stones are hard, and that water is wet, and he remains convinced for most of the novel that two plus two equals four—but a list of 'true' statements does not amount to a description of truth. For many of Orwell's contemporaries, descriptions of this kind were either redundant or mistaken. According to A. J. Ayer—a philosopher that Orwell regarded as a 'great friend'—platitudes such as 'p is true = p' exhaust the meaning of a word such as truth. 'Truisms are true', Winston believes, but, unfortunately, truth is also truistic: it is whatever is the case—a banal, even hollow conclusion. However, in the face of truth-deniers such as O'Brien, Winston thinks that there are substantive principles of truth that are worth defending. At times, he seems to believe—although much of this remains implicit in the novel— that truth is the way our statements *correspond* with the world; sometimes it is the way our beliefs *cohere*; yet at other points it is a set of statements which can be properly *verified*. But the novel suggests that none of these criteria are sufficient and when cast as wholesale theories of truth, they seem to fail.

Throughout much of the novel, Winston is convinced that there is a world that exists independently of beliefs. Reality, he maintains, is 'external' and beliefs are accountable to it. This realist commitment does not necessarily mean that truth should be cast as a form of correspondence between our beliefs on the one hand and a set of independent facts on the other, but it remained an attractive option to many of Orwell's contemporaries and, perhaps, to Orwell himself. However, long before Winston enters Room 101, this theory faces problems that are basic to its very formulation. The notion of an external world is itself a belief—if it is not, it cannot stand as a candidate in any bid for truth-status. But to say that this belief (in an external reality) is true, because it corresponds with an independent reality, is to argue in a circle: it presupposes what is at issue—namely correspondence with an external something. Nor is it clear what correspondence really is: if it implies an identity between reality and its representation, then it undermines the very distinction between facts and thoughts that Winston is so keen to defend. If correspondence means a kind of likeness, then the terms of this comparison are problematically vague. It would seem that further criteria are necessary for determining the nature of likeness, and these will need other criteria in turn.

Yet Winston feels that much of reality is simply given to him through sensory awareness. Rather like Orwell himself, Winston is a convinced empiricist—a firm believer in the 'evidence of your senses', or the 'evidence of your eyes and ears', as the key foundation for knowledge. Orwell often worried that empiricism was being written off by the philosophically sophisticated as 'vulgar philistinism'. He noted, moreover, that modern science was revealing that the 'real world is something quite other than what it appears to be to our senses'. Immediate sensory knowledge thus turned out to be suspect: 'I know that my inkpot, the table and myself are not solid objects but merely wavering masses of electrons, and what appear to me as shapes and colours are in fact illusions'. From this sceptical position it was a slippery slope to complete epistemic nihilism—or so he claimed. Mistrust of one's eyes and ears quickly led to an unhinged assertiveness, allowing one to claim, for instance, that Trotsky had sided with the Whites in the Russian Civil War. It was thus important—for political as much as epistemic reasons— to assert the validity of a certain kind of sensory knowledge: 'My point is that we live on the macroscopic plane and must not be argued into denying the evidence of our senses because the sub-microscopic world is in fact different from what our senses tell us'.

Winston too will not be argued into denying his senses. Indeed, so trustful is he of his perceptions that he is prepared to waive the rules of arithmetic when they conflict with sensory evidence: thus, in Room 101, he 'sees' five fingers when mathematical logic suggests that there could only be four. But this flouting of logic, one might argue, is potentially an indictment of the notion of an immediate sensory knowledge. Perceptions in the novel are not only unreliable as a source of true belief; they are also insufficient evidence of anything external to themselves. Pushed by O'Brien to demonstrate the existence of a mind-independent world, Winston struggles. 'The belief that nothing exists outside your own mind—surely there must be some way of demonstrating that it was false?' But this demonstration eludes Winston (unfortunately, no copies of Lenin's *Materialism and Empirio-Criticism* lie around the waiting rooms of the Ministry of Love). In the end, Winston's view of truth as a kind of correspondence seems to culminate in little more than confusion.

But Winston has other criteria of truth available to him. For instance, he sets great store in logical consistency as well as a broader form of coherence between beliefs. The test of truth here is not the way our beliefs correspond to an independent reality; rather, it is the way these beliefs fit with each other in a coherent and comprehensive system. The Party repeatedly flouts the most basic prerequisites of this kind of truth. It sponsors doublethink— the 'power of holding two contradictory beliefs in one's mind simultaneously, and accepting both of them'. But this seems to violate the basic grammar of belief. For something to be believed, it must be held to be true (it is difficult to see how one can 'tell deliberate lies while genuinely believing in them'), and for something to be true, it must at least make sense. Yet much of what the Party endorses is totally senseless. In some situations, it encourages its members 'to *believe* that black is white', but literal nonsense of this kind cannot form the basis of a belief. Here the text strains to depict a world that has turned its back on truth altogether. As Wittgenstein maintained, we cannot say what an illogical world would look like and Orwell clearly struggles to describe how it looks.

These logical constraints on what the novel can imagine or on what its readers find plausible ultimately tend to confirm an epistemological thesis: coherence is a constitutive principle of thought itself and a reality that has no need for it is largely unthinkable. Yet if logical coherence is a necessary feature of truth in *Nineteen Eighty-Four*, it also remains an insufficient criterion. There is, after all, a grim consistency in much of the Party's principles and actions. These principles are a bleak parody of Marxist-Leninist tenets: a) there is a truth immanent to human history; b) the proletariat is the category through which this truth is fully constituted and described; c) the Party is the concrete embodiment of the proletariat's will. For O'Brien, the deduction is clear: what 'the Party holds to be truth, *is* truth'. This at least is coherent within a set of premises, yet it makes a mockery of truth. Winston feels that O'Brien's arguments are coherent and even unanswerable, but he also regards them as 'mad'. Truth, it would seem, requires something more than the simple absence of contradictory beliefs.

The appeal of coherence models of truth stems from their ability to connect truth with justification. Winston also appeals to other canons of justification, such as the use of empirical evidence ('How can I help seeing what is in front of my eyes?'). As we shall see, however, his tendency to equate 'truth' with empirical verification ultimately leads him to despair. Verificationism was a popular position in the 1940s, although it was more plausibly presented as a theory of meaning than of truth. For Ayer, it was a semantic issue: 'a sentence is factually significant to any given person, if, and only if, he knows how to verify the proposition which it purports to express'. He acknowledged that there were different ways of verifying claims, but he believed that an empirical observation must ground our statements if they are to mean anything. Orwell sometimes subscribed to a similar theory of meaning, albeit with less philosophical self-consciousness. He maintained, for instance, that words which lack an empirical referent are devoid of sense: terms like 'romantic, plastic, values, human, dead, sentimental, natural, vitality . . . are strictly meaningless, in the sense that they not only do not point to any discoverable object, but are hardly even expected to do so by the reader'.

Such tests of meaning were extraordinarily reductive, but they had obvious uses: they allowed Orwell to attack much of the pretentious jargon that had dominated the criticism of art and the discussion of politics. Verificationism, for some, was also a challenge to the verbiage of metaphysics; according to Ayer, metaphysical statements were neither tautologies nor empirical hypotheses and were thus strictly meaningless. However, the demand for verification itself was not a tautology, nor was it verifiable; thus, it failed to satisfy its own test for meaning. Moreover, the stricture was either too permissive—an empirical description could be applied to a host of wrong-headed claims (theories of the sun's movement around the earth could invoke some weak form of 'evidence')—or too severe (many of Einstein's claims, for instance, were untestable for Orwell's contemporaries). Winston is caught between both these extremes. He believes that many of our most basic beliefs are meaningful, but they are not—in Oceania at least—verifiable. He knew, for instance, that the Party did not create aeroplanes and yet this is no longer demonstrable. In Oceania, 'you could prove nothing. There never was any evidence'. But, according to an extreme verificationism, claims that can never be proven or can appeal to no canon of evidence are utterly meaningless.

But not all verificationism is so crude. What really matters, some of its advocates argued, is that Winston's beliefs about the past are *in principle* verifiable, even if they are no longer practically demonstrable. This allows for convictions to remain meaningful even if they cannot be shown to be true.

However, in the context of Winston's strongly empirical view of human understanding—his trust in the 'evidence of your senses' as the foundation for all epistemic claims—the verification of historical descriptions remains problematic even in principle. Since the Spanish Civil War, the problem of historical verification seemed to have obsessed Orwell—indeed, by 1944, he feared that 'history has in a sense ceased to exist'—and he revisited the problem in *Nineteen Eighty-Four*. As O'Brien maintains, the past seems to lack an empirical status: 'Does the past exist concretely, in space? Is there somewhere or other a place, a world of solid objects, where the past is still happening?'. Winston turns to the sense-data of memory as a form of verification, but his mental records are potentially mistaken. As he puts it: 'I don't know with any certainty that any other human being shares my memories'. He seems to rule out the possibility of memory being self-validating: the correctness of one private image of the past cannot be established by simply insisting on the veracity of another.

Construed as strictly private sensations, memories are not simply unreliable; lacking public means of validation, they are arguably meaningless. The idea that ideas have to be publicly communicable if they are to be meaningful (a view often associated with Wittgenstein) had a certain currency in the 1940s, although such 'publicism' also had its critics—it had 'the effect of driving out Reason from the private incommunicable worlds of non-scientific experience'. Indeed, Orwell was profoundly committed to the notion of private, incommunicable worlds. This could make him profoundly suspicious of language ('Everyone who thinks at all has noticed that our language is practically useless for describing anything that goes on inside the brain'). It could also make him fairly despairing about communication, leading him to insist on the 'practical impossibility of understanding others or being understood'. In *Nineteen Eighty-Four*, of course, this incommunicability has its attractions. Convinced that public life is thoroughly corrupt, he takes refuge in 'the inner heart, whose workings were mysterious even to yourself'. Even Winston lacks epistemic access to this private world and its contents cannot be fully described in his or anybody else's language. Winston's inner life is a mystery—yet a space so 'impregnable' to standards of verification or description might easily be written off as nonsense.

Oceania, of course, does not lack verified beliefs: documentary evidence, photographs, and statistics constitute an elaborate system of verification. But, as Orwell makes painfully clear, these practices are also deeply incoherent.

Evidence is usually at odds with its own presuppositions and people construct facts while claiming to track them (Winston, for instance, writes a report about a purely fictional Comrade Ogilvy). Systems of proof are not rationally constrained by the way the world is. 'Anything could be true' in Oceania because everything can be proven. But this merely illustrates how 'proof' has been severed from truth. To conflate the true with the verified in this setting is to relinquish one's grip on reality. In Oceania, therefore, verificationism is an utterly inadequate criterion of truth: it either sets the bar too high, asking for proof where none is available, or it sets it too low, and identifies the proven with the true. One might argue that nothing is ever really proved here, since all forms of justification are incoherent and as capricious as the regime they stem from. A coherent system, one might add, would be a sufficient measure of truth. But the problem of verifying this system would still remain and there would be no non-circular way of doing so. One might appeal to ideal standards of verification, but it would be difficult to know what would make these standards ideal outside of their being true. Verificationism begins by reducing truth to verified beliefs, but it ends up making true beliefs criterial for verification.

The seeming virtue of much verificationism is that it appears to make justification independent of consensus: it sets tests for truth that operate independently of what the majority of people might happen to believe. But perhaps this simply pushes the issue of consensus further back: arguably, any truth-test (whether it involves an appeal to coherence or correspond-ence) derives its ultimate authority from the consensus it engenders and one might feel that there is no way of determining that any test has been met outside of the agreement it produces. Here consensus is not just a con-dition, but the criterion of justification. Winston, however, is horrified by this view. Truth, he feels, has nothing to do with consensus—majorities are often mistaken, while he remains committed to 'a truth that nobody would ever hear'. Sanity may be a statistical issue ('Perhaps a lunatic was simply a minority of one'), but truth, he feels, is not reducible to what most people believe. His investment in the objectivity of the past may make him a luna-tic, but this prospect does not trouble him: 'the horror was that he might also be wrong'. He later equates truth with sanity, but insists that neither is a product of consensus: 'if you clung to the truth even against the whole world, you were not mad'. 'Sanity', he ultimately concludes, 'is not statistical' and membership of a minority, even a minority of one, did not make one wrong. By the end of the novel, however, Winston seems to have abandoned this conviction. He has become accountable to his leaders and can no longer account for the world.

In the end, Winston abandons his defence of objective truth, but that is not to say that the novel does. It promotes no comprehensive theory of truth, while also exposing the shortcomings of some classical positions. Theories of correspondence, coherence, verification, and consensus fail in *Nineteen Eighty-Four* as total descriptions of truth and the novel suggests— although one can hardly say it demonstrates—that these theories will always fall short. But this form of failure simply indicates that truth is not exhausted by our theories. For figures like Orwell, truth seems to be less an object of thought than its simple horizon; it eludes our grasp, but it places basic constraints on our thinking which even maniacs like O'Brien struggle to slough off. On the one hand, truth demands that we show how the world is answerable to our beliefs and to our particular systems of justification (this is where coherentism and verificationism work well), but it must also show how our conceptual schemes are answerable to the world and are constrained by its existence—hence, perhaps, the intuitive appeal of correspondence theories. However, the governors of Oceania acknowledge few of these rational demands and their refusal to do so leads to moral and political disaster.

The value of truth

In Oceania, it would appear that Lenin's fantastic Machians have taken over and that radical idealism has triumphed. The credo comes in different guises: 'reality is not external'; 'Nothing exists except through human consciousness'; 'All happenings are in the mind'; 'Outside man there is nothing'; 'Reality is inside the skull'. And so forth. O'Brien is alive to the solipsistic implications of these nostrums, but he also dismisses the problem: 'This is not solipsism. Collective solipsism, if you like. But that is a different thing: in fact, the opposite thing'. O'Brien's rejection of a mind-independent reality leads him to repudiate all external restrictions on the will. He makes no concessions to the friction of the world: 'I could float off this floor like a soap bubble if I wished to'. So O'Brien cannot even tolerate gravitational laws and claims a kind of freedom that many Christians had denied even to God.

It was often argued that 'God himself cannot effect, that twice two should not be four'. The laws of logic and of nature were binding even for God. For many voluntarists, however, this was tantamount to a denial of God's omnipotence: God was the author of nature's laws, not their subject, and could alter their content through a simple reflex of his will. The Party is a secular parody of this voluntarist God: 'God is power' and the Party officials are 'the priests of power'. The link Orwell drew between religious and political fanaticism was, of course, an old trope. Russell always believed that Bolshevism was a religion because its dogmas, he claimed, 'went beyond or were contrary to evidence'. As he put it in 1920: 'One who believes... that the free intellect is the chief engine of human progress, cannot but be fundamentally opposed to Bolshevism, as much as to the Church of Rome'. Orwell was a great admirer of Russell's 'very rare book' on Bolshevism, and throughout his own writings an aggressive anti-Catholicism travels hand in hand with anti-communism.

Yet the Church of Rome never professed to 'make the laws of Nature'. O'Brien's confidence in his world-constituting powers is in part a product of his anti-realism. Admittedly, even Winston grows sceptical of spatial metaphors, which suggest that 'somewhere or other, outside oneself, there was a "real" world where "real" things happened'. It seems that if the world is to be intelligible, it must disclose itself within a conceptual scheme—and this scheme has no literal spatial limit. But this simply means that reality is thinkable; it does not entail that the world is exclusively mental, nor does it suggest that there are no constraints on how it might be conceived. O'Brien may question the realism of mathematics, but it remains a rule-governed activity nonetheless; his flouting of its rules yields simple nonsense. Winston also believes that thoughts are rationally constrained by the independent existence of the world. He regards stones as hard and water as wet because the world dictates that we deem them so. The world's independence from thoughts is arguably a rational requirement of thought itself: without this independence, his concepts would lack content, and without content, they would not really be thoughts. But this realism remains largely intuitive— Winston, partly to his credit, is 'no metaphysician' and he remains helpless in the face of O'Brien's sceptical line of questioning.

O'Brien may triumph over Winston in the end, but Orwell had often suggested that those who resisted the constraints of truth would ultimately come a cropper. This had been the line taken in the face of Nazi lies and pseudoscience in the 1940s. As John Strachey argued in 1941, nature does not forgive: 'If we break its laws, because we have not had the self-control, perseverance and ability to learn them, the non-human universe will relentlessly destroy us'. It was vitally important, therefore, that 'we should all agree that two and two make four'—without unity on this fundamental point, human beings would perish. Stanley Baldwin had made a similar case against the Russians in the '20s.

> Whatever be the case in a world of Einsteins, or in Russia, over most parts of the world two and two are still believed to make four. Without that knowledge or in the belief that two and two may in a certain environment make five, you may indeed upset a constitution, but you will never make an engine, nor, if you were in possession of a ship, could you bring it into any port in the world. Those, therefore, who would navigate the ship of State, if they would avoid shipwreck, had better base their sailing orders on this platitudinous verity.

Orwell also insisted on the practical importance of mathematical platitudes. When drawing the blueprint of an aeroplane, 'two and two have to make four'. So there were, it seemed, real limits to Hitler's power ('He can't say that two and two are five, because for the purposes of, say ballistics they have to make four'). But Orwell then went on to propose that in some future world 'two and two could become five if the fuhrer wished it'. The reasons why accuracy might be so easily disregarded in this dark future were not wholly obvious, but he clearly restaged his concerns in *Nineteen Eighty-Four*. Once again, there initially appear to be insurmountable, practical constraints on what can be believed. As Goldstein explains: 'Physical facts could not be ignored. In philosophy, or religion, or ethics, or politics, two and two might make five, but when one was designing a gun or an aeroplane they had to make four. Inefficient nations were always conquered sooner or later, and the struggle for efficiency was inimical to illusions'. However, Goldstein declares that the codependent virtues of accuracy and efficiency are no longer necessary in Oceania. This assessment does not strictly square with Oceanic life—clearly, the need for accuracy still exists ('When we navigate the ocean, or when we predict an eclipse', O'Brien confides, 'we often find it convenient to assume that the earth goes round the sun and that the stars are millions upon millions of kilometres away'). Nonetheless, the epistemic norms that make for practical success in one domain are—through the force of doublethink—suspended in another. In Oceania, accuracy has only an instrumental value and when it does not serve a purpose, it can be set aside.

For Winston, however, truth cannot be suspended in this way: it is not only built into the fabric of thought, it is also the very fulcrum of freedom. As he famously puts it: '*Freedom is the freedom to say that two plus two make four. If that is granted, all else follows*'. Some have argued that truth is not really the issue here at all, but freedom of speech: according to Richard Rorty, for instance, the crucial point is not that Winston's sums are true, but that they can be freely asserted. Yet this seems to overlook Orwell's own views of the matter. He worried about 'the crushing not only of freedom of thought but of the concept of objective truth'. Indeed, the discussion about intellectual freedom was often a disguised debate about truth: as he put it in 1945, 'the controversy over freedom of speech and of the Press is at bottom a controversy of the desirability, or otherwise, of telling lies'.

The codependency of truth and freedom seems to be a key theme of *Nineteen Eighty-Four*. As the novel makes clear, the social practice of truth presupposes freedom of expression as well as freedom of assent. This freedom is clearly not a sufficient guarantor of truth, as the intellectuals who write 'mentally dishonest propaganda' confirm every day. Nonetheless, free discussion facilitates the discovery, confirmation, and maintenance of true speech or knowledge. One does not need to be a verificationist to appreciate that if something is to have truth-status it must be capable of being shared with others. One might even stipulate conditions for the proper sharing of views and present these in turn as conditions of epistemic justification. According to Orwell, 'it is possible to hold true beliefs for the wrong reasons' and clearly, therefore, the procedures for arriving at truth may be as important as its content. As O'Brien fails to appreciate, the use of torture can never give rise to justified belief. Or as Orwell's beloved Milton once put it: 'A man may be a heretic in the truth; and if he believe only because his pastor says so, or the Assembly so determines, without knowing other reason, though his belief be true, yet the very truth he holds becomes his heresy'. Winston's ultimate capitulation to Pastor O'Brien makes this point in painful detail.

The truth may need freedom, but Orwell also suggests that freedom needs truth. It provides citizens with tools for scrutinizing their masters and holding them to account. The price of freedom, Orwell liked to iterate, was 'eternal vigilance', but it also required a civic concern for accuracy and objectivity. Truth placed rational restrictions on power by committing both rulers and ruled to the same canons of justification; here all were bound to the same anonymous sovereign. Playing by the rules entailed a certain sense of epistemic fairness or 'mental decency', forcing everyone to trust in the compelling power of reason rather than brute force. This may sound like a very sanitized account of public argument and was arguably at odds with Orwell's own rhetorical method. The aggression of some of his speech acts ('I think Sartre is a bag of wind and I am going to give him a good boot') might seem to put pressure on the distinction between rational argument and force. Orwell played to win and, as we have seen, he could play fast and loose with rules of evidence in his pursuit of 'essential' truth or—less euphemistically—victory. Nonetheless, in an age of universal 'Bully-worship', he repeatedly extolled the political benefits of certain epistemic virtues like accuracy, coherence, and the appeal to evidence.

Orwell's defence of 'intellectual decency' found a receptive home in *Polemic*—a liberal and defiantly anti-communist journal published between 1945 and 1947. The editor of the magazine—Humphrey Slater—attempted to make the connection between political and epistemic virtue by drawing upon Karl Popper's defence of rationalism. The public use of reason, Popper argued, presupposed the cultivation of civic virtues like tolerance and humility:

> rationalism is an attitude of readiness to listen to critical arguments and to learn from experience. It is fundamentally an attitude of admitting that 'I may be wrong and you may be right, and by an effort, we may get nearer to the truth'.

For Popper and *Polemic*, this 'attitude of reasonableness' was informed 'by the belief that in the search for truth we need co-operation and that, with the help of argument, we can attain something like objectivity'. Orwell often promoted the importance of independence rather than cooperation (in *Polemic 2*, he arguably did both, urging others 'to stand alone'), but his contributions to the magazine generally chimed with its editorial line on rationalism. Even good prose, he suggested, was 'the product of rationalism'—a tradition characterized above all by a belief in freedom of inquiry and expression.

Orwell's defence of objectivity in the 1940s was entirely in line with *Polemic*'s case for realism. As an editorial in *Polemic 5* announced: 'We believe that any future society must assume that there is an objective universe existing independently of our feeling about it'. Metaphysical realism, in other words, was a key basis for civilized life—an argument that Orwell would make his own in *Nineteen Eighty-Four*, largely by focusing on the disastrous consequences that stem from its denial. In fact, Orwell's own contributions to *Polemic* in the mid '40s set the tone for much of what appeared in the novel. In *Polemic 1*, for instance, he stressed the political importance of objectivity and argued that it could be achieved through '*moral* effort'. In *Polemic 2*, he claimed that totalitarianism demands a 'disbelief in the very existence of objective truth', while in an editorial for *Polemic 3*, he argued that the pursuit of objectivity was best served by the cultivation of 'liberal values'.

Orwell's defences of what he called 'naive realism' and 'the evidence of one's senses' were also entirely in line with Bertrand Russell's views (another contributor to *Polemic*). Indeed, Russell would make an extraordinarily bold set of connections between ethics and epistemology in the 1940s. 'Empiricism', he insisted in *Philosophy and Politics*, 'is to be commended not only on the ground of its greater truth, but also on ethical grounds'. Committed as it was to ideas of verification and falsifiability, empiricism provided the epistemic foundations for a rational and non-dogmatic form of authority. Indeed, in Russell's eyes: 'The only philosophy that affords a theoretical justification of democracy is empiricism'. Orwell owned Russell's pamphlet and he appears to have continued its defence of empiricism in *Nineteen Eighty-Four*. The case Winston makes for 'the evidence of your eyes and ears' may fail, yet for much of the novel he holds fast to the connection between epistemic and political virtue. Here reason and freedom travel hand in hand—or so it would seem. Yet many thinkers have thought this a bad marriage, finding something deeply authoritarian in a view that would cast reason as a prerequisite of freedom. It is to this issue that I now turn.

Truth and freedom

The freedom that truth both presupposes and guarantees, in Orwell's eyes, might appear to be strictly 'negative': it implies an absence of coercion in the formation of belief. People seek truth, moreover, in order to preserve this independence from those who exercise power. Here truth and freedom are independent goods and have a purely instrumental relationship. But when Winston claims that '*Freedom is the freedom to say two plus two make four,*' he seems to cast truth not only as a means to freedom, but also as its fundamental constituent. Human beings, he suggests, are reason-seeking animals and the concept of truth is internal to reason itself, serving as its ground and regulative ideal. To deprive human beings of their relationship to truth—as O'Brien does to Winston—is thus to deprive them of their reason and their basic orientation in the world. The broken creature that emerges from Room 101 only serves to bolster the belief that reason is a fundamental constituent of human agency, serving as the basis for what we might call a 'positive' form of freedom. The measure of a civilized polity, we might conclude, is that it enables its citizens to be free by helping them to cultivate reason and their relationship to truth.

Some citizens, however, might balk at this account of freedom (Richard Rorty certainly did). Not only does it fuse two distinct goods (freedom and truth), it allows a sense of their interdependence to erode a more minimal or 'negative' interpretation of freedom—freedom, say, as an absence of impediments to action. This 'negative' liberty might easily find itself overwhelmed in a more ambitious pursuit of truth-cum-freedom. Isaiah Berlin provided a satirical account of how this subversion happens not long after Orwell's death: 'Only the truth liberates, and the only way in which I can learn the truth is by doing blindly today, what you, who know it, or coerce me, to do, in the certain knowledge, that only thus will I arrive at your clear vision, and be free like you'. It is difficult to imagine who would ever speak in this way (Winston Smith, perhaps, after he has emerged from Room 101, besotted with O'Brien and Big Brother); arguably, truth would always elude such a blind follower and certainly most procedural conceptions of truth would preclude this type of uncritical advocacy. But Berlin was firmly convinced that there was a connection between positive liberty and certain forms of authoritarianism. The claim demands some attention, because Berlin would ultimately enlist Orwell's work as evidence for his thesis.

Berlin clearly struggled to provide a consistent distinction between 'positive' and 'negative' freedom, but his main point was that 'negative' freedom was a minimalist principle: it simply implied an absence of impediments to action and was radically neutral about what actions should be undertaken or what ends they should serve. 'Positive' freedom, on the other hand, was less agnostic about what ends our actions should pursue, often modelling an account of freedom's purposes around a substantial theory of the human being. A somewhat aspirational portrait of the human as an *ens rationis*, for instance, allowed reason to be cast as the ground, constituent, or, indeed, goal of freedom. Moreover, in this schema, freedom was not to be conceived as an absence of constraints. The constraining hand of reason, after all, was not a limitation of freedom; it was its enabling condition. So Winston feels that his self-subjection to a rational law ($2 + 2 = 4$) is not a check to his liberty; it is a rule that allows him to use his freedom well.

Not everyone, of course, has found the laws of arithmetic so emancipating. Consider, for instance, Turgenev's arresting prayer—'Great God, grant that twice two be not four'. Dostoevsky also took issue with the tyranny of sums: as his narrator puts it in *Notes from Underground*, 'Twice two is four is...an intolerable thing'. Like all coercive laws, it 'stands in your path and defies you'. Isaiah Berlin was very sympathetic to this libertarian and anti-rationalist perspective. He did not chafe at mathematical laws, but he clearly believed there were authoritarian elements in rationalist conceptions of freedom. While rationalists from Plato to Kant may have identified freedom with the sovereignty of reason, Berlin found reason an uncompromising sovereign: it tolerates no exceptions to itself and demands total unanimity from its constituents (Berlin made much of Fichte's claim that 'No one has...rights against reason').

Significantly, this oppressive uniformity was also something Orwell feared. As we saw in Chapter 1, he proclaimed that a rationalist utopia would entirely preclude freedom. Indeed, for all his defence of 'rationalism' in *Polemic*, he would go on to argue in the same magazine that under the government of reason the individual would be under continuous pressure to 'behave and think the same way as everyone else'. Swift's Houyhnhnms, for instance, subscribe voluntarily to 'the dictates of "Reason"', but their society, nonetheless, has a 'totalitarian' character. Under the government of absolute reason 'there can be no freedom and no development'. It is no surprise, therefore, that Berlin saw Orwell as a key ideological ally.

Berlin's account of rationalists, however, could sometimes appear as fanciful as Swift's Houyhnhnms. According to Berlin, 'rationalist' conceptions of rationality depend on three assumptions: 'in the first place, that, as in the sciences, all genuine questions must have one true answer and one only, all the rest being necessarily errors; in the second place, that there must be a dependable path towards the discovery of these truths; in the third place that the true answers, when found, must necessarily be compatible with one another and form a single whole, for one truth cannot be incompatible with another'. This leads him to the conclusion that reason demands total unanimity from its practitioners. However, standards of rationality—even for the most zealous type of rationalist—are more permissive than Berlin suggests. Reason may track the truth, but it is not identical with it: methods of rational justification serve as a 'dependable path', yet the path is distinct from the destination. Even those who believe that there is 'one true answer' do not necessarily maintain that there is only one reasonable answer, for the same norms of justification (principles of coherence, verification, and practical efficacy) can yield different responses to the same question. But the reason that Berlin lampoons acknowledges no such latitude: the 'pronouncements of reason'—and not just its norms or methods—'must be the same in all minds'. Moreover, this one-dimensional reason believes that it can coerce others in the name of freedom. Orwell, he felt, 'is excellent on this'. Thus, for Berlin, the terrible inversion of *Nineteen Eighty-Four*—'Freedom is Slavery'—seems to mark an indictment of 'positive' or rationalist schemes of liberty.

Berlin's interpretation is all too bald, and I will suggest why in a moment. But it is worth acknowledging that many of the novels that influenced *Nineteen Eighty-Four*—Koestler's *Darkness at Noon* (a 'masterpiece' in Orwell's eyes) or Yevgeny Zamyatin's *We* (which Orwell endorsed in 1946)—make the same association between rationalism and authoritarianism and it is easy to think of *Nineteen Eighty-Four* as a continuation of this anti-rationalist tradition. The Party leaders in *Darkness at Noon*, for instance, rule 'in the name of universal reason' and 'differ from all others in [their] logical consistency'. They have replaced 'decency by reason', supplanting an unmethodical moralism with a rigorous consequentialism. For instance, Comrade Rubashov believes he has 'burnt the remains of the old, illogical morality from his consciousness with the acid of reason'. Such reason, he believes, liberates, but for others it is indistinguishable from servitude ('We brought you freedom, and it looks in our hands like a whip').

Zamyatin's 'OneState' is equally authoritarian: it is a regime pledged to 'infallible reason' and a rigidly monistic conception of truth: 'Truth is one, and the true path is one'. Freedom is not identified with reason in *We*; in fact, the two are radically opposed. For instance, the novel's narrator disparages the 'primitive state known as freedom' and presents it as 'disorganized wildness'; constraint, he suggests, is a condition of rationality and a properly civilized life: 'Man ceased to be a wild animal only when we built the first wall'. Moreover, law-governed activity is repeatedly contrasted with freedom. *We*'s narrator, for example, derives pleasure from the sense of necessity contained in rational laws. He also celebrates the 'dance' of causal connection. The dance is beautiful precisely 'because it is *nonfree* movement, because all the fundamental significance of the dance lies precisely in its aesthetic subjection, its ideal nonfreedom'. The truths of mathematics also appear to embody this form of delightful restriction. The sonnet 'Happiness' is, in part, a paean to mathematical necessity:

> *Forever enamoured are two plus two,*
> *Forever conjoined in blissful four.*
> *The hottest lovers in all the world:*
> *The permanent weld of two plus two . . .*

Zamyatin thus follows the example of Turgenev and Dostoevsky in associating mathematical laws with the evisceration of freedom—a state of affairs that receives ironic praise in *We* (here young couples prefer to tackle math problems together than to tackle each other).

It is striking, therefore, that the rules of arithmetic in *Nineteen Eighty-Four* are used to come to a seemingly opposite conclusion: for Winston Smith, $2 + 2 = 4$ marks the realization of freedom, not its obliteration. Thus, freedom is eroded when 'two plus two' are no longer 'conjoined in blissful four': when these mathematical necessities are forbidden, Winston is driven out of his mind and out of an intelligible world. Winston ceases to be a free agent when he is no longer a rational one.

Given the explicit alignment of rationality and freedom in *Nineteen Eighty-Four*, it may seem strange that Berlin believed that Orwell was on his side in his criticisms of 'positive freedom'. However, Berlin had clearly some grounds for thinking so. As O'Brien points out, the government in Oceania is not interested in 'negative obedience', but rather in something much more positive. His authority is no longer modelled around the precept 'Thou shalt not', but on the dictum 'Thou *art*'. The regime, therefore, seeks to reconstitute the self in what might be cast as a grotesque parody of 'positive', 'perfectionist', or, indeed, 'rationalist' schemes of freedom. 'I shall make you perfect', O'Brien declares, and he equates perfection with a particular type of enlightenment. Room 101—significantly enough, the 'place where there is no darkness'—is where this ultimate knowledge is instilled. The task in this laboratory is to burn 'all evil and illusion out of' the cognitive sinner. In Room 101, therefore, we find a grim enactment of John 8:32: 'Then you will know the truth, and the truth will set you free'.

Nineteen Eighty-Four might seem to stand, therefore, as a terrible indictment of those who would conflate freedom with truth or reason. O'Brien casts himself as a fundamentalist of reason who cannot tolerate the possibility that 'an erroneous thought should exist anywhere in the world'. Here Orwell seems to repeat the line he adopted in his essay on Swift: reason is potentially totalitarian and can make terrible inroads on our most basic liberties. Yet *Nineteen Eighty-Four* is about the abuse of reason as much as it is about the distortion of freedom—indeed, there seems to be a deep connection between these processes. After all, O'Brien may despise erroneous thoughts, but most of the errors in the book are his. Many of his basic claims (for instance, that two plus two are sometimes 'three' and sometimes 'five') are unintelligible; his use of evidence is incoherent (so he uses a photograph as evidence of a past that 'never existed'); as we have seen, his methods of persuasion (like torture) will never yield justified belief; and his conception of truth (what 'the Party holds to be truth, *is* truth') violates deep intuitions about what the concept entails. Like Winston, we may struggle to make full or interesting sense of our intuitions about truth, but they are basic to how we reason and hold others to account.

To this extent, truth is a regulative ideal of reason; but, as Winston Smith suggests, our reason also regulates our freedom. One might conclude, therefore, that *Nineteen Eighty-Four* illustrates how positive and specifically rationalist conceptions of freedom can be abused, but the novel also invokes a positive scheme of liberty—namely, a basic form of rational self-rule—to track this abuse. After all, it is impossible to make sense of the conclusion of Orwell's novel without some sense of the connection between reason and freedom being in place. O'Brien invokes the language of freedom when predicting Winston's ultimate capitulation—'When finally you surrender to us, it must be of your own free will'—but this discourse of the will is entirely misplaced. The language of choice is an abomination in the face of torture and sustained imprisonment. The wreck that emerges from Room 101 is no longer a free agent, because he is incapable of rational dis-crimination. This is borne out by his terrible math, '$2 + 2 = 5$', and by his concluding rapture: 'He loved Big Brother'. We experience this conviction as sad because we read it as a sign that he has lost his mind and with it his freedom. Moreover, the way we chart key elements of this cognitive and moral disaster is through our own basic hold on truth.

5

Happiness

'Happiness', Orwell admitted, 'is notoriously difficult to describe', but he believed that it was equally hard to experience—at least in the modern world. As he put it in 1946: 'no honest person claims that happiness is *now* a normal condition among adult human beings'. The diagnosis owed something, perhaps, to recent events—the Second World War had produced more dead than any conflict in human history; 3.5 million homes had been destroyed in London; 30 per cent of Britain's national stock had been damaged or destroyed—but even before hostilities had commenced, Orwell would remark upon the unhappiness of his epoch. 'There's something gone out of us', George Bowling remarks in 1939. 'It's a kind of vital juice that we've squirted away ... empty places in our bones where the marrow ought to be'. Similarly bleak assessments of the existential weather proliferated throughout the 1930s. 'But how can one be "happy"?', a character asks herself in *The Years* (1936). 'On every placard at every street corner was Death; or worse— tyranny; brutality; torture; the fall of civilisation; the end of freedom'. Woolf clearly gestured to the political basis of the collective gloom—namely, the rise of totalitarianism across Europe and the lurch towards war—but less than six years earlier, Bertrand Russell had struggled to find an 'external cause' for the unhappiness that he perceived everywhere. For Russell, the problem was primarily cognitive—the sad product of 'mistaken habits' founded on 'mistaken views'. In *The Conquest of Happiness* (1930)—Russell's self-help book for a troubled age—he outlined 'a cure for the ordinary day-to-day unhappiness from which most people in civilised countries suffer'. Fortunately, with a little discipline, clarity, and effort, happiness was an eminently achievable end.

Not everyone was convinced—least of all, perhaps, Russell himself (shortly after penning *The Conquest of Happiness*, Russell lapsed into years of unhappiness, or so he later reported). In Freud's sober estimate—also published in 1930—the notion 'that man should be "happy" is not included in the plan of

"Creation" '. Human psychology did not allow for it—at least in a sustainable form. Orwell, too, would have his doubts. He sometimes cast happiness as a value, sometimes as a feeling, but the value often proved difficult to instantiate, while the feeling tended to be short-lived ('One thing I've noticed about the human mind', George Bowling opines, 'is that it goes in jerks. There's no emotion that stays by you for any length of time'). Orwell also cast happiness as a reprieve from pain and therefore as something radically incomplete, since it required suffering for its basic existence; 'The inability of mankind to imagine happiness except in the form of *relief*', he concluded, amounted to a serious problem for those who wanted a better world. He suggested, too, that there was something self-defeating about the pursuit of happiness: making a fetish of this all-singing, all-dancing condition was, in fact, a recipe for depression. So there were psychological limits—indeed, Orwell would cast them as physiological constraints—to how much happiness we might enjoy. When one did the maths, the results could be dispiriting: 'on balance', he concluded, 'life is suffering'.

But Orwell often appeared to worry less about the psychological viability of happiness than about its moral status. He was hardly the first to suggest that the 'doctrine of morals' and 'the doctrine of happiness' might lead in different directions, but it could produce in Orwell's writing a very austere vision of moral and political life. The precept he derived somewhat idiosyncratically from *King Lear*—'Give away your lands if you want to, but don't expect to gain happiness by doing so'—reflected Orwell's very confirmed sense of the disjunction between the good and the happy person. The same rift is also evident in his important essay published in *Tribune* in December 1943: 'Can Socialists be Happy?' Orwell's question contains an ambiguous modal verb (at least if everyday use is anything to go by): it queries not only the psychological possibility of happiness, but also its moral permissibility under certain conditions. So was it okay to feel happy in Christmas 1943? Orwell took pains to remind his readers that throughout the festive period 'thousands of men will be bleeding to death in the Russian snows, or drowning in icy waters, or blowing one another to pieces with hand grenades on swampy islands of the Pacific; homeless children will be scrabbling for food among the wreckage of German cities'. In the face of such circumstances, he implied that it would be difficult for anyone to feel upbeat; indeed, he suggests that it might even be indecent to feel so.

He was hardly the only one in the 1940s to wonder about the propriety of happiness. Theodor Adorno—another gloomy sage of socialism—was

obsessed by this question and his vividly articulated qualms shed light on
Orwell's unhappiness with happiness. In much of Adorno's writings, happiness
is a key constituent of the good life, but partly for that reason, he seemed to
regard it as a moral obscenity in an evil world. Behind modern admonitions
to be happy he discovered a denial of our own and other people's suffering,
as well as a distraction from its political basis. Indeed, in 1944 he claimed
that there was a direct connection between the 'gospel of happiness' and the
concentration camps. Only by appeal to this gospel, he argued, could he and
his countrymen repress the screams of pain that emanated from Poland. In
the face of such horror, no socialist—or vaguely principled person—could
be authentically happy. This concept of authentic happiness helps us to
make sense of Adorno's paradoxical proposals to renounce happiness 'for the
sake of happiness'. Yet the 'negation of all false happiness' in Adorno is so
thoroughgoing that it can occasionally seem that gloom itself has become
an ethical principle. He would berate others—Huxley, for instance—for
turning their backs on true happiness in their puritanical resistance to false
versions, but his own position could be just as extreme. 'All contemplation
can do', he opined in *Moralia*, is 'to trace the ambiguity of melancholy in
ever new configurations'. Elsewhere, he acknowledged that there was a
happiness to be found in contemplating one's own unhappiness, since
thought itself was gratifying, but it is easy to see how this self-consciousness
could make unhappiness worse. Adorno's 'melancholy science', as he liked
to term it, represents an interesting phase in the history of philosophy: only
the good man can be truly happy, Socrates began; the good *deserved* to be
happy, Kant insisted, even if there was little evidence to suggest that they
were; only the unhappy can be good, Adorno frequently implies—at least in
a 'wrong world'.

Orwell sounded equally gloomy notes in the 1940s. Indeed, readers would
object to his catalogues of woe ('those not-so-cheerful aspects of the
modern world over which he licks wry lips'); yet the criticisms did little to
keep the bleakness at bay. 'Since about 1930', he proclaimed in 1944, 'the
world has given no reason for optimism whatever'. Nothing lay in sight,
he added, 'except a welter of lies, hatred, cruelty and ignorance, and beyond
our present troubles loom vaster ones which are only now entering into
the European consciousness'. In the face of the 'goofy optimism' of others,
Orwell liked to play the role of a socialist Cassandra, taking no small pride
in the fact that he had known for years 'that the future must be catastrophic'.
Gordon Comstock exultantly predicts the bombing of London, while George

Bowling foresees the 'bombs, the food-queues, the rubber truncheons, the barbed wire, the coloured shirts, the slogans, the enormous faces, the machine-guns squirting out of bedroom windows'. The famous boot stamping on a face forever caps the premonitions of evil. Like Adorno, Orwell sometimes implied that one had an obligation to be gloomy in iniquitous settings. In a system so unjust as capitalism—Orwell regarded it as 'evil'—'we ought to be discontented'. Some of his bitterest irony is reserved for those who exude good cheer in bad climes (consider Parsons in *Nineteen Eighty-Four*, whose unquenchable good spirits are a clear sign of his moral coarseness). Happiness is for dupes—or so it can sometimes seem. Gordon Comstock recoils from the bliss of the modern consumer—'The idiotic grinning face, like the face of a self-satisfied rat'—projected onto billboards. Indeed, grins in Orwell are almost always false or foolish: 'what is behind the grin?' Comstock's answer: 'Desolation, emptiness, prophecies of doom'. Surrounded by false cheer, Comstock wears his own misery as a badge of virtue—until, of course, he becomes a sucker like the rest of them.

But, significantly, Orwell would also take issue with an austere moralism (arguably his own), which would abjure happiness in the name of justice. In April 1946, for instance, he rounded on socialist killjoys who believed that 'any pleasure in the actual process of life encourages a sort of political quietism'. According to Orwell, however, life afforded some benign joys that one ought to savour:

> is it politically reprehensible, while we are all groaning, or at any rate ought to be groaning, under the shackles of the capitalist system, to point out that life is frequently more worth living because of a blackbird's song, a yellow elm tree in October, or some other natural phenomenon which does not cost money and does not have what the editors of Left-wing newspapers call a class angle?

Even here Orwell found it difficult to relinquish the thought that one has an obligation to be unhappy in exploitative environments—one 'ought to be groaning, under the shackles of the capitalist system'—but he none-theless maintained that nature's pleasures were to be enjoyed. He admitted that one should not rest content with compensatory joys ('we ought not simply to find out ways of making the best of a bad job'); however, he also added that it was a serious mistake to 'kill all pleasure in the actual process of life'. Such enjoyment, after all, played a part in furnishing us with an understanding of the good. In other words, without a visceral sense of joy, socialists would have no idea of the type of society they should attempt to build.

The tacit assumption behind Orwell's defence of nature's pleasures is that some form of happiness is a goal of socialism—indeed, this was a repeated theme of his writings. *Animal Farm* is, perhaps, a fictional endorsement of this possibility—here, for a time, the 'animals were happy as they never conceived it possible to be'. This happiness is admittedly short-lived, and such ill luck might trigger doubts about the possibility of felicity as a sustainable public good. Yet throughout the 1940s, Orwell repeatedly denounced the dogmatic 'disbeliever in the possibility of happiness'. So while he accepted in 1946 that happiness was not a normal condition among adult human beings, he also added that 'it *could* be made normal', provided there was sufficient political will. Thus, he had no truck with 'pessimists'—that is, 'Those who deny that a planned society can lead either to happiness or to true progress'. But even here there was a significant ambiguity: was 'true progress' a synonym for happiness or were they entirely discrete values, testifying, perhaps, to a tragic rupture in our basic concept of the good life? Orwell struggled to make up his mind and this made him sponsor very different ideas about the ultimate purpose of politics.

Happiness and other values

Orwell put the matter boldly in 1941: 'the destiny and therefore the true happiness of man lies in a society of pure communism'. His investment in 'happiness' as a goal reflected in some senses a very ancient outlook on politics. The aim of Plato's republic was to foster happiness, while the object of politics, for Aristotle, was *eudaimonia*—or a happiness that stems from the pursuit of virtue. Not all moderns were inclined to believe that virtuous living was such good fun; nonetheless, many would continue to conceive of politics as an organized pursuit of happiness. 'The object of the State', Edmund Burke maintained, 'is the happiness of the whole'. His nemesis, Paine, argued the same: government should have 'no other object than the general happiness'. These may have been little more than rhetorical gestures, outlining a fairly empty desire for desirable government. But in the nineteenth century, figures like Jeremy Bentham aimed for a more rigorous science of happiness that would underwrite politics. The golden rule of utilitarianism—the greatest happiness of the greatest number—was, of course, notoriously vulnerable to criticism. Many pointed to the problem of the double maximum (the greatest quantity or the widest distribution of happiness?); others queried

Bentham's blithe confidence in the measurability and optimization of felicity; numerous critics disputed his contention that it was reducible to pleasure. James Fitzjames Stephens summed up the more general problem: 'To base a universal moral system on the assumption that there is any one definite thing, or any one definite set of things, which can be denoted by the word happiness is to build on the sand'.

However, the sands of happiness were stable enough ground for many socialists. As William Morris urged: 'Do not let us fix our standard of endeavour by the misery which has been but rather by the happiness that might be'. According to the Fabian Graham Wallas, society was essentially a 'Happiness Organisation' and the aim of socialism was to see happiness maximized. Or, as Laski explained: 'The citizen seeks for happiness, and the state, for him, is an institution which exists to make his happiness possible'. In 1935 G. D. H. Cole put the case emphatically: 'The reason—the only valid reason—for being a Socialist is the desire, the impassioned will, to seek the greatest happiness and wellbeing of the greatest number'. Some on the Left would complain that socialists over-relied on Bentham for their concept of the greatest good; however, many continued to conceive of the good in distinctly utilitarian terms.

Orwell was also inclined to think that the greatest happiness principle was a 'good slogan', although in the middle of the war he proposed an alternative credo: 'Better an end with horror than a horror without end'. Here and elsewhere he found it easier to envision a *summum malum* rather than a *summum bonum* of pure felicity (hell, he suggested, was much easier to conceive of than paradise). Yet, even after the ravages of war, he remained convinced that happiness was the question around which 'all serious political controversy really turns'. His desire in 1946 to see happiness normalized had something in common with the utilitarian aim to see it maximized, although, as we shall see, he had a very different conception of what happiness involved than Bentham. Orwell admitted that the arrival of happiness under socialism would not be immediate—particularly if this was judged in terms of material benefits—nonetheless, it would be the best means of ensuring public felicity in the long run.

Not all socialists were convinced of the likelihood or even the coherence of this prediction—indeed, the scepticism may have been shared by Orwell himself. R. H. Tawney, one of the few left-leaning theorists for whom Orwell had any regard, had argued in 1925 that happiness was an unserviceable political goal: 'to say that the end of social institutions is happiness is to say that they have no common end at all'. Happiness, for Tawney, was individual: something so subjective could never serve as a viable criterion of the common good. Other socialists conceded that happiness was an individual matter, while also arguing that there were 'prerequisites of happiness' that were basic to everyone. According to Cole, for instance, these conditions of felicity were 'physical health, security of mind and body; and reasonable comfort in the supply of material needs'—the distribution of which was fundamentally a political question. It is probable if not absolutely clear that Orwell believed that there were universal or quasi-objective prerequisites for a happy life. 'Man needs warmth, society, leisure, comfort and security', he declared, while the miserable Gordon Comstock makes the case—*ad nauseam*—that no happiness can be found in a capitalist world without money.

Yet Orwell had ambivalent views on most of these goods. If, as Huxley contended, modern happiness was 'generally identified with comfort'—the great utilitarian maxim having degenerated into 'the greatest comfort of the greatest number'—then Orwell had little interest in this slippered content-ment (more on this later). His views on security were similarly mixed. He sometimes cast it as a means to happiness, partly by stressing the terrible effects of its absence. Take the frazzled citizens of *Coming Up for Air*—'Nerves worn all to bits'—who each day fear the sack, not to mention the arrival of the rubber-truncheon boys. Indeed, the political and economic paranoia that can be found in so much of Orwell's fiction goes some way to vindi-cating Tawney's claim that 'security is fundamental, and almost the gravest indictment of our civilization is that the mass of mankind are without it'. But as Bertrand Russell pointed out, a 'secure life is not necessarily a happy life', and Orwell, too, would also stress the difference. Not only did people aspire to more than comfort and safety, in Orwell's eyes, they frequently courted 'struggle and self-sacrifice'. Hitler and Mussolini had recognized this fact. Indeed, as far as Orwell was concerned, 'Fascism and Nazism are psychologically far sounder than any hedonistic conception of life'.

As we shall see, Orwell struck different poses about hedonism (he some-times cast it as an inadequate theory of happiness; at other moments, it simply exposed the inadequacy of happiness itself), but it certainly made him wonder about the ultimate aim of political action. Even if this object was happiness, he was far from convinced that it could be coherently pursued as either a public or private end. In 1944, for instance, he reasserted what Sidgwick had called 'the fundamental paradox of Hedonism'. 'Men can only be happy', Orwell declared, 'when they do not assume that the object of life is happiness'. Of course, the psychological viability of abandoning happiness as a goal in order to best secure it is open to question. It had been a particularly thorny issue within utilitarianism. For utilitarians like J. S. Mill, happiness was the only true end: 'happiness is desirable, and the only thing desirable, as an end; all other things being only desirable as means to that end'. Yet, as Mill recognized, this risked giving a purely instrumental significance to objects and activities that people ordinarily conceived to have intrinsic value—say cultural excellence, moral integrity, truth and truthfulness. To treat these goods as purely instrumental to happiness is potentially to deplete the world of much of its value. 'We are happy in something', Hobhouse argued in 1924, 'and the something must be worthwhile. Take from it its intrinsic value and our happiness becomes an illusion'. Treating everything as a mere means to contentment is a basis for melancholy.

Orwell thus concluded that the direct pursuit of happiness was self-undermining. As he put it in 1943: 'Happiness hitherto has been a by-product, and for all we know it may always remain so'. This is the psychology which informed his assertion in December 1943 that the goal of socialism was not happiness, but something more substantive, namely 'human brotherhood'. This struck some readers as a deeply invidious either/or: '*Not* happiness, *but* human brotherhood—what an extraordinary antithesis', wrote one respondent. Though he courted the grimness of the existential choice, Orwell was not necessarily viewing fraternity and felicity as rivals; indeed, he often seemed to assume that there was a very substantive happiness to be enjoyed from making fellowship one's primary aim. The rapture of his days in Spain bears this out. But, as we have already seen, the actual practice of brotherhood in Orwell is often a much trickier and less fond affair than his eulogies about it would tend to suggest. Happiness may depend on other intrinsic values for its own existence, but it does not always live in harmony with these ends. If its relationship to brotherhood was not always fraternal, it could also find itself at odds with freedom. Indeed, when Orwell ruled out happiness as the goal of socialism in 1943, the pseudonym he chose for the occasion—'John Freeman'—was apposite, for it pointed to another troublesome conflict of ends.

Orwell's doubts about the compatibility of happiness and freedom were stoked by his reading of Yevgeny Zamyatin's *We*. In the novel, the problem is given a quasi-biblical dimension by the poet R-13:

> The old legend about Paradise—that was about us, about right now. Yes! Just think about it. Those two in Paradise, they were offered a choice: happiness

without freedom, or freedom without happiness, nothing else. Those idiots chose freedom. And then what? Then for centuries they were homesick for the chains. That's why the world was so miserable, see? They missed the chains. For ages! And we were the first to hit on the way to get back to happiness... We helped God finally overcome the Devil—because that's who it was that pushed people to break the commandment and taste freedom and be ruined. It was him, the wily serpent. But we gave him a boot to the head! Crack! And it was all over: Paradise was back. And we're simple and innocent again, like Adam and Eve.

The guiding principle of Zamyatin's State, Orwell concludes, 'is that happiness and freedom are incompatible'. The text seems to have made a significant impression on Orwell, for in *Nineteen Eighty-Four* we discover the same either/or. Here the Party assumes (or rather Winston assumes this is its view) that 'the choice for mankind lay between freedom and happiness, and that, for the great bulk of mankind, happiness was better'. The mass of mankind does not choose wisely—or so Winston seems to think.

The choice between happiness and freedom may, of course, be a deeply false one, and may function as an indictment of the regime that enlists it. True happiness, one may feel, cannot thrive in conditions of unfreedom. This is the point that Orwell made in a radio play for the BBC in 1946. Here a resuscitated Darwin and his colleague Robert Fitzroy (the captain of *The Beagle*) discuss the possibility of happy slaves. Orwell's Fitzroy recalls visiting an estate where he heard every slave without exception declare 'that he was perfectly happy and had no wish to be free'. But Darwin has no truck with this observation: of course, a slave would feel obliged to embrace his chains in the face of his oppressor. In *Nineteen Eighty-Four*, freedom has become slavery, and happiness, therefore, seems to have been exiled from the State. There is certainly something grimly ironic in Big Brother's claims to have installed a 'new, happy life'—even if it is simply a pale echo of some of Stalin's claims. The sincerity of Big Brother's commitment to happiness may be queried, but there is something even more worrying if its mantra is sincere.

Happiness may presuppose freedom in Orwell's eyes, but this would also imply that there are limits to how much one might hope to legislate for felicity or directly foster it as a public good. A sense of those limits is apparent in the much-rehearsed lines of the American Declaration of Independence—lines which Orwell significantly cites in the appendix to *Nineteen Eighty-Four*: '*We hold these truths to be self-evident, that all men are created equal, that they are endowed by their Creator with certain unalienable Rights, that among these are Life, Liberty, and the pursuit of Happiness*'. Here the role of government is to guarantee the *pursuit* of happiness, not the end product itself. There is, after all, something counterproductive in prescribing happiness for people, since a condition of that happiness, one might argue, is that people should be allowed to pursue their own view of what it involves. However well intentioned, the imposition of happiness by a government jeopardizes that good and its necessary prerequisite: freedom. Kant, for instance, had spelled out the authoritarian potential of happiness: 'The sovereign wants to make the people happy in accordance with his concepts and becomes a despot; the people are not willing to give up their universal human claim to their own happiness and become rebels'. This, in effect, becomes the basic plot trajectory of the modern dystopian novel from Zamyatin to Huxley.

'Everybody's happy nowadays', Huxley's Lenina jauntily reports, but this happiness is deeply inimical to freedom—and thus, perhaps, to true happiness. What constitutes true happiness is a point of dispute throughout *Brave New World*, but Bernard Marx is convinced that it is agent-relative: being happy in one's 'own way' is essential to being happy. Huxley's Savage, on the other hand, famously claims the 'right to be unhappy', believing this to be a corollary of his freedom. But again, perhaps, this is a fairly drastic either/or—involving, as Huxley presents it, 'voluntary crucifixion'—and functions as a critique of the regime that produces this invidious choice. As H. G. Wells summed it up, happiness is inconceivable without freedom in the modern utopia. The dystopias of Zamyatin and Huxley bear this out partly by exposing a fatal severance between these ideals. *Nineteen Eighty-Four* also contains this terrible schism. It is best embodied in the parody of the beatific vision that concludes the novel ('But it was all right, everything was all right, the struggle was finished... He loved Big Brother'). Winston has attained happiness at the expense of freedom. If readers experience this ending as a tragic one, it is partly because they retain the belief that true happiness presupposes some sort of liberty.

The codependency of freedom and happiness for Orwell is advertised, perhaps, in the title of his *Tribune* column of the 1940s, 'As I Please'. The phrase suggests that it is pleasing to be free while freedom entails doing as one pleases. Yet, as we have seen in Chapter 1, it is open to debate whether this pleasant licence amounts to a very satisfactory version of freedom. For certain rationalists, at least, freedom and, indeed, happiness itself presupposes some critical independence from one's own desires. Pleasure, after all, can enslave and this is a prospect Orwell repeatedly encourages us to consider in his repeated attacks on 'hedonism'. As he put it, 'the highest happiness does *not* lie in relaxing, resting, playing poker, drinking and making love simultaneously', although perhaps everyone would find these endeavours irksome if attempted at the same time. Throughout his life, he remained utterly convinced of 'the falsity of the hedonistic attitude of life'—both as a psychological theory and as an account of value—yet his views on pleasure were much more complicated than his bald denunciations of hedonism might initially lead us to conclude.

Hedonism and its discontents

'It is better to be a human being dissatisfied than a pig satisfied; better to be Socrates dissatisfied than a fool satisfied'—or so J. S. Mill famously concluded. Many of Orwell's characters seem to think the same: Gordon Comstock is no Socrates, but he clearly recoils from the contentment of fools: he has no intention of becoming a 'docile little porker, sitting in the money-sty, drinking Bovex'; John Flory is also a hero of disaffection in a world of 'Dull, boozing, witless porkers'. Hedonism, in Orwell's eyes, is essentially a 'Pig-Philosophy'—to adopt Hobhouse's phrase. He had no interest in happiness if it meant a life of mindless pleasure. 'Much of what goes by the name of pleasure', he complained in 1946, 'is simply an effort to destroy conscious-ness'. The soma-besotted inhabitants of *Brave New World* helped to make this point to much of Orwell's generation. Here, as Orwell noted, 'the hedonistic principle is pushed to its utmost' and happiness has been reduced to a very vacuous form of gratification. Orwell expressed mixed feelings about Huxley's 'hedonistic Utopia'. He declared it a 'brilliant caricature of the present', but he also doubted its predictive power. He maintained, too, on very little evi-dence, that it was plagiarized (from Zamyatin's *We*). Yet Orwell shared all of Huxley's misgivings about hedonism: an addiction to pleasure, he seemed to believe, was incompatible with a fully autonomous life.

Orwell also worried about the moral rectitude of pleasure. In *The Conquest of Happiness*, Bertrand Russell had assured his readers that 'the acts to be recommended from the point of view of the hedonist are on the whole the same as those to be recommended by the sane moralist'. For a self-declared hedonist, Russell was remarkably sketchy about the exact extent to which the goals of enjoyment and righteousness overlapped and he placed some interesting if arbitrary boundaries on what one might legitimately do for fun. Certainly, if the high jinks of the young George Bowling are anything to go by—'We used to catch toads, ram the nozzle of a bicycle pump up their backsides, and blow them up till they burst'—it is easy to see how the paths of pleasure and virtue might diverge. Bowling and his fellow outlaws may be particularly repugnant ('Killing things—that's about as near to poetry as a boy gets'), yet there is a much-remarked-upon sadistic streak that runs across Orwell's writing and some would say his character. From the projected 'joy' of driving a bayonet into a Buddhist priest's guts to Winston's fantasies of torturing, raping, and killing Julia, people, as we have already noted, get their kicks in disturbing ways in his work. The sadism clearly illustrates the moral hazards of making pleasure a criterion of the good—let alone a sufficient one. Often, of course, Orwell's fun is pretty benign—in 1946, for instance, he stressed the salutary delights of contemplating toads rather than exploding them. Yet he would continue to insist that life was about more than having a 'good time'.

Orwell's mistrust of a 'good time' did not amount to an apology for asceticism. As A. J. Ayer and others insisted, 'he was no enemy to pleasure'. He may have been tortured by guilt when he overstepped the mark, or so Anthony Powell confided, yet he openly defended the value of an old-fashioned 'debauch' against the evangelists of moderation. In fact, he repeatedly disparaged saintly restraint: 'No doubt, alcohol, tobacco and so forth are things that a saint must avoid, but sainthood is also a thing that human beings must avoid'—an attitude that partly explains his mixed feelings about Gandhi. In *A Clergyman's Daughter*, moreover, hedonism is not without its attractions, particularly when the alternative is a sort of self-punishing piety. Mr Warburton is a committed pleasure-seeker—'to me', he declares, 'it seems the merest common sense to have a bit of fun while the going's good'. This outlook is exposed for what it is—'That's just hedonism'—but Warburton is unapologetic. Every school of ethics, he declares, is on some level hedonistic. Christians were the biggest hedonists of all: they searched for eternal happiness while atheists like Warburton are content with a finite share. Indeed, every do-gooder is a covert pleasure-seeker. 'Ultimately we're all trying for a bit of fun', Warburton declares, 'but some people take it in such perverted forms'. 'Your notion of fun', he tells Dorothea, 'seems to be massaging Mrs Pither's legs'.

Warburton cynically extends the concept of fun so that it covers virtually everything and thus says practically nothing at all. Yet on many fronts he offers a serious challenge to the moral assumptions of the novel's central protagonist. He takes issue with her strong sense of responsibility ('Hypertrophy of the sense of duty—that's what's the matter with you'), a dutifulness that must increasingly become its own justification as her religious faith declines. He puts pressure, too, on Dorothy's commitment to a higher meaning outside of pleasure:

> What do you want with a meaning? When I eat my dinner I don't do it for the greater glory of God; I do it because I enjoy it. The world's full of amusing things—books, pictures, wine, travel, friends—everything. I've never seen any meaning in it all, and I don't want to see one. Why not take life as you find it?

There is an attractive pragmatism here that abandons the need for meta-physical depth and all the existential hand-wringing this entails. The search for a bigger meaning—outside enjoyment itself—merely perpetuates feelings of meaninglessness.

Yet Warburton's determination to enjoy himself also exposes the moral hazards of hedonism. He embarks on acts of sexual harassment and assault, for instance, with disturbing urbanity. His shamelessness, at the very least, is an ambiguous attribute. Warburton may turn out to be a better friend to Dorothy than many of the moralists of Knype Hill, but she cannot bring herself to wed him or to share his vision of life. Ironically, her refusal to wed this aging satyr makes some genuflection to his outlook on things—the decisive trigger for rejecting him is that she cannot bear to be held in the arms of a 'fattish, oldish man'. Hedonic satisfaction—or its opposite—becomes a criterion for key decision-making. Dorothy comes no closer to finding a substantive sense of life's meaning at the end of the novel and the narrator insinuates that there is no such meaning to be found. Yet the emptiness of a purely hedonistic existence is something she cannot bear. Nor, it seems, could Orwell. He too was a non-believer, but he rued the disenchantment of the world caused by the decline of religion. 'One cannot have any worth-while picture of the future', he wrote in 1944, 'unless one realises how much we have lost by the decay of Christianity'. He did not want its return; nor, however, did he want the hedonism, which, he felt, had established itself in its wake.

Orwell's criticisms of a hedonistic outlook repeatedly associate it with a coarse form of sensualism. Yet principled hedonists since the days of Epicurus had distinguished between mental and physical pleasures and had often pri-oritized the former. Mill, too, would discriminate between higher and lower pleasures, although the extent to which he remained a consistent hedonist in doing so remains a matter of dispute. Even the lecherous Warburton can include books, art, travel, and friendship in his list of life's joys. So Orwell's depiction of hedonism as a grossly carnal attitude is a reductive view of a supposedly reductive viewpoint. However, he insisted in 1941 that there was a coarse little sensualist inside all of us:

> There is one part of you that wishes to be a hero or a saint, but another part of you is a little fat man who sees very clearly the advantages of staying alive with a whole skin. He is your unofficial self, the voice of the belly protesting against the soul. His tastes lie towards safety, soft beds, no work, pots of beer and women with 'voluptuous' figures. He it is who punctures your fine attitudes and urges you to look after Number One, to be unfaithful to your wife, to bilk your debts, and so on and so forth. Whether you allow yourself to be influenced by him is a different question. But it is simply a lie to say that he is not part of you [...]

Mill and Bentham had managed to combine a hedonistic theory of value with a demanding altruism—a position that is also taken up by Huxley's Mustapha Mond ('Happiness is a hard master—particularly other people's happiness'). Yet Orwell simply collapses hedonism into egotism in his portrait of our inner sensualist, and would round upon 'a hedonistic, what-do-I-get-out-of-it attitude to life' elsewhere in his work. Moreover, obesity would remain a crude symbol of moral inadequacy throughout his writing. His portrait of the portly George Bowling indicates that he could look affectionately enough on the everyday pleasure-seeker, but he could also turn from him in disgust. He had no desire to make 'the world safe for little fat men'.

Unfortunately, key elements of socialism wanted to make the world safe for the morally flabby. 'Outside Soviet Russia', he complained, 'left-wing thought has generally been hedonistic, and the weaknesses of the Socialist movement springs partly from this'. Once again, this hedonism is belly-led. 'Most Socialists', he argued, 'are content to point out that once Socialism has been established we shall be happier in a material sense, and to assume that all problems lapse when one's belly is full'. This outlook was deeply mistaken: at best, the satisfaction of material wants provided conditions for the attainment of happiness, but this should not be confused with happiness itself. Indeed, when making this argument, Orwell spoke less of happiness as such than the pursuit of one's true vocation. It is only when we have got away from drudgery and exploitation, he averred, 'that we shall really start wondering about man's destiny and the reason for his existence'. Orwell sometimes identified the pursuit of one's telos with happiness, but he was also keen to distinguish this well-being from 'the sloppy idealization of the physical side of life'. The sloppiness is roundly mocked in the hymn to Napoleon in *Animal Farm*: '*Fountain of happiness! / Lord of the swill-bucket . . . / Thou art the giver of / All that thy creatures love*'. Socialism, it seems, should aim higher than this.

But his critique of a crude materialism should not be made to sound too ethereal. While he insisted in 1937 that 'man is not, as the vulgarer hedonists seem to suppose, a kind of walking stomach' (bear in mind that it was Orwell himself who had insisted that a 'human being is primarily a bag for putting food into'), his response was to list the other sensory organs available to man—'he has also got a hand, an eye and a brain'. The full use of these faculties was essential for a truly satisfying life. This was the higher material-ism (one that carried unacknowledged echoes of both Marx and Morris) that informed his critique of the 'vulgar' version.

Orwell moreover, often aspired to what Morris had called 'a non-ascetic simplicity of life'. His search for the simplicity partly accounts for his deep unease with modern luxury. A man, he insisted, 'only stays human by preserv-ing large patches of simplicity in his life', but luxury and its ornate wants connive against this existential peace. Paradoxical as it may sound, luxury was a type of asceticism for Morris: it was the 'sworn foe' of true pleasure, and expressed a 'sickly discontent with the simple joys of the lovely earth'. True happiness, therefore, necessitated 'the extinction of luxury'. Orwell admitted in 1949 to the 'Impossibility of envisaging life without luxuries', yet he had repeatedly worried—often in a very Morrisite vein—about their morally corrosive effects. Early commentators on luxury had emphasized a distributive justice within opulence itself—rich people's excess furnished incomes for many. Orwell, however, dwelt on the ways in which luxury perpetuates inequality partly by facilitating snobbish distinctions. Since lux-uries were by definition exclusive goods and 'can't be distributed to every-body', he sometimes suggested that they should be entirely done away with. Yet he also disapproved of the democratization of opulence in the form of 'cheap luxuries'.

Orwell's war on luxury could sound fairly snobbish itself: he often seemed to object less to the distribution of wealth than to its 'sheer vulgar fatness'. But his campaign also expressed a very dogged commitment to self-sufficiency as a prerequisite or expression of happiness. This not only required inde-pendence from others, but also demanded some independence from one's own desires. To be self-sufficient, it seemed, one needed enough to be happy and one needed to be happy with enough. But what exactly was enough?

'Luxury is itself a necessity', Chesterton had pointedly quipped: 'man does not live by bread alone' but, at the very least, 'by bread and butter'.

In his own life and writings, Orwell often wanted both his bread and butter. Yet he continued to campaign in somewhat circular fashion against 'unnecessary luxuries'. It clearly pained him to think in 1937 that 'a luxury is nowadays almost always cheaper than a necessity'—an observation that triggered worried reports about the price of milk. He enjoyed the moral clarity of the Second World War ('How much rubbish this war will sweep away') and found people 'happier' under more austere conditions. He clearly felt there was something demoralizing about the sight of opulence during the war: 'The lady in the Rolls-Royce car is more damaging to morale than a fleet of Göring's bombing-planes'. He rued the fact that the government did not do more in the war to lure people away from the 'luxury trades to productive work'. On the other hand, he supported its imposition of luxury taxes, even if it made him wince at the price of cigarettes. In the famous fairy story he composed during the war, Orwell's animals also bravely attempt to institute sumptuary laws. Sadly, there will be no ribbons after the revolution.

As we have seen, Orwell's animals impose laws against luxury in an attempt to restrict desire to the level of need. But this proves to be a tricky business on 'Animal Farm'. It would appear to be an even trickier issue under capitalism— a system arguably predicated on the manufacture as much as the satisfaction of desire. Here true and false wants were often indistinguishable. Modern advertising, moreover, was frequently judged to play a key role in the manufacture of false want—and this is often how it functions in Orwell's writing. In Gordon Comstock's eyes, advertising is 'the dirtiest ramp that capitalism had yet produced'. Towards the end of *Keep the Aspidistra Flying*, Comstock leafs through a magazine in fascinated horror:

> Quickly he flicked over the shiny pages. Lingerie, jewellery, cosmetics, fur coats, silk stockings flicked up and down like the figures in a child's peepshow. Page after page, advert after advert. Lipsticks, undies, tinned food, patent medicines, slimming cures, face-creams. A sort of cross-section of the money world. A panorama of ignorance, greed, vulgarity, snobbishness, whoredom, and disease.

Lingerie and lipstick may not float Comstock's boat, but they capture, nonetheless, the erotic spell of the commodity in general. The capitalist peep show certainly triggers disgust, but it may also stoke desire in Comstock (it should be noted that the man badly wants to get laid). Comstock continues, at any rate, with his vigorous leafing. The caption he subsequently stumbles upon—'Flick, flick. Britons never shall be slaves!'—is not without its ironies, for it is clear that advertising itself enslaves. It undermines self-sufficiency by aggravating desire; in thrall to our own appetites, we find ourselves mastered by others. Thus, we are transformed into 'the little docile cit' that Comstock despises and yet is destined to be.

These jeremiads against the vulgar hedonism of a capitalist system were two a penny in the 1930s and '40s and Comstock hits many of the usual targets, from newspapers to magazines to radios. He feels some ambivalence about the 'soggy attraction' of cinema. There is something vaguely pleasurable, he suggests, about the annihilation of the self that occurs in a picture palace:

> To sit on the padded seat in the warm smoke-scented darkness, letting the flickering drivel on the screen gradually overwhelm you—feeling the waves of its silliness lap you round till you seem to drown, intoxicated, in a viscous sea— after all, it's the kind of drug we need. The right drug for a friendless people.

Orwell's account of the culture industry was often more affectionate than Comstock's, but he also dwelled on the narcotic power of mass amusement— its cancellation of 'that dreaded thing, thought'. The entertainment industry, he argued, aspired to a kind of foetal state. In a wry piece on pleasure resorts, he showed how the amusement park seeks to recreate womb-like conditions. In the modern pleasure dome, 'one was never alone, one never saw daylight, the temperature was always regulated, one did not have to worry about work or food, and one's thoughts, if any, were drowned by a continuous rhythmic throbbing'. Of course, this is all very Huxley and raises many of the same themes that Orwell's old schoolteacher had raised some fourteen years earlier: the evisceration of thought, the taboos against solitude, and the terrible passivity of the new happiness.

True happiness, Huxley insisted, was not passive: like the old *eudaimonia*, it required an active life as a condition of its realization. But, as Huxley explained in 1926, the modern pleasure industry connived against this active well-being:

> The cinema, the gramophone, the wireless are distractions; but they do nothing to satisfy men's desire for self-assertion and self-expression; they give him none of that happiness which comes from the consciousness of something personally accomplished.

Indeed, for many thinkers in the socialist tradition, happiness was a practice as much as it was a psychological state (as Morris had argued, 'the pleasurable exercise of our energies is...the cause of all happiness'). Here work could be pleasurable, while pleasure could be industrious. But according to Orwell, this virtuous activity was undermined by much of what passed for pleasure. In 1946, for instance, he rounded on amusements such as film, radio, and, oddly enough, aeroplanes for their deleterious effects on 'man': they tended 'to weaken his consciousness, dull his curiosity, and, in general, drive him nearer to the animals'. Clearly, it was better to be a man dissatisfied—at least when that man was Orwell—than a satisfied beast.

But it was the political effects of modern pleasure-seeking that worried Orwell the most. Indeed, the link between consumerism and political subjugation was remarkably direct in his work. As he famously opined: 'It is quite likely that fish and chips, art-silk stockings, tinned salmon, cut-price chocolate (five two-ounce bars for sixpence), the movies, the radio, strong tea and the Football Pools have between them averted revolution'. The hyperbole was distinctively Orwell's, but the argument was fairly antique: fish and chips had simply replaced Juvenal's bread and circuses. The politically corrosive effects of luxury, after all, were a standard refrain of republicanism for almost two millennia. For many civic humanists, active citizenship was the source of the highest happiness imaginable; yet this happiness could be easily tossed aside for a life of corrupt pleasure. Thus, the interests of the *patria* and therefore one's own long-term interests would be sacrificed to an irrational hedonism. Orwell recycled many of the same worries. Hedonism, he complained during the war, left no room 'for patriotism and the military virtues'—a valour he later cast as a 'spiritual need'. This vigorous sense of virtue made him bemoan the pudginess of modern times. 'The tendency of mechanical progress', he complained, 'is to make your environment safe and soft; and yet you are striving to keep yourself brave and hard'—the use of the second person seeks to befriend, while also managing to coerce. But the message itself wasn't particularly inclusive: 'softness is repulsive'.

Partly because of its moral and political weaknesses, Orwell convinced himself that a hedonistic society was unlikely to last. As he put it in 1941: 'A nation trained to think hedonistically cannot survive amid peoples who work like slaves and breed like rabbits, and whose chief national industry is war'. This was issued as a warning to England in the face of German military might: the little fat men needed to get on the treadmill. Yet the rise of fascism—and the consequent military effort to defeat it—helped to persuade Orwell that Huxley had been entirely wrong about the future. In November 1943, for instance, he insisted that people had overestimated the likelihood of 'a "Brave New World"—i.e. a completely materialistic vulgar civilisation based on hedonism'. This prospect had passed and the world was threatened by a new type of politics. Here society would derive its conditions of unity, not from the collective pursuit of pleasure, but from 'some kind of rabid nationalism and leader-worship kept going by literally continuous war'.

Nineteen Eighty-Four is, in part, a portrait of this new dispensation. The Party, after all, intends to eviscerate all 'enjoyment of the process of life'—a histrionic, if not demented, repudiation of hedonism. Or perhaps hedonism simply has an alternative content in the novel—cruelty or power is now the new fun and 'All competing pleasures will be destroyed'. As Warburton pointed out, some people get their kicks in perverse forms. If sadism is a type of hedonism in Orwell's dystopia—memorably summed up in 'ecstasy of fear and vindictiveness' that characterizes the collective hate sessions—it exposes once again the moral hazards of pleasure-seeking. Other glimpses of his earlier attacks on 'vulgar hedonism' can also be seen throughout the novel. The proles, for instance, commit themselves to mindless fun—porn, gambling, and alcohol—often meted out by the State, in what is a fairly lurid reiteration of the bread-and-circuses thesis.

But, on other levels, Big Brother has succeeded all too effectively in putting an end to a good time. Indeed, the taboo on pleasure in the novel invests this state with an iconoclastic, even emancipatory function. This is clearly the case with sex. Given that the Party has ambitious aims of removing all pleasure from the sexual act ('We shall abolish the orgasm'), the celebration of sexual delight is a rebellious gesture. As I have previously mentioned, the exultant lovemaking between Winston and Julia is certainly cast in this light: 'Their embrace had been a battle, the climax a victory. It was a blow struck against the Party'. There is perhaps a residual puritanism in the notion of fucking for freedom: the pleasure derived from the illicit strengthens the taboo. Admittedly, Orwell was far from alone in investing sex with political significance in the 1940s. According to Adorno, for instance, the sexual act was the 'idea' or ur-symbol of happiness: in its reciprocal and consensual nature it conjoined freedom and equality and, when this delight was pursued as its own end, it represented the purest form of pleasure. In *Nineteen Eighty-Four*, eroticism—or sex uncoupled from its reproductive function—is a similarly non-instrumental pleasure in a grimly instrumental world, although this presumably puts limits on how the practice might be co-opted for political ends.

So Orwell expresses very mixed views of pleasure in *Nineteen Eighty-Four*. Sex, as we have seen, is a symbol of happiness, which presupposes equality and freedom as conditions of authentic pleasure. Orwell clearly continues to worry about irrational pleasure-seeking, mediating many of his concerns through the figure of Julia—the famous 'rebel from the waist downwards'. Though Julia remains fairly acute in her plotting for fun, she delegates the hassle of moral principles and systematic thought to her more discerning lover. Julia is, in many respects, a sexist stereotype and an aging male's fantasy (a twenty-six-year-old woman who delights in an older man with a varicose ulcer and five false teeth, and gamely conspires to send him love notes on his way to the lavatory), yet she is the repository of Orwell's concerns about an unreflective hedonism. Authority, he suggests, has little to fear from those who shirk the discipline of thought and a systematic politics in their devotion to somatic delight.

Yet there is a heroism, too, in Julia's commitment to joy—pursued at considerable hazard to herself—and it reflects a strong conviction that the pleasant is good and that this good is worth dying for. Indeed, the value of pleasure is built into the fabric of *Nineteen Eighty-Four*, partly through the ubiquity of its opposite. From the smell of boiled cabbage at the opening of the narrative, to the foul-tasting gin throughout, to the basic appearance of people ('Nearly everyone was ugly'), existence in Oceania is subjected to a sustained aesthetic critique. The Party may wish to retire the distinction between beauty and ugliness, but the contrast is alive and well within the narrative voice. The canteen in the Ministry of Truth says it all:

> its walls grimy from the contact of innumerable bodies; battered metal tables and chairs…bent spoons, dented trays, coarse white mugs; all surfaces greasy, grime in every crack; and a sourish, composite smell of bad gin and bad coffee and metallic stew and dirty clothes.

Orwell may have drawn his canteen from his days in the BBC and many of the novel's details—from its war-torn buildings to the use of rationing—reflect the ravages of post-war Britain. This may queer the historical target of Orwell's satire, but the case against the fictional regime remains clear: its deep unpleasantness functions as a quasi-moral indictment of everything it represents. 'Always in your stomach and in your skin', the narrator explains, 'there was a sort of protest, a feeling that you had been cheated of something that you had a right to'. Sometimes, it seems, the belly gets justice right.

So in *Nineteen Eighty-Four* Orwell gives two cheers to pleasure. Julia re-sensitizes Winston to many of life's joys—the delights of real coffee and of fine chocolate—and she exults in goods such as perfume and make-up. The novel communicates little sense of how some of these fine goods may have been bound up with a different order of oppression. At one point, the narrative degenerates into a quaint advertisement from the cosmetics industry: 'With just a few dabs of colour in the right places she had become not only very much prettier, but, above all, far more feminine'—the 'above all' marking the high point of a very patriarchal aesthetic. Yet the beauty products and the coffee emphasize the peculiar pleasure and indeed, as Chesterton would have it, the necessity of luxury. Winston, too, is an enthusiast of fine goods, revelling in the smooth, creamy paper of his beautiful book and old-fashioned ink pen. His attraction to these items depends in part upon on their historical character: they attest to the objectivity of the past in a time when this is being denied. But it is the sheer uselessness of some of these goods that constitutes their appeal to Winston (however Orwell himself may have inveighed against 'useless luxuries' during the war). Take the famous piece of glass-embedded coral, for instance: 'The thing was doubly attractive because of its apparent uselessness'. The object may have been intended as a paperweight, but Winston wants to believe that it has never truly served as one.

In the 1930s and '40s commentators throughout Europe had criticized the instrumentalism of the modern world—every object reduced to a mere means for the subject's preordained uses. In *Nineteen Eighty-Four*, Orwell also gets in on the act, rebuking a crudely means–ends attitude to life. The paperweight, it seems, is its own end. In its glorious self-sufficiency, it operates as a sort of symbol of happiness—the only state, it is often thought, that does not aspire to be something else. Of course, its uselessness makes it a luxury and even a form of fetish. Yet it also represents what Adorno once called 'the utopia of the qualitative'—the unique particularity of the thing reasserts itself over the purely comparative value of exchange relationships— a utopia which can only express itself in a distorted form in the modern world, namely through a type of commodity fetishism. Junk, for Orwell, came close to such a utopia: the object's apparent worthlessness supplied it with worth; increasingly shorn of its exchange value, the thing is restored to the dignity of itself. Of course, junk in *Nineteen Eighty-Four* does not transcend the realm of exchange—Winston pays a seemingly high price for his coveted items—but it nonetheless possesses a potent aura. Indeed, objects from old clocks to mahogany beds are saturated with a very intimate significance throughout the novel: they may be little more than 'junk', but they reveal a more complicated attitude to luxury in Orwell than his war-time tirades against 'useless luxuries' might at first suggest.

Winston Smith is no Gandhi: he likes sex and shopping, and longs for a world where he can go around 'talking trivialities and buying odds and ends for the household'. His interest in 'stuff' may simply attest to the 'jackdaw inside all of us'—an innocent acquisitiveness that Orwell spoke up for in 1946. Winston's delight in certain possessions may also reflect Orwell's conviction that small-scale ownership was compatible with a substantive form of socialism. But the pursuit of luxury in *Nineteen Eighty-Four* reveals a more ambivalent view on the acquisitive society than his jeremiads against little fat men might initially suggest. If he had taken issue in 1940 with 'the "commonsense" outlook which takes the hedonism of the human animal for granted', he seems to worry in his final novel that hedonism is no longer common sense. It leads him to stress the value of pleasure and its integral role in a good life. The good, however, is not reducible to pleasure and the novel seems to place a considerable emphasis on the idea that there are worthy and unworthy pleasures—a bland but very defensible thesis. So sex *en plein air* is fine; stamping on people's faces isn't so good. Pleasure has a sadistic side in Orwell, but, as we shall see, it also has its masochistic dimensions. Indeed, the truly happy life for Orwell involves its fair share of toil, hardship, and pain.

The search for utopia

'All efforts to describe *permanent* happiness', Orwell opined, 'have been failures'. He took considerable pains to attack fantasies of an eternal good time, rehashing the hackneyed factoid that utopia meant 'no place' as much as it meant the 'good place'. All descriptions of paradise, he suggested, have been flops. Mt. Olympus is disarmingly 'homelike', but it is also banal and no one would want to reside there. Depictions of the Christian heaven, on the other hand, have yielded little but kitsch—familiar processions 'of gold, precious stones and endless hymns'. More earth-bound visions of bliss have been equally unsatisfactory. The happy life of Charles IX commemorated by Voltaire—essentially an endless round of feasting, drinking, hunting, and lovemaking—would sicken anyone after a while. Orwell also objected to Wells's visions of a pain-free world: 'We all want to abolish the things Wells wants to abolish. But is there anyone who actually wants to live in a Wellsian

Utopia?' It is no surprise that Wells deemed Orwell a 'shit'—not least because the young giant-killer had clearly ignored Wells's earlier remarks on the irreducibility of suffering and the secondariness of happiness. Orwell was equally unkind to William Morris. In Morris's worthy nowhere: 'Everyone is kindly and reasonable, all the upholstery comes from Liberty's, but the impression left behind is of a sort of watery melancholy'. Orwell had claimed in 1942 that all humour presupposes 'evil'—since in a perfect world there would be nothing to laugh at. The frequent cruelty of his own wit (whether aimed at Wells's 'paradise of little fat men' or Morris's 'goody-goody version' of the same thing) proved the point on many levels.

Happiness, like humour, is dependent on imperfection in Orwell's eyes. This is where utopians go wrong: they fail to see that well-being is a fundamentally relative condition and derives its identity from the fact of suffering. Dickens, he argued, easily grasped this existential truth: his vision of happiness acknowledged suffering, partly by being an explicit reprieve from it. In the Cratchit household, for instance, the 'steam of the Christmas pudding drifts across a background of pawnshops and sweated labour, and in a double sense the ghost of Scrooge stands beside the dinner table'. Such festivity is finite and derives its value primarily from contrast. Orwell concluded that Dickens was virtually unique among modern writers in his ability to produce a convincing vision of happiness; its plausibility stemmed from its incompleteness.

Happiness in Orwell is equally incomplete, if not always equally convincing, yet it plays a key role in his writing. Orwell's sunnier moments often occur in a bucolic setting. In the middle of *Coming Up for Air*, for instance, George Bowling plays host to a rare feeling: 'What I felt was something that's so unusual nowadays that to say it sounds like foolishness. I felt *happy*'. The uplift is a complex state, but it is essentially a product of being in the countryside on a beautiful spring day. Throughout Orwell's fiction we discover moments of similar elation. In *A Clergyman's Daughter*, for instance, Dorothy experiences 'a mystical joy in the beauty of the earth'. In a particularly heady moment, she languishes in a hedge, finds herself enveloped by vegetation, and has an almost erotic encounter with a piece of fennel:

> Dorothy pulled a frond of the fennel against her face and breathed in the strong sweet scent. Its richness overwhelmed her, almost dizzied her for a moment. She drank it in, filling her lungs with it. Lovely, lovely scent—scent of summer days, scent of childhood joys, scent of spice-drenched islands in the warm foam of oriental seas!

The authenticity of such joy may, of course, be questionable. It is notable, for instance, that a moment of sensuous particularity is described in a very generalized key: the specific content of the moment is lost to a series of cliches. The repeated use of plural terms—'summer days', 'childhood joys', etc.—only confirms the non-specific quality of the scene, while the hand-me-down exoticism of 'spice-drenched islands' and 'oriental seas' betrays the imaginative poverty of this vision of fulfilment. Happiness can only be construed as an escapist fantasy—a lacquered delight that concedes its unreality in the very attempt to attest to its existence.

The sugary prose may simply illustrate the peculiar difficulty of representing happiness. After all, to describe this hallowed state is arguably to step outside it. People blasphemed against their own happiness, Adorno argued, in their attempts to avow its existence: the mediation of concepts spoiled the raw immediacy of total contentment. So the labours of thought, or at least of original writing, one might argue, are necessarily abandoned in Orwell during moments of supreme bliss. The striking thing about happiness in his fiction is often its discursive banality, with characters reduced to a repetitive jabber in moments of elation—Dorothy 'was happy, happy!', Flory 'was happy, happy', Elizabeth 'was happy, happy'. But significantly, much of this tongue-tied rapture is triggered by contact with nature. So Dorothy swoons in a hedge and ends up kissing a frond of fennel. A sight of flowers provokes a 'pang of unreasonable happiness' in lovers in *Burmese Days*. In *Keep the Aspidistra Flying*, Gordon and Rosemary also find themselves 'extravagantly happy' on a countryside walk. The trip Winston and Julia make to the countryside is a little oasis of joy in a relentlessly grim novel. Here, as we have noted, Orwell's recurrent fantasy of outdoor sex (or what Cyril Connolly called 'cold pastoral') is finally consummated. Through such noble savagery a whole civilization is annihilated—at least in Winston's hopeful eyes.

As I have earlier argued, however, the dream of pastoral happiness is usually exposed as an unsustainable fantasy in Orwell. He was also aware that a romantic commitment to nature was generally symptomatic of a certain alienation from it: 'those who really have to deal with nature have no cause to be in love with it'. In fact, true country folk, he believed, have an aggressively utilitarian attitude to the world ('Real rustics are not conscious of being picturesque, they do not construct bird sanctuaries, they are uninterested in any plant or animal that does not affect them directly'). The husbands of the earth are often clueless about its contents: they confuse frogs with toads (seemingly a significant offence in Orwell's books) and make the naive assumption that all snakes are poisonous. Here nature is entirely disenchanted. On the other hand, Orwell had little time for the 'shallow pantheism' of committed nature-worshippers. George Bowling similarly dislikes those who preach the simple life and a 'roll in the dew before breakfast'. And yet he remains deeply susceptible to nature's charms. The simple sight of primroses makes him weak at the knees.

Significantly, Orwell's personal writings contain the same spots of joy. The itemizing of nature's everyday wonders is a key feature of his diaries ('Crocuses now full out. One seems to catch glimpses of them dimly through a haze of war news'). Accused of being negative during the war, Orwell would pay homage to the Woolworth's rose—an affordable but very authentic form of pleasure and one that could be enjoyed in urban environments. The public happiness that nature provides is also a key theme of 'Some Thoughts on the Common Toad' (1946). Here he makes the remarkable claim that by preserving a 'love of such things as trees, fishes, butterflies and . . . toads, one makes a peaceful and decent future a little more probable'. Conversely, an obsession with concrete and steel makes one susceptible to hatred and authoritarianism. In these moments, Orwell clearly believes that there are worthy and unworthy pleasures. He yearns for a future where 'the sort of pleasure one gets from finding the first primrose will loom larger than the sort of pleasure one gets from eating an ice to the tune of a Wurlitzer'. Orwell recognized, of course, that this fond talk would raise some heckles. 'I know by experience', he claimed, 'that a favourable reference to "Nature" in one of my articles is liable to bring me abusive letters'. His war-time encomium on the Woolworth's rose, for instance, was dismissed by one contemporary reader as 'bourgeois nostalgia'. Orwell struggled to see what was 'bourgeois' about a liking for flowers, but the nostalgic element in his paeans to nature is often internally acknowledged within his own work.

George Bowling, for instance, nurses an avowedly 'sentimental' view of his bucolic youth. His nostalgia famously collects around the concept of fishing:

> As soon as you think of fishing you think of things that don't belong to the modern world. The very idea of sitting all day under a willow tree beside a quiet pool—and being able to find a quiet pool to sit beside—belongs to the time before the war, before the radio, before aeroplanes, before Hitler. There's a kind of peacefulness even in the names of English coarse fish. Roach, rudd, dace, bleak, barbel, bream, gudgeon, pike, chub, carp, tench. They're solid kind of names. The people who made them up hadn't heard of machine-guns, they didn't live in terror of the sack or spend their time eating aspirins, going to the pictures and wondering how to keep out of the concentration camp.

The voodoo surrounding fish names is idiosyncratic, but it steers him to the conclusion that fishing 'is the opposite of war'—presumably, not a view shared by many fish. In search of the lost happiness that fishing represents, Bowling returns to the scenes of his youth in Binfield (arguably modelled on Orwell's own salad days in Henley and Shiplake). Inevitably, the pond on which he caught his first fish has been drained and built over, 'as though the countryside had been buried by a kind of volcanic eruption from the outer suburbs'. Binfield House has become a mental hospital, while its waterways are now a rubbish dump. 'What's the good of trying to revisit the scenes of your boyhood?', Bowling asks. 'They don't exist'.

Orwell may ruthlessly expose the anachronism in his own—or at least in his characters'—vision of happiness, yet he would also criticize the 'widespread idea that nostalgic feelings about the past are inherently vicious'. Indeed, in texts like *Coming Up for Air* and *Nineteen Eighty-Four*, nostalgia is in many respects politically salutary: memory may be fallible, but it remains foundational to people's sense of a better world. However, Orwell's own hankering for better times could produce moments of wistfulness and even atavism—at least where happiness was concerned. He had little doubt, for instance, 'that primitive peoples, untouched by capitalism and industrialism, are happier than civilised men'. The physiognomy of contentment was fairly obvious to this keen student of faces: 'among primitive peoples . . . the faces that you see are predominantly happy; in no great city of the West is this true'. Some of Orwell's historical speculation yielded less damning conclusions about modernity: he conceded in 1944, for instance, that 'it was quite possible that a modern factory-worker is . . . "happier" than, say, a mediæval serf or Roman slave', although perhaps this was not much of a concession. 'One does not have to be a mediævalist', he insisted, 'to feel that the modern world has something seriously wrong with it'. As he contended, one glance out of a window—at least in any urban centre—would give the most confirmed optimist pause for thought.

Back in 1928, Aldous Huxley refused to be drawn into the question of whether moderns were happier than their predecessors, but he posed a related question: 'how far is highly developed technology compatible with individual happiness?' This question would be asked several times throughout the 1930s and '40s and it drew some dark answers. As Middleton Murry put it in 1944: 'The crisis in the life of man lies in his failure to respond to the ever more insistent challenge of the machine'. In his review of *Adam and Eve*, Orwell criticized Murry for exaggerating 'the "dehumanising" effects of the machine', yet it was Orwell himself who had earlier stressed 'the tendency of the machine to make a fully human life impossible'. Throughout the 1940s, Orwell was particularly obsessed with the ways in which the machine had 'frustrated the creative instincts and degraded aesthetic feeling'. He also emphasized the ways in which it had destroyed the immanent pleasures of work.

Again, this was an all-too-common lament. Both Ruskin and Morris had repeatedly argued that the mechanization of production had undermined the self-expressive dimensions of work—or the peculiar 'happiness of labour'—and similar arguments would do the rounds throughout the interwar years. As Huxley put it in 1929: 'Creative work, of however humble a kind, is the source of man's most solid, least transitory happiness. The machine robs the majority of human beings of the very possibility of this happiness'. In an attempt to recuperate this contentment, figures like Edmund Blunden and H. J. Massingham would recommend 'a return to husbandry': small-scale ownership of land, the cultivation of traditional arts and crafts, and the restoration of hand labour. Through husbandry, Massingham insisted, man's 'work is a form of play, his workshop is a shrine of quality, and beauty emanates from it as an inevitable by-product'—a self-delighting labour that is lost to the modern factory hand.

Orwell often insisted that there were limits to the ways in which labour could be conceived as play ('an enormous amount of dull and exhausting work has to be done by unwilling human muscles'). Yet he wrote a sympathetic review of Massingham's edited collection *The Natural Order* in 1945: 'No thinking person would deny that Mr. Massingham and his associates have a strong case'. Here he proclaimed himself deeply receptive to the view that 'a truly human life—and, consequently private happiness and international peace—is only possible on a basis of hand labour and wide distribution of property'. Rehearsing the arguments of England's new husbandmen, he stressed the dignity of skilled and self-directed work, and juxtaposed this with the degradation of mechanized labour. Like Massingham—and, indeed, Murry—he presented work as the telos of a fully human life: 'Man', as he put it, 'is a working animal, his work is and must be the central factor in his life'. Unfortunately, however, much modern labour is 'soul-destroying' and affords no scope for self-expression. Summoning up an image that might have come from Lang's *Metropolis*, he outlined the spirit-crushing boredom of standing 'eight hours a day beside a conveyor belt, tightening up the same nut over and over again'.

Machines not only eroded the joys of production for Orwell, they also evacuated the pleasures of consumption. In 1937, for instance, he decried the 'frightful debauchery of taste that has...been effected by a century of mechanisation'. The corruption of the palate was a particular preoccupation:

> In the highly mechanised countries, thanks to tinned food, cold storage, synthetic flavouring matters, etc., the palate is almost a dead organ... what the majority of English people mean by an apple is a lump of highly-coloured cotton wool from America or Australia; they will devour these things, apparently with pleasure, and let the English apples rot under the trees.

This meditation on apples may make Orwell sound like a would-be member of the British Soil Association (founded in 1946), but they illustrate the extent to which his critique of modernity was an aesthetic one. Orwell's tastes, however, could be exacting. Consider his famous speculation about the effects of preserved food in *The Road to Wigan Pier* ('We may find in the long run that tinned food is a deadlier weapon than the machine gun') or the arresting description of frankfurters in *Coming Up for Air* ('Bombs of filth bursting inside your mouth'). The sausage-eating occurs amidst the din of newspaper revelations about a murder involving a woman's severed legs: moral and aesthetic horror get mixed up during the act of mastication, producing an overwhelming sense of disgust. The frankfurter Bowling eats is, in fact, an ersatz sausage—fish serving as a substitute for meat. It leaves Bowling with the impression that he has bitten into the modern world: 'That's the way we're going nowadays. Everything slick and streamlined, everything made out of something else'. In modern times, objects have lost their *quidditas* and have ceased to be themselves. One is surrounded by a 'sort of phantom stuff that you can't taste and can hardly believe in the existence of'.

Orwell's search for authenticity in a machine age reveals once again the important role of pleasure in his conception of the good life, but it could also yield a cranky dissatisfaction with much of the modern world. His list of reprehensible goods, for instance, was extraordinarily catholic:

> In a healthy world there would be no demand for tinned food, aspirins, gramophones, gas-pipe chairs, machine guns, daily newspapers, telephones, motorcars, etc. etc.; and on the other hand there would be a constant demand for the things the machine cannot produce. But meanwhile the machine is here, and its corrupting effects are almost irresistible.

But for all of his contempt for 'machine-civilisation', Orwell always professed to abjure ludditism. As he put it in 1945, 'the machine and the machine civilisation are here and cannot be got rid of'. In fact, he felt that there was a hypocrisy built into many pleas for the simple life: 'Rejection of the machine is, of course, always founded on tacit acceptance of the machine'. Non-industrialized countries, he argued, were 'helpless' in a military sense: murderous machines were a condition of sovereign independence in the modern world. The mechanization of production may have undermined creativity in the workplace, but some jobs were irredeemably boring and should, he insisted, be done by machines. 'It makes one sick', he argued in 1937, 'to see half a dozen men sweating their guts out to dig a trench for a water-pipe, when some easily devised machine would scoop the earth out in a couple of minutes'. Perhaps with his days as a *plongeur* in mind, he presented dishwashing as another candidate for extinction: it was an 'uncreative and life-wasting job'. It was by no means perverse, therefore, that 'the vast majority of modern men prefer the machine civilisation'.

So Orwell readily accepted that 'it is impossible to "go back"'. He also insisted in *The Road to Wigan Pier* that 'a dislike of the mechanised future does not imply the smallest reverence for any period of the past'. Yet his image of happiness was frequently suffused with an Edwardian or Victorian must. Anthony Powell would comment on his friend's 'Victorianism', while Cyril Connolly famously declared him a revolutionary in love with 1910. Orwell himself spoke fondly of 'the golden years between 1890 and 1914'. Of course, Orwell was not alone in his wistfulness or in his discontent with the present. Connolly himself would complain in 1944 that happiness is 'a lost art'. Russell, who had set off like some existential mountaineer on *The Conquest of Happiness* in 1930, ultimately despaired about its prospects in the modern world. To be born after 1914, he concluded late in life, is to be 'incapable of happiness'. For many of the illuminati, therefore, modernity had failed to furnish proper conditions for sustainable happiness, although the problem may have stemmed from the very expectation itself. The search for utopia is always liable to produce despair. Orwell would continue to hope—presenting left-wing utopians as the best upholders of socialist traditions—but by the end of the 1940s, the political basis for such hope could seem fairly elusive. If *Nineteen Eighty-Four* is anything to go by, project happiness was in a bad state.

Joy on Jura

Orwell, I have argued, had mixed views on happiness. He generally regarded it as one value among many and not necessarily the most important one. After all, the writing of novels, he often insisted, was incompatible with happiness, yet he persisted in writing books. This may have simply reflected his conviction that there were psychological limits to the ways in which happiness could be pursued as a direct end—a fact that applied to politics as much as it did to private life. I want to conclude by considering how Orwell's theories of happiness may have influenced or played themselves out in his personal life—or at least his writing about it. In P. G. Wodehouse's eyes, he was 'a gloomy sort of chap'; others like Malcolm Muggeridge disagreed, finding Orwell a 'happy man' in his own eccentric way.

The striking thing about Orwell's letters and diaries is their lack of reference to his own happiness. Arguably, he had absorbed Mill's advice better than anyone. 'Ask whether you are happy', the philosopher had opined, 'and you cease to be so'. Orwell rarely asked. In the rare moments that he did turn his gaze upon himself, the results could be pretty dispiriting. As he confided to Anthony Powell in 1948: 'It's my birthday today—45, isn't it awful. I've also got some more false teeth, and . . . a lot more grey in my hair'. Even here, however, the focus is largely on externals, and this remains the case throughout much of his letters and journals. Orwell's 'domestic diaries' may have had an avowedly practical purpose, but the extent of their absorption in the raw mundanities of subsistence is fairly remarkable: 'Cylinder of Calor Gas gave out today. Put on a new one. The last has gone only for 12 days . . . Runner beans & late peas very poor, no doubt owing to drought. 5 eggs'. Even Orwell's most enthusiastic followers—like Christopher Hitchens—have found some of these entries tough going. Nonetheless, this anatomy of the mundane sheds some interesting light on the question of happiness.

This is particularly true of the diaries he wrote on Jura between 1946 and 1948. Perhaps a rain-soaked island in the Hebrides was not the best place of residence for a man in poor health. Indeed, some biographers detect a suicidal impulse behind the retreat—one that reflects Orwell's 'inner need to sabotage his chance for a happy life'. Yet there is reason to believe he found some contentment there. He had for a long time fantasized about Jura ('Thinking always of my island in the Hebrides', he confided to his diary in 1940), and finally managed a visit in 1945. He decided to rent a house near Barnhill from 23 May 1946 to 13 October 1946 and he would spend much of 1947 on the island. After some time in hospital, he returned to the island in 1948, until poor health forced a final retreat in January 1949. Orwell's ostensible reason for visiting Jura was that he wanted to complete a novel (*Nineteen Eighty-Four*) and wished to withdraw from the distractions of his London life. He was also fairly upbeat about the conditions: 'The weather here is as disgusting as in England, but it isn't quite so cold and a little easier to get fuel'. He celebrated the sparseness of the population ('This island, which is as large as a small county, only has 300 people on it'). It could get lonely at times, but he exulted in the island's beauty.

It is hard to say definitively that Orwell enjoyed himself on Jura, so shorn of subjective commentary or introspection the diaries tend to be. Orwell often lists a series of perceptions, usually of the natural world: 'Honeysuckle almost over. Dead shrew on the path. Corn ripening in places. Candytuft almost over'. The absence of a pronoun may simply reflect a commitment to economy, but it also chimes with Uncle Bertie's self-help from the 1930s: as Russell had argued, happiness is best found by forgetting about oneself and by taking an interest in things outside the ego. Orwell certainly takes an interest in the world. Consider his deliberations about goats ('Saw 3 wild goats. They were about 400 yards away, & at that distance looked definitely black. Somewhat heavy moments, compared with the deer') or his reflections on wild birds ('Large hovering hawk of some kind—in style of flight somewhat like a larger edition of a kestrel, but flaps its wings more slowly—always about behind the house. Presumably some kind of buzzard'). These might be an anorak's musings—indeed, Anthony Powell believed that Orwell affected a quasi-scientific interest in nature to mask the naive joy it produced in him. But underneath his endless botanizing is a clear sense of wonder ('The common wild rose of these parts is now coming into blossom. A white flower with tendency to pink at the edges. Bud large & very beautiful, with bright pink tip. Leaves have a faint sweetbriar smell'). The synthesis of 'scientific observation' and a 'love of Nature', which he admired in Darwin's prose, was evidently something to which he aspired in his own journals.

Jura may have allowed Orwell to affect some notional return to nature, yet the diaries do not yield a sentimental portrait of its goodness. Signs of its violence are everywhere: 'Found a dead rabbit in the lane, newly killed, with the back of its neck torn out & backbone exposed. Probably hoodie crows'. Orwell hears it reported that gulls and hoodies attack vulnerable sheep—a fact that appears to be confirmed when he stumbles upon a lamb in a poor state 'oozing blood from the mouth'. The animal dies, having being neglected by its mother from the start. There is, perhaps, a latent sympathy here, but Orwell participates in nature's violence casually enough: 'Killed very large snake', 'shot a very young rabbit in the garden', 'Killed a mouse in the larder', 'killed another snake (small one)', 'killed an enormous rat in the byre'. Rats are a particular obsession—'I hear that recently two children at Ardlussa were bitten by rats (in the face, as usual)'—and they will famously make their way into *Nineteen Eighty-Four*. The gruelling hardship of subsisting within or alongside nature is borne out throughout the diaries. Orwell has to contend with the elements ('Chicken-house blown off its base... Shall have to fix it down with guy ropes'), with the birds ('The chaffinches have evidently destroyed all the turnips, so I shall have to re-sow'), and with the beasts ('All the small plants I put in—pansies, lupins, cheddar pinks & cabbages—have completely disappeared, evidently owing to rabbits'). Survival here is tough work.

But work was also something that Orwell extolled. In January 1947, he circulated Marcus Aurelius' reflections on humanity's true vocation to readers of *Tribune*. This advice, he suggested, should be written out and placed on walls opposite people's beds:

> In the morning when thou risest unwillingly, let this thought be present—
> I am rising to the work of a human being. Why then am I dissatisfied if I am
> going to do the things for which I exist and for which I was brought into the
> world? Or have I been made for this, to lie in the bed-clothes and keep myself
> warm?—But this is more pleasant—Dost though exist then to take thy pleas-
> ure, and not at all for action or exertion? Dost thou not see the little plants,
> the little birds, the ants, the spiders, the bees working together to put in order
> their several parts of the universe? And art thou unwilling to do the work of a
> human being, and dost thou not make haste to do that which is according to
> thy nature?

Here Orwell champions stoic duty over idle pleasure. Yet the joy that can be derived from gruelling labour is a repeated refrain in his writing. This is true of his Jura journals, but it can also be seen in his fiction.

Consider his account of hop-picking in *A Clergyman's Daughter*: 'As the afternoon wore on you grew almost too tired to stand... Yet you were happy, with an unreasonable happiness. The work took hold of you and absorbed you... It gave you a physical joy, a warm satisfied feeling inside you'. More sedentary intellectuals—or those who could be bothered to intellectualize sedentariness—sometimes suggested that happiness 'goes beyond doing' and involves something akin to the indolence of beasts. '*Rien faire comme une bête,* lying on water and looking peacefully into the sky' was the epitome of hap-piness for Adorno. Perhaps this is the peace that George Bowling derives from fishing (though fishing may have been too strenuous and purposive for Adorno's tastes). Nonetheless, Orwell's notion of happiness usually presup-posed some form of activity and effort as its fundamental element: it was a practice as much as it was a psychological state. Yet it also yielded a kind of animal pleasure, with self-consciousness eviscerated through sheer fatigue. Take the joy that Flory and Elizabeth derive from a hunt in *Burmese Days*: 'They were happy with that inordinate happiness that comes of exhaustion and achievement, and with which nothing else in life—no joy of either the body or the mind—is even able to be compared'.

Jura provided Orwell with many opportunities for delightful exhaustion—not least his attempts to wrest a vegetable garden from 'virgin jungle'. Presumably this, too, was a source of joy ('Outside my work', he confided in 1940, 'the thing I care most about is gardening, especially vegetable gardening'). The return to husbandry—so loudly extolled by Massingham and Blunden throughout the 1940s—could be quietly pursued on Jura. Moreover, the self-sufficiency fetishized by England's new husbandmen could be brought to impressive lengths on the island. Take Orwell's entry from 28 May 1946: 'Yesterday made a trestle for sawing logs... Today made a sledge—primitive substitute for wheelbarrow... Started building incinerator out of stone'. Orwell made a sledgehammer out of a bough of mountain ash, a mustard spoon from bone, and cast a plug for a bathroom basin out of lead ('There is something in this operation that I do wrong'). The detailing of this very practical creativity, he believed, gave 'island' literature its unique charm. He insisted that even 'a dismal book like *Robinson Crusoe*... becomes interesting when it describes efforts to make a table, glaze earthenware and grow a patch of wheat'. Orwell's Jura diaries contain plenty of these details, although perhaps not all readers would share his conviction that the technicalities of subsistence made 'island literature' more exciting than courtroom dramas.

Still, the relentless domesticity of the Jura diaries is one of their conceptually interesting features: for such a self-consciously political writer, the journal is insistently apolitical, at least in its denotative content. Like Winston Smith's diary—also penned in Jura—the Jura journals seem to insist on the limit of politics—committing themselves to a private space that, notionally at least, exceeds public power. Of course, privacy must be paid for and is not without its political preconditions: the farm in Barnhill was partly funded by an 'investment' of £1,000 by Richard Rees (the entire island was owned by his Etonian comrade David Astor). Though dependent on other people's finance, Orwell's island retreat allowed him to indulge the Rousseauian dimensions of his personality (Rousseau, too, was a lover of islands and cast his time on St Pierre in Lake Brienne as the happiest time of his life). Total independence could never be regained (as Huxley maintained, 'there are no

Crusoes'), but a stoic self-sufficiency might be attempted—with, of course, a little help from one's friends. Though he had companions and benefactors, there was, perhaps, something anti-social in Orwell's dream of self-dependence. If George Bowling is anything to go by, Orwell was aware of the misanthropy that could lurk behind the embrace of nature: 'Sentimental, you say? Anti-social? Oughtn't to prefer trees to men?' But Bowling's response—like Orwell's perhaps—is unapologetic: 'I say it depends what trees and what men'. In 1943 Orwell prioritized brotherhood over happiness, but on Jura this hierarchy might seem to have become reversed.

'Jura killed Orwell'—or so we are told. His health certainly depreciated on the island ('[I] thought I'd probably got T.B. but like a fool I decided not to go to a doctor as I knew I'd be stuck in bed'). Writing from his hospital bed in East Kilbride in 1949, Orwell's sense of the future—not just his own—was fairly bleak. Another global conflict, he believed, was imminent: 'This stupid war is coming off in about 10–20 years, and this country will be blown off the map whatever else happens. The only hope is to have a home with a few animals in some place not worth a bomb'. Jura may have been this unworthy space, although it was also an island on which Orwell seemed to have enjoyed considerable happiness. The character he created there—Winston Smith—believes there is 'no such thing as happiness', but there was much in Orwell's own life at the time that appears to contradict this claim. Yet the Jura diaries—relentlessly domestic, aggressively apolitical—might also suggest that Orwell had lost confidence in happiness as a public good. The socialist dream of planning for happiness certainly seemed to have been put on hold.

Conclusion
On consistency

'The human mind has an almost infinite capacity for being inconsistent', Huxley observed in 1927. Orwell's life and writing are a testament to these mental powers. 'He had a lynx eye for humbug and inconsistency', his friend Richard Rees declared, but one doesn't need lynx-like powers to spot the discrepancies in Orwell's politics. To use one of his own expressions, he was a 'change-of-heart man'. In the 1930s, for instance, he suggested that 'fascism' and 'capitalist democracy' were flipsides of the same false coin; by 1940, he had dismissed such views as crude and harmful. He was on the side of pacifists in the 1930s, but declared them objectively pro-Nazi in the '40s. However, he would soon condemn this functionalist method of argument as intellectually dishonest. He insisted on the importance of honesty, yet he felt that lies were justifiable for political ends. If this was hypocritical, then even his views on hypocrisy were two-faced: it was politically benign, but it was also vicious.

Orwell's notorious notes about 'crypto-communists' and fellow travellers could be viewed as hypocrisy of the more vicious sort. He was a man who could hang out with Stephen Spender and then coolly conclude in his notebook: 'Sentimental sympathiser & very unreliable. Easily influenced'. And, as if to suggest how Spender might be influenced, Orwell added the observation: 'Tendency towards homosexuality'. His remarks about Kingsley Martin ('very dishonest') or Richard Crossman ('too dishonest to be an outright F. T.' [i.e. fellow-traveller]) never seemed to have sparked doubts about his own honesty or trustworthiness.

'I always knew he was two-faced', the Marxist historian Christopher Hill declared when he learned about the list of thirty-five names that Orwell submitted to the Information Research Department of the Foreign Office. Yet the list has had its defenders. As Timothy Garton Ash points out, when

Orwell submitted his information to Celia Kirwan in May 1949, the Cold War was just heating up—the USSR had taken over Czechoslovakia and its forces were in the process of blockading Berlin. Orwell had never disguised his hatred of the USSR and he clearly believed that the extension of its power would wreak political and moral disaster. So he was, perhaps, a very principled form of snitch. Nonetheless, his surveillance work for the Foreign Office certainly sits uneasily alongside his criticisms of Big Brother and the Thought Police. If you were a prominent left-wing critic of the liberal order in the 1940s, there was a strong probability that George Orwell was watching you.

He remains, for many, 'a paradox'—a self-appointed 'advocatus diaboli' of the Left who believed that 'to defend Socialism it is necessary to start by attacking it'; a disciple of brotherhood who loathed a good cross section of his brothers; a socialist egalitarian who decried 'the personal inferiority of many individual Socialists'; a revolutionary and an internationalist who also claimed that 'No real revolutionary has ever been an internationalist'; an intellectual who despised intellectuals. 'To accept an orthodoxy', he insisted, 'is always to inherit unresolved contradictions', but to oppose opinions for heresy's sake was also to generate them. So he became a utopian when surrounded by 'realists' and a 'realist' when confronting utopians. In the face of other people's moralism, he could sound like an economic determinist, but against the fatalism and cynicism of others he stressed the importance of moral effort. Orwell, it seems, was alert to his own perversity. Indeed, according to Anthony Powell, he liked to 'draw attention to the contradictions in his own point of view'.

It is easy to take a dim view of Orwell's inconsistencies—seeing them as a testimony to a kind of arrogance, complacency, or opportunism that was both expressed and disguised by a relentless rhetoric of certitude. Yet the paradox of Orwell should not be viewed in simply personal terms. His shortcomings express a more obdurate set of difficulties or—to adopt the parlance of his time—'social contradictions'. Understandably, many have recoiled from the cant of contradiction—a discursive universe in which a butterfly is the negation of an egg (as Engels would have it) and even 'motion is a contradiction' (Plekhanov). As far as Bertrand Russell was concerned, this type of jargon deployed logical categories in 'ways that no self-respecting logician can approve'. As we saw in Chapter 4, contradictions are a property of sentences not of the world as such; and it is a fantasy to suggest that our social realities are structured like a sentence or a logical argument. Yet social worlds are in part constituted by belief, and Orwell's world, I have argued, involved a series of strong political beliefs—many of which were mutually entailing, but many of which failed to add up. 'The civil status of a contradiction, or its status in civil life': this, Wittgenstein proposed, was the key philosophical problem. And it is the problem that repeatedly expresses itself across Orwell's life and writing.

Orwell nursed deep convictions about liberty, equality, solidarity, truth, and happiness, but these commitments did not produce a unified view of justice or the good. Such unity, one might argue, is always liable to elude us. In fact, Orwell's contemporary Isaiah Berlin deemed the very notion of a unified good to be incoherent; the word 'good' necessarily entailed a preference between different and incompatible values. Characteristically enough, Orwell felt that political life usually entailed a choice of evils rather than a choice of goods, but it is clear that his life was shaped by difficult and unavoidable moral choices. So, faced with apparent tensions between liberty and equality in the early '40s, he sometimes backed equality even if it seemed to involve a type of 'serfdom'. In other contexts, however, a very negative conception of liberty seemed to take priority over all other values. This sharp-elbowed ideal had little to do with brotherhood, yet Orwell made loud fraternal noises, even prioritizing brotherhood over happiness. On the island of Jura, however, these priorities were arguably reversed. So throughout his life Orwell struggled to answer the question that faces all moderns: 'Which of the warring gods should we serve?' Like most of us, he ended up serving different masters at one and the same time.

This could make his politics look like a mess. But it was also, one can argue, a noble mess—the result of a principled refusal to jettison the basic values that justice should serve, even if they were liable to culminate in confusion. So a commitment to justice and charity made him want to kill fascists in Spain; an appeal to the same principles also accounts for his refusal to kill them—at least when they had their trousers down. This type of inconsistency has certainly had its defenders, while moral clarity has often proved to be pretty brutal in what it is prepared to set aside. Indeed, for some liberals, total consistency frequently breeds fanaticism, while inconsistency has been judged a 'source of tolerance'. Perhaps this is the tolerance that Orwell practised when he defended P. G. Wodehouse and Kipling or when he admitted to liking Hitler. Of course, his attitude to Hitler may reveal a certain consistency—a steadfast refusal to engage in the hatred that Nazis had practised—but it was also liable to produce some moral reflux. Isn't it contradictory to tolerate those who don't do toleration?

If the very question presupposes that we should get worked up about contradiction, then Orwell often appeared to endorse such a presumption. He was, after all, a great critic of political 'schizophrenia' and doublethink. In *Animal Farm* and *Nineteen Eighty-Four*, he appeared to defend consistency as a core principle and emphasized the moral and political dangers of its abandonment. This raises troubling questions about his own inconsistencies and doubletalk. Contrary to what many have assumed, Orwell provides few solutions to our political difficulties, although this was never really his job. As Hilary Putnam once suggested, the writer's task is not to deliver solutions, but to engage in 'the imaginative re-creation of moral perplexities'. I have dwelt on the element of perplexity in Orwell's life and work because it is easily buried under the weight of his own certitude and the militancy of some of his followers. Of course, even perplexity needs to be sure about something, and Orwell was right, I feel, to subscribe to the core principles I have explored in this book. Their pursuit may have repeatedly ended in failure, but, as he liked to suggest, not all failures are the same.

Notes

INTRODUCTION

Orwell season on the BBC: For an account of Orwell's very mixed views of the BBC, see Melissa Dinsman, *Modernism at the Microphone: Radio, Propaganda, and Literary Aesthetics* (London: Bloomsbury, 2015), 97–120; Douglas Kerr, 'Orwell's BBC Broadcasts: Colonial Discourse and the Rhetoric of Propaganda', *Textual Practice*, 16.3 (2002): 473–90; C. Fleay and M. L. Sanders, 'Looking into the Abyss: George Orwell at the BBC', *Journal of Contemporary History*, 24 (1989): 503–18.

broadsheet journalism: On the controversy, see 'George Orwell was a Snazzy Dresser and Certainly Not a Snarler', *The Guardian*, 11 August 2016.

'What would Orwell say?': On this point, see Anna Vaninskaya, 'The Orwell Century and After: Rethinking Reception and Reputation', *Modern Intellectual History*, 5.3 (2008): 597–617. See, too, John Rodden, 'On the Ethics of Admiration and Detraction', *Midwest Quarterly* (46.3): 284–98.

George Orwell's 1984': Hansard, House of Lords, 23 June 1972, vol. 332, 534.

1984 come to life': Hansard, House of Lords, 24 March 1983, vol. 440, 1282.

dream come true': Hansard, House of Commons, 3 December 1990, vol. 182, 109.

'an Orwellian nightmare': Hansard, House of Commons, 29 January 2004, vol. 656, 407.

Orwell would have shuddered': Hansard, House of Lords, 26 November 2015, vol. 767, 853.

either in Parliament or elsewhere: 'I often find that comparisons with Orwell's dystopia are at best inappropriate and at worst over the top', Tom Harris observed in 2001. Hansard, House of Commons, 30 October 2001, vol. 373, 834. Alex Carlile also criticized the 'hackneyed analogies'. See Hansard, House of Commons, 25 January 1984, vol. 52, 1000.

this position for some time: *Times Educational Supplement*, 21 July 2015.

cheerleaders in the US: 'George Orwell's "1984" is Suddenly a Best-Seller', *New York Times*, 25 January 2017. On the reception of Orwell in America, see, in particular, John Rodden, *The Unexamined Orwell* (Austin, TX: University of Texas, 2011), 15–118.

political and cultural achievements: Isaac Deutscher, 'The Mysticism of Cruelty', *Heretics and Renegades* (London: Hamish Hamilton, 1955), 35–50; 'Will Self

Declares George Orwell the "Supreme Mediocrity" ', *The Guardian*, 1 September 2014. For a lengthier takedown, see Scott Lucas, *Orwell* (London: Haus, 2003).

nimbus of spookiness: 'Do You Know What "Orwellian" Means?' *The Guardian*, 11 November 2014. Rodden noted that the word implies 'obfuscatory language', but he also argues that it is often an instance of such language. John Rodden, *The Politics of Literary Reputation: The Making and Claiming of 'St. George' Orwell* (Oxford: Oxford University Press, 1989), 37.

served 'human liberty': Richard Rorty, 'The Last Intellectual in Europe: George Orwell', in *Contingency, Irony, and Solidarity* (Cambridge: Cambridge University Press, 1989), 169–88, 170.

collective illusions: As Orwell put it in *The Left News* in 1941: 'a widespread illusion, capable of influencing public behaviour, is itself an important fact' George Orwell, *Complete Works of George Orwell*, ed. Peter Davison, 20 vols. (London: Secker & Warburg, 1986–98), 12.378–9. All subsequent references are to this edition.

traditions of political thought: Among the many monographs on Orwell's politics, I have found Robert Colls' *English Rebel* (Oxford: Oxford University Press, 2013), Stephen Ingle's *The Social and Political Thought of George Orwell: A Reassessment* (London: Routledge, 2008), and John Newsinger's *Orwell's Politics* (London: Macmillan, 1999) particularly helpful.

p.3 **make it known:** (17.371). See Philip P. Bliss and Ira D. Sankey, *Gospel Hymns: No. 2* (New York: Biglow & Main; Chicago, IL: John Church & Co., n.d.), 88.

political beliefs: But for a useful effort to situate Orwell within a wider terrain, see Ben Clarke, *Orwell in Context: Communities, Myths, Values* (Basingstoke: Palgrave, 2007). For attempts to place him within a set of socialist traditions, see Philip Bounds, *Orwell and Marxism* (London: Tauris, 2009); John Rodden, 'Orwell, Marx, and the Marxists', in *Scenes from an Afterlife: The Legacy of George Orwell* (Wilmington, DE: ISI Books, 2003), 177–94; Alex Zwerdling, *Orwell and the Left* (New Haven, CT: Yale University Press, 1974).

such a history: He appears, for instance, in the *Routledge Dictionary of Twentieth-Century Political Thinkers*, ed. Robert Benewick and Philip Green (London: Routledge, 1992), 177–8, but is absent from most major anthologies of modern political thought.

writing into an art': (18.319).

p.4 **knowledge regarding them':** Leo Strauss, *What is Political Philosophy?* (Chicago, IL: University of Chicago Press, 1959), 12. Initially given as a lecture, 'What is Political Philosophy?' was published in *Iyyun* in April 1955 and in *The Review of Politics* in 1957. The essay was modified when published in book form.

strive after': (18.318).

always wrong': (5.138).

'feeling of partisanship': (18.319).

better than others': (17.155).

p.5 **quibbles and abstractions':** (18.421).

think too deeply': (11.104).

forbidden by law': (20.52).

'they show their wisdom': Bertrand Russell, *Philosophy and Politics* (London: Cambridge University Press, 1947), 7.

from Russia, Italy, and Germany: Edmund Burke, *Reflections on the Revolution in France*, in *The Writings and Speeches of Edmund Burke*, ed. Paul Langford, 9 vols. (Oxford: Oxford University Press, 1981–2015), 8.53–293, 197. Indeed, Herbert Samuel invoked Burke in 1945 to claim that it 'is with an armed doctrine that we are at war'. Quoted in Thomas. L. Akehurst, *The Cultural Politics of Analytical Philosophy: Britishness and the Spectre of Europe* (London: Continuum, 2010), 79.

'a psycho-analysis': Bertrand Russell, 'Scylla and Charybdis, or Communism and Fascism', in *In Praise of Idleness and Other Essays* (London: George Allen & Unwin, 1935), 109–20, 116. He flew in the face of his own strictures by repeatedly relating Germany's political fanaticism to its philosophical idealism. On this point, see Akehurst, *The Cultural Politics of Analytical Philosophy*.

an abstract theory: Orwell, for instance, would present authoritarian rule in Russia and Germany as the 'dictatorship of theorists' (12.141).

bottomless pit': Stanley Baldwin, 'Political Education', in *On England and Other Addresses* (London: Philip Allan, 1926), 147–59, 150–1. Orwell was highly critical of Baldwin as a leader ('one could not even dignify him with the name of stuffed shirt' (12.402)).

races have succumbed': Stanley Baldwin, *An Interpreter of England* (London: Hodder & Stoughton, 1939), 19.

use of logic': (12.399).

nation of philosophers': (16.227).

bit like a philosophy: Russell, *Philosophy and Politics*, 7.

moral 'evasion': (11.105).

practices are wrong: (12.315).

form of totalitarianism': (12.55). Orwell denied that he attacked ' "intellectuals" or "the intelligentsia" *en bloc*' (13.399), but his criticisms were often remarkably unqualified. For an account of Orwell's views on intellectuals, see Stefan Collini, *Absent Minds* (Oxford: Oxford University Press, 2006), 350–74.

different and rival directions: He disparaged the 'common sense' of H. G. Wells (12.537) and C. E. M. Joad (12.178)—a philosopher who had attempted to make 'common sense' a foundation for ethics and politics.

'elementary common sense': (5.159).

could be 'shallow': (12.172).

sadly insufficient: (11.311, 12.178).

as people imagined: (13.159).

theoretically innocent: Gollancz voiced his criticisms in a preface to *The Road to Wigan Pier*, reprinted in *Complete Works*, 5.216–25.

basic fact: (5.195).

rules of common sense': Leon Trotsky, 'Their Morals and Ours', *The New International*, 4.6 (1938): 163–73, 166.

like a scoundrel': (10.307). For Shaw's use of the phrase, see *New Statesman*, 8.450 (7 October 1939): 483–4. In September 1943 Orwell suggested that Shaw had abandoned common decency as his guide (15.243). On the links between Shaw and Orwell's O'Brien, see Ingle, *The Social and Political Thought of George Orwell*, 153–4.

a 'disgusting murderer': (12.552). Orwell would be identified as a 'Trotskyist' after his time with the Workers' Party of Marxist Unification (POUM) in the Spanish Civil War ('Gollancz won't have any more to do with me', he told Jack Common, 'now I am a Trotskyist' (11.93)). On Orwell's exposure to Trotskyist ideas, see John Newsinger, 'The American Connection: George Orwell, Literary Trotskyism and the New York Intellectuals', *Labour History Review*, 64.1 (1999): 23–43.

intellectually sophisticated: Indeed, contemporaries would comment on his 'acuteness as an observer' and 'his infantilism as a theorist'. Dwight Macdonald, 'The British Genius', *Partisan Review*, 9.2 (1942): 166–8.

p.8   **nonsense is stripped off":** (5.205).

what is just: Harold Laski, 'The Road to Wigan Pier', *The Left News*, 11 (1937): 275–6.

on their side': ibid., 276.

irreconcilable meanings: (17.425).

cracks and limitations: On disputable ideals, see W. B. Gallie, 'Essentially Contested Concepts', in *Philosophy and the Historical Understanding*, 2nd ed. (New York: Schocken Books, 1968), 157–91.

in later life: (18.319). See Rayner Heppenstall, *Four Absentees* (London: Barrie & Rockcliff, 1960), 32. Also Bernard Crick, *George Orwell: A Life* (London: Secker & Warburg, 1980), 102.

p.9   **chapters of the book:** 'All through the Christian ages, and especially since the French Revolution', Orwell declared, 'the Western world has been haunted by the idea of freedom and equality'. A few sentences later, he associated these values with 'the idea of human brotherhood' (12.55).

moral foundations: As he put it in 1946, socialism was a credo pledged to 'liberty and equality and drew its inspiration from the belief in human brotherhood' (18.62).

'human brotherhood': (18.62).

out of the world': (13.504).

in the community: For an account of both justice and happiness as a 'perfect unity of diverse elements', see Plato, *The Republic*, ed. G. R. F. Ferrari, trans. Tom Griffith (Cambridge: Cambridge University Press, 2000), 141.

at each other's throats: As Tawney pointed out, liberty, equality, and fraternity were often regarded in England as 'antithetic' and dismissed as 'a hybrid abortion'. R. H. Tawney, *Equality* (London: George Allen & Unwin, 1931), 237–8.

interpretations of freedom: Harold Laski, *A Grammar of Politics* (London: Allen & Unwin, 1925), 161.

equalization of power: Hence, Laski argued that the 'achievement of equality would be harmful without the maximum of decentralisation'. Ibid., 170–1.

egalitarian ethos: Fraternity, for Michelet, was an expression of liberty and equality, but for Louis Blanc, it was a bulwark against the narrow individualism that might arise from both. On this point, see Linda Orr, 'French Romantic Histories of the Revolution: Michelet, Blanc, Tocqueville—A Narrative', *The Eighteenth Century*, 30.2 (1989): 123–42. On the vice of individualism and on egalitarian peevishness, see Alexis de Tocqueville, *Democracy in America* (London: Everyman, 1994), Book 2, 96–9.

human brotherhood': (12.126).

freedom would suffer: As Arthur Koestler maintained, 'the greater the distance from intimacy and the wider the radius of the circle, the more warming became the radiations of this lonely man's great power of love'. *The Observer*, 29 January 1950, 4.

the police state': (18.58). This is, in part, offered as a ventriloquization of F. A. Voigt.

Eeyore of the left: As he put it in 1947: 'A Socialist today is in the position of treating an all but hopeless case' (19.163).

vanity, ambition, and vengeance: (18.318).

much more than himself': Raymond Williams, *Orwell* (London: Fontana, 1971), 82.

a century and a half': E. H. Carr, *The Twenty Years' Crisis: An Introduction to the Study of International Relations* (London: Macmillan, 1939), 80. Or as Laski reported in 1933, 'Our generation seems to have lost its scheme of values'. Harold Laski, *Democracy in Crisis* (London: George Allen & Unwin, 1933), 16.

'the Good Man': G. B. Shaw, *Collected Letters*. Volume 1: *1874–1897*, ed. Dan. H. Laurence (London: Max Reinhardt Ltd, 1965), 266. For all his disparagement of the good man, Shaw remained very much a moralist and would promote socialism as the basis for 'a higher morality'. G. B. Shaw, 'Socialism and Human Nature', in *The Road to Equality: Ten Unpublished Lectures and Essays, 1884–1918*, ed. Louis Crompton (Boston, MA: Beacon Press, 1971), 89–102, 90. On Shaw's contradictory politics, see Gareth Griffith, *Socialism and Superior Brains: The Political Thought of Bernard Shaw* (London: Routledge, 1993).

not too good': (13.30).

'absolute right and wrong': (16.106).

an earlier epoch: (10.524–5).

undermining one another': (12.31).

the 'Marxist decade': F. R. Leavis, 'Retrospect of a Decade', *Scrutiny*, 9.1 (June 1940): 70–2, 71.

awareness of his ideas: Isaac Deutscher proclaimed that Orwell knew nothing about dialectical materialism. See Isaac Deutscher, '"1984": The Mysticism of Cruelty', 45. Yet Zwerdling argued that he had 'read Marx with care and understanding'. Zwerdling, *Orwell and the Left*, 20. For a discussion of the impact of English Marxism on Orwell, see Bounds, *Orwell and Marxism*.

consciousness of us all': (11.105). However, Cole would claim in 1938 that 'British socialism had grown up in almost complete ignorance of Marx'. G. D. H. Cole, *Socialism in Evolution* (London: Penguin, 1938), 159.

with Marx or against him': Christopher Caudwell, *Studies in a Dying Culture* (London: John Lane, 1938), 13.

follower of Karl Marx': G. D. H. Cole, 'Marxism and the World Situation Today', in J. Middleton Murry, John Macmurray, N. A. Holdaway, and G. D. H. Cole,

Marxism (London: Chapman & Hall, 1935), 208–40, 240. Or as Macmurray put it: 'To be a dogmatic Marxist is to repudiate Marxism'. John Macmurray, *The Philosophy of Communism* (London: Faber, 1933), 61.

not for the dog: As his wife Eileen declared to Norah Myles: 'We called him Marx to remind us that we had never read Marx and now we have read a little and taken so strong a personal dislike to the man that we can't look the dog in the face when we speak to him'. Peter Davison (ed.), *The Lost Orwell* (London: Timewell Press, 2006), 72.

antithesis, and synthesis': (5.164).

'superior smiles': (5.160).

'polysyllables': (5.201).

'Marxist prigs': (5.197).

the 'gramophone' mind: He condemned the 'Socialist gramophone' in December 1937 (11.105). On 12 July 1940 he was quite hopeful that the 'human gramophone…is now disappearing even from Socialist tracts' (12.211). Ellipsis mine.

Marxist towards literature': (5.207). For a more damning account of 'Marxist literary criticism', see his review of Philip Henderson's *The Novel To-Day* (10.533–4). In 1941, however, he claimed that 'the most lively' literary criticism had come from Marxists writers (12.484). He lauded the subtlety of Edmund Wilson's Marxism. For his review of *The Wound and the Bow*, see 13.314–16. He also endorsed the 'lively criticism' of Christopher Caudwell, Philip Henderson, and Edward Upward (12.484).

moral sense': (12.315).

style of argument: Karl Marx and Friedrich Engels, *Collected Works*, 50 vols. (London: Lawrence & Wishart, 1975–2000), 6.312–40. Significantly, Marx's attack on Karl Heinzen's 'moralising criticism' was offered in the name of a truly 'critical morality'.

p.13 | **to leave behind:** ibid., 6.494–5.

all **morality':** ibid., 5.419. The italics are mine.

it seemed to be: On this point, see Allen W. Wood, *Karl Marx* (London: Routledge, 1981), 125–264; Steven Lukes, *Marxism and Morality* (Oxford: Clarendon, 1985); Rodney G. Peffer, *Marxism, Morality and Social Justice* (Princeton, NJ: Princeton University Press, 1990).

exploitation of labour': V. I. Lenin, 'The Tasks of the Young Leagues' (1920), *Collected Works*, 45 vols. (London: Lawrence & Wishart; Moscow: Progress Publishing, 1960–80), 32.283–99, 294.

a class character': Trotsky, 'Their Morals and Ours', 170, 165.

killed in Spain): Caudwell, *Studies in a Dying Culture*, 96.

'secondary illusions': ibid., xx.

Hebrew prophet': Tawney, 'Christianity and the Social Revolution', 160.

p.14 | **moral considerations whatsoever:** Victor Gollancz, 'On Political Morality', in *The Betrayal of the Left*, ed. Victor Gollancz (London: Victor Gollancz, 1941), 265–301, 273.

tremendous crash': (12.31).

forms may be': (12.141).

sense of social causation: In a throwaway remark in 1936, Orwell admitted that 'The statement that "every ideology is a reflection of economic circumstances" explains a good deal', but he clearly departed from this type of explanation throughout much of his work (10.478).

its causal significance: (12.244).

systems of thought': (16.71).

exclusively moral': (12.22).

world would be decent" ': (12.23).

a platitude as it sounds': (12.31).

historically contingent convictions: For a book-length study of Orwell's ideas of decency, see Anthony Stewart, *Orwell, Doubleness and Decency* (London: Routledge, 2003). See also Stephen Ingle, 'The Politics of Decency', in *George Orwell: A Political Life* (Manchester: Manchester University Press, 1993), 36–56.

to think similarly': Laski, 'The Road to Wigan Pier', 276.

middle-class notions': (5.149).

'bourgeois illusion': (13.396).

the middle classes: On this point, see R. H. Tawney, 'We Mean Freedom' (1945), in *The Attack and Other Papers* (London: Allen & Unwin, 1953), 82–100.

type of cant: Caudwell, *Studies in a Dying Culture*, xvii.

and so forth': (5.154). Ellipsis mine.

the upper classes': (16.207).

found in the world: This view is advanced despite his conviction that 'the average of human behaviour differs enormously from country to country' (12.392).

'Everyone knows': (12.397).

his eyes knows': (12.392).

his brain knows': (5.158).

not a fool knows': (5.175). For a discussion of the 'authoritarian' character of Orwell's generalizations, see Roger Fowler, *The Language of George Orwell* (Basingstoke: Macmillan, 1995), 47–8. See also Ingle, *The Social and Political Thought of George Orwell*, 24–5.

morally sound': (12.141).

'all decent people': (18.264).

'all sensitive people': (18.32).

fools or scoundrels': (5.148).

different views: On this ostracism of the reader, see Daphne Patai, *The Orwell Mystique: A Study in Male Ideology* (Amherst, MA: University of Massachusetts Press, 1984), 10.

weakening of religion: (16.107). Orwell stated his position on Trotskyism in May 1945: 'The fact that Trotskyists are everywhere a persecuted minority, and that the accusation usually made against them, *i.e.* of collaborating with the Fascists, is obviously false, creates an impression that Trotskyism is intellectually and morally superior to Communism; but it is doubtful there is much difference' (17.152). According to Borkenau, 'Trotsky is the Arch-Fascist; Stalin is Only his Pupil'. Franz Borkenau, *The Totalitarian Enemy* (London: Faber, 1940), 225–6.

'any transcendental belief': (12.140). Figures like Trotsky were adamant that 'The theory of eternal morals can in nowise survive without god'. Trotsky, 'Their Morals and Ours', 164.

God in his life: On Orwell's complicated attitudes to religion, see Michael Brennan, *George Orwell and Religion* (London: Bloomsbury, 2016).

acting a part': Anthony Powell, *To Keep the Ball Rolling: The Memoirs of Anthony Powell*. Volume 1: *Infants of the Spring* (London: Heinemann, 1976), 140. According to Raymond Williams, Orwell's 'only successful character' was Orwell. Williams, *Orwell*, 82.

p.16 expression of a face': (12.397).

'supra-class morals': Trotsky, 'Their Morals and Ours', 171.

something else?': (12.244).

specific ideas: As he put it in *The German Ideology*: 'The ideas of the ruling class are in every epoch the ruling ideas... The ruling ideas are nothing more than the ideal expression of the dominant material relations, the dominant material relations grasped as ideas; hence of the relations which make the one class the ruling one, therefore, the ideas of its dominance'. Marx and Engels, *Collected Works*, 5.59.

conclusions were false': (16.398-9).

their motives': (16.398).

views on the matter: (13.40). He repeated this anti-pacifist argument in 1942, presenting it as 'elementary common sense' (13.396).

p.17 brought forward again: (16.495). In *Tribune* in November 1945 he again criticized this functionalism as 'dishonest' (17.398).

foresee their actions': (16.495).

predictive science: As Orwell argued in July 1940: 'Marxian Socialists... have failed to foresee dangers that were obvious to people who had never heard the name of Marx' (12.212). Ellipsis mine. He reiterated the position a month later: 'during the past twenty years the predictions of the Marxists have usually been not only wrong but, so to speak, more sensationally wrong than those of much simpler people' (12.245).

followers of Nostradamus: (16.415).

among idealists now': Stephen Spender, *Forward from Liberalism* (London: Victor Gollancz, 1937), 157. Huxley made a similar complaint in the same year: 'Essentially all the new moralities, Communist, Fascist, Nazi or merely Nationalist, are singularly alike. All affirm that the end justifies the means; and in all the end is the triumph of a section of the human species over the rest'. See Aldous Huxley, *Ends and Means: An Enquiry into the Nature of Ideals and into the Methods Employed for their Realization* (London: Chatto & Windus, 1937), 283.

man over man': Trotsky, 'Their Morals and Not Ours', 172. Ellipsis mine.

"sacredness of human life" ': Leon Trotsky, *The Defence of Terrorism: A Reply to Karl Kautsky* (London: Allen & Unwin, 1921), 60. Shaw too would challenge the 'dogma of the unconditional sacredness of human life'. See G. B. Shaw, 'Preface' to *On the Rocks*, in *The Collected Works of Bernard Shaw* (London: Constable, 1934), 31.145–91, 149.

systematically exploited: Trotsky, *The Defence of Terrorism*, 59. These arguments may have convinced Orwell that Trotsky was as responsible for the Russian dictatorship 'as any man now living'. He added that there was no certainty he would be 'preferable to Stalin' (11.317).

fight against exploitation: On this point, see his letter to Naomi Mitchison in June 1938 (11.163–4).

an authoritarian mindset: (16.190).

the Old Bolsheviks': (16.397). Arthur Koestler, *Darkness at Noon*, trans. Daphne Hardy (London: Jonathan Cape, 1940), 226.

a 'masterpiece': (16.395).

'Yes.': (9.179–80).

service of revolution: Famously, the one sacrifice they refuse to make for the revolution is to separate from one another (5.180).

'Spain 1937': (12.103–4).

cause they believe in': (12.490).

forms of justification: On Orwell's 'austere version of consequentialism' during the war, see John Stone, 'George Orwell on Politics and War', *Review of International Studies*, 43.2 (2017): 221–39.

to use violence': (12.422). See also his perfect willingness 'to use violence' in February 1941 (12.381).

if it is necessary': (12.272).

cellars of the Ogpu': (16.397).

transplanted to England': (12.426).

ramifications for everyone: (15.295).

not always very clear: For an account of Orwell's attitudes to realism to which I am indebted, see Ian Hall, 'A Shallow Piece of Naughtiness: George Orwell and Political Realism', *Millennium: Journal of International Studies*, 36.2 (2008), 191–215.

'Might is Right': (15.296).

'the game of Macchiavelli [*sic*.]: (15.295).

Otto von Bismarck: (16.184). See, for instance, Friedrich Meinecke, *Machiavellism: The Doctrine of Raison d'État and its Place in Modern History*, trans. Douglas Scott (London: Transaction 1988). See, too, James Burnham, *The Machiavellians: Defenders of Freedom* (London: Putnam & Co., 1943).

Blood and Iron': Quoted in John Bew, *Realpolitik: A History* (New York: Oxford University Press, 2015), 47. Ellipsis mine.

to promote their ends: On the importance of 'blood and iron' for Bolsheviks, see Trotsky, *The Defence of Terrorism*, 60.

the same for Stalin: Georg Lukács, *Lenin: A Study on the Unity of His Thought*, trans. Nicholas Jacobs (London: Verso, 2009), 73. Leonard Woolf presented Stalin as one of 'the ultra-Realists of Socialism'. See Leonard Woolf, *Barbarians at the Gate* (London: Victor Gollancz, 1939), 61.

realist grounds: (15.295). On the policy of appeasement, see Ian Hall, 'Power, Politics and Appeasement: Political Realism in British International Thought', *The British Journal of Politics and International Relations*, 8.2 (2006): 174–92.

ultimate arbiter: 'Morality can only be relative, not universal. Ethics must be interpreted in terms of politics; and the search for an ethical norm outside politics is doomed to frustration'. Carr, *The Twenty Years' Crisis*, 28.

'Appeaser only': (20.244).

name in the 1940s: According to Orwell, Burnham's 'key concept is realism' (19.104).

'power politics': See his review in January 1944 (16.72–4) and also the later appraisal of *The Machiavellians* and the *Managerial Revolution* in 1946 (18.268–84).

science of power: On this point, see also Ignazio Silone, *The School for Dictators*, ed. Gwenda David and Eric Mosbacher (London: Jonathan Cape, 1939), 17–19. For Orwell's review of Silone, see 11.353–5.

restrain power': Burnham, *The Machiavellians*, 182. Orwell cited this phrase in an exchange with Burnham in the *Tribune* (16.63).

p.21 **chance of taking root:** As Burnham put it: 'It is only when there are several different major social forces, not only subordinate to any one social force, that there can be any assurance of liberty'. Burnham, *The Machiavellians*, 184.

explanation of their meaning: Burnham disagreed with the view that Machiavelli tries to 'divorce ethics from politics'. Machiavelli, he believed, eschewed a crude moralism in the name of objectivity, but he ultimately wished to use this science for ethical ends—namely, the instantiation of freedom. See Burnham, *The Machiavellians*, 27–8.

aimed to debunk': (16.73).

test of material success': (16.74).

does *not* pay': (15.295–6).

universal religion': (11.311).

wishful thinking: 'Power philosophies, when account is taken of their social consequences, are self-refuting'. Bertrand Russell, *Power* (London: Allen & Unwin, 1938), 273. For Orwell's review of Russell, see 11.311–12.

p.22 **it is an end':** (9.276).

epitomizes the point: 'The love of power is part of normal human nature, but power-philosophies are, in a certain precise sense, insane'. Russell, *Power*, 270.

now called "realism"': (18.284).

tend to become true': (16.204).

under a thin disguise': (13.152).

bully-worship himself: Orwell, for instance, did not like mixing in literary circles for fear that friendship would hinder the 'intellectual brutality' he liked to practise in his writing. On this point, see Collini, *Absent Minds*, 358.

folly of "realism"': (17.344).

its efficacy': (16.72).

unserviceably geriatric: Carr, *The Twenty Years' Crisis*, 15.

p.23 **feet in the mud':** (15.201).

above the trees: Any responsible reformer, he insisted in 1946, needed to steer a path been 'Machiavellianism, bureaucracy and Utopianism' (18.62).

Socialism from Utopianism': (16.35).

inherently reactionary': (12.464).

unpleasant facts': (18.316).

'pious hope': (11.311).

'fantasy world': (17.148).

'masturbation fantasy': (12.199).

'wish-thinking': (16.74).

Socialist movement with Machiavellianism': (18.62).

Socialist tradition': (18.62).

'woolly-minded Utopianism': (19.422).

Lawrence and Wishart': (12.381).

'Utopian dreamers': (18.62).

'Marxist realism': (12.125).

pay of the boss': (12.244).

24 | dim glimpses': (15.213).

positive purpose': In 1939 G. D. H. Cole also stressed that socialism rested on 'an unquenchable belief in human decency'. See Cole, *Socialism in Evolution*, 247.

its own contradictions': Gollancz, *The Betrayal of the Left*, 273.

its worst form: 'Socialism and Ethics (III)—by a Marxist', *The Left News*, 58 (April 1941), 1698.

simply relative: ibid., 1696.

restored to politics': (16.150).

class deception': Trotsky, 'Their Morals and Ours', 165.

truth about power': Burnham, *The Machiavellians*, 182.

virtue in England: On Orwell's acceptance of hypocrisy, see David Runciman, *Political Hypocrisy: The Mask of Power, from Hobbes to Orwell and Beyond* (Princeton, NJ: Princeton University Press, 2008), 168–93.

'moral code': (15.294).

25 | handkerchief industry': Cyril Connolly, *The Evening Colonnade* (London: Bruce & Watson, 1973), 382. Ellipsis mine.

august ideals: Carr, *Twenty Years' Crisis*, 127. Orwell noticed the same tendency in his discussion of Dickens—a moralist who 'despises politics' (12.23).

'monstrous harlequinade': (11.358).

'dirty, degrading business': (19.292).

'sordid' process: (17.424).

hatred and schizophrenia': (17.428).

'horror of politics': (12.148).

"keep out of politics" ': (11.167).

literature by politics': (19.288).

political matters: Indeed, in 1949 he defended the controversial decision to award Mussolini's cheerleader, Ezra Pound, the Bollingen Prize for poetry: 'since the judges have taken what amounts to the "art for art's sake" position, that is, the position that aesthetic integrity and common decency are two separate things, then at least let us keep them separate' (20.101). He had earlier claimed that 'one has the right to expect ordinary decency even of a poet' (16.81), insisting that Pound clearly failed to meet these expectations.

attraction to modernism: He struck contradictory attitudes about modernism, berating its reactionary politics, but also arguing that it contained 'no politics in the narrower sense' (12.97). For an analysis of Orwell's views on modernism, see Rae's 'Mr. Charrington's Junk Shop: T. S. Eliot and Modernist Poetics in *Nineteen Eighty-Four*', *Twentieth Century Literature*, 43.2 (Summer 1997): 196–220; Vincent Sherry, 'George Orwell and T. S. Eliot: The Sense of the Past', *College Literature*, 14.2 (1987): 85–100.

pure aestheticism': (12.486).

political attitude': (18.318).

p.26 **illusions of Liberalism':** (14.281).

interpretation of everything': Stephen Spender, 'Preface' to *The Temple* (London: Faber, 1988), xi, xii.

evils of our times': (17.11).

an unpolitical age': Spender, *Forward From Liberalism*, 27. Or as Leonard Woolf put it: 'Happy the country and era—if there can ever have been one—which has no politics'. Leonard Woolf, *An Autobiography of the Years 1919–39* (London: Hogarth Press, 1968), 27.

influence of Marx: It was certainly with people like Spender and Auden in mind that MacNeice observed: 'Marx was to the poets of the thirties what Rousseau was to the poets of the Romantic Revival'. Louis MacNeice, *The Strings are False: An Unfinished Autobiography* (London: Faber, 1965), 169.

owners of property': John Strachey, *The Theory and Practice of Socialism* (London: Victor Gollancz, 1936), 197. Strachey would run again for Parliament, serving as an MP from 1945 to 1963. Harold Laski, *Reflections on the Revolution of Our Time* (London: Allen & Unwin, 1943), 332.

'impotence of all politics': Laski, *Reflections on the Revolution of Our Time*, 110.

critique of power: For some commentators, this extension of politics was, in fact, its emasculation, for it eviscerated the distinctive logic of the political. See Carl Schmitt, *Political Theology: Four Chapters on the Concept of Sovereignty*, trans. George Schwab (Chicago, IL: University of Chicago Press, 2005), 65. See Hannah Arendt, *The Human Condition* (Chicago, IL: University of Chicago Press, 1958), 33.

hand-wringing about handkerchiefs: (17.428).

p.27 **so Orwell maintained:** (19.288).

liberal element in his thought: On Orwell's interest in anarchism, see David Goodway, *Anarchist Seeds Beneath the Snow: Left-Libertarian Thought and British Writers from William Morris to Colin Ward* (Liverpool: Liverpool University Press, 2006), 123–48.

individual was an illusion: (12.502).

from the bourgeois age': (12.110–11).

Liberalism alive': (19.288).

p.28 **best of its purposes:** Michael Oakeshott in 'The Claims of Politics', *Scrutiny*, 8.2 (September 1939): 146–51, 148. In 1940 Spender would also argue that 'Politics have necessarily a restricted view of life'. See Stephen Spender, 'A Look at the Worst', *Horizon*, 2.9 (September 1940): 103–17, 114.

collective action possible: (17.427).

child's Meccano set': (17.376).

generally bad writing: (17.427).

literary integrity': (19.291).

destroy yourself as a writer': (19.292).

.29   keep out of politics': (12.105).

he repeatedly insisted: (11.167). Or as he argued in 1945: 'no one describable as an
      intellectual *can* keep out of politics' (17.154–5). He made a similar point in 1948:
      'no thinking person can or does genuinely keep out of politics, in an age like the
      present one' (19.291).

lapse of taste': (12.98).

worship of the meaningless': (12.98). See also 10.533. He defended modernism—or
      at least Joyce, Eliot, and Woolf—from these charges of vacuity. He admired 'emphasis
      on technique' (12.484), but he also suggested their work retained a broader moral
      'purpose' (12.98). However, he also averred that what 'purpose they have is very
      much up in the air' (12.97).

truly neutral': (12.95).

are the same thing': (10.533).

not all propaganda is art: (12.47). See also 12.297. In 1941 he claimed that 'propa-
      ganda in some form or other lurks in every book' (12.486), and later professed
      that 'All art is to some extent propaganda' (14.65). He was also keen to insist that
      not all propaganda is political (12.297).

a social movement': Leon Trotsky, 'Art and Politics', *Partisan Review*, 5.3 (June
      1938): 3–11, 11.

30   critics ever since: (18.320).

non-utilitarian' endeavour: (18.318).

workmanlike smell: (18.320).

would consider irrelevant': (18.319).

inexhaustibly instrumental world: Theodor Adorno, *Aesthetic Theory*, trans.
      C. Lenhardt (New York: Routledge and Kegan Paul, 1984), 322.

lifeless books': (18.320).

'democratic Socialism': (18.319). For an impressively literal interpretation of Orwell's
      political apology for this own writing, see Alex Woloch, *Or Orwell: Writing and
      Democratic Socialism* (Cambridge, MA: Harvard University Press, 2016).

dialectical materialism: (5.206).

literary men ever happens': (11.359).

emotionally lived events: W. H. Auden, *Spain* (London: Faber & Faber, 1937), 11.
      W. H. Auden, 'In Memory of W. B. Yeats', in *Collected Poems*, ed. Edward Mendelson
      (London: Faber & Faber, 1976), 247–9, 248.

31   self-indulgent gloom': MacNeice, *The Strings are False*, 134.

hanging out with tramps: (5.143).

use of the imagination': Henry James, 'Preface' to 'The Lesson of the Master', in
      Henry James, *The Art of the Novel*, ed. Richard P. Blackmur (New York: Charles
      Scribner's Sons, 1934), 223. James' remark is discussed at length in Martha

Nussbaum's 'Perception and Revolution: *The Princess Casamassima* and the Political Imagination', in *Love's Knowledge: Essays on Philosophy and Literature* (Oxford: Oxford University Press, 1990), 195–219.

'compassionate citizenship': On these themes, see Martha Nussbaum, *Political Emotions: Why Love Matters for Justice* (Cambridge, MA: Harvard University Press, 2013).

real suffering: Jean-Jacques Rousseau, *Politics and the Arts: Letter to M. D'Alembert*, trans. Allan Bloom (Ithaca, NY: Cornell University Press, 1968), 17.

existence of conflict: As Rousseau suggested, antagonism is the basic condition of politics: if there were no conflict, 'everything would run by itself, and politics would cease to be an art'. Jean-Jacques Rousseau, *The Social Contract and Other Later Political Writings*, ed. and trans. Victor Gourevitch (Cambridge: Cambridge University Press, 1997), 60.

not Orwell's credo: E. M. Forster, 'The Long Run', *New Statesman and Nation* (10 December 1938), 971–2, 972.

literary vitality': (15.292).

p.32 | **context of art**: For an account of the senses in which intention does and doesn't matter in art, see Stanley Cavell, 'A Matter of Meaning It', in *Must We Mean What We Say?* (Cambridge: Cambridge University Press), 213–38.

no need to do it': Louis MacNeice, 'Poetry To-day', in *The Arts To-day*, ed. Geoffrey Grigson (London: John Lane, 1935), 25–67, 25.

incarnated in experience': Judith Shklar, '*Nineteen Eighty-Four*: Should Political Theory Care?', *Political Theory*, 13.1 (1985): 5–18, 7.

Orwell's writing: Of course, Orwell's most famous biographer, Bernard Crick, was a political theorist, though his engagement with his writing was not particularly theoretical. See Crick, *Orwell*. For a more conceptual treatment, see Bernard Crick, 'Orwell and English Socialism', in *George Orwell: A Reassessment*, ed. P. Buitenhuis and Ira B. Nadel (London: Macmillan, 1988), 3–22. For other politico-philosophical approaches to Orwell, see Michael Walzer, 'George Orwell's England', in *The Company of Critics: Social Criticism and Political Commitment in the Twentieth Century* (New York: Basic Books, 1988): 117–35; Runciman, *Political Hypocrisy*, 168–93.

the actual world': Shklar, '*Nineteen Eighty-Four*: Should Political Theory Care?', 7.

p.33 | **'conviction without understanding'**: Plato, *Gorgias*, trans. Robin Waterfield (Oxford: Oxford University Press, 1994), 17.

without foundation: As Isaac Deutscher maintained in the '50s: '1984 . . . has frightened millions of people. But it has not helped them to see more clearly the issues with which the world is grappling; it has not advanced their understanding'. Ellipsis mine. See Deutscher, '"1984"—The Mysticism of Cruelty', 49.

beliefs it serviced: On the formal complexity of Orwell's writing, see, in particular, Woloch, *Or Orwell*. See, too, Loraine Saunders, *The Unsung Artistry of George Orwell: The Novels from Burmese Days to Nineteen Eighty-Four* (Aldershot: Ashgate, 2008).

CHAPTER I

p.35 **great hurrah-concept:** Though freedom and liberty have sometimes been distinguished, I shall treat them here as synonyms. Orwell seemed to have done the same.

individuals and organisations': (19.431).

'rootless freedom': (3.249).

'unthinkable': (2.69).

the modern world: (4.52).

fast asleep': (7.11).

all the difference': (8.75).

that was freedom': (9.294).

lack of freedom: (3.297).

p.36 **nobody is free':** (5.158).

disbelieving in liberty': (18.425).

feature of the 1930s: 'Do not be deluded by the abstract word Freedom!', Marx declared, but few in the '30s seemed to heed the warning. See Marx and Engels, *Collected Works*, 6.463.

it might be defended: Malcolm Muggeridge, *The Thirties: 1930–1940 in Great Britain* (London: Hamish Hamilton, 1940), 317–18. Ellipsis mine.

carried on its name': Spender, *Forward from Liberalism*, 45. Spender suggested that the word liberty was little more than a positive emotion, yet he still went on to insist that it was the most 'meaningful abstract noun in the language'. Ibid., 171–2.

believe in freedom now': E. M. Forster, 'The Menace to Freedom', in *Two Cheers for Democracy* (London: Edward Arnold, 1951), 9–11, 10.

spit on freedom': (12.462).

Goddess of Liberty': Martin Clark, *Mussolini* (London: Routledge, 2005), 78. Many picked up on the paradox: 'Fascism tells us that we must abandon freedom because it has not made us free'. Spender, *Forward from Liberalism*, 45.

37 **right sort of folk):** Adolf Hitler, *Mein Kampf: Eine kritische Edition*, ed. Christian Hartmann, Thomas Vordermayer, Othmar Plöckinger, and Roman Töppel, 2 vols. (Berlin: Instituts für Zeitgeschichte München-Berlin, 2016), 2.969.

Stalin's project: Strachey, *The Theory and Practice of Socialism*, 156.

freedom was absolute: Woolf, *Barbarians at the Gate*, 63.

hesitate to employ them': Friedrich Hayek, *The Road to Serfdom* (London: Routledge, 2001), 14.

meaningless words: (17.425).

'freedom for the other fellow': (17.257). He attributed this comment to Rosa Luxemburg. Orwell appears to have drawn his sense of this remark from Luxemburg's account of the Russian Revolution. 'Freedom is always and exclusively freedom for the one who thinks differently'. See Rosa Luxemburg, *The Russian Revolution*, trans. Bertram Wolfe (New York: Workers Age Publishers, 1940), 45.

many on the Left: On this codependency, see Harold Laski, *Socialism and Freedom* (London: Fabian Society, 1925), 9.

'terror of the boss': (7.176).

'terror of the sack': (7.76).

terror of unemployment': (13.509).

as his master': (6.83).

he is acted upon': (5.44).

a classless society': (17.372). As Huxley put it in 1931, 'the rich can buy large quantities of freedom; the poor must do without it'. Aldous Huxley, 'Boundaries of Utopia', in *Complete Essays*, ed. Robert. S. Baker and James Sexton, 6 vols. (Chicago, IL: Ivan R. Dee, 2001), 3.124–9, 124.

freedom elsewhere': (17.29).

disenfranchised human beings': (11.360).

freedom that he destroys': (10.504).

p.38   same property in others: Jean-Jacques Rousseau, 'Lettres de La Montagne: VIII', *Oeuvres Complètes de Jean-Jacques Rousseau*, 4 vols. (Paris: Houssiaux, 1852), 3.81. G. W. F. Hegel, *Phenomenology of Spirit*, trans. A. V. Miller (Oxford: Oxford University Press, 1979), 111–19.

yellow faces behind': (10.504).

don't agree with niggers': Christopher Hollis, *A Study of George Orwell* (London: Hollis & Carter, 1956), 27.

wheels of despotism': (2.69).

individual and the community': (12.502).

anti-social entity: To oppose an 'abstract man' to an 'abstract community', Laski contended, leads 'to the common injury of both'. Laski, *A Grammar of Politics*, 43.

broader social organism: (12.125). He put it in less absolute terms in 1941: 'war brings it home to the individual that he is *not* altogether an individual' (12.421).

only a cell': (9.276).

p.39   illusion of being autonomous': (12.502).

never clearly defined': (17.310).

the word himself: Laski, 'The Road to Wigan Pier', 275–6. For Gollancz' criticisms, see 5.216–25.

sleek professors': (12.315).

freedom of the will: (16.203).

reconciled with one another': (17.245).

set of freedoms: (12.394).

p.40   'political liberty': (17.370).

liberty as a fraud: (12.377).

and you're all right"': (1.167).

conditions for its existence: On the political limits of 'inner freedom', see Hannah Arendt, 'What is Freedom?', in *Between Past and Future: Eight Excursus in Political Thought* (London: Penguin, 2006), 142–69, 145–6.

inside your skull': (9.29).

can't get inside you': (9.174).

'all is money': (4.14).

freedom with it': (4.165).

.41 **Marxist of the 1930s:** Comstock's polemic has much in common with Marx's reflections on the 'Power of Money' in *The Philosophic and Economic Manuscripts* (1844): 'The extent of the power of money is the extent of my power. Money's properties are my—the possessor's—properties and essential powers... Money is the supreme good, therefore its possessor is good'. Ellipsis mine. See Marx and Engels, *Collected Works*, 3.324.

it kills thought': (4.53).

hand and brain': (4.168). Ellipsis mine.

ever been his': (4.266).

every human being' (4.267).

thesis in the 1930s: Engels drew on Hegel to make the point. Marx and Engels, *Collected Works*, 25.105. For some of its uses in the '30s, see C. Day Lewis, 'A Time to Dance', in *A Time to Dance and Other Poems* (London: Hogarth Press, 1935), 31–64, 57; Caudwell, *Studies in a Dying Culture*, 206. The phrase would be continued to be used in the '40s. See 'Archimedes' (pseud.), 'The Freedom of Necessity I, II, III, IV', *Horizon* (July 1942): 16–33; ibid. (August 1942): 97–107; ibid. (October 1942): 267–98; ibid. (November 1942): 355–70; Harold Laski, *Reflections on the Revolution of Our Time*, 336.

might suggest otherwise: Caudwell, *Studies in a Dying Culture*, 209. Ellipsis mine.

'positive' concept: On aspects of the debates, see Michael Freeden, *Liberalism Divided: A Study in British Political Thought, 1914–1939* (Oxford: Clarendon Press, 1986).

42 **Freudian age):** As Gilbert Murray noted in 1932: 'The Faculty of Reason is very much down in the world. Its stock is low'. Gilbert Murray, 'A Plea for Reason', *The Rationalist Annual*, ed. Charles A. Watts (London: The Rationalist Press Association, 1932), 3–6, 3. For the impact of Freud on the 1930s, see Richard Overy, *The Morbid Age: Britain and the Crisis of Civilization, 1919–1939* (London: Allen Lane, 2009), 136–47.

Harold Laski's: It was, after all, 'the age of Laski'—even in the eyes of his critics. See Max Beloff, 'The Age of Laski', *The Fortnightly Review*, 167 (1950): 378–84.

absence of restraint'): Harold Laski, *A Grammar of Politics*, 142.

power to expand': Laski, *Liberty and the Modern State*, 13.

fast for Laski: See Harold Laski, *Authority in the Modern State* (New Haven, CT: Yale University Press, 1919), 54; Laski, *Reflections on the Revolution of Our Time*, 316.

positive freedom': ibid., 358.

purpose of freedom': Laski, *Liberty and the Modern State*, 14.

43 **a 'negative' matter:** ibid., 11. Earlier he claimed, however, that 'there is a sense in which Rousseau's paradox... may in the end be true that men must be forced to be free'. Ellipsis mine. See Laski, *Authority in the Modern State*, 108. Rousseau made the same claim. See Rousseau, *The Social Contract and Other Later Political Writings*, 53.

'positive' sense of the State: (15.271).

State interference': (18.496).

'FREEDOM IS SLAVERY': (9.18).

'positive' schemes of freedom: This was the certainly Isaiah Berlin's reading of *Nineteen Eighty-Four*. See Ramin Jahanbegloo (ed.), *Conversations With Isaiah Berlin* (London: Peter Halban, 1992), 41.

rules of ancient liberty': (17.259). The line is drawn from Sonnet XII. See John Milton, *The Complete Works of John Milton*. Volume III: *The Shorter Poems*, ed. Barbara Kiefer Lewalski and Estelle Haan (Oxford: Oxford University Press, 2012), 241.

with breaking rules': (7.66).

George Bowling: (19.336).

p.44   Bogs and Precipes': John Locke, *Two Treatises of Government*, ed. Peter Laslett (Cambridge: Cambridge University Press, 1988), 305.

it was silent: Thomas Hobbes, *Leviathan*, ed. Richard Tuck (Cambridge: Cambridge University Press, 1996), 152.

beg the question: Jeremy Bentham, *The Works of Jeremy Bentham*, ed. John Bowring, 11 vols. (Edinburgh: Tait, 1843), 2.503.

more anarchic waters: Indeed, in Isaac Deutscher's eyes, Orwell always remained 'a simple-minded anarchist'. Deutscher, 'The Mysticism of Cruelty', 45. Orwell's large collection of anarchist pamphlets—containing works by Godwin, Kropotkin, Berkman, Woodcock, etc.—certainly communicates an interest in anarchism, though it puts pressure on the idea that it was entirely unschooled.

'sentimental nonsense': (5.137).

at that moment': (1.10).

people from violence': (5.137).

'absolute': (17.257).

not permissive enough: Shaw also argued that the 'notion that the absence of legislation means the absence of compulsion is an old fallacy of socialism'. Shaw, 'Freedom and the State', in *The Road to Equality*, 37–54, 39–40.

system of law: (18.424).

p.45   as everyone else: (18.424–5).

no development': (18.425).

obtained by men': Caudwell, *Studies in a Dying Culture*, 213.

bourgeois thought': ibid., 179.

p.46   Noble Savage': (16.43).

the din of towns: (12.204).

the money-god: (4.165).

sex in the open air: According to Powell, Orwell himself showed some fascination with the idea of 'having' a woman in a park. Anthony Powell, *Infants of the Spring* (London: Heinemann, 1976), 134.

squalid and ugly': (4.157).

'lunatic asylum': (7.228).

dejectedly concludes: (7.238).

'to please himself": (9.230).

p.47   normal or decent': (1.3).

people from work': (1.3).

have no meaning': (4.227).

do not exist': (4.233).

they cry libertie': See John Milton, 'XII', in *The Complete Works of John Milton. Volume III: The Shorter Poems*, 241.

.48 was so disapproving: Matthew Arnold, *Culture and Anarchy*, ed. Stefan Collini (Cambridge: Cambridge University Press, 1993), 81–101; Laski, *Socialism and Freedom*, 12.

what one wants': Caudwell, *Studies of a Dying Culture*, 225. Shaw also viewed liberty as a type of license or what he preferred to call 'leisure': 'If you can at any moment in the day say "I can do as I please for the next hour" then for that hour you are at liberty'. G. B. Shaw, *The Intelligent Woman's Guide to Socialism and Capitalism* (London: Constable & Co., 1928), 320. Liberty entailed: 'freedom from any obligation to do anything except just what we like', ibid., 77.

we want to do': (7.82).

harmful to ourselves: L. T. Hobhouse, *The Elements of Social Justice* (London: George Allen, 1922), 50.

oneself is freedom': Rousseau, *The Social Contract and Other Later Political Writings*, 53.

altered from outside': (9.171).

locus of his freedom: (9.293).

49 avoid joining in': (9.16).

radio hypnosis': (13.499).

things they don't want': (7.131).

plebs and gentlemen: (9.94).

intellectual stimulant': (9.89).

50 slave of a passion': Hobhouse, *The Elements of Social Justice*, 50.

'self-mastery': In 1951 Harold Laski would also regard 'self-mastery as one of the essential conditions of a free society'. Harold Laski, *Reflections on the Constitution: The House of Commons, the Cabinet, the Civil Service* (Manchester: Manchester University Press, 1951), 9.

emotions, interests, impulses': ibid., 57. Ellipsis mine.

young Kingsley Martin: Martin, *Father Figures: A First Volume of Autobiography, 1897–1931* (London: Hutchinson, 1966), 110, 112.

its warring constituents: For the argument that Freud advocates 'self-mastery', see Paul Roazen, *Encountering Freud: The Politics and Histories of Psychoanalysis* (New York: Transaction, 1990).

passions and fantasies: Caudwell, *Studies in a Dying Culture*, 207.

form of freedom: Or as J. D. Bernal put it in 1929: 'Rationalism strove to make the super ego the dominant partner; it never succeeded, not only because its standard was too high to allow any outlet for the primitive forces, but because it was itself too arbitrary, too tainted with distorted primitive wishes ever to be brought into correspondence with reality'. J. D. Bernal, *The World, the Flesh and the Devil* (London: Cape, 1970 [1929]), 54.

'Shooting an Elephant': (10.502).

51 would never do so': (9.17).

pleasure and desire: For Freud, this repression was arguably a condition of civilization. See Sigmund Freud, *Civilisation and its Discontents*, in *The Penguin Freud Library.* Volume 12: *Civilisation, Society and Religion*, trans. James Strachey, ed. Albert Dickson (London: Penguin, 1991). But it was judged to have been brought to an unbearable form under capitalism as well as totalitarianism. See Caudwell, *Studies in a Dying Culture*, 64.

this repressive hypothesis: This was noted long ago: see Paul Roazen, 'Orwell, Freud, and 1984', *Virginia Quarterly Review*, 54 (1978): 675–95.

abolishing the orgasm: (9.280).

animals are free': (9.75).

remained sane': (9.163).

cannot become conscious': (9.74).

being true agents: As Ayer explained: 'The ground for taking ignorance to be restrictive of freedom is that it causes people to make choices which they would not have involved if they had seen what the realization of their choices involved'. A. J. Ayer, 'The Concept of Freedom', *Horizon* (April 1944), 228–37.

to become sane': (9.263).

making the case against them: For the critique of positive liberty as a model of political freedom, see Isaiah Berlin, 'Two Concepts of Freedom', in *Four Essays on Liberty* (Oxford: Oxford University Press, 1969), 118–72. For his comments on Orwell, see Ramin Jahanbegloo (ed.), *Conversations with Isaiah Berlin*, 41.

| p.52 | **desire for death':** (18.426).

who are deeply unfree: (7.25).

a new idea': (7.168).

Orthodoxy is unconsciousness': (9.56).

own free will': (7.115).

| p.53 | **everlasting idiocies':** (7.82).

our element': (7.15).

maggot in his heart': (4.70).

epoch of fear': (12.91).

enemy of freedom': Harold Laski, 'Democracy in War Time', in *Victory or Vested Interest?*, ed. G. D. H. Cole (London: Routledge, 1942), 38–56, 53. See also Laski, *A Grammar of Politics*, 149.

all happened together: Tawney, 'We Mean Freedom', in *The Attack and Other Papers*, 82–100, 90.

blood like leeches': (7.10). The very title of *Coming Up for Air* seems to endorse Cyril Connolly's opinion that 'England is…a grey little fey little island from which the air is slowly being pumped out, and in which breathing will become difficult unless equality of opportunity and fraternity of outlook be added to the liberty of opinion which those of us who have a little money can still afford'. Ellipsis mine. Cyril Connolly, 'We English Again', *The New Statesman and Nation* (10 December 1938): 972–4, 974.

get the sack': (7.15).

bum-suckers': (7.13).

dog that sees the whip': (7.15).

they weren't secure': (7.110).

mankind are without it': Tawney, *The Acquisitive Society* (London: G. Bell & Sons, 1921), 83. See, too, Laski, *Reflections on the Revolution of Our Time*, 17. Orwell insisted that since the 1930s 'security has never existed'—it had been entirely shattered by Hitler and the Great Depression (12.485).

not worth having': Laski, *Liberty in the Modern State*, 14. Ellipsis mine.

'more security': (17.339).

Friedrich Hayek: For a discussion of Orwell and Hayek, see Andrew Farrant, 'Hayek, Orwell, and *The Road to Serfdom*', in *Hayek: A Collaborative Biography. Part VI: Good Dictators, Sovereign Producers and Hayek's 'Ruthless Consistency'* (London: Palgrave, 2015), 152–82.

sacrifice their liberty': Hayek, *The Road to Serfdom*, 136.

freedom's gravest threats: ibid., 124.

liberty nor safety': ibid., 137.

great deal of truth': (16.149).

'tyranny': (16.149).

'dead': (12.429).

security to liberty': (12.249).

economic security?': (13.164).

war-preparation entails': (11.240, 11.245).

the conflict itself: Emma Robinson, 'George Orwell, Internment and the Illusion of Liberty', *Literature and History*, 25.2 (2014): 35–50.

diminution of liberty': (12.463).

'War Socialism': (12.534).

dominate the 1940s: As Judt argued, planning would become 'the political religion of post-war Europe'. Tony Judt, *Postwar: A History of Europe Since 1945* (London: Pimlico, 2007), 67.

high road to serfdom: Laski saw planning as the precondition for a positive form of freedom. See Laski, *Reflections on the Revolution of Our Time*, 351. For the broader debates about planning on the Left, see Richard Toye, *The Labour Party and the Planned Economy* (Woodbridge: Boydell, 2003).

a planned society': (19.87).

'a planless one': (12.410).

worst man wins': (12.413).

the world is going': (12.460).

any say in the matter': (16.149).

by some other name': (18.59).

slavery than the alternative': (18.102).

totalitarianisation of our economy': (12.477).

any previous age: (12.503).

before long': (12.123).

'we are all socialists now': Hayek, *The Road to Serfdom*, 5.

non-democratic kind: (12.461). 'National Socialism *is* a form of Socialism, *is* emphatically revolutionary, *does* crush the property-owner just as surely as it crushes the worker' (12.159). This position was articulated in a supportive review of Borkenau's *The Totalitarian Enemy*. According to Borkenau, 'Fascism is undoubtedly the most extreme political form of the most extreme type of Socialism'. See Franz Borkenau, *The Totalitarian Enemy* (London: Faber, 1940), 104.

individual liberty': (15.271).

race of oligarchs': (15.271).

'monstrous error': Harold Laski, *Faith, Reason and Civilisation* (London: Victor Gollancz, 1944), 168.

freedom in doing so': (16.191).

important than anything else': (18.71).

'individualism': (9.85).

empty term of abuse: (17.372).

indignity of living for others: Oscar Wilde, 'The Soul of Man Under Socialism', in *The Complete Works of Oscar Wilde* (London: Harper Collins, 1999), 1174–97.

individuality in the workers': G. D. H. Cole, *Self-Government in Industry* (London: G. Bell & Sons, 1918), 24.

p.58 to use their rights': Tawney, *The Acquisitive Society*, 51.

abolish liberty the better': C. D. Burns, 'The Conception of Liberty', *Journal of Philosophical Studies*, 3.10 (1928), 186–97, 195.

men into the mire': Caudwell, *Studies in a Dying Culture*, 19.

a sick soul': Spender, *Forward From Liberalism*, 65. Spender would also argue for socialism on the grounds that it was the only means of ensuring a fully authentic individualism.

Huxley declared in 1929: Aldous Huxley, 'This Community Business', in *Complete Essays*, 3.221–5, 222. Ellipsis mine.

'individualist': Forster, 'What I Believe', in *Two Cheers for Democracy*, 65–73, 72.

'egotism and selfishness': Hayek, *The Road to Serfdom*, 14.

individualist position': ibid., 63.

animal in a trap': (5.79).

'individualism': As John Macmurray put it in 1933: 'Beyond a certain point the development of individualism means the destruction of individuality'. Macmurray, *The Philosophy of Communism*, 96.

the chief incentive': (18.57).

swallowed by the masses: (16.210).

a 'sinking ship': (17.21).

p.59 independence and creativity: (12.530).

heterogeneous ideas imaginable': Max Weber, *The Protestant Ethic and the 'Spirit' of Capitalism and Other Writings*, ed. and trans. Peter Baehr and Gordon C. Wells (London: Penguin, 2002), 133.

'tirades against "individualism"': (17.380).

'petit-bourgeois individualism': (17.372).

Burns claimed in 1928: On later political uses of the Crusoe myth, see Joseph Slaughter, *Human Rights Inc.: The World Novel, Narrative Form and International Law* (New York: Oxford University Press, 2007), 59–63.

regulation was interference': Burns, 'The Conception of Liberty', 189.

the asocial individual: Friedrich Hayek, *Individualism: True and False* (Dublin: Hodges and Figgis, 1946), 7.

a creative meaning': Laski, *Liberty and the Modern State*, 20; Laski, *Faith, Reason and Civilisation*, 67. Ellipsis mine.

'unfree alone': Caudwell, *Studies in a Dying Culture*, 211.

experience of war: (12.534).

altogether an individual': (12.421).

race, creed, class': (12.126).

the classless society': (16.478).

emotionally at sea': W. H. Auden, 'Problems of Education', in *Prose*, ed. Edward Mendelson, 6 vols. (Princeton, NJ: Princeton University Press, 1996–2015), 1.27–8, 28.

Christian mysticism: John Middleton Murry, 'The New Man', in *Marxism*, 99–119, 105.

everything to gain: ibid., 104.

Choose!: John Middleton Murry, *The Necessity of Communism* (London: Jonathan Cape, 1932), 118.

arises fanaticism': ibid., 113–14.

the "individual"': John Middleton Murry, 'On Marxism in General', *Marxism*, 3–24, 12. Ellipses mine.

a mere 'cell': (9.276).

all-powerful and immortal': (9.276–7). Ellipsis mine.

the loving breast!': (9.311).

a mere cell: (12.125).

self-surrender: (16.478).

with the community"': (17.380).

collective and immortal': (9.261).

such contempt would lead: Eugene Lyons, *Assignment in Utopia* (New York: Harcourt, Brace & Co., 1937), 646. For Orwell's review published in the *New English Weekly* in June 1938, see 11.158–60.

cited by Orwell in 1946: (18.177).

inside your skull': (9.29).

being understood': (12.129).

even to yourself': (9.174).

personal to himself: Laski, *Liberty in the Modern State*, 31. He would also claim that the 'true self is the self that is isolated from his fellows'; ibid., 25.

individualist' by disposition: (15.271). In 1944 Laski would celebrate the fact that the 'individualist world is unlikely to survive'. See Harold Laski, *Will Planning Restrict Freedom?* (Cheam: Architectural Press, 1944), 27. But he had also complained that we 'lack a healthy individualism which might give us the courage to experiment with ourselves'. Harold Laski, 'A Plea for Equality', in *The Dangers of Obedience and Other Essays* (New York and London: Harpers, 1930), 207–37, 228.

can be free *inside*': (16.172).

social in their constitution': Michael Oakeshott, 'Review of *The State and the Citizen*, by J. D. Mabbott', *Mind*, 58 (1949): 378–89, 386. Ellipsis mine.

p.63   very valuable thing': (9.144).

chosen for you from above: (12.394).

'obstructive nuisance': (12.31).

p.64   crossword-puzzle fans': (12.394).

'the liberty of the ancients': See Benjamin Constant, 'The Liberty of the Ancients Compared with that of the Moderns', in *Political Writings*, ed. Biancamaria Fontana (Cambridge: Cambridge University Press, 1988), 308–28.

a private context': Laski, *A Grammar of Politics*, 25.

shared with so many': Hobhouse, *Elements of Justice*, 89.

a tedious affair: See Auden, 'The Unknown Citizen', in *Collected Poems*, 252–3.

exploding like bombs: Auden, *Spain*, 11.

Blifil-Gordon for ever!': (3.35).

p.65   a disgusting spectacle?': (3.38).

Mr. Blifil-Gordon!': (3.36). Ellipsis mine.

keep your overcoat on': (7.151).

fifteen or sixteen people': (7.151).

this kind of thing?': (7.152).

'born chairman': (7.152).

shooting out slogans': (7.153).

Fascism': (7.153).

p.66   the more he likes it: (7.156–7).

Democracy-Fascism-Democracy': (7.153–4).

pond of Binfield House: As Hannah Arendt pointed out, moderns are 'inclined to believe that freedom begins where politics ends'. See Arendt, 'What is Freedom?', in *Between Past and Future*, 148.

p.67   so thoughtlessly pursued: Tocqueville, *Democracy in America*, Book 2, 98–9.

chaps like himself: (7.158).

'just plain foolishness': (7.169).

'Hitler matters': (7.166).

they're all for it': (7.239).

p.68   under their noses': (7.168).

"eternal vigilance"': (19.431).

they weren't secure': (7.110).

England's the whole world': (7.168).

'are paralysed': (7.169).

'Fascism–democracy dogfight': (12.102).

"We spit upon Freedom"': (12.462).

p.69   instinctive wisdom': (17.165).

'is Nosey Parker': (12.394).

conscripted, "co-ordinated" ': (12.394).

Stop him!': (7.183). Ellipsis mine.

what's coming to them': (7.26). Ellipsis mine.

something that's got to happen': (7.238).

and lets things happen to him': (12.91).

initiative and responsibility': Laski, 'The Recovery of Citizenship', in *The Dangers of Obedience and Other Essays*, 59–90, 59.

intellectual atmosphere': (19.423).

CHAPTER 2

becoming a reality': (12.430). This chapter draws on previously published material: David Dwan, 'Orwell's Paradox: Equality in *Animal Farm*', ELH, 79.3 (2010): 655–83.

psychological difficulties may be': (16.74). This claim would also be reiterated in the political theory he attributes to Goldstein in *Nineteen Eighty-Four* (9.211–12).

of the concept: As Tawney remarked in his famous study of the ideal: 'It is obvious that the word "Equality" possesses more than one meaning and that controversies surrounding it arise partly, at least, because the same term is employed with different connotations'. Tawney, *Equality*, 46. For some discussion of the ambiguities, see Douglas Rae, *Equalities* (Cambridge, MA: Harvard University Press, 1981); Peter Westen, *Speaking Equality* (Princeton, NJ: Princeton University Press, 1990); Thomas Nagel, *Equality and Partiality* (Oxford: Oxford University Press, 1991); Nils Holtug and Kasper Lippert-Rasmussen (eds.), *Egalitarianism: New Essays on the Nature and Value of Equality* (Oxford: Clarendon, 2006); and Stewart White, *Equality* (Oxford: Blackwell, 2006).

his contemporaries: (17.425).

more equal than others': (8.90).

a general concept: The extent to which the paradox is really Orwell's is a matter of some dispute. It is possible he borrowed the phrase from Philip Guedalla's 'A Russian Fairy Tale', in *The Missing Muse* (New York: Harper & Brothers, 1930). See Richard Mayne, 'The Gentleman Beneath', *Times Literary Supplement*, 26 November 1982, 1292.

persons are naturally equal': William Morris, *The Unpublished Lectures of William Morris*, ed. Eugene D. LeMire (Detroit, MI: Wayne State University Press, 1969), 217.

of equal value': R. H. Tawney, 'Christianity and the Social Revolution' (1935), in *The Attack and Other Papers*, 157–92, 182–3.

to consideration and to respect': Tawney, *Equality*, 47.

in Orwell's writing: For Hayek, respect is an intrinsically restricted good. See Friedrich Hayek, *Law, Legislation and Liberty: The Mirage of Social Justice* (London: Routledge & Kegan Paul, 1976), 99.

'the gangster and the pansy': (11.244).

wolfing bacon': (1.133). Ellipsis mine.

flatten the Jew's nose': (1.16).

'Race-prejudice': (19.465).

Indians are inferior to Europeans': (13.276). For a discussion of Orwell's racist attitudes, see Patai, *The Orwell Mystique*, 105.

except physical strength': (16.271).

tribe of high-minded women': (5.169).

keep lodging-houses': (4.24).

reminded one of boiling-fowls': (1.184).

nagging, feminine clamour': (3.1).

many individual Socialists': (5.202).

many fear and detest': Hobhouse, *The Elements of Social Justice*, 48.

human rights for granted': (12.411).

links all socialists': W. A. Lewis, *Principles of Economic Planning* (London: Dobson, 1949), 10. Cited in Ben Jackson, *Equality and the British Left: A Study in Progressive Political Thought, 1900–64* (Manchester: Manchester University Press, 2007), 155. 'Equality', Shaw insisted, 'is the best touchstone for distinguishing your real Socialist from your virtuously indignant pitier of the poor'. Shaw, 'The Simple Truth about Socialism', in *The Road to Equality,* 155–94, 194.

p.73 Marx wholeheartedly endorsed: For an account of Marx as a sceptic of equality, see Alan Wood, 'Marx and Equality', in *Analytical Marxism*, ed. John Roemer (Cambridge: Cambridge University Press, 1986), 283–303. Norman Geras prefers to emphasize Marx's ambivalence for the principle; see 'The Controversy about Marx and Justice', in *Literature of Revolution: Essays on Marxism* (London: Verso, 1986), 3–57. See also G. A. Cohen, *Self-Ownership, Freedom and Equality* (Cambridge: Cambridge University Press, 1995), 116–43.

the Workers' International: Marx and Engels, *Collected Works*, 20.14, 441.

reactionary ideal: ibid., 24.86–7.

in the name of justice: Adorno also decried an 'equality in which differences perish'. Theodor Adorno, *Negative Dialectics*, trans. E. B. Ashton (New York: Continuum, 2007), 309.

deeply invidious results: Marx and Engels, *Collected Works*, 24.86–7.

rather than equal': ibid., 24.87.

on some other level: According to Laski: 'Equality does not mean that the differences of men are to be neglected; it means only that those differences are to be selected for emphasis which are deliberately relevant to the common good'. Harold Laski, 'A Plea for Equality', in *The Dangers of Obedience and Other Essays* (New York and London: Harpers, 1930), 207–37, 232.

highly inegalitarian outcomes: See J. S. Mill, *Utilitarianism*, in *The Collected Works of John Stuart Mill*, ed. J. M. Robson, 33 vols. (London and Toronto: University of Toronto Press, 1963–9), 10.203–60, 257. Sidney and Beatrice Webb also declared that this was the credo of Soviet Russia. Sidney and Beatrice Webb, *Soviet Communism: A New Civilisation?*, 2 vols. (London: Longman, 1935), 2.1035.

irrational concern in the 1930s: This point was made in detail in 1937 by Borkenau. See Borkenau, *The Totalitarian Enemy*, 150–2.

if you were a minority: Bertrand Russell, 'What is Democracy?', in *What is Democracy?* (London: National Peace Council, 1946), 14–16, 15. Orwell owned this pamphlet. See British Library, SS.29.2.

mastery and subordination': Tawney, *Equality*, 152.

.74 open to question: (9.229).

in the 1920s and '30s: Engels had once promoted communism as the triumph of 'real equality' over inauthentic versions, but he too distanced himself from such rhetoric. Marx and Engels, *Collected Works*, 3:398. As he declared in 1875: 'The concept of a socialist society as a realm of equality is a one-sided French concept'. Whatever the historical value of equality as a principle, it now 'produced nothing but mental confusion'. Marx and Engels, *Collected Works*, 45.64.

strides to vanquish: J. V. Stalin, *Collected Works*, 13 vols. (Moscow: Foreign Languages Publishing House, 1952–5), 13.121.

one of inequality': Sidney and Beatrice Webb, *Soviet Communism: A New Civilisation?*, 2.702.

a socialist objective': Lyons, *Assignment in Utopia*, 419. Orwell reviewed the book positively in June 1938 (11.158–60).

the same charge: Leon Trotsky, *The Revolution Betrayed: What is the Soviet Union and Where is it Going?*, trans. Max Eastman (London: Faber, 1937), 110–15. In 1937 Max Eastman would also proclaim that 'the experiment in socialism in Russia is at an end'. See Max Eastman, *The End of Socialism in Russia* (London: Secker & Warburg, 1937), 46.

to do with equality': Goldstein argues in *Nineteen Eighty-Four* that from 1900 socialism increasingly abandons both liberty and equality as its fundamental goals (9.211).

grab-motive left intact': (6.83).

means nothing at all': (6.84). See also his review of Jack Common's *The Freedom of the Streets*, where he declared that 'the mystique of proletarian Socialism is the idea of equality' (11.162).

other political values: As he put it in *The Road to Wigan Pier*: 'the only thing he [Wells] cares to imagine is inequality' (5.188).

substituted for another (economic)': E. F. M. Durbin, *The Politics of Democratic Socialism* (London: Routledge, 1940), 270.

75 ruled by stoats': (5.200).

air of equality': (6.83).

militia uniform': (6.3).

to have wildly exaggerated: See Paul Preston, 'Lights and Shadows in George Orwell's *Homage to Catalonia*', *Bulletin of Spanish Studies*, Published Online, 23 October 2017.

supercilious bastard': Quoted in Richard Baxell, *Unlikely Warriors: The Extraordinary Story of the Britons Who Fought in the Spanish Civil War* (London: Aurum Press, 2012), 187.

everyone else "*Comrade*"': (6.3).

Are we not all comrades?': (6.7).

complete equality': (6.26).

p.76 argue with the officer': (6.7).

'comradeship': (6.27).

away from egalitarianism': (16.52).

it was not far from it': (6.83).

when running an army: In 1939 Orwell suggested that plans to 'democratise' the British military would 'rob the army of efficiency for five or ten years'—an impossible cost when the aim was to 'stop Hitler' (11.406).

symptomatic of the problem: (6.190).

agents such as the USSR: On the role of Russia, see Stanley G. Payne, *The Spanish Civil War, the Soviet Union and Communism* (New Haven, CT: Yale University Press, 2004).

account of the P.O.U.M "line"': (11.256).

p.77 so is Fascism': (6.203).

dictatorship had passed': (6.132–3).

would have foreseen': (11.333). However, in different polemical circumstances in 1941 he claimed that the 'Spanish Republican Government...from the very beginning of the civil war, outraged every principle of Democracy' (12.463).

Tweedledum and Tweedledee': (11.77).

depress me horribly': (12.5).

a Stalinist mantra: (13.68).

most of his writing life: (18.319).

developed form of democracy': Strachey, *The Theory and Practice of Socialism*, 137. For Trotsky, the task of communism was to supplant a purely 'formal democracy' with 'pure democracy'. Leon Trotsky, *The History of the Russian Revolution*, trans. Max Eastman (London: Victor Gollancz, 1936), 36–67. According to Stalin: 'Democracy in Capitalist countries...is democracy for the strong, democracy for the propertied minority. In the U.S.S.R., on the contrary, democracy is democracy for the toilers, that is democracy for all'. See Joseph Stalin, *The New Democracy: Stalin's Speech on the New Constitution* (London: Lawrence & Wishart, 1936), 22.

p.78 Capitalist democracy': (11.169).

negated by its capitalist setting: As he put it: 'British democracy is very far from being a sham' (12.363); 'British Democracy is *not* altogether a sham' (12.381); British democracy 'is less a fraud than it sometimes appears' (12.400).

'genuine democracy': (12.345).

'democratic': (12.381).

democratic means': (12.377). It was hardly a surprise, therefore, that he regarded the 'problem of making fundamental changes by democratic methods' to be the burning issue of his time (11.332).

the socialist movement suffers from': G. D. H. Cole, *The Left News*, 70 (April 1942), 2069–73, 2072.

claimed to be its champion: (17.425).

'organic popular democracy': See *The New Democracy: Stalin's Speech on the New Constitution*, 22. Stalin's remarks are also cited in E. H. Carr, *Democracy in International Affairs* (Nottingham: University College, 1945), 4. On Franco, see Stanley G. Payne, *The Franco Regime, 1936–75* (Madison, WI: University of Wisconsin Press, 1987), 355.

edifying spectacle': (19.292).

they know nothing about': (13.69).

most active in the debates': (8.19).

'aristocracy of orators': See Hobbes, *The Elements of Law, Natural and Politic*, ed. J. C. A. Gaskin (Oxford: Oxford University Press, 2008), 120.

·79 Parliamentary democracy': (13.291).

'relatively unimportant': (16.68).

not altogether a sham': (12.381).

absurd to call Britain democratic': (16.71). He produced a slightly extended version of this in May 1944: 'If democracy means either popular rule or social equality, it is clear that Britain is not democratic' (16.214). According to Schumpeter, it was always absurd to think that democratic government embodies 'the will of the people'. Joseph A. Schumpeter, *Capitalism, Socialism, and Democracy* (London and New York: Routledge, 1992), 254.

conduct of the government': (13.67).

part of the price: Tawney, 'Christianity and the Social Revolution', in *The Attack and Other Papers*, 165–6.

80 preferred to equality': Tawney, *Equality*, 238.

English people desire': (16.217).

'more social equality': (13.302).

they want equality': (18.62).

more important than anything else': (18.71).

makes democracy impossible': (16.71).

set about this': (16.181).

'treacherous minority': (12.422).

81 principles of human conduct': William Godwin, *Selections from Political Justice*, ed. George Woodcock (London: Freedom Press, 1943), 20. British Library, SS.4.39.

'parable-art': Auden, 'Psychology and Art To-day', in *Prose*, I.93–105, 104. According to Meyer, Orwell initially presented his tale as 'a kind of parable'. See Michael Meyer, *Not Prince Hamlet: Literary and Theatrical Memoirs* (London: Secker & Warburg, 1989), 68.

Russian communism: For a detailed account of the way the novella tracks events in Soviet history, see Alok Rai, *Orwell and the Politics of Despair* (Cambridge: Cambridge University Press, 1988), 81–112.

pretend anything else': (19.234). This was not an uncontroversial position at the time. In 1947 Laski was still insisting that 'The Russian Revolution is the greatest, and the most beneficent event in modern history since the French Revolution'. Harold Laski, *The Webbs and Soviet Communism* (London: Fabian Society, 1943), 8.

'monstrous inequality': Leon Trotsky, *I Stake My Life!—Dewey Reports on the Moscow Trials* (London: Workers International League, 1937), 21. Orwell owned this pamphlet: see British Library, SS.3.50.

'little anti-Stalin book': (17.120).

'a variation of Bonapartism': Trotsky, *The Revolution Betrayed*, 278. The ex-Trotskyite Burnham would also equate Stalinism with Bonapartism. See Burnham, *The Machiavellians*, 176–9. 'With Trotsky', Bertrand Russell declared, 'the comparison with Napoleon was forced upon one'. Bertrand Russell, *The Practice and Theory of Bolshevism* (London: George Allen & Unwin, 1920), 43.

wider application': (18.507).

short work of these distinctions: G. K. Chesterton, 'Introduction', in *Aesop's Fables* (London: Heinemann, 1912), v–xi, vii.

p.82 | peculiarly extended life: According to Isaac Rosenberg, the scope of the novella is 'over-extended' and distorts the facts it depicts. See Isaac Rosenfeld, *Nation*, 7 September, 1946, 273–4, in *The Critical Heritage*, ed. Jeffrey Meyers (London: Routledge & Kegan Paul, 1975), 201–4, 204.

so ideologically problematic: For praise of its 'permanence', see Williams, *Orwell*, 74.

liberty and equality: (12.196).

circular account of revolution: For some consideration of the different ideas of revolution at work in the fable, see V. C. Letemendia, 'Revolution on Animal Farm: Orwell's Neglected Commentary', *Journal of Modern Literature*, 18.1 (1992): 127–37.

that is, badly': (8.34).

radical change is impossible: As he put it in 1940: 'The mental connexion between pessimism and a reactionary outlook is no doubt obvious enough' (12.98).

vindicated by history: (12.150).

'reactionary bromide': Northrop Frye, 'Turning New Leaves', *Canadian Forum* (December 1946): 211–12, in Jeffrey Meyer (ed.), *George Orwell: The Critical Heritage*, 206–9, 208.

power instinct': (17.344). Ellipsis mine. Writing from his prison cell prior to execution, Bukharin declared that the 'lust for power' would disappear in the egalitarianism of the future, but Orwell never seemed to have possessed this confidence. For Bukharin's views, see Nikolai Bukharin, *The Prison Manuscripts: Socialism and its Culture*, trans. George Shriver (London, New York, Calcutta: Seagull Books, 2006), 146.

p.83 | root-and-branch change: For a particularly scathing account of the book, see Stephen Sedley, 'An Immodest Proposal', in *Inside the Myth. Orwell: Views from the Left*, ed. Christopher Norris (London: Lawrence & Wishart, 1984), 155–62. In 1938 Orwell declared it 'an unfortunate fact that any hostile criticism of the present Russian regime is liable to be taken as propaganda *against Socialism*' (11.159).

against America': (19.180). For a brief history of the book's reception, see John Rodden, *George Orwell: The Politics of Literary Reputation* (New Brunswick, NJ: Transaction, 2002), 19–26, 384–7, 394–8.

handled sufficiently well': Letter from William Empson to George Orwell, 24 August 1945; quoted in Gordon Bowker, *George Orwell* (London: Little, Brown, 2003), 336.

and vice versa: William Empson, *The Listener*, 16 September, 1965, 422. Quoted in John Haffenden, *William Empson*. Volume II: *Against the Christians* (Oxford: Oxford University Press, 2006), 498.

non-human beings?: According to Stewart Cole, Orwell's answer to this question is an ethically complacent 'no'. *Animal Farm* rests upon 'an unbridgeable ontological gulf between human and nonhuman animals' that is sustained even as it is being ostensibly overcome by the conventions of the fable. See Stewart Cole, ' "The True Struggle": Orwell and the Specter of the Animal', *Literature Interpretation Theory*, 28.4 (2017): 335–53, 337.

'All men are created equal': *In Congress, July 4, 1776. A Declaration by the Representatives of the United States of America, in General Congress Assembled* (Boston, MA: John Gill, and Powars, and Willis, 1776), 1.

abstractions in algebra': Chesterton, 'Introduction', in *Aesop's Fables*, vii.

as a value: For an account of the distinction between descriptive and normative concepts of equality, see Bernard Williams, 'The Idea of Equality', in *Problems of the Self* (Cambridge: Cambridge University Press, 1973), 230–49.

things ought to be: (8.6).

grounds the norm: On this point, see Williams, 'The Idea of Equality', 97.

first-rate intelligence': (8.2).

admiration of everybody': (8.18).

he does all his mischief" ': (8.22).

question against them: (8.6).

life of his carcase': (5.162). According to Greenblatt, 'Orwell in *Animal Farm* loves animals only as much or as little as he loves human beings'. See Stephen Greenblatt, 'Orwell as Satirist', in *George Orwell: A Collection of Critical Essays*, ed. Raymond Williams (Englewood Cliffs, NJ: Prentice Hall, 1974), 103–18, 107.

'miserable, laborious and short': (8.3).

rich exploit the proletariat: (19.88).

'All animals are equal': (8.6).

equivalent to racism and sexism: Peter Singer, 'All Animals are Equal', *Philosophical Exchange*, 1.5 (1974): 243–57.

priority over animals: Cole, ' "The True Struggle": Orwell and the Specter of the Animal', 339.

like animals': (9.74).

one species of animal': (13.504).

bees or coral insects?': (11.417).

'human equality': (12.430).

bag for putting food into': (5.84).

equality of human beings: Hobbes, *Leviathan*, 87.

equality of man': W. H. Auden and Christopher Isherwood, 'In Time of War', in *Journey to a War* (London: Faber, 1939), 14.

idea of equality': (12.430).

souls are equal before God: Huxley was keen to insist that 'men's equality before God', did not imply 'their equality as among themselves'. Aldous Huxley, 'The Idea of Equality', in *Complete Essays*, 2.150–66, 151.

'fully human life': (14.254).

'more human or less human': (18.32).

'a human and an inhuman world': (5.204).

'deeply human atmosphere': (5.108).

more 'human' than capitalism: (12.41).

behave as human beings': (6.4).

equal respect and concern: Indeed, 'the basis of socialism', Orwell insisted, 'is humanism', and 'animalism' in *Animal Farm* is arguably a coded version of both. Its fundamental tenet—'All animals are equal' (8.6)—is, for Orwell, a disguised humanism. This puts him on the same page as the early Marx, for whom 'communism . . . equals humanism'. See Marx and Engels, *Collected Works*, 3.296.

even inhuman types': (5.169).

vague as it was winsome: According to one sweeping assessment, 'Orwell represents the confused and self-destructive motives of a liberal humanism finally run aground on its own bankrupt ideology'. Christopher Norris, 'Language, Truth and Ideology: Orwell and the Postwar Left', in *Inside the Myth*, 245–62, 245.

p.88 | line of criticism: Marx, *Collected Works*, 6.330.

professes to indict: (13.153).

radical political change: (16.294).

human nature, can change': (14.160). The underlying premise of socialism, he declared in 1946, is that 'human nature is fairly decent to start with and is capable of indefinite development' (18.62).

couple of generations': (16.294).

breed of hornless cows': (11.317).

not completely empty: For a philosophical defence of this position, see Bernard Williams in 'The Idea of Equality', 99–101.

not human beings': (12.122). Despite his own chauvinistic moments, he deplored a type of racism in which the other is 'looked upon as a different kind of animal' (12.121). He lamented the fact that 'the white race can't, in fact, look on the negro quite as a human being' (12.153).

aren't human beings': (12.123).

into the world to destroy': (12.430).

belief in human *inequality*': (12.411). Nazi propaganda explicitly rejected a 'socialism of equality' for a 'God-given inequality'. See Wolfgang Bialas and Lothar Fritze, *Nazi Ideology and Ethics* (Cambridge: Cambridge Scholars, 2014), 27.

Nordic man is fully human': (12.411).

different categories of men': (19.465).

p.89 | more about this later): In *Animal Farm*, for instance, a 'new class system is born based on *biological* inequality'. Paul Kirschner, 'The Dual Purpose of *Animal Farm*', *The Review of English Studies*, 55.222 (2004): 759–86, 769.

treat them equally': Hayek, *Individualism: True and False*, 15.

the same manner to all': ibid., 16.

All to the good: Hesiod, *Works and Days* and *Theogony*, trans. Stanley Lombardo, introd. Robert Lamberton (Indianapolis, IN; Cambridge: Hackett, 1993), 31–2.

which was which': (8.95).

to think the same: Macmurray, *The Philosophy of Communism*, 93.

.90 the form of justice: (8.15).

legal understanding: (8.21).

one for the poor': (12.397). Laski claimed the same in 1925: 'there is one law for the rich and one law for the poor'. Laski, *Socialism and Freedom*, 8.

impartially administered': (12.397).

.91 not particular, but universal': Tawney, *Equality*, 238.

action was permissible: See, in particular, Immanuel Kant, *Groundwork of the Metaphysics of Morals*, ed. Mary J. Gregor (Cambridge: Cambridge University Press, 1997), 26–32.

.92 imagined it in detail: On this point, see Barbara Herman, *The Practice of Moral Judgment* (Cambridge, MA: Harvard University Press, 1993), 116–19. See also Allen W. Wood, *Kant's Ethical Thought* (Cambridge: Cambridge University Press, 1999), 89. Those committed to the ideal of a Kantian farm might still argue that killing could not be universalized on a practical basis because not everyone— those, for instance, who are killed—could adopt it as a maxim. Nor is it certain, they might add, that a state of universal war can be coherently willed. If a necessary constituent of rational willing is that one desires the satisfaction of one's ends, it would be difficult to see what ends could be secured in such a belligerent environment.

93 very necessary': Shaw, 'Preface' to *On the Rocks*, in *The Works of Bernard Shaw* (London: Constable 1931), 31.145–91, 148.

animal *without cause*': (8.61).

without self-contradiction: (8.15).

point of view': (19.88).

94 a porcine Marx: Jeffrey Meyers, *Orwell: Life and Art* (Urbana, IL: University of Illinois Press, 2010), 117.

incoherent in its application: (8.6). Old Major also declares that 'we are all brothers' (8.6). But Marx took issue with the initial credo of the Communist League—'All men are brothers' (Marx purportedly declared that there were many men whose brother he did not wish to be). The League's motto was consequently changed to 'Proletarians of all countries—unite'. See David McLellan, *Karl Marx: His Life and Thought* (London: Harper & Row, 1973), 172.

'fair distribution': Marx and Engels, *Collected Works*, 24.85.

each according to his needs!': ibid., 24.87.

throughout the 1930s: V. I. Lenin, *The State and Revolution*, in *Collected Works*, 25.381–492, 468. See *The New Democracy: Stalin's Speech on the New Constitution*, 13. For its uses on the Left, see Harold Laski, *Communism* (London: Williams & Norgate, 1927), 177–8; J. A. Hobson, *Wealth and Life: A Study in Values* (London: Macmillan & Co., 1929), 220–2.

egalitarian values: Strachey, *The Theory and Practice of Socialism*, 112. See also Sidney and Beatrice Webb, *Soviet Communism*, 702.

most appropriate to them': Tawney, *Equality*, 51–2.

principles of the USSR: Stalin, *The New Democracy: Stalin's Speech on the New Constitution*, 13.

protecting the weak': (8.58).

according to its needs: Elsewhere, Orwell would claim that ' "Communism" meant a free and just society based on the principle of "to each according to his needs" ' (19.268–9).

possible to be': (8.18).

well-being of a pig': (8.23).

p.95   nobody should have them': (16.102).

'luxury feeding': (13.303).

drink alcohol', etc.: (8.15).

people with empty bellies': (5.82).

the surface of life': (5.83).

nothing had happened': (8.19).

p.96   dealing with such figures: Shaw, 'Preface' to *On the Rocks*, 160. 'A great many people would have to be put out of existence simply because it wastes other people's time to look after them'. George Bernard Shaw, 'Eugenics Education Society Lecture', *The Daily Express*, 4 March 1910. Cited in Dan Stone, *Breeding Superman: Nietzsche, Race and Eugenics in Edwardian and Interwar Britain* (Liverpool: Liverpool University Press, 2002), 127.

a matter of course': G. B. Shaw to G. Wallas, 5.6.1928, Wallas Papers 1/89. Cited in Jackson, *Equality and the British Left: A Study in Progressive Thought*, 45. Indeed, in a 1931 broadcast to Americans, Shaw suggested that individuals should be forced to justify their existence on a regular basis before a qualified jury: if they failed to do so, they should 'be summarily and painlessly terminated'. George Bernard Shaw, *Look, You Boob! What Bernard Shaw Told the Americans about Russia! His Famous Broadcast* (London: The Friends of the Soviet Union, 1931), 12.

principle of socialism': Lenin, *Collected Works*, 27.391.

kind of compulsion': (19.438).

at different times': Strachey, *The Theory and Practice of Socialism*, 134.

blaming for bad work': ibid., 131.

communism of the future: Marx and Engels, *Collected Works*, 24:87.

'an acute positive pleasure': (8.18).

'sordid' labour: (8.35).

minds with conversation': (8.32). Ellipsis mine.

p.97   First Class': (8.28).

Second Class': (8.28–9).

need of both systems: He distinguishes between these types of equality in a foot-note to the *Second Discourse*. See Jean-Jacques Rousseau, *The Discourses and Other Early Political Writings*, ed. Victor Gourevitch (Cambridge: Cambridge University Press, 1997), 221–2.

'Animal Hero, Second Class': (18.55).

inducement to perform it': Tawney, *Equality*, 156.

in Plato's eyes: Plato, *The Republic*, 127.

p.98   assume the leadership': (8.17).

superior virtue: (16.282–3).

beneficial upbringing: Anthony Crosland, *The Future of Socialism* (London: Jonathan Cape, 1956), 236.

leadership for themselves: Sidney and Beatrice Webb, *The Decay of Capitalist Civilisation*, 3rd ed. (London: George Allen & Unwin, 1923), 124.

'rational conversation': Adam Smith, *An Inquiry into the Nature and Causes of the Wealth of Nations*, 2 vols., ed. R. H. Campbell, A. S. Kinner, and W. B. Todd (Oxford: Oxford University Press, 2002), vol. 2, 781.

physical monster': Marx and Engels, *Collected Works*, 3.44, 220.

a plausible prediction: ibid., 5.47.

differences of wealth': (9.212).

modern social structures: James Burnham, *The Managerial Revolution: What is Happening in the World* (New York: John Day Co., 1941), 73.

clearly attest: For his criticisms of this fatalism, see 16.61. For his praise of Burnham's 'intellectual courage' and diagnostic powers, see 19.99.

'the paradise of the able': See George Bernard Shaw, 'Socialism and Superior Brains', in *The Works of Bernard Shaw*, 30.261–95, 286.

equal opportunity: According to Crosland, 'the creation of equal opportunities may merely serve to replace a remote elite (based on lineage) by a new one (based on ability and intelligence)'. Crosland, *The Future of Socialism*, 233.

source of injustice': See Trotsky, *The Revolution Betrayed*, 259. Ellipsis mine.

the present system: (5.159).

attraction to this form: Chesterton, 'Introduction', in *Aesop's Fables*, v.

the political sphere: Schumpeter, *Capitalism, Socialism, and Democracy*, 262.

dictatorship of theorists': (12.141).

'dictatorship of the prigs': (5.170).

a millimetre nearer': (9.210).

'we are all brothers': (8.6).

CHAPTER 3

as well as I liked him: (6.1–2). Ellipses mine.

human brotherhood: On the different origins and ethical valences of 'solidarity' and 'brotherhood', see Steinar Stjerno, *Solidarity in Europe: The History of an Idea* (Cambridge: Cambridge University Press, 2004), 25–30.

'human equality': (12.430).

may bear this out: Norman Kelvin (ed.), *William Morris on Art and Socialism* (Mineola, NY: Dover, 1999), 17. L. T. Hobhouse also argued that solidarity embodies 'the real meaning of equality'. See L. T. Hobhouse, 'Liberalism', in *Liberalism and Other Writings*, ed. James Meadowcroft (Cambridge: Cambridge University Press, 1994), 58.

stupendous intellectual feat': (6.1).

'pathetic reverence': (6.1).

imply their equality': Huxley, 'The Idea of Equality', in *Complete Essays*, 2.151.

'the necessary murder': (12.103–4).

context of war: As Auden put it in a letter to Monroe Spears in May 1963: 'To kill another human being is always murder and should never be called anything else'. But he also conceded that 'If there is such a thing as a just war, then murder can be necessary for the sake of justice'. See Monroe K. Spears, *The Poetry of W. H. Auden* (New York: Oxford University Press, 1963), 157.

p.105   sake of loyalty': (20.8).

callousness towards another': (19.41).

competitive prestige': (17.442).

'great modern disease': (19.92).

human brotherhood': (12.126).

'friendship with the world': Roy Walker (ed.), *The Wisdom of Gandhi in His Own Words* (London: Dakers, 1943), 16. Orwell's copy of this contained the interesting inscription 'To George Orwell—who seems to need it'. See British Library, 1899.SS.1.

'not an abstraction': (12.126).

to mean something': (13.502).

p.106   see him again': (6.2). Ellipsis mine.

No power can disinherit': (13.512).

confidence to the test: Bertrand Russell, *Roads to Freedom: Socialism, Anarchism and Syndicalism* (London: Allen & Unwin, 1918), 159.

poisonous to literature': (19.291). As Collini argues, 'Orwell's constant idealization of the true writer as a lonely rebel rests upon an implicit binary opposition between "individual integrity" and "collective self-deception"'. Collini, *Absent Minds*, 367.

conceptions of fellowship: Orwell, in this respect, was very similar to the early Shaw. In 1885 Shaw dismissed all 'fraternity mongering' on 'individualist' grounds. He was, he argued, 'nobody's comrade'. See Joseph O. Baylen, 'George Bernard Shaw and the Socialist League: Some Unpublished Letters', *International Review of Social History*, 7.3 (1962): 426–40, 431–2.

community singing': (12.99).

community life very much': Auden, 'Problems of Education', in *Prose*, 1.27.

p.107   so Orwell believed: (12.55).

as it is aesthetic: (13.509).

blackleg in strike: (5.107).

all altruism and all justice': (4.109).

creatures with black faces': (2.122).

a dead cat': (1.130).

ye are brethren': Matthew, 23:8, KJV.

p.108   to be immortal: (12.125–6). Ellipsis mine.

euphemized this may be: For Carl Schmitt, this friend–enemy distinction was the constitutive principle of political life. A universal solidarity, therefore, would seem to involve a total transcendence of politics. Carl Schmitt, *The Concept of the Political*, trans. George Schwab (Chicago, IL: University of Chicago Press, 1996), 26–7.

them that hate you': Matthew, 5:44, KJV.

in certain circumstances': (12.456).

only a cell': (12.125).

illiberal implications: The subordination of the individual to the community was sometimes an explicit feature of English socialism. As Sidney Webb explained, socialism meant 'the real recognition of fraternity, the universal obligation of personal service, and the subordination of individual ends to the common good'. Sidney Webb, *Socialism in England* (London: Swan Sonnenschein, 1890), 10.

cut your fingernails?: (9.276).

from the loving breast': (9.311).

I care nothing of all': James Fitzjames Stephens, *Liberty, Equality, Fraternity*, 2nd ed. (London: Smith, Elder & Co., 1874), 304.

some are Cains': Marx and Engels, *Collected Works*, 6.519. Jones is quoted in Hal Draper, *Karl Marx's Theory of Revolution*, 6 vols. (New York: Monthly Review Press, 1977–c.2005), 4.38.

esteem as brothers: See Steinar Stjerno, *Solidarity in Europe*, 44–6.

109   contradictory class interests': Marx and Engels, *Collected Works*, 10.58.

'we are all brothers': (8.6).

Marx's stated views: The fraternal ethos of Orwell's noble pig—and the fact that it is derived from a dream—has much more in common with William Morris. Of course, the theme of fraternity would continue to be strongly advanced within English socialism. As Hardie put it, 'Socialism means fraternity, founded on justice'. Quoted in Kenneth O. Morgan, *Keir Hardie: Radical and Socialist* (London: Wiedenfeld & Nicolson, 1975), 207.

all countries, unite!': See Draper, *Karl Marx's Theory of Revolution*, 4.37. Shaw was equally uninterested in universal brotherhood under unjust conditions: 'So far from idealizing fraternity, we show the working class that they must utterly refuse to fraternise with those who deny them the rights of social equals'. Shaw, 'Socialism and Human Nature', in *The Road to Equality*, 89–102, 101.

partisan or class-specific: Thus, Engels would call for 'the brotherhood of the workers' to stand firm against 'the brotherhood of the bourgeoisie'. Marx and Engels, *Collected Works*, 6.390.

'universal brotherhood swindle': ibid., 11.180.

fact of life': ibid., 3.212.

spheres of society': ibid., 3.186.

domination in general: ibid., 6.212; also 6.506.

real interests are opposed': (5.212).

to act together': (5.211).

110   'the class-difficulty': (5.208).

hierarchy of classes': (5.208).

account of class struggle: According to Stalin, however, 'mankind is divided into rich and poor, into property owners and exploited'. See G. Bernard Shaw, H. G. Wells, J. M. Keynes, Ernst Toller, and others, *The Stalin-Wells Talk: The Verbatim Report and Discussion* (London: New Statesman and Nation, 1934), 9.

a fountain pen': (5.213).

with the mouse': (5.212).

people are the same': (5.214).

Asiatic coolies': (13.153).

so vast: (16.23).

p.111 | I would answer': (1.113–14). Ellipsis mine.

captain above a private: (1.69).

any demonstration of it: (1.76).

slaves of them': (1.117).

Marxist smell: (5.208).

so Marx contended: Marx and Engels, *Collected Works*, 11.187.

'class interests': ibid., 6.211.

another pompous expression: (5.163).

p.112 | education of the masses': (16.398).

cannot become conscious': (9.74). Marx suggested that revolution was intrinsically educative: 'the revolution is necessary, therefore, not only because the *ruling* class cannot be overthrown in any other way, but also because the class *overthrowing* it can only in a revolution succeed in ridding itself of all the muck of ages and become fitted to found society anew', Marx and Engels, *Collected Works*, 5.53.

philanthropic bourgeois: ibid., 24.264.

historical movement as a whole: ibid., 6.494.

the working class: On this point, see Valentine Cunningham, *British Writers of the Thirties* (Oxford: Clarendon, 1988), 211.

Marx-quoting type': (5.171).

the Lower Orders': (5.167).

the working class?': (5.162). Ellipsis mine.

p.113 | to commit suicide': (5.157).

get through it': (5.145).

'pernicious rubbish': (5.149).

make an effort': (5.150).

against their tyrants': (5.138).

'the lowest of the low': (5.142).

vulnerable to this outlook himself: According to Stephen Spender, Orwell 'was really classless', but many have had their doubts. See Spender, *World Review* (June 1950): 51–4, in *George Orwell: The Critical Heritage*, 134–7, 134.

towards the light': (13.506).

p.114 | '*emotional* Socialism': (5.225).

political significance: For a recent defence of the politics of compassion, see Martha C. Nussbaum, *Political Emotions: Why Love Matters for Justice* (Cambridge, MA: Belknap Press, 2013), 137–60. See also Martha Nussbaum, 'Compassion: The Basic Social Emotion', *Social Philosophy and Policy*, 13 (1996): 27–58.

Nothing very much': (13.501).

p.115 | fascism or anti-fascism: As Hume put it in the *Treatise*: ''Tis certain, that the imagination is more affected by what is particular, than by what is general; and that the sentiments are always mov'd with difficulty, where their objects are, in any degree, loose and undetermin'd'. See David Hume, *Treatise of Human Nature*, ed. David Fate Norton and Mary J. Norton (Oxford: Oxford University Press, 2000), 370.

species in general: Rousseau, *The Discourses and Other Early Political Writings*, 153. For a discussion of the limits of sympathy in Rousseau, see Richard Boyd, 'Pity's Pathologies Portrayed: Rousseau and the Limits of Democratic Compassion', *Political Theory*, 32.4 (2004): 519–46.

our hearts to humanity': Jean-Jacques Rousseau, *Émile*, trans. Allan Bloom (London: Penguin, 1991), 221.

murder to children: (9.11). In Rousseau, it is market women who intercede in brawls to keep the combatants from murdering each other. The philosopher and the prudent man simply walk on by. Rousseau, *The Discourses and Other Early Political Writings*, 154.

claims of persons': Harold Laski, *Faith, Reason and Civilisation*, 113.

116 | some people's books: Schmitt, *The Concept of the Political*, 26–7.

intolerable wrongs': (12.117).

cruelty to men': Rousseau, *Émile*, 253. However, Rousseau also encouraged readers 'to love all men, even those who despise men'; ibid., 228.

learn to hate': Quoted in Kevin Morgan, *Harry Pollitt* (London: Lawrence and Wishart, 1985), 133.

expect from justice: (16.138).

justice in political life: Rousseau would also argue that pity must either cede to or be tempered by justice: 'To prevent pity from degenerating into weakness, it must, therefore, be generalized and extended to the whole of mankind. The one yields to it only insofar as it accords with justice, because of all the virtues, justice is the one that contributes most to the common good of men'. Rousseau, *Émile*, 253.

117 | responsible for them: (5.136).

administer it ruthlessly': (5.137).

118 | one world less: (10.208–9).

that abominable noise': (10.208).

suffering of others is a relief': Judith Shklar, *Ordinary Vices* (Cambridge, MA: Belknap Press, 1984), 36.

the job was done': (10.210).

119 | moderated by it: Rousseau, *The Discourses and Other Early Political Writings*, 152.

to snigger': (10.210).

a hundred yards away: (12.210).

120 | suffering as he does': Rousseau, *Émile*, 221.

people want to kick you': (1.49).

the experiences of others: Rousseau, *Émile*, 223.

does nothing morally': George Eliot, Letter to Charles Bray, 5 July 1859, in *Collected Letters*, ed. Gordon S. Haight, 6 vols. (New Haven, CT: Yale University Press), 3.111.

'compassionate citizenship': See Nussbaum, *Political Emotions*, 21. See also Martha Nussbaum, *Poetic Justice: The Literary Imagination and Public Life* (Boston, MA: Beacon Press, 1996); Martha Nussbaum, *Love's Knowledge: Essays on Philosophy and Literature* (Oxford: Oxford University Press, 1990), 168–219.

fellow sufferers': Richard Rorty, *Contingency, Irony, and Solidarity*, xvi.

worst sort of evil: This is what Rorty (drawing on Shklar) argues about Orwell—ibid., 169–88.

expense of the living': Jean-Jacques Rousseau, *Politics and the Arts: Letter to M. D'Alembert*, trans. Allan Bloom (Ithaca, NY: Cornell University Press, 1968), 17.

p.121 anywhere near them': (5.131).

become one of them': (5.141).

first contact with poverty': (1.13).

one of its constituents: (5.106).

p.122 I have ever seen': (5.15).

understands her plight: (5.15).

for his insults': Morgan, *Harry Pollitt*, 4.

mean grievances': (5.14).

a visceral disgust: For a discussion of disgust in Orwell, see William Ian Miller, *An Anatomy of Disgust* (Cambridge, MA: Harvard University Press, 1997), 235–54.

predominantly olfactory: On the olfactory nature of Orwellian disgust, see John Sutherland, *Orwell's Nose: A Pathological Biography* (London: Reaktion Books, 2016).

'*the lower classes smell*': (5.119).

than the upper classes': (5.121).

dishonest to deny': (17.204).

you will hate him: (5.119).

our sense of smell': (5.121). See Somerset Maugham, *On a Chinese Screen* (London: Heinemann, 1922), 142.

p.123 disgusted me very much': (1.132).

base animality of others: Nussbaum, *Political Emotions*, 186.

time to time': (10.405).

belief in human dignity: In a broadcast for the BBC, he imagines Swift in contemporary London surrounded once again by 'the same hideous faces, unshapely bodies and ill-fitting clothes' (14.158). However, he also criticizes Swift for only seeing the 'dirty and ridiculous' side of human character (14.161).

that is humanity': (9.285).

'impudent social parasites': (1.204–5).

'spiritual halitosis': (4.102).

defeated by love: Nussbaum, *Political Emotions*, 211.

p.124 will of love is done': W. H. Auden and Christopher Isherwood, *On the Frontier*, in *The Complete Works of W. H. Auden: Plays and Other Dramatic Writings, 1928–38*, ed. Edward Mendelson (Princeton, NJ: Princeton University Press, 1988), 357–418, 418. John Strachey continued to argue in this key in the '40s: the aim was 'to establish, for the first time, the authority of love upon this earth'. John Strachey, *A Faith to Fight For* (London: Victor Gollancz, 1941), 93.

'universal love' in the '30s: As Auden put it in 1946, 'one thing, and one thing only, is serious: loving one's neighbour as one's self'. Auden, 'Address on Henry James', in *Prose*, 2.296–303, 2.302. Or, allowing for human fallibility, the rule became: 'You shall love your crooked neighbour / With your crooked heart'. W. H. Auden, 'As I Walked Out One Evening', in *Collected Poems*, 133–5, 135.

desirable end': Spender, *Forward from Liberalism*, 170.

reducible to 'love': Murry, *The Necessity of Communism*, 115.

realities of class conflict: See, in particular, Marx and Engels, 'Circular against Kriege', *Collected Works*, 6.36–51.

everything remains unchanged: ibid., 21.289. For a discussion of these critiques of 'sentimental socialism', see Draper, *Karl Marx's Theory of Revolution*, 4.22–40.

neighbourly love: See Anna Vaninskaya, *William Morris and the Idea of Community: Romance, History and Propaganda, 1880–1914* (Edinburgh: Edinburgh University Press, 2010), 143.

took to their hearts: Francis Johnson, *Keir Hardie's Socialism* (London: ILP, 1922), 10–11.

perversion and unrest': Caudwell, *Studies in a Dying Culture*, 148.

love one another or die': W. H. Auden, 'September 1, 1939', in *The Early Auden*, ed. Edward Mendelson (London: Faber, 1981), 245–6.

particular love-summons: As is well known, Auden later regarded 'September 1, 1939' as 'the most dishonest poem that I have ever written'. Richard Davenport-Hines, *Auden* (London: Heinemann, 1995), 319.

'Love the Beloved Republic': Forster, 'What I Believe', in *Two Cheers for Democracy*, 67.

does not work': ibid., 44.

onerous form of loyalty: (18.424–5).

freely assented to: 'But love is a feeling [*Empfindung*], that is, ethical life in its natural form. In the state, it is no longer present. There, one is conscious of unity as law; there, the content must be rational, and I must know it'. G. W. F. Hegel, *Elements of the Philosophy of Right*, ed. Allen W. Wood, trans. H. B. Nisbet (Cambridge: Cambridge University Press, 1991), 199.

respect and justice': Stephens, *Liberty, Equality, Fraternity*, 274.

potentially totalitarian: (18.424).

love of Big Brother': (9.280).

founded upon hatred': (9.279).

deliberate method of rule: Borkenau, *The Totalitarian Enemy*, 137.

plumber's blow-flame': (12.159).

a blow-lamp': (9.16).

against the Party': (9.133).

Julia! Not me!': (9.300). Ellipsis mine.

'All you care about is yourself': (3.305).

'He loved Big Brother': (9.311).

'privacy, love and friendship': (9.32).

making love go public: W. H. Auden, 'A Bride in the 30's', in *Collected Poems*, 128–30, 129.

sense of brotherhood: As he put it in 1937, 'I am not one of your fashionable pansies like Auden and Spender' (11.67).

insufficient virtue: Aristotle, *The Nicomachean Ethics*, ed. and trans. Roger Crisp (Cambridge: Cambridge University Press, 2000), 144. Of course, the moral purity and intimate nature of this type of friendship is easily exaggerated: such amity, Aristotle admitted, was generally motivated by estimates of utility or personal advantage, although it could eventually evolve into something more ethically substantive. On this point, see E. Irrera, 'Between Advantage and Virtue: Aristotle's Theory of Political Friendship', *History of Political Thought*, 26.4 (Winter 2005): 565–85. Jill Frank, *A Democracy of Distinction: Aristotle and the Work of Politics* (Chicago, IL: Chicago University Press, 2005), 138–80. See, too, Bernard Yack, 'Community and Conflict in Aristotle's Political Philosophy', *The Review of Politics*, 47.1 (1985): 92–112.

his verse and Spender's: Auden, 'Introduction to *The Portable Greek Reader*', in *Prose*, 2.354–77, 370. Michael Roberts, 'Preface', in *New Signatures* (London: Hogarth, 1932), 7–20, 19. MacNeice would also comment on the 'Greek' quality of such comradeship. Louis MacNeice, 'Poetry To-day', in *The Arts To-day*, ed. Geoffrey Grigson (London: John Lane, 1935), 25–67, 57. Auden, however, was often struck by 'the unlikeness of the Greeks to ourselves'. Auden, 'Introduction to *the Portable Greek Reader*', in *Prose*, 2.363–4.

betray my country': E. M. Forster, 'What I Believe', in *Two Cheers For Democracy*, 68.

identification with the State: Even here, however, Auden hopes that such intimate love can be made to embrace 'mankind's *imperium*'. Auden, 'New Year Letter', in *Collected Poems*, 198–243, 224.

inflaming our loneliness': Auden, 'T. E. Lawrence', in *Prose*, 1.61–2, 62.

partial and selective: Auden, 'A Summer Night', in *Collected Poems*, 117–19, 117.

a people's army': W. H. Auden, *Spain* (London: Faber & Faber, 1937), 10.

our bowels yearn': W. H. Auden, *The English Auden: Poems, Essays and Dramatic Writings, 1927–39*, ed. Edward Mendelson (London: Faber, 1977), 422.

these yearning bowels: Read, however, admired the 'downright, comrade-like' tone of Auden's work. Herbert Read et al., 'Sixteen Comments on Auden', *New Verse*, 26–7 (November 1937): 23–9, 28.

idealisation of homosexuality': Louis MacNeice, 'Poetry To-day', in *The Arts To-day*, ed. Geoffrey Grigson (London: John Lane, 1935), 25–67, 57. Ellipsis mine.

'Nancy poets': (5.31).

an immediate liking': (6.1).

p.128 | **a dead cat':** (5.169).

school at Letchworth: (5.161–2).

'ordinary decent person': (5.169).

'Keep Off!': Sean O'Casey, 'Rebel Orwell', *Sunset and Evening Star* (London: Macmillan, 1954), 124–42, 126. O'Casey had been incensed by Orwell's scathing criticisms of *Drums under the Window* (17.331–2). For O'Casey's response to the review, see 17.333–4.

is sick': Theodor Adorno, *Minima Moralia: Reflections on a Damaged Life*, trans. E. F. N. Jephcott (London: Verso, 2005), 51.

measure of solidarity': ibid., 37, 26.

p.129 | **gulp of shame?:** (5.208).

for humbug': (6.83).

solidarity-making: See Monica Ozouf, *Festivals and the French Revolution* (Cambridge, MA: Harvard University Press, 1988).

the German State: See Malte Rolf, *Soviet Mass Festivals, 1917–91* (Pittsburgh, PA: University of Pittsburgh Press, 2013). Peter Reichal, 'Festival and Cult: Masculine and Militaristic Mechanisms of National Socialism', in *Shaping the Superman: Fascist Body as Political Icon*, ed. J. A. Mangan (London: Frank Cass, 1999), 153–68.

within his lifetime: According to its Director General, Gerald Barry, the event was 'a new-fashioned variation on the old-fashioned theme of patriotism'. Gerald Barry, 'The Festival of Britain', *The Adelphi* (1951): 205. Quoted in F. M. Leventhal, 'A Tonic to the Nation: The Festival of Britain, 1951', *Albion*, 27.3 (1995): 445–53, 449.

interests of power: Aldous Huxley, *Brave New World*, ed. David Bradshaw (London: Vintage, 2007), 73.

general delirium': (9.19).

no longer fraternal': Cited in Monica Ozouf, 'Fraternity', in *A Critical Dictionary of the French Revolution*, ed. François Furet and Monica Ozouf, trans. Arthur Goldhammer (Cambridge, MA: Harvard University Press, 1989), 697–703, 700. Ellipsis mine.

know the reason': (9.32).

130 | little bastards': (7.90).

worried about its decline: In 1930 Bertrand Russell maintained that 'the failure of the family to provide the fundamental satisfaction which in principle it is capable of yielding is one of the most deep-seated causes of the discontent which is prevalent in our age'. Bertrand Russell, *The Conquest of Happiness* (London: Routledge, 2012), 130. Auden observed in 1934 that 'the family is rapidly ceasing to be the natural social unit'. Auden, 'The Group Movement and the Middle Classes', in *Prose*, 1.47–54, 49.

for the affections: Middleton Murry, *Adam and Eve: An Essay Towards a New and Better Society* (London: Dakers, 1944), 209.

love your family?"': Richard Rees, *Fugitive from the Camp of Victory* (London: Secker & Warburg, 1961), 144.

Orwell's egalitarianism: Marx and Engels, *Collected Works*, 26.181.

the woman or the baby': (5.75).

a Eurasian spy!': (9.25).

Winston concludes: (9.26).

children own the parent': H. G. Wells, *Socialism and the Family* (London: A. C. Fifield, 1906), 31.

more vital centuries: ibid., 30.

131 | voiced in the 1930s: On literary attempts to rework the concept of the family, see Barry McCrea, *In the Company of Strangers: Family and Narrative in Dickens, Conan Doyle, Joyce, and Proust* (New York: Columbia University Press, 2011).

bourgeois family must go: Alick West, *Crisis and Criticism* (London: Lawrence & Wishart, 1937), 65–6.

modern world: (18.78).

family loyalty': (9.225).

relations are personal': Auden, *The Prolific and the Devourer*, in *Prose*, 2.409–58, 422.

more than others': (20.8). Or as Wells put it in 1933: 'To love everybody is simply not to love at all', and Orwell clearly adopted a similar line. H. G. Wells, *The Open Conspiracy and Other Writings* (London: Waterlow & Sons, 1933), 181.

is a family': (12.401). Shaw would also urge his readers to 'think of the whole country as a big household, and the whole nation as a big family'. He also believed that the family was very badly managed. Shaw, *The Intelligent Woman's Guide to Socialism and Capitalism*, 50.

p.132 out on Friday': (6.187).

roar of bombs: (6.187).

'Hitler matters': (7.166).

"not our business"': (17.59).

'sturdy islanders': (12.34).

p.133 a storm of fury: (5.82).

exist any longer': (12.473).

done nothing': (13.506).

a myth': (16.399).

lip-service to solidarity': (13.506).

much appeal': (13.39).

with foreigners': Hume, *Treatise of Human Nature*, 371.

particular object': David Hume, *An Enquiry Concerning the Principles of Morals*, ed. Tom L. Beauchamp (Oxford: Oxford University Press, 1998), 116.

primary relationships: Adam Smith, *The Theory of Moral Sentiments*, ed. Knud Haakonssen (Cambridge: Cambridge University Press, 2002), 270.

p.134 his own interests': (13.289).

'an evil religion': (15.135).

decencies can vanish': (17.153).

everyone is a nationalist': (16.415).

ugly fact of nationalism: For a more systematic attempt to do the same, see Maurizio Viroli, *For Love of Country: An Essay on Patriotism and Nationalism* (Oxford: Oxford University Press, 1995). For a critique of the arbitrariness of this endeavour, see Bernard, 'The Myth of the Civic Nation', in Ronald Beiner (ed.), *Theorizing Nationalism* (Albany, NY: SUNY Press, 1999), 103–18.

militarily and culturally': (17.142).

kind of internationalism': (12.398).

'liberty, equality, and internationalism': (19.164).

is international Socialism': (13.381).

p.135 people had imagined': (12.428).

World State': (12.537). Ellipsis mine.

own nationality': (12.406).

an internationalist': (12.428).

England in a phrase: (12.401).

'family settlement': Edmund Burke, *Reflections on the Revolution in France*, in *Writings and Speeches*, 8.314.

deliberation or choice: Huxley would make the same point in 1928: family life 'is good for you precisely because you have not chosen your companions but have them casually thrust upon you by the whim of chance'. Huxley, 'The Decline of the Family', in *Complete Essays*, 2.116–19, 117.

.136 bears are not philosophers': Edmund Burke, 'Letter to a Member of the National Assembly', in *Writings and Speeches*, 8.294–335, 315.

nation of philosophers': (16.227).

the deracinated': (12.103).

fond talk: For a critique of the familial metaphor as a sentimental myth of a deracinated intellectual, see Williams, *Orwell*, 24–8.

'emotional unity': (12.400).

family image': See Auden, 'The Group Movement and the Middle Classes', in *Prose*, 1.49. Interestingly, Auden could also conceive of Englishness in familial terms. As he put it with characteristic ambivalence: 'English life is for me a family life, and I love my family but I don't want to live with them'. Quoted in Humphrey Carpenter, *W. H. Auden: A Biography* (London: Faber, 1981), 243.

137 the authorities': (12.394).

constitutionalism and legality': (12.397).

marked characteristic': (12.395).

'world-famed hypocrisy': (12.393).

CHAPTER 4

139 counted for very little: (20.75). This chapter draws on previously published material: David Dwan, 'Truth and Freedom in Orwell's *Nineteen Eighty-Four*', *Philosophy and Literature*, 34.2 (2010): 381–93.

out of the world': (13.504).

enemy utters it': (13.500).

history is falsified': (16.415).

hatred and schizophrenia': (17.428).

methodical way': R. G. Collingwood, *An Essay on Metaphysics* (Oxford: Clarendon, 1940), 135, 140.

meaning of truth': Hayek, *The Road to Serfdom*, 167.

remembered best: Note, for instance, the most recent collection of Orwell's views on the matter, George Orwell, *Orwell on Truth* (London: Harvill Secker, 2018).

dark indeed: For a contextualization of the poor maths, see Matthew Taunton, '2 + 2 = 5: The Politics of Number in Writing about the Soviet Union', *Textual Practice*, 29.5 (2015): 993–1016.

'orgies of lying': (12.527).

truth about anything': (11.239).

.40 modern times': (12.471).

lunatic beliefs': (17.148).

'age of lies': (17.11).

to tell lies': (11.114).

'brute truth': (19.290). Here, for instance, was Orwellian honesty in 1937: 'By the way, tell your pansy friend Spender that I am preserving specimens of his war-heroics and that when the time comes when he squirms for shame at having written it, as the people who wrote the war-propaganda in the Great War are squirming now, I shall rub it in good and hard' (11.67).

'gutless Kipling': (5.170). 'W. H. Auden on George Orwell', *The Spectator*, 7438 (16 January 1971): 18–19, 19.

'almost inhuman': On this reputation for honesty, see Collini, *Absent Minds*, 358. For Koestler on Orwell's honesty, see *The Observer*, 29 January 1950, 4, in Meyers (ed.), *George Orwell: The Critical Heritage*, 296–9, 296. In Malcolm Muggeridge's eyes, Orwell had 'an utterly honest mind'. Malcolm Muggeridge, *The Chronicles of Wasted Time*, 2 vols. (London: Collins: 1972–3), 1.273.

love of truth': For Bertrand Russell, see *World Review*, June 1950, in Meyers (ed.), *George Orwell: The Critical Heritage*, 299–301, 301.

exemplary way': Lionel Trilling, 'George Orwell and the Politics of Truth', in *The Opposing Self: Nine Essays in Criticism* (London: Secker & Warburg, 1955), 151–72, 171.

his best work': Kingsley Amis, 'One World and Its Way', *Twentieth Century*, 158 (1955): 168.

'*essentially* true': Frank Kermode, 'The Essential Orwell', *London Review of Books*, 3.1 (22 January 1981): 5–6; repr. in *The Uses of Error* (London: Collins, 1990), 317–26.

p.141 | to be so': (13.229).

otherwise have been': (14.214). He had praised the BBC for its truthfulness in the 1940s. As he declared in 1941: 'The BBC, in spite of its foreign propaganda and the unbearable voices of its announcers, is very truthful' (12.472).

best propaganda: (15.85).

telling the truth: (13.229).

and why': (13.229).

to be truthful': (15.xxiv).

idea of a lie: (13.504).

persecution defeats itself': (19.289). His suggestion that this was one of the fantasies of liberalism overlooked the fact that liberals had criticized the same optimism. 'It is a piece of idle sentimentality', J. S. Mill opined, 'that truth, merely as truth has any inherent power, denied to error, of prevailing against the dungeon and the stake'. See Mill, 'On Liberty', in *The Collected Works of John Stuart Mill*, 18.213–310, 238.

cannot tell the truth': Edward Upward, 'A Marxist Interpretation of Literature', in *The Mind in Chains*, ed. C. Day Lewis (London: Frederick Muller, 1937) 39–56, 49.

'double-think': Bertrand Russell, 'Symptoms of Orwell's 1984', in *Portraits from Memory* (London: Allen & Unwin, 1956), 203–10, 209.

is very simple': (13.499). But he also mocked Richard Acland for his confidence in the simplicity of truth (15.104).

what truth is: For other discussions of the question of truth in Orwell, to which I am indebted, see Rorty, 'The Last Intellectual in Europe: Orwell on Cruelty', in *Contingency, Irony, and Solidarity*, 169–88; James Conant, 'Freedom, Cruelty, and Truth: Rorty Versus Orwell', in *Rorty and his Critics*, ed. Robert B. Brandom (Oxford: Blackwell, 2000), 268–342. Also Marcus Morgan, 'Revisiting Truth and Freedom in Orwell and Rorty', *Philosophy and Social Criticism*, 41.8 (2015): 853–65. For a short but insightful discussion of truth in *Nineteen Eighty-Four*, see Bernard Williams, *Truth and Truthfulness: An Essay in Genealogy* (Princeton, NJ: Princeton University Press, 2002), 146–8. See also Stephen Ingle, 'Lies, Damned Lies and Literature: George Orwell and "The Truth"', *British Journal of Politics and International Relations*, 9.4 (2007): 730–46.

p.142 'objective science': Burnham, *The Machiavellians: Defenders of Freedom*, 164.

force, fraud, and lies: According to Burnham, 'Power politics is the only kind of politics there is'. James Burnham, *The Struggle for the World* (London: Jonathan Cape, 1947), 147. Orwell often entertained the belief that 'in the long run an evasion of truth is always paid for' (18.143), but when Bertrand Russell made this argument against power-philosophies in 1938, he declared himself unconvinced: 'The view that "the truth is great and will prevail", Orwell announced, 'is a prayer rather than an axiom' (11.312).

condition of power: Thomas Hobbes, *Leviathan, sive de materia, forma, & potestate civitatis ecclesiasticæ et civilis* (London: John Tomson, 1676), 133. Carl Schmitt, *The Crisis of Parliamentary Democracy*, trans. Ellen Kennedy (Cambridge, MA: MIT Press, 1988), 43. Schmitt, *Political Theology*, 33, 52.

succour in Hobbes: Carl Schmitt, *The Leviathan in the State Theory of Thomas Hobbes*, trans. George Schwab and Erna Hilfstein (Chicago, IL: University of Chicago Press, 2008).

his successors: Hobbes, *Leviathan*, 92.

Europe in the process: Edmund Burke, *An Appeal from the New Whigs to the Old Whigs*, in *Writings and Speeches*, 4.365–477, 470.

143 absolute and unsweeping': Russell, *The Practice and Theory of Bolshevism*, 121.

search for truth': Michael Oakeshott, *Rationalism in Politics and Other Essays* (Indianapolis, IN: Liberty Fund, 1991), 428.

that truth was: 'Anyone who helps to put peace on the map', he declared in 1938, 'is doing useful work', but he increasingly recognized the limitations of this position (11.154). For the shifts in Orwell's attitude to pacifism, see Ingle, *The Social and Political Thought of George Orwell*, 80–2.

social cohesion: Plato, *Laws*, ed. and trans. Trevor J. Saunders (London: Penguin, 1970; rev. 2004), 149. For Plato, lies were a type of medicine. See Plato, *The Republic*, 69, 75, 107, 157.

themselves be deceived': Machiavelli, *The Prince*, ed. Quentin Skinner and Russell Price (Cambridge: Cambridge University Press, 1988), 62.

price of truth: Burnham, *The Machiavellians*, 200–1.

unifying lie': See W. H. Auden and Christopher Isherwood, 'In Time of War', in *Collected Poems*, 189.

public life possible: (12.397).

during the war: (12.397).

a virtuous sham: He would also declare that 'even in England it is not exactly profitable to speak and write the truth' (12.378).

no commitment to it at all: For Orwell's defence of hypocrisy, see Runciman, *Political Hypocrisy*, 168–93.

p.144 'humbug can be dropped': (12.401).

'disgusting': (13.500).

ad nauseam: Thucydides, *The Peloponnesian War*, trans. Martin Hammond (Oxford: Oxford University Press, 2009), 150. Burnham, *The Machiavellians*, 174. To a large extent, Orwell deemed the idea of popular self-rule to be mythical also: see Chapter 2.

hypocritical words: (18.163).

and so forth': (17.373).

Nazi forms of misinformation: See, for instance, his review of Tangye Lean's *Voices in the Darkness* in *Tribune*, 30 April 1943 (15.84–6), or his endorsement of Robert Brady's *The Spirit and Structure of German Fascism* (17.325). He also possessed a wide range of anti-Nazi pamphlets.

was ignored': (16.61). He reiterated the same arguments in May 1946. Mistakes of the magnitude of invading Russia 'are most likely to be made, in countries where public opinion has no power' (18.283).

objective truth': (16.89).

world has ever seen': John Strachey, *A Faith to Fight For* (London: Victor Gollancz, 1941), 33.

p.145 objective truth: Russell, *Power*, 270.

'absolute truth': Karl Popper, *The Open Society and its Enemies*, 2 vols. (London and New York: Routledge, 2002); Carr, *Democracy in International Affairs*, 16.

zealots of truth: Or, as he put it in 1938, 'The Soviet government, when it seized power, reverted to the teaching of the Catholic Church in its great days: that it is the business of Authority to propagate Truth, both by positive teaching and by the suppression of all rival doctrines'. Russell, *Power*, 121.

political polemic: (12.538).

'the scientific sense': Adolf Hitler, *Mein Kampf*, trans. James Vincent Murphy (London: Hurst & Blackett, 1939), 216.

'on the community': Hermann Rauschning, *Hitler Speaks: A Series of Political Conversations with Adolf Hitler on his Real Aims* (London: Thornton Butterworth, 1939), 220–1. For a discussion of Rauschning's influence on Orwell, see George Watson, 'Orwell's Nazi Renegade', *The Sewanee Review*, 94.3 (1986): 486–95.

"Jewish science" etc'.: (13.504).

objective truth': (12.504).

ᵖ.146 one can appeal: (9.290).

moral norms: E. H. Carr, *Propaganda in International Politics* (Oxford: Clarendon, 1939), 9; Hayek, *The Road to Serfdom*, 157.

a minor official': (17.371).

atomization of the world': (16.415).

world from another': (17.148).

immediate circle': (16.415).

'Oceania is the world': (9.277).

the rest of the world': Lyons, *Assignment in Utopia*, 632.

Moscow show trials: Orwell owned a copy of the Dewey report on the Moscow show trials. Here the commission found 'after a careful study of the relevant material that the Prosecutor's argument is based upon systematic distortion of history'. John Dewey, *I Stake My Life! Dewey Report on the Moscow Show Trials* (London: Workers International League, 1938), 21. British Library, SS.3.53.

the class struggle': Leon Trotsky, 'Their Morals and Ours', *The New International*, 4.6 (1938): 163–73, 169. But for a highly critical account of deceit under Stalinism, see Leon Trotsky, *The Stalin School of Falsification*, trans. Max Shachtman (New York: Pioneer Publishers, 1937). See, too, Leon Trotsky, 'The Priests of Half-Truth', *Socialist Appeal*, 2.16 (16 April 1938): 1, 4.

147 world communism had won: Leon Trotsky, 'Their Morals and Ours', *The New International*, 4.6 (1938): 163–73, 169.

the Soviet scene': Lyons, *Assignment in Utopia*, 240.

will make five': (11.311).

social change': Burnham, *The Machiavellians*, 165.

communist power is true: Burnham, *The Struggle for the World*, 135. Orwell reviewed the book for *The New Leader* in March 1947 (19.96–105).

148 monsters and cataclysms': (19.105).

'old-style democracy': (19.99).

worries about truth: In *The Managerial Revolution*, Burnham had predicted the emergence of three superstates permanently at loggerheads and organized on oligarchical lines. For a discussion of Burnham's influence, see R. B. Reaves, 'Orwell's "Second Thoughts on James Burnham" and *1984*', *College Literature*, 11.1 (1984): 13–21.

'doublethink': Lyons would also proclaim that dialectical materialism 'is the smuggest and most convenient philosophy ever adapted by a ruling caste to its political needs. It finds a bogus consistency in the most startling inconsistencies'. Lyons, *Assignment in Utopia*, 423.

'black-moustachio'd face': (9.4).

eternal truths"': Marx and Engels, *Collected Works*, 6.504.

thinking in practice': ibid., 5.3.

really were the case: For an account of Marx as a pragmatist, see Leszek Kolakowski, 'Karl Marx and the Classical Definition of Truth', in *Toward a Marxist Humanism: Essays on the Left Today*, trans. Jane Zielonko Peel (New York: Grove Press, 1968), 38–66. For a critique of Kolakowski's interpretation, see Wood, *Karl Marx*, 181–4.

works in practice': Upward, 'A Marxist Interpretation of Literature', in *The Mind in Chains*, 47.

what is harmful': Koestler, *Darkness at Noon*, 217.

is fairly clear: Russell associated this first position with pragmatism. According to Russell: 'Pragmatism, in some of its forms, is a power-philosophy. For pragmatism insists "a belief is true" if its consequences are pleasant'. Russell, *Power*, 268.

p.149 'thought and existence': Georg Lukács, *History and Class Consciousness*, trans. Rodney Livingstone (London: Merlin, 1971), 204. For a British defence of an idealist Marxism, see John Lewis, *Marxism and Modern Idealism* (New York: International Publishers, 1945).

nowhere else': (9.261).

common sense: See Akehurst, *The Cultural Politics of Analytical Philosophy*, 34, 111.

intellectual genealogy: Bertrand Russell, *Philosophy and Politics*, 7.

not external': (9.261).

hard-headed realist: Marx and Engels, *Collected Works*, 3.337.

independent of him': ibid., 3.336.

mind-independent reality: On this point, see Wood, *Karl Marx*, 189–94.

views on truth were: Marx and Engels, *Collected Works*, 5.3.

reality outside ourselves': ibid., 27.287.

p.150 of reality': ibid., 25.596.

final and ultimate truth': ibid., 25.84.

does not equal 4': ibid., 25.538.

they were rarer still: ibid., 25.81.

apart from platitudes': ibid., 25.83.

error and truth': ibid., 25.85.

eternal truths': Cited in V. I. Lenin, *Materialism and Empirio-Criticism: Critical Comments on a Reactionary Philosophy*, in *Collected Works*, 14.17–362, 122.

p.151 foundation of knowledge: ibid., 69–70. Ellipsis mine.

orthodox Leninism: (16.89).

independent of our mind': C. P. S. U. (B), *History of the Communist Party of the Soviet Union, Short Course* (Moscow: Foreign Languages Publishing House, 1939), 112.

'objective truth': ibid., 113.

universal class: As Marx put it, the proletariat is 'a class of civil society which is not of civil society, an estate which is the dissolution of all estates, a sphere which has a universal character because of its universal suffering'. See Marx and Engels, *Collected Works*, 3.186.

determining what is right': Cited in Roy Medvedev, *Let History Judge: The Origins and Consequences of Stalinism* (New York: Columbia University Press, 1989), 187.

is truth': (9.261).

two and two are five': (13.504).

p.152 there was untruth': (9.226).

'great friend': (18.242).

such as truth: See, in particular, A. J. Ayer, *Language, Truth and Logic* (New York: Dover, 1952).

hollow conclusion: (9.84).

accountable to it: (9.83).

.153 your senses': (9.83).

eyes and ears': (9.84).

'vulgar philistinism': (17.374).

in fact illusions': (17.369).

senses tell us': (17.369).

it was false?': (9.279).

.154 both of them': (9.223).

make sense: (9.223).

basis of a belief: (9.221).

how it looks: Ludwig Wittgenstein, *Tractatus Logico-Philosophicus* (London and New York: Routledge, 2001), 12.

is truth': (9.261). For a similar formula, see Koestler, *Darkness at Noon*, 40.

'mad': (9.268).

contradictory beliefs: This partly explains Russell's deep hostility to Hegel: 'Hegelians maintain that truth does not consist in agreement with fact but in the mutual consistency of the whole system of our beliefs'. As far as Russell was concerned, this made it impossible to discern historical truth from coherent fiction. See Russell, *Power*, 267.

.155 my eyes': (9.263).

purports to express': Ayer, *Language, Truth and Logic*, 35.

philosophical self-consciousness: Orwell, as I have suggested, was often scathing about philosophy—see Ingle, *The Social and Political Thought of George Orwell*, 124–5.

by the reader': (17.425). Ellipsis mine.

strictly meaningless: For the suggestion that newspeak might be read as a logical extension of Ayer's views, see Shklar, '*Nineteen Eighty-Four*: Should Political Theory Care?', *Political Theory*, 13.1 (1985): 5–18, 11–12.

any evidence': (9.39).

156 your senses': (9.83).

ceased to exist': (16.191).

past is still happening?': (9.260).

my memories': (9.162).

non-scientific experience': John Needham, 'Biology and Mr. Huxley', *Scrutiny*, 1.18 (May 1932): 76–9, 78.

inside the brain': (12.128).

being understood': (12.129). In 1940 Orwell speculated that a language might be invented that would redeem us from this 'star-like isolation' (12.129). All one needed to do, he suggested, was to take the step of 'coining names for the unnamed things that exist in the mind' (12.132). Yet the act of naming unnamed things might seem to require the very names one hopes to coin.

even to yourself': (9.174).

57 can be proven: (9.291).

would ever hear': (9.30). Stephen Ingle's proposal that we reduce 'objective truth' to 'societal or consensual truth' seems to miss out on this strand of the novel. See Ingle, 'Lies, Damned Lies and Literature: George Orwell and "the Truth"', 743.

also be wrong': (9.83).

not mad': (9.226).

make one wrong: (9.227).

not external': (9.261).

human consciousness': (9.278).

in the mind': (9.291).

there is nothing': (9.278).

inside the skull': (9.277).

opposite thing': (9.279).

if I wished to': (9.277).

should not be four': Hugo Grotius, *The Rights of War and Peace*, ed. Richard Tuck, 3 vols. (Indianapolis, IN: Liberty, 2005), 1:155.

p.159 'the priests of power': (9.276). In an article written in 1945, Orwell claimed that a 'totalitarian state is in effect a theocracy' (17.374).

Church of Rome': Russell, *The Practice and Theory of Bolshevism*, 114–15.

on Bolshevism: (19.128).

anti-communism: As he put it in 1945: 'Obviously there are considerable resemblances between political Catholicism...and Communism' (17.145). Or, as he declared a year later, 'the Catholic and the Communist are alike in assuming that an opponent cannot be both honest and intelligent' (17.372). For a discussion of Orwell's anti-Catholicism, see: John Rodden, 'Orwell on Religion: The Catholic and Jewish Questions', *College Literature*, 11 (1984): 44–58, and 'George Orwell and British Catholicism', *Renascence*, 41 (1989): 143–68; Leroy Spiller, 'George Orwell and British Catholicism', *Logos*, 6 (2003): 150–63; Lawrence Dugan, 'Orwell and Catholicism', *Modern Age*, 8.3 (2006): 226–40. See, too, Brennan, *George Orwell and Religion*.

laws of Nature': (9.277).

things happened': (9.291).

might be conceived: On this point, see John McDowell, *Mind and World* (Cambridge, MA: Harvard University Press, 1996), 24–45.

line of questioning: (9.260).

relentlessly destroy us': John Strachey, *A Faith to Fight For*, 82.

p.160 two and two make four': John Strachey, 'Totalitarianism', *The Left News*, 55 (January 1941): 1603–8, 1604.

platitudinous verity: Stanley Baldwin, 'Truth and Politics', in *On England and Other Addresses*, 75–92, 81.

to make four': (17.380).

fuhrer wished it': (16.191).

inimical to illusions': (9.206).

kilometres away': (9.278).

all else follows': (9.84).

p.161 freely asserted: Rorty, 'The Last Intellectual in Europe: Orwell on Cruelty', in *Contingency, Irony, and Solidarity*, 176. Orwell was certainly an advocate of free

speech and he believed that the human personality would atrophy without it
(16.172–3). Significantly, his support for the principle was not unqualified: 'it
means that everyone shall have the right to say and to print what he believes to
be the truth, provided only that it does not harm the rest of the community in
some quite unmistakable way' (17.257). So freedom was constrained by the
notion of harm—and what constituted harm was left open.

objective truth': (16.180).

telling lies': (17.372).

confirm every day: (13.399).

wrong reasons': (20.75).

becomes his heresy': John Milton, *Complete Poems and Major Prose*, ed. Merritt
Y. Hughes (Indianapolis, IN: Hackett, 1957), 739.

'eternal vigilance': (19.431).

'mental decency': (16.365).

a good boot: (19.457).

162 | **'bully-worship':** (11.311).

certain epistemic virtues: Bertrand Russell, for instance, was 'an essentially *decent*
intellect' and citizens had much to learn from his brand of tolerant but tough-
minded reasonableness (11.312).

'intellectual decency': (17.379).

nearer to the truth': Incidentally, this edition carried essays by Orwell ('The Prevention of Literature' (4–13)) and by Russell ('The Problem of Universals' (21–34)).

something like objectivity': 'Editorial', *Polemic*, 2 (1946): 2. Hugh Trevor-Roper
would also review Popper's book in *Polemic*, 3 (1946): 59–65.

'to stand alone': (17.371).

inquiry and expression: (17.378).

feeling about it': *Polemic*, 'Editorial', 5 (1946): 2.

'*moral* effort': (17.155).

objective truth': (17.374).

'liberal values': (18.267).

163 | **'naive realism':** (17.369).

one's senses': (17.374).

on ethical grounds': Russell, *Philosophy and Politics*, 26.

is empiricism': ibid., 20.

eyes and ears': (9.84).

two make four': (9.84).

164 | **Rorty certainly did):** Rorty, 'The Last Intellectual in Europe: Orwell on Cruelty',
in *Contingency, Irony, and Solidarity*, 176.

be free like you': Berlin, 'Two Concepts of Liberty', in *Four Essays on Liberty*, 118–72,
151–2.

forms of authoritarianism: This link, he suggested, was historically contingent, but
it was not completely arbitrary—the logical structure of such liberty meant that it
was more susceptible to authoritarian perversion than negative forms of freedom.

'negative' freedom: For a view of these 'false starts' upon which my own account
of Berlin depends, see Quentin Skinner, 'A Third Concept of Liberty', *London
Review of Books*, 24.7 (April 2002): 16–18.

not four': Ivan Turgenev, 'Prayer', in *Dream Tales and Prose Poems*, trans. Constance Garnett (London: William Heinemann, 1897), 323–4.

defies you': Fyodor Dostoevsky, *Notes from Underground and the Double*, trans. Ronald Wilks (London: Penguin, 2009), 31. Ellipsis mine.

p.165 | **from its constituents**: Isaiah Berlin, 'Two Concepts of Liberty', in *Four Essays on Liberty*, 151.

no development': (18.424–5).

incompatible with another': Isaiah Berlin, 'The Pursuit of the Ideal', in *The Proper Study of Mankind*, ed. Henry Hardy and Roger Hausheer (London: Chatto & Windus, 1997), 1–16, 5.

p.166 | **excellent on this'**: See Ramin Jahanbegloo (ed.), *Conversations with Isaiah Berlin*, 41.

'Freedom is Slavery': (9.6).

in Orwell's eyes: (16:395).

endorsed in 1946': (18:13–16).

logical consistency': Koestler, *Darkness at Noon*, 99, 100.

rigorous consequentialism: ibid., 169.

acid of reason': ibid., 246. Despite Rubashov's emphasis on reason, however, Orwell concluded that 'objective truth [had] long ceased to have any meaning for him' (16:396).

like a whip': Koestler, *Darkness at Noon*, 62.

true path is one': Yevgeny Zamyatin, *We*, trans. Clarence Brown (London: Penguin, 1993), 65, 172.

the first wall': ibid., 3, 13, 91.

ideal nonfreedom': ibid., 6.

two plus two…: ibid., 65.

p.167 | **a rational one**: As John Gray argued in an essay on Isaiah Berlin, even negative liberty presupposes some weak form of reason. See 'On Negative and Positive Liberty', *Political Studies*, 28 (1980): 507–26.

"Thou *art*"': (9.267).

knowledge is instilled: (9.256).

cognitive sinner: (9.267).

anywhere in the world': (9.267).

are unintelligible: (9.263).

'never existed': (9.259).

is **truth'**: (9.261).

own free will': (9.267).

p.168 | **'2 + 2 = 5'**: (9.303).

'He loved Big Brother': (9.311).

CHAPTER 5

p.169 | **difficult to describe'**: (18.427).

human beings': (18.425).

damaged or destroyed: On casualties, see Richard Bessel, 'Death and Survival in the Second World War', in *The Cambridge History of the Second World War*: Volume 3:

Total War: Economy, Society and Culture, ed. Michael Geyer and Adam Tooze (Cambridge: Cambridge University Press, 2015), 252–76. On the economic damage, see Timothy Smith, 'Renegotiating the Social Contract', in *The Cambridge History of the Second World War*, Vol. 2, 552–74, 573.

ought to be': (7.177). Ellipsis mine.

throughout the 1930s: On the self-conscious gloominess of the epoch, see Richard Overy, *The Morbid Age: Britain Between the Wars* (London: Penguin, 2009).

end of freedom': Virginia Woolf, *The Years* (Oxford: Oxford University Press, 2009), 369.

countries suffer': Russell, *The Conquest of Happiness*, 5. Some of Russell's earlier pronouncements seem to suggest that happiness was a political issue. As a young man, 'it appeared to me obvious that the happiness of mankind should be the aim of all action'. Bertrand Russell, *Autobiographies* (London: Routledge, 2010), 33. This would seem to include political action.

achievable end: In fact, he once insisted that felicity, in his own case, could be achieved by two good bowel movements a day. Ibid., 440.

170 **plan of "Creation":** Sigmund Freud, *Civilisation and its Discontents*, in *The Penguin Freud Library*. Volume 12: *Civilisation, Society and Religion*, trans. James Strachey, ed. Albert Dickson (London: Penguin, 1991), 262.

length of time': (7.194).

form of *relief*': (16.42).

recipe for depression: (16.399).

we might enjoy: As he argued in 1942, 'a "perfect" society only becomes thinkable if the human mind and even the human physiology are somehow got rid of' (14.254).

'life is suffering': (19.64).

moral and political life: On the distinction between 'the doctrine of morals' and 'the doctrine of happiness', see Immanuel Kant, *The Critique of Practical Reason* (1788), in *Practical Philosophy*, trans. Mary J. Gregor (Cambridge: Cambridge University Press, 1996), 133–272, 173, 214, 244.

happiness by doing so': (19.63).

'Can Socialists be Happy?': (16.37–45).

German cities': (16.43).

171 **its political basis:** Adorno, *Minima Moralia*, 63. See, too, Adorno, *Aesthetic Theory*, 311.

concentration camps: Adorno, *Minima Moralia*, 63.

sake of happiness': Adorno, *Aesthetic Theory*, 18.

an ethical principle: Adorno, *Negative Dialectics*, 353.

just as extreme: Theodor Adorno, *Prisms*, trans. Samuel and Shierry Weber (Cambridge, MA: MIT Press, 1981), 103–4.

ever new configurations': Adorno, *Minima Moralia*, 121.

one's own unhappiness: Theodor Adorno, 'Resignation', in *The Culture Industry: Selected Essays on Mass Culture*, ed. J. M. Bernstein (London and New York: Routledge, 2001), 198–204, 203. The happiness to be derived from contemplation is, of course, an old theme. See, in particular, Aristotle, *Nicomachean Ethics*, 198.

'melancholy science': Adorno, *Minima Moralia*, 15.

Socrates began: 'I maintain that a man and a woman are happy if they are honourable and good, but miserable if they are vicious and wicked'. Plato, *Gorgias*, trans. Walter Hamilton, ed. Chris Emlyn-Jones, rev. ed. (London: Penguin, 2004), 43.

suggest that they were: According to Kant, morality 'is not properly the doctrine of how we are to *make* ourselves happy but of how we are to become *worthy* of happiness'. Kant, *Critique of Practical Reason*, in *Practical Philosophy*, 244.

'wrong world': Adorno, *Negative Dialectics*, 352. Significantly, Shaw seemed to take this as a reason for doing away with 'the Good Man'. 'Virtue', he declared, 'is only a mask for the revolting features of Unhappiness'. Shaw, *Collected Letters*, 1.266.

licks wry lips': (16.185).

European consciousness': (16.399).

'goofy optimism': (4.4).

must be catastrophic': (12.182).

p.172 **bedroom windows':** (7.238).

ought to be discontented': (18.240).

self-satisfied rat': (4.14).

projected onto billboards: Adorno had much the same views on laughter: 'in wrong society laughter is a sickness'. Adorno, *Dialectic of Enlightenment*, trans. John Cumming (London: Verso, 1997), 112.

prophecies of doom': (4.16).

a class angle?: (18.239).

process of life': (18.240).

p.173 **possible to be':** (8.18).

possibility of happiness': (18.425).

political will: (18.425).

true progress': (18.57).

pure communism': (12.459).

outlook on politics: As G. D. H. Cole noted: 'Happiness has a long history, both as a political principle and as a guide to individual living'. G. D. H. Cole, *The Next Ten Years in British Social and Economic Policy* (London: Macmillan, 1929), 19.

pursuit of virtue: The object of rule is 'to make the whole city as happy as possible'. Plato, *The Republic*, 111–12. See, too, Plato, *The Laws*, trans. Tom Griffith, ed. Malcolm Schofield (Cambridge: Cambridge University Press, 2016), 48. For Aristotle's account of public happiness, see Aristotle, *Nicomachean Ethics*, 4, 20. Also Aristotle, *The Politics*, in *The Politics and The Constitution of Athens*, ed. Stephen Everson (Cambridge: Cambridge University Press, 1996), 167–73.

happiness of the whole': Edmund Burke, *The Writings and Speeches of Edmund Burke*. Volume IV: *Party, Parliament and the Dividing of the Whigs, 1780–1794*, ed. P. J. Marshall and Donald Bryant (Oxford: Oxford University Press, 2015), 492.

general happiness': Thomas Paine, '*Rights of Man*', in *Political Writings*, ed. Paul Kuklick (Cambridge: Cambridge University Press, 2000), 155–263, 206.

underwrite politics: As Bentham put it, the 'happiness of individuals, of whom a community is composed...is the end and the sole end which the legislator ought to have in view'. Ellipsis mine. Jeremy Bentham, *The Principles of Morals and Legislation* (New York: Prometheus Books, 1988), 24.

vulnerable to criticism: Jeremy Bentham, *A Fragment on Government*, ed. Ross Harrison (Cambridge: Cambridge University, 1988), 3, 116.

174 **build on the sand':** Stephens, *Liberty, Equality, Fraternity*, 286.

happiness that might be': William Morris, 'Art and Labour', in *The Unpublished Lectures of William Morris*, ed. Eugene D. Lemire (Detroit, MI: Wayne State University, 1969), 94–118, 113.

happiness maximized: Graham Wallas, *The Great Society* (London: Macmillan, 1914), 343.

happiness possible': Harold Laski, *Liberty and the Modern State* (London: Faber, 1930), 79. According to Leonard Woolf, happiness was the object of modern democracy, while democracy dictated that it should be equitably distributed. See Leonard Woolf, 'What is Democracy?' and 'Happiness', in *The Modern State* (London: George Allen, 1933), 15–27, 28–39.

greatest number': G. D. H. Cole, *The Simple Case for Socialism* (London: Victor Gollancz, 1935), 16. See, too, 'The Case for Political Benthamism', in Cole, *The Next Ten Years*, 16–21. Laski also claimed to follow Bentham in arguing 'that social good means the avoidance of misery and the attainment of happiness'. Laski, *A Grammar of Politics*, 24.

greatest good: 'As far as the English socialists, in particular, are concerned', Tawney complained, 'they have taken the criterion of public well-being straight from Bentham almost without question'. See R. H. Tawney, *R. H. Tawney's Commonplace Book*, ed. J. M. Winter and D. M. Joslin (Cambridge: Cambridge University Press, 1972), 63.

utilitarian terms: As Evan Durbin put it: 'To those of us who were brought up in the liberal and democratic traditions of British political life a certain form of utilitarianism is bred in our bones'. Durbin, *The Politics of Democratic Socialism*, 329. See, too, Ben Jackson, 'The Uses of Utilitarianism: Social Justice, Welfare Economics and British Socialism, 1931–48', *History of Political Thought*, 25.3 (2004): 508–35.

horror without end': (12.118).

controversy really turns': (18.425).

the long run: (12.459).

75 **no common end at all':** Tawney, *The Acquisitive Society*, 32.

the common good: Kant similarly believed that happiness is 'really not fit for any determinate principle at all'. See Immanuel Kant, 'On the Common Saying: That May be Correct in Theory, But It is of No Use in Practice', in *Practical Philosophy*, 273–310, 300.

political question: Cole, *The Simple Case for Socialism*, 16–17.

comfort and security': (18.32).

the greatest number': Huxley, 'Ideas and the Machine Tool', in *Complete Essays*, 3.294–95, 295.

rubber-truncheon boys: (7.177).

'mankind are without it': Tawney, *The Acquisitive Society*, 83.

stress the difference: Bertrand Russell, *Authority and the Individual* (London: Routledge, 2010 [1949]), 60. This slightly jarred with his earlier assertion that: 'Economic security would do more to increase the happiness of civilized communities than any other change that can be imagined, except the prevention of war'. Russell, 'The Case for Socialism', in *In Praise of Idleness*, 121–56, 135.

'conception of life': (12.118). In *Mein Kampf*, for instance, Hitler mocked the 'bourgeois virtues of peacefulness and order' while simultaneously advocating self-denial, sacrifice, and 'the joy of giving one's self in the service of others'. He also extolled the 'renunciation of the worldly pleasures that wealth can purchase'. See Adolf Hitler, *Mein Kampf* (London: Hurst & Blackett Ltd, 1939), 240, 238, 245.

paradox of Hedonism': Henry Sidgwick, *The Methods of Ethics*, repr. 7th ed. (Indianapolis, IN: Hackett, 1981), 48.

p.176 'life is happiness': (16.399).

means to that end': J. S. Mill, *Utilitarianism*, in *The Collected Works of John Stuart Mill*, 10.234.

'becomes an illusion': Hobhouse, *The Elements of Social Justice*, 18.

always remain so': (16.42). As Mill put it, 'I never, indeed, wavered in the conviction that happiness is the test of all rules of conduct, and the end of life. But I now thought that this end was only to be attained by not making it the direct end'. J. S. Mill, *Autobiography*, in *The Collected Works of John Stuart Mill*, 1.1–290, 145.

'human brotherhood': (16.42).

wrote one respondent: (16.44).

Yevgeny Zamyatin's *We*: Zamyatin was himself indebted to Dostoevsky, who had also queried the compatibility of freedom and happiness. See Fyodor Dostoyevsky, *The Brothers Karamazov*, trans. David McDuff, rev. ed. (London: Penguin, 2003), 318.

p.177 like Adam and Eve: Yevgeny Zamyatin, *We*, trans. Clarence Brown (London: Penguin, 1993), 61. Ellipsis mine.

are incompatible': (18.14).

the same either/or: As he admitted in a letter to Gleb Struve, *We* inspired him to turn to dystopian writing (16.99).

'happiness was better': (9.275).

regime that enlists it: As Adorno once argued, 'the objective possibility of happiness, but also the subjective capacity for happiness, can only be achieved in freedom'. See Adorno, *Minima Moralia*, 91. For Marcuse, there was ultimately no distinction between the values: 'happiness…at root, is freedom'. Ellipsis mine. Herbert Marcuse, *Negations*, trans. Jeremy J. Shapiro (London: Free Association Books, 1988), 180.

'no wish to be free': (18.189).

the face of his oppressor: Darwin was a passionate critic of slavery, although in 1832 he had no problem in believing in the possibility of 'happy and contented' slaves. See Charles Darwin, *Voyage on the Beagle*, ed. Janet Browne and Michael Neve (London: Penguin, 1989), 62. On Darwin and the question of slavery, see Adrian Desmond and James Moore, *Darwin's Sacred Cause: Race, Slavery and the Quest for Human Origins* (London: Allen Lane, 2009).

'new, happy life': (9.61).

Stalin's claims: For accounts of Stalin as the 'creator of people's happiness', see Jeffrey Brooks, *Thank You, Comrade Stalin!: Soviet Public Culture from Revolution to Cold War* (Princeton, NJ: Princeton University Press, 2000), 66, 94, 149, 186, 225.

the pursuit of Happiness': (9.325).

become rebels': Kant, 'On the Common Saying: That May be Correct in Theory, But It is No Use in Practice', in *Practical Philosophy*, 301.

essential to being happy: Huxley, *Brave New World*, 79.

corollary of his freedom: ibid., 212.

this invidious choice: ibid., 215.

modern utopia: H. G. Wells, *A Modern Utopia*, ed. Gregory Claeys (London: Penguin, 2005), 28–30.

'He loved Big Brother': (9.311). Ellipsis mine.

doing as one pleases: On this point, see Alex Woloch, *Or Orwell*, 318.

'hedonism': For an overview of hedonism in his work, to which I am indebted, see Gregory Claeys, 'Industrialism and Collectivism in Orwell's Literary and Political Development', *Albion: A Quarterly Journal Concerned with British Studies*, 18.2 (1986): 219–45.

making love simultaneously': (18.32).

'attitude of life': (12.118).

famously concluded: Mill, *Utilitarianism*, in *The Collected Works of John Stuart Mill*, I.212.

drinking Bovex': (4.14). He struggles to complete his book of poems *London Pleasures*, partly because he seems to operate as if there are no authentic London pleasures.

porkers': (2.31).

Hobhouse's phrase: Hobhouse, *The Elements of Social Justice*, 17.

destroy consciousness': (18.32).

form of gratification: (12.211).

'hedonistic Utopia': (12.126).

of the present': (12.211).

the sane moralist': Russell, *The Conquest of Happiness*, 174.

do for fun: For instance, he insisted: 'I can not advocate any happiness based upon what seem to me to be false beliefs', but the grounds for this inability were not spelled out. Russell, *The Conquest of Happiness*, 106.

virtue might diverge: (7.70).

as a boy gets': (7.75).

his character: Rayner Heppenstall, for instance, recorded the look of 'sadistic exaltation' in Orwell's face when being beaten by him by shooting stick. See Rayner Heppenstall, 'The Shooting Stick', *The Twentieth Century*, 157.938 (April 1955), 367–73, 371.

Buddhist priest's guts: (10.502).

killing Julia: (9.17).

'good time': (12.118).

enemy to pleasure': A. J. Ayer, *Part of My Life* (London: Collins 1977), 287.

evangelists of moderation: (18.518). Powell, *Infants of the Spring*, 134.

must avoid': (20.8).

feelings about Gandhi: This did not dissuade V. S. Pritchett from regarding him as 'a kind of saint'. V. S. Pritchett, *New Statesman* (28 January 1950): 96. Cited in Meyers (ed.), *George Orwell: The Critical Heritage*, 294–6, 294. Or, as Rees put it in 1951, he was 'one of those self-mortifying saints who kissed the sores of lepers'. Cited in Rodden, *The Politics of Literary Reputation*, 325.

Warburton is unapologetic: (3.285).

a limited share: Orwell would also claim that Christians were 'self-interested and hedonistic' (19.64). See, too, the portrait of Sugarcandy Mountain in *Animal Farm* (8.10–11).

Mrs Pither's legs': (3.285).

p.181 **life as you find it?:** (3.275–6).

oldish man': (3.283).

decay of Christianity': (16.113).

matter of dispute: On this point, for instance, see Robert T. Long, 'Mill's Higher Pleasures and the Choice of Character', *Utilitas*, 4.2 (1992): 279–97. See, too, Michael Hauskeller, 'No Philosophy for Swine: John Stuart Mill on the Quality of Pleasures', *Utilitas*, 23.4 (2011): 428–46. For a defence of the coherence of Mill's hedonism, see Jonathan Riley, 'Interpreting Mill's Qualitative Hedonism', *Philosophical Quarterly*, 53.212 (2003): 410–18.

p.182 **not part of you:** (13.29).

demanding altruism: Cole suggested that Bentham's 'greatest happiness' principle was 'merely altruism camouflaged under an egoistic name'. Cole, *The Next Ten Years*, 20.

other people's happiness': Huxley, *Brave New World*, 200.

attitude to life': (12.428).

throughout his writing: Gordon Comstock notes the 'fatty degeneration of the spirit that goes with wealth' (4.90) and decries the 'fat-bellied triviality' (4.16) of modern culture. Incidentally, he also disparages fat people for trying to play down the fact of their own fatness (4.25). His creator, meanwhile, railed against the 'fat-bellied version of "progress"' (5.176) and 'the fat-bellied type of perfectionism' (5.189) that informed much progressive thought.

little fat men': (5.195).

partly from this': (15.6).

one's belly is full': (16.113). This was a commonly broadcast argument—one made also by Russell in 1916. See Bertrand Russell, *Principles of Social Reconstruction*, 15th ed. (London: Unwin, 1971), 31.

reason for his existence': (16.113).

telos with happiness: (12.459).

p.183 **physical side of life':** (10.404).

thy creatures love': (8.63). Ellipsis mine.

walking stomach': (5.184).

putting food into': (5.84).

eye and a brain': (5.184).

simplicity of life': William Morris, 'The Society of the Future', in *William Morris: Artist, Writer, Socialist*, ed. May Morris, 2 vols. (Oxford: Blackwell, 1936), 2.443–68, 462.

existential peace: (18.32).

extinction of luxury': Morris, 'The Society of the Future', 458.

life without luxuries': (19.445).

incomes for many: The classic text here was Bernard Mandeville's, *The Fable of the Bees: or, Private Vices Publick Benefits*, 6th ed., 2 vols. (London: J Tonson, 1729). For a survey of key features of the debate, see István Hont, 'The Early Enlightenment Debate on Commerce and Luxury', in *The Cambridge History of Eighteenth-Century Political Thought*, ed. Mark Goldie and Robert Wolker (Cambridge: Cambridge University Press, 2006), 377–418.

snobbish distinctions: Orwell seemed to take a much more Fabian line: 'your ease and luxury are paid for by the misery and want of others! Your superfluities are the parents of poverty'. See Margaret Cole, *The Story of Fabian Socialism* (London: Heinemann, 1961), 7.

done away with: (16.102).

'cheap luxuries': (5.83).

'sheer vulgar fatness': (19.376).

184 'by bread and butter': G. K. Chesterton, 'The Necessity of Luxury', *The Open Review*, July 1906, in *The Man Who was Orthodox: A Selection from the Uncollected Writings*, ed. A. L. Maycock (London: Dennis Dobson, 1963), 153–4, 154.

'unnecessary luxuries': (12.175).

price of milk: (5.82).

war will sweep away': (12.184).

austere conditions: (13.42).

bombing-planes': (12.418).

productive work': (12.199).

luxury taxes: (13.275).

price of cigarettes: (13.308). He repeatedly criticized people's attempts to get around sumptuary laws. See, for example, 13.303.

often indistinguishable: 'The indistinguishability of true and false needs', Adorno claimed, 'is an essential part of the present phase'. Adorno, *Prisms*, 109.

capitalism has yet produced': (4.55). Travelling through the underground, Orwell would also find himself 'sickened by the advertisements, the silly staring faces and strident colours, the general frantic struggle to induce people to waste labour and material by consuming useless luxuries or harmful drugs' (12.184).

whoredom, and disease: (4.262).

185 shall be slaves!': (4.262).

little docile cit': (4.51).

friendless people: (4.78).

dreaded thing, thought': (18.31).

foetal state: According to Adorno, 'happiness is nothing other than...an after-image of the original shelter within the mother'. Ellipsis mine. See Adorno, *Minima Moralia*, 112.

rhythmic throbbing': (18.31).

its realization: This is itself a fairly ancient line of argument. As Aristotle argued, 'happiness is some sort of activity'—namely, an activity in accordance with virtue. See Aristotle, *Nicomachean Ethics*, 16. Bertrand Russell would also claim that utopians consistently overlooked that 'man's happiness depends upon activity'. Russell, *Principles of Social Reconstruction*, 66. Or as he put it in 1956: 'It is impossible to be happy without activity'. See Bertrand Russell, 'The Road to Happiness', in *Portraits from Memory and Other Essays* (London: Allen & Unwin, 1956), 198–202, 200. Laski would make the connection between activity and happiness in Aristotle explicit. See Harold Laski, *The Foundations of Sovereignty and Other Essays* (London: Allen & Unwin, 1921), 39.

personally accomplished: Huxley, 'On Making Things Too Easy', in *Complete Essays*, 2.55–8.

cause of all happiness': William Morris, 'The Socialist Ideal', in *The Collected Works of William Morris*, ed. May Morris, 24 vols. (London: Longman's, 1915), 23.255–63, 260. Ellipsis mine.

p.186 nearer to the animals': (18.32).

averted revolution': (5.83).

happiness imaginable: As Aristotle argued, neither beasts nor children can be truly called happy because they cannot engage in politics. See Aristotle, *Nicomachean Ethics*, 16.

military virtues': (12.118).

'spiritual need': (12.272).

brave and hard': (5.181).

'softness is repulsive': (5.182).

industry is war': (12.428).

p.187 based on hedonism': (15.308).

continuous war': (15.308).

process of life': (9.280).

will be destroyed': (9.280).

fear and vindictiveness': (9.16).

abolish the orgasm': (9.280).

against the Party': (9.133).

strengthens the taboo: Nowhere is this more evident, perhaps, than in their naughty lovers' talk: 'I hate purity! I hate goodness!... Well then, I ought to suit you, dear. I'm corrupt to the bones' (9.132). Ellipsis mine.

purest form of pleasure: Adorno, *Minima Moralia*, 217.

p.188 waist downwards': (9.163).

everyone was ugly': (9.63).

beauty and ugliness: (9.280).

dirty clothes: (9.62). Ellipsis mine.

a right to': (9.62).

p.189 far more feminine': (9.149).

necessity of luxury: On the necessity of luxury, see also Peter Kropotkin, *The Conquest of Bread and Other Writings*, ed. Marshall S. Shatz (Cambridge: Cambridge University Press, 1995), 94.

apparent uselessness': (9.99).

preordained uses: See Theodor Adorno and Max Horkheimer, *Dialectic of the Enlightenment*, trans. John Cumming (London: Verso, 1997). See, too, Heidegger on the tyrannical reign of the 'Gestell'. Martin Heidegger, *Basic Writings*, ed. David Farrell Krell (London: Routledge, 2011), 227.

something else: As Aristotle put it: 'And some activities are necessary, that is, worth choosing for the sake of something else, while others are worthy of choice in themselves; clearly happiness must be classed as one of those worthy of choice in themselves and not as one of those worth choosing for the sake of something else. For happiness lacks nothing, but is self-sufficient'. Aristotle, *Nicomachean Ethics*, 193.

commodity fetishism: Adorno, *Minima Moralia*, 121.

inside all of us': (18.19).

animal for granted': (12.178).

defensible thesis: The position is a familiar one. As Aristotle argued: 'the pleasure proper to a virtuous activity is good, and that proper to a wicked one is bad, because appetites for noble objects are to be praised, those for disgraceful things blamed'. Aristotle, *Nicomachean Ethics*, 191.

'have been failures': (16.39). According to Adorno, 'to be always the same is the essence of unhappiness'. Adorno, *Negative Dialectics*, 352.

have been flops: Russell, too, would argue that all utopias have been mind-numbingly dull. See Russell, *Principles of Social Reconstruction*, 66. Orwell would draw attention to Russell's critique of utopianism in 1946 (18.58).

after a while: Voltaire himself recognized that hedonism brought diminishing returns. Candide only decides to stay in El Dorado for a month. Voltaire, *Candide, or Optimism*, trans. Theo Cuffe, introd. Michael Wood (London: Penguin, 2005).

Wellsian Utopia?': (16.39).

a 'shit': (13.249).

secondariness of happiness: On the irreducibility of suffering, see H. G. Wells, *The Time Machine*, ed. Patrick Parrinder (London: Penguin, 2005), 32. 'The world', Wells declared, 'has a purpose greater than happiness'. See H. G. Wells, *Anticipations of the Reaction of Mechanical and Scientific Progress Upon Human Life and Thought*, 2nd ed. (London: Chapman, 1902), 318.

of watery melancholy': (16.40).

nothing to laugh at: (14.254).

little fat men': (5.180).

the same thing: (16.40).

the dinner table': (16.39).

primarily from contrast: (16.42). Freud would claim something similar: 'We are so made that we can derive intense enjoyment only from a contrast'. See Freud, *Civilisation and its Discontents*, 264.

I felt *happy*': (7.171).

beauty of the earth': (3.56).

foam of oriental seas!: (3.55).

p.192 total contentment: Adorno, *Minima Moralia*, 112. This strains against his own contention that contemplation is a source of joy. Adorno, 'Resignation', in *The Culture Industry*, 203.

Dorothy 'was happy, happy!': (3.55).

Flory 'was happy, happy': (2.156).

Elizabeth 'was happy, happy': (2.214).

Burmese Days: (2.84).

countryside walk: (4.141).

finally consummated: Connolly's phrase is reported by Powell. See Powell, *Infants of the Spring*, 134–5.

in love with it': (16.129).

affect them directly': (16.129).

p.193 nature-worshippers: (15.135).

before breakfast': (7.228).

nature's charms: (7.173).

weak at the knees: (7.172).

war news': (13.249).

little more probable': (18.240). Ellipsis mine.

of a Wurlitzer': (18.240).

abusive letters': (18.239).

'bourgeois nostalgia': (16.78).

concentration camp: (7.76).

p.194 by many fish: (7.84).

outer suburbs': (7.211).

'They don't exist': (7.230).

inherently vicious': (19.397). On the question of nostalgia, see Joseph Brooker, 'Forbidden to Dream Again: Orwell and Nostalgia', *English*, 55 (Autumn 2006): 281–97; Patricia Rae, 'There'll Be No More Fishing This Side of the Grave: Radical Nostalgia in George Orwell's *Coming Up for Air*', in *Modernism and Nostalgia: Bodies, Locations, Aesthetics*, ed. Tammy Clewell (Houndmills, Basingstoke: Palgrave, 2013), 149–65.

civilised men': (12.460).

is this true': (12.460). Ellipsis mine.

Roman slave': (16.434). Ellipsis mine.

wrong with it': (17.27). He had also insisted in *The Road to Wigan Pier* that 'a dislike of the mechanised future does not imply the smallest reverence for any period of the past' (5.194).

individual happiness?': Huxley, 'Whither Are We Civilizing', in *Complete Essays*, 2.102–7, 105.

some dark answers: Stuart Chase's inquiry was particularly popular. See Stuart Chase, *Men and Machines* (New York: Macmillan, 1929). See, too, Charles Wood, *Successful Living in this Machine Age* (London: J. Cape, 1932).

challenge of the machine': Murry, *Adam and Eve*, 197.

effects of the machine': (16.434).

life impossible': (5.178).

aesthetic feeling': (17.403).

interwar years: See, for instance, John Ruskin, *The Stones of Venice*, ed. William Morris (Hammersmith: Kelmscott Press, 1892), ii.

possibility of this happiness': Huxley, 'Spinoza's Worm', in *Complete Essays*, 2.319–34, 331. 'Creative work alone brings man fulfillment', Middleton Murry also declared. See Murry, *Adam and Eve*, 207.

modern factory hand: H. J. Massingham (ed.), *The Natural Order: Essays in the Return to Husbandry* (London: J. M. Dent, 1945), 37.

human muscles': (19.334).

a strong case': (17.28). He was more critical of the anachronistic features of George Stapledon's ruralism (16.72).

distribution of property': (17.27).

factor in his life': (17.28). As Murry also put it, 'Man needs to work in order to fulfill his own humanity'. Murry, *Adam and Eve*, 206.

over again': (17.28).

century of mechanisation': (5.189). Ellipsis mine.

rot under the trees: (5.189–90).

machine gun': (5.91).

something else': (7.24).

the existence of': (7.22).

almost irresistible: (5.190).

'machine-civilisation': (5.189).

cannot be got rid of': (17.28).

acceptance of the machine': (15.214).

modern world: (17.28).

couple of minutes': (5.183).

life-wasting job': (17.43).

machine civilisation': (17.28).

"go back"': (5.194). The impossibility of going back seems to have been conceded by almost everyone. See Murry, *Adam and Eve*, 206.

period of the past': (5.194).

in love with 1910: Anthony Powell, *Infants of the Spring*, 135. Connolly, *The Evening Colonnade*, 378.

between 1890 and 1914': (12.191).

'a lost art': Cyril Connolly, *The Unquiet Grave: A Word Cycle by Palinurus* (London: Curwen Press, 1944), 92.

'incapable of happiness': Russell, *Autobiographies*, 561.

socialist traditions: (18.62).

incompatible with happiness: (10.344).

persisted in writing books: In 1946 he famously compared book-writing to 'a long bout of some painful illness' (18.320).

his own eccentric way: Muggeridge, *Chronicles of Wasted Time*, 2.232.

cease to be so': Mill, *Autobiography*, in *The Collected Works of John Stuart Mill*, 147.

grey in my hair': (19.394). Ellipsis mine.

5 eggs': (19.194). Ellipsis mine.

entries tough-going: Christopher Hitchens, 'The Importance of Being Orwell', *Vanity Fair*, 9 July 2012.

a happy life': On Orwell's 'death-wish', see Heppenstall, *Four Absentees*, 176.

some contentment there: Rees, *Fugitive from the Camp of Victory*, 148, 149.

diary in 1940: (12.188).

his London life: For a discussion of the circumstances of its composition, see Paul Delany, 'Orwell on Jura: Locating *Nineteen Eighty-Four*', *University of Toronto Quarterly*, 30.1 (2011): 78–88.

p.199 300 people on it': (19.126).

Candytuft almost over': (19.191).

things outside the ego: Russell, *The Conquest of Happiness*, 6.

compared with the deer': (18.322).

some kind of buzzard': (18.321).

it produced in him: Powell, *Infants of the Spring*, 134.

faint sweetbriar smell': (18.333).

his own journals: (18.183).

Probably hoodie crows': (18.378).

from the mouth': (19.137).

very large snake': (19.176).

rabbit in the garden': (19.153).

mouse in the larder': (19.140).

another snake (small one)': (18.368).

rat in the byre': (19.141). 'Orwell's hunting instinct', according to Bowker, 'had more than a trace of cruelty about it'. Bowker, *George Orwell*, 368.

p.200 as usual)': (19.156).

into *Nineteen Eighty-Four*: For more on this issue, see D. J. Taylor, 'Orwell and the Rats', in *Orwell: The Life* (London: Chatto & Windus, 2003), 143–7.

guy ropes': (19.136). Ellipsis mine.

have to re-sow': (19.140).

owing to rabbits': (19.8).

according to thy nature?: (19.7–8). This is drawn from the beginning of book 5 in Aurelius' *Meditations*. For a modern translation, see Marcus Aurelius, *Meditations*, trans. Martin Hammond (London: Penguin, 2006), 35.

feeling inside you': (3.113–14). Ellipses mine.

happiness for Adorno: Adorno, *Minima Moralia*, 157.

p.201 able to be compared': (2.179).

vegetable gardening': (12.148).

out of stone': (18.314). Ellipses mine.

I do wrong': (19.143).

its unique charm: 'Some desert-island stories', Orwell opined, 'are worse than others, but none is altogether bad when it sticks to the actual concrete details of the struggle to keep alive' (12.233).

patch of wheat': (12.233). Ellipsis mine.

time of his life): Jean-Jacques Rousseau, *Reveries of a Solitary Walker*, trans. Russell Goulbourne (Oxford: Oxford University Press, 2011), 49.

.202 'there are no Crusoes': Huxley, 'One and Many', in *Complete Essays*, 2.302–19.

what trees and what men': (7.229). In March 1944 Orwell argued that nature-worship carried to extreme lengths is 'inherently anti-social' (16.129).

so we are told: Robert MacFarlane, *The Wild Places* (London: Granta, 2007), 140.

not worth a bomb': (19.240–1).

considerable happiness: Perhaps Jura was that place not worth a bomb, although during the Second World War, he recalled an unpromising story of a woman who rented an island in the Hebrides to escape the *Luftwaffe*, only to find herself killed by a stray RAF bomb. 'Good if true' was Orwell's tough assessment of the tale (12.188).

such thing as happiness': (9.142).

CONCLUSION

203 being inconsistent': Huxley, 'The Idea of Equality', in *Complete Essays*, 2.151.

Orwell's own writing: Rees, *Fugitive from the Camp of Victory*, 153.

'change-of-heart man': (12.97).

towards homosexuality': (20.255).

'very dishonest': (20.250).

his own honesty: (20.244).

the Foreign Office: Cited in Timothy Garton Ash, 'Orwell's List', *New York Review of Books*, 50.14 (September 2003), repr. Timothy Garton Ash, *Facts are Subversive* (London: Atlantic Books, 2009), 356–73.

had its defenders: See Christopher Hitchens, *Orwell's Victory* (London: Allen Lane, 2002), 111–21. See Garton Ash, 'Orwell's List'.

204 Orwell was watching you: On the broader context, see James Smith, *British Writers and MI5 Surveillance 1930–1960* (Cambridge: Cambridge University Press, 2012). See, too, Frances Stonor Saunders, *The Cultural Cold War: The CIA and the World of Arts and Letters* (New York: The New Press, 1999).

'a paradox': Richard J. Voorhees, *The Paradox of George Orwell* (West Lafayette, IN: Purdue University Press, 1960); Williams, *Orwell*, 39, 73, 87.

attacking it': (5.160).

individual Socialists': (5.202).

an internationalist': (12.428).

unresolved contradictions': (19.291).

point of view': Powell, *Infants of the Spring*, 135.

of an egg: Marx and Engels, *Collected Works*, 25.126.

'motion is a contradiction': G. V. Plekhanov, *Fundamental Problems of Marxism*, trans. Julius Katzer (Moscow: Progress Publishers, 1962), 92.

logician can approve': Russell, *Philosophy and Politics*, 19.

205 key philosophical problem: Ludwig Wittgenstein, *Philosophical Investigations: The German Text with a Revised English Translation*, trans. G. E. M. Anscombe (Oxford: Blackwell, 2002), 43.

always liable to elude us: On how we might agree about the procedures of justice while disagreeing about its substance, see Stuart Hampshire, *Justice is Conflict* (Princeton, NJ: Princeton University Press, 2000).

incompatible values: This made the idea of a unified good incoherent in Berlin's eyes. Some among the great goods, he argued, cannot live together. See Isaiah Berlin, 'The Pursuit of the Ideal', in *The Crooked Timber of Humanity*, 13–14.

a choice of goods: (19.292).

should we serve?': This was Weber's question in what seemed like a very polytheistic modernity. See Max Weber, 'Science as a Vocation', in *From Max Weber: Essays in Sociology*, ed. and trans. H. H. Gerth (London: Routledge, 1991), 129–56, 153.

'source of tolerance': Leszek Kolakowski, 'In Praise of Inconsistency', in *Toward a Marxist Humanism*, 211–20, 213.

p.206 moral perplexities': Hilary Putnam, 'Literature, Science and Reflection', in *Meaning and the Moral Sciences* (London: Routledge, 1978), 83–94, 87.

Bibliography

'100 fiction books all children should read before leaving secondary school—according to teachers'. TES, 31 July 2015. https://www.tes.com.

Adorno, Theodor. *Prisms*. Translated by Samuel Weber and Shierry Weber (Cambridge, MA: MIT Press, 1981).

Adorno, Theodor. *Aesthetic Theory*. Translated by C. Lenhardt (New York: Routledge and Kegan Paul, 1984).

Adorno, Theodor. *Dialectic of Enlightenment*. Translated by John Cumming (London: Verso, 1997).

Adorno, Theodor. 'Resignation'. In *The Culture Industry: Selected Essays on Mass Culture*, edited by J. M. Bernstein (London and New York: Routledge, 2001), 198–204.

Adorno, Theodor W. *Minima Moralia: Reflections on a Damaged Life*. Translated by E. F. N. Jephcott (London: Verso, 2005).

Adorno, Theodor W. *Negative Dialectics*. Translated by E. B. Ashton (New York: Continuum, 2007).

Akehurst, Thomas L. *The Cultural Politics of Analytical Philosophy: Britishness and the Spectre of Europe* (London: Continuum, 2010).

Archimedes (pseudonym). 'The Freedom of Necessity I'. *Horizon* (July 1942): 16–33.

Archimedes (pseudonym). 'The Freedom of Necessity II'. *Horizon* (August 1942): 97–107.

Archimedes (pseudonym). 'The Freedom of Necessity III'. *Horizon* (October 1942): 267–98.

Archimedes (pseudonym). 'The Freedom of Necessity IV'. *Horizon* (November 1942): 355–70.

Arendt, Hannah. *The Human Condition*. Charles R. Walgreen Foundation Lectures (Chicago, IL: University of Chicago Press, 1958).

Arendt, Hannah. 'What is Freedom?' In *Between Past and Future: Eight Excursus in Political Thought* (London: Penguin Books, 2006), 142–69.

Aristotle. *The Politics and the Constitution of Athens*. Edited by Stephen Everson (Cambridge: Cambridge University Press, 1996).

Aristotle. *The Nicomachean Ethics*. Edited and translated by Roger Crisp (Cambridge: Cambridge University Press, 2000).

Arnold, Matthew. *Culture and Anarchy and Other Writings*. Edited by Stefan Collini (Cambridge: Cambridge University Press, 1993).

Ash, Timothy Garton. *Facts are Subversive* (London: Atlantic Books, 2009).

Auden, W. H. *Spain* (London: Faber & Faber, 1937).

Auden, W. H. *Collected Poems*. Edited by Edward Mendelson (London: Faber & Faber, 1976).

Auden, W. H. *The English Auden: Poems, Essays and Dramatic Writings, 1927–1939*. Edited by Edward Mendelson (London: Faber & Faber, 1977).

Auden, W. H. *The Early Auden*. Edited by Edward Mendelson (London: Faber, 1981).

Auden, W. H. *Prose*. Edited by Edward Mendelson, 6 vols. (Princeton, NJ: Princeton University Press, 1996–2015).

Auden, W. H., and Christopher Isherwood. In *Journey to a War* (London: Faber & Faber, 1939).

Auden, W. H., and Christopher Isherwood. *On the Frontier*. In *The Complete Works of W. H. Auden: Plays and Other Dramatic Writings, 1928–1938*, edited by Edward Mendelson (Princeton, NJ: Princeton University Press, 1988), 357–418.

Aurelius, Marcus. *Meditations*. Translated by Martin Hammond (London: Penguin, 2006).

Ayer, A. J. 'The Concept of Freedom'. *Horizon* (April 1944): 228–37.

Ayer, A. J. *Language, Truth and Logic* (New York: Dover Publications, Inc., 1952).

Ayer, A. J. *Part of My Life* (London: Collins, 1977).

Baldwin, Stanley. *On England and Other Addresses* (London: Philip Allan & Co., 1926).

Baldwin, Stanley. *An Interpreter of England: The Falconer Lectures* (London: Hodder & Stoughton, 1939).

Baxell, Richard. *Unlikely Warriors: The Extraordinary Story of the Britons Who Fought in the Spanish Civil War* (London: Aurum Press, 2012).

Baylen, Joseph O. 'George Bernard Shaw and the Socialist League: Some Unpublished Letters'. *International Review of Social History*, 7.3 (1962): 426–40.

Beloff, Max. 'The Age of Laski'. *The Fortnightly Review*, 167 (1950): 378–84.

Benewick, Robert, and Philip Green, eds. *The Routledge Dictionary of Twentieth-Century Political Thinkers* (London: Routledge, 1992).

Bentham, Jeremy. *The Works of Jeremy Bentham*, 11 vols. (Edinburgh: W. Tait, 1843).

Bentham, Jeremy. *A Fragment on Government*. Edited by Ross Harrison (Cambridge: Cambridge University Press, 1988).

Bentham, Jeremy. *The Principles of Morals and Legislation* (New York: Prometheus Books, 1988).

Berlin, Isaiah. 'Two Concepts of Freedom'. In *Four Essays on Liberty* (Oxford: Oxford University Press, 1969), 118–72.

Berlin, Isaiah. 'The Pursuit of the Ideal'. In *The Proper Study of Mankind*, edited by Henry Hardy and Roger Hausheer (London: Chatto & Windus, 1997), 1–16.

Bernal, J. D. *The World, the Flesh and the Devil: An Inquiry into the Future of the Three Enemies of the Rational Soul* (London: Cape Editions, 1970).

Bew, John. *Realpolitik: A History* (New York: Oxford University Press, 2015).

Bialas, Wolfgang, and Lothar Fritze. *Nazi Ideology and Ethics* (Newcastle-upon-Tyne: Cambridge Scholars Publishing, 2014).

Bliss, Philip P., and Ira D. Sankey. *Gospel Hymns*, 2 vols. (New York: Biglow & Main; Chicago, IL: John Church & Co., n.d.).

Borkenau, Franz. *The Totalitarian Enemy* (London: Faber & Faber, 1940).

Bounds, Philip. *Orwell and Marxism: The Political and Cultural Thinking of George Orwell* (London: Tauris Academic Studies, 2009).

Bowker, Gordon. *George Orwell* (London: Little, Brown, 2003).

Boyd, Richard. 'Pity's Pathologies Portrayed: Rousseau and the Limits of Democratic Compassion'. *Political Theory*, 32.4 (2004): 519–46.

Brennan, Michael G. *George Orwell and Religion* (London: Bloomsbury, 2016).

Brooker, Joseph. 'Forbidden to Dream Again: Orwell and Nostalgia'. *English*, 55.213 (2006): 281–97.

Brooks, Jeffrey. *Thank You, Comrade Stalin!: Soviet Public Culture from Revolution to Cold War* (Princeton, NJ: Princeton University Press, 2000).

Bukharin, Nikolai. *The Prison Manuscripts: Socialism and its Culture*. Translated by George Shriver (London, New York, Calcutta: Seagull Books, 2006).

Burke, Edmund. *The Writings and Speeches of Edmund Burke*. Edited by Paul Langford, 9 vols. (Oxford: Oxford University Press, 1981–2015).

Burnham, James. *The Managerial Revolution: What is Happening in the World* (New York: John Day Co., 1941).

Burnham, James. *The Machiavellians: Defenders of Freedom* (London: Putnam, 1943).

Burnham, James. *The Struggle for the World* (London: Jonathan Cape, 1947).

Burns, C. D. 'The Conception of Liberty'. *Journal of Philosophical Studies*, 3.10 (1928): 186–97.

Carpenter, Humphrey. *W. H. Auden: A Biography* (London: Faber & Faber, 1981).

Carr, E. H. *Propaganda in International Politics* (Oxford: Clarendon Press, 1939).

Carr, E. H. *The Twenty Years' Crisis, 1919–1939: An Introduction to the Study of International Relations* (London: Macmillan, 1939).

Carr, E. H. *Democracy in International Affairs* (Nottingham: University College, 1945).

Caudwell, Christopher. *Studies in a Dying Culture* (London: John Lane, 1938).

Cavell, Stanley. 'A Matter of Meaning It'. In *Must We Mean What We Say?: A Book of Essays* (Cambridge: Cambridge University Press, 1976).

Chase, Stuart. *Men and Machines* (New York: Macmillan, 1929).

Chesterton, G. K. 'Introduction'. In *Aesop's Fables* (London: Heinemann, 1912), v–xi.

Chesterton, G. K. 'The Necessity of Luxury'. In *The Man Who was Orthodox: A Selection from the Uncollected Writings*, edited by A. L. Maycock (London: Dennis Dobson, 1963), 153–4.

Claeys, Gregory. 'Industrialism and Collectivism in Orwell's Literary and Political Development'. *Albion: A Quarterly Journal Concerned with British Studies*, 18.2 (1986): 219–45.

Clark, Martin. *Mussolini* (London: Routledge, 2005).

Clarke, Benjamin. *Orwell in Context: Communities, Myths, Values* (Basingstoke: Palgrave Macmillan, 2007).

Clayton, Philip. 'George Orwell was a Snazzy Dresser and Certainly Not a Snarler'. *The Guardian*, 11 August 2016.

Cohen, G. A. *Self-Ownership, Freedom, and Equality* (Cambridge: Cambridge University Press, 1995).

Cole, G. D. H. *Self-Government in Industry* (London: G. Bell & Sons, 1918).

Cole, G. D. H. *The Next Ten Years in British Social and Economic Policy* (London: Macmillan, 1929).

Cole, G. D. H. *The Simple Case for Socialism* (London: Victor Gollancz, 1935).

Cole, G. D. H. *Socialism in Evolution* (London: Penguin Books, 1938).

Cole, G. D. H. *The Left News*, 70 (April 1942): 2069–73.

Cole, Margaret. *The Story of Fabian Socialism* (London: Heinemann, 1961).

Cole, Stewart. '"The True Struggle": Orwell and the Specter of the Animal'. *Literature Interpretation Theory*, 28.4 (2017): 335–53.

Collingwood, R. G. *An Essay on Metaphysics* (Oxford: Clarendon Press, 1940).

Collini, Stefan. *Absent Minds: Intellectuals in Britain* (Oxford: Oxford University Press, 2006).

Colls, Robert. *George Orwell: English Rebel* (Oxford: Oxford University Press, 2013).

Conant, James. 'Freedom, Cruelty, and Truth: Rorty versus Orwell'. In *Rorty and his Critics*, edited by Robert B. Brandom (Oxford: Blackwell, 2000).

Connolly, Cyril. 'We English Again'. *The New Statesman and Nation*, 10 December 1938, 972–4.

Connolly, Cyril. *The Unquiet Grave: A Word Cycle by Palinurus* (London: Curwen Press, 1944).

Connolly, Cyril. *The Evening Colonnade* (London: Bruce & Watson, 1973).

Constant, Benjamin. 'The Liberty of the Ancients Compared with that of the Moderns'. In *Political Writings*, edited by Biancamaria Fontana (Cambridge: Cambridge University Press, 1988), 308–28.

C. P. S. U. (B). *History of the Communist Party of the Soviet Union, Short Course* (Moscow: Foreign Languages Publishing House, 1939).

Crick, Bernard. *George Orwell: A Life* (London: Secker & Warburg, 1980).

Crick, Bernard. 'Orwell and English Socialism'. In *George Orwell: A Reassessment*, edited by P. Buitenhuis and Ira B. Nadel (London: Macmillan, 1988), 3–22.

Crosland, Anthony. *The Future of Socialism* (London: Jonathan Cape, 1956).

Cunningham, Valentine. *British Writers of the Thirties* (Oxford: Clarendon Press, 1988).

Darwin, Charles. *Voyage on the Beagle*. Edited by Janet Browne and Michael Neve (London: Penguin Books, 1989).

Davenport-Hines, Richard. *Auden* (London: Heinemann, 1995).

Davison, Peter, ed. *The Lost Orwell: Being a Supplement to The Complete Works of George Orwell* (London: Timewell, 2006).

Delany, Paul. 'Orwell on Jura: Locating *Nineteen Eighty-Four*'. *University of Toronto Quarterly*, 30.1 (2011): 78–88.

Desmond, Adrian, and James Moore. *Darwin's Sacred Cause: Race, Slavery and the Quest for Human Origins* (London: Allen Lane, 2009).

Deutscher, Isaac. 'The Mysticism of Cruelty'. In *Heretics and Renegades* (London: Hamish Hamilton, 1955), 35–50.

Dewey, John. *I Stake My Life! Dewey Report on the Moscow Show Trials* (London: Workers International League, 1938).

Dinsman, Melissa. *Modernism at the Microphone: Radio, Propaganda, and Literary Aesthetics during World War II* (London: Bloomsbury Academic, 2015).

Dostoyevsky, Fyodor. *The Brothers Karamazov*. Translated by David McDuff. Rev. ed. (London: Penguin Books, 2003).

Dostoyevsky, Fyodor. *Notes from Underground and the Double*. Translated by Ronald Wilks (London: Penguin Books, 2009).

Draper, Hal. *Karl Marx's Theory of Revolution*, 6 vols. (New York; London: Monthly Review Press, 1977–2005).

Dugan, Lawrence. 'Orwell and Catholicism'. *Modern Age*, 8.3 (2006): 226–40.

Durbin, E. F. M. *The Politics of Democratic Socialism: An Essay on Social Policy* (London: George Routledge & Sons, 1940).

Eastman, Max. *The End of Socialism in Russia* (London: Martin Secker & Warburg, 1937).

Eliot, George. *The George Eliot Letters*. Edited by Gordon S. Haight, 6 vols. (New Haven, CT: Yale University Press, 1954–78).

Farrant, Andrew. 'Hayek, Orwell, and "The Road to Serfdom"'. In *Hayek: A Collaborative Biography. Part VI: Good Dictators, Sovereign Producers and Hayek's 'Ruthless Consistency'*, edited by Robert Leeson (London: Palgrave Macmillan, 2015), 152–82.

Fleay, C., and M. L. Sanders. 'Looking into the Abyss: George Orwell at the BBC'. *Journal of Contemporary History*, 24.3 (1989): 503–18.

Flood, Alison. 'Will Self Declares George Orwell the "Supreme Mediocrity"'. *The Guardian*, 1 September 2014.

Forster, E. M. 'The Long Run'. *New Statesman and Nation*, 10 December 1938, 971–2.

Forster, E. M. *Two Cheers for Democracy* (London: Edward Arnold, 1951).

Fowler, Roger. *The Language of George Orwell* (Basingstoke: Macmillan Press, 1995).

Frank, Jill. *A Democracy of Distinction: Aristotle and the Work of Politics* (Chicago, IL: University of Chicago Press, 2005).

Freeden, Michael. *Liberalism Divided: A Study in British Political Thought, 1914–1939* (Oxford: Clarendon Press, 1986).

Freud, Sigmund. 'Civilisation and its Discontents'. In *The Penguin Freud Library* Vol. 12: *Civilisation, Society and Religion*. Translated by James Strachey, edited by Albert Dickson. Vol. 12: *Civilisation, Society and Religion* (London: Penguin Books, 1991).

de Freytas-Tamura, Kimko. 'George Orwell's "1984" is Suddenly a Best-Seller'. *The New York Times*, 25 January 2017.

Frye, Northrop. 'Turning New Leaves', *Canadian Forum* (December 1946). In *George Orwell: The Critical Heritage*, edited by Jeffrey Meyers (London: Routledge, 1975), 211–12.

Gallie, W. B. *Philosophy and the Historical Understanding*. 2nd ed. (New York: Schocken Books, 1968).

Geras, Norman. 'The Controversy about Marx and Justice'. In *Literature of Revolution: Essays on Marxism* (London: Verso, 1986), 3–57.

Geyer, Michael, and J. Adam Tooze. *The Cambridge History of the Second World War*, 3 vols. (Cambridge: Cambridge University Press, 2015).

Godwin, William. *Selections from Political Justice*. Edited by George Woodcock (London: Freedom Press, 1943).

Gollancz, Victor. *The Betrayal of the Left: An Examination and Refutation of Communist Policy from October 1939 to January 1941: With Suggestions for an Alternative and an Epilogue on Political Morality* (London: Victor Gollancz, 1941).

Goodway, David. *Anarchist Seeds beneath the Snow: Left-Libertarian Thought and British Writers from William Morris to Colin Ward* (Liverpool: Liverpool University Press, 2006).

Gray, John. 'On Negative and Positive Liberty'. *Political Studies*, 28 (1980): 507–26.

Greenblatt, Stephen. 'Orwell as Satirist'. In *George Orwell: A Collection of Critical Essays*, edited by Raymond Williams (Englewood Cliffs, NJ: Prentice Hall, 1974), 103–18.

Griffith, Gareth. *Socialism and Superior Brains: The Political Thought of Bernard Shaw* (London: Routledge, 1993).

Grotius, Hugh. *The Rights of War and Peace*. Edited by Richard Tuck, 3 vols. (Indianapolis, IN: Liberty, 2005).

Guedalla, Philip. 'A Russian Fairy Tale'. In *The Missing Muse* (New York: Harper & Brothers, 1930).

Haffenden, John. *William Empson*. Volume II: *Against the Christians* (Oxford: Oxford University Press, 2006).

Hall, Ian. 'Power Politics and Appeasement: Political Realism in British International Thought'. *The British Journal of Politics and International Relations*, 8.2 (2006): 174–92.

Hall, Ian. 'A Shallow Piece of Naughtiness: George Orwell and Political Realism'. *Millennium: Journal of International Studies*, 36.2 (2008): 191–215.

Hampshire, Stuart. *Justice is Conflict* (Princeton, NJ: Princeton University Press, 2000).

Hauskeller, Michael. 'No Philosophy for Swine: John Stuart Mill on the Quality of Pleasures'. *Utilitas*, 23.4 (2011): 428–46.

Hayek, Friedrich. *Individualism: True and False* (Dublin: Hodges Figgis Ltd, 1946).

Hayek, Friedrich. *Law, Legislation and Liberty: The Mirage of Social Justice* (London: Routledge & Kegan Paul, 1976).

Hayek, Friedrich. *The Road to Serfdom* (London: Routledge, 2001).

Hegel, G. W. F. *Phenomenology of Spirit*. Translated by A. V. Miller (Oxford: Oxford University Press, 1979).

Hegel, G. W. F. *Elements of the Philosophy of Right*. Edited by Allen W. Wood, translated by H. B. Nisbet (Cambridge: Cambridge University Press, 1991).

Heidegger, Martin. *Basic Writings*. Edited by David Farrell Krell (London: Routledge, 2011).

Heppenstall, Rayner. 'The Shooting Stick'. *The Twentieth Century*, 157.938 (April 1955): 367–73.

Heppenstall, Rayner. *Four Absentees* (London: Barrie & Rockliff, 1960).

Herman, Barbara. *The Practice of Moral Judgment* (Cambridge, MA: Harvard University Press, 1993).

Hesiod. *Works and Days* and *Theogony*. Translated by Stanley Lombardo, introduction by Robert Lamberton (Indianapolis, IN; Cambridge: Hackett, 1993).

Hitchens, Christopher. *Orwell's Victory* (London: Allen Lane, 2002).

Hitler, Adolf. *Mein Kampf*. Translated by James Vincent Murphy (London: Hurst & Blackett, 1939).

Hitler, Adolf. *Mein Kampf: Eine Kritische Edition*. Edited by Christian Hartmann, Thomas Vordermayer, Othmar Plöckinger, and Roman Töppel (Berlin: Instituts für Zeitgeschichte München-Berlin, 2016).

Hobbes, Thomas. *Leviathan, sive de materia, forma, & potestate civitatis ecclesiasticæ et civilis* (London: John Tomson, 1676).

Hobbes, Thomas. *Leviathan*. Edited by Richard Tuck (Cambridge: Cambridge University Press, 1996).

Hobbes, Thomas, and Thomas Gaskin. *The Elements of Law, Natural and Politic*. Edited by J. C. A. Gaskin (Oxford: Oxford University Press, 2008).

Hobhouse, L. T. *The Elements of Social Justice* (London: Allen & Unwin, 1922).

Hobhouse, L. T. *Liberalism and Other Writings*. Edited by James Meadowcroft (Cambridge: Cambridge University Press, 1994).

Hobson, J. A. *Wealth and Life: A Study in Values* (London: Macmillan and Co., 1929).

Hollis, Christopher. *A Study of George Orwell* (London: Hollis & Carter, 1956).

Holtug, Nils, and Kasper Lippert-Rasmussen, eds. *Egalitarianism: New Essays on the Nature and Value of Equality* (Oxford: Clarendon Press, 2007).

Hont, István. 'The Early Enlightenment Debate on Commerce and Luxury'. In *The Cambridge History of Eighteenth-Century Political Thought*, edited by Mark Goldie and Robert Wolker (Cambridge: Cambridge University Press, 2006), 377–418.

Horkheimer, Max. *Dialectic of the Enlightenment*. Translated by John Cumming (London: Verso, 1997).

House of Lords. *Hansard: House of Lords Debates*. Westminster, London: United Kingdom Parliament, 1995. 23 June 1972 sess. Vol. 332. 534.

House of Lords. *Hansard: House of Lords Debates*. Westminster, London: United Kingdom Parliament, 1995. 24 March 1983 sess. Vol. 440. 1282.

House of Lords. *Hansard: House of Lords Debates*. Westminster, London: United Kingdom Parliament, 1995. 25 January 1984 sess. Vol. 52. 1000.

House of Lords. *Hansard: House of Lords Debates*. Westminster, London: United Kingdom Parliament, 1995. 3 December 1990 sess. Vol. 182. 109.

House of Lords. *Hansard: House of Lords Debates*. Westminster, London: United Kingdom Parliament, 1995. 30 October 2001 sess. Vol. 373. 834.

House of Lords. *Hansard: House of Lords Debates*. Westminster, London: United Kingdom Parliament, 1995. 29 January 2004 sess. Vol. 656. 407.

House of Lords. *Hansard: House of Lords Debates*. Westminster, London: United Kingdom Parliament, 1995. 26 November 2015 sess. Vol. 767. 853.

Hume, David. *An Enquiry Concerning the Principles of Morals*. Edited by Tom L. Beauchamp (Oxford: Clarendon Press, 1998).

Hume, David. *Treatise of Human Nature*. Edited by David Fate Norton and Mary J. Norton (Oxford: Oxford University Press, 2000).

Huxley, Aldous. *Ends and Means: An Enquiry into the Nature of Ideals and into the Methods Employed for Their Realization* (London: Chatto & Windus, 1937).

Huxley, Aldous. *Complete Works*. Edited by Robert S. Baker and James Sexton, 6 vols. (Chicago, IL: Ivan R. Dee, 2001).

Huxley, Aldous. *Brave New World*. Edited by David Bradshaw (London: Vintage, 2007).

Ingle, Stephen. *George Orwell: A Political Life*. (Manchester: Manchester University Press, 1993).

Ingle, Stephen. *The Social and Political Thought of George Orwell: A Reassessment* (London: Routledge, 2006).

Ingle, Stephen. 'Lies, Damned Lies and Literature: George Orwell and "The Truth"'. *The British Journal of Politics and International Relations*, 9.4 (2007): 730–46.

Irrera, E. 'Between Advantage and Virtue: Aristotle's Theory of Political Friendship'. *History of Political Thought*, 26.4 (Winter 2005): 565–85.

Jackson, Ben. 'The Uses of Utilitarianism: Social Justice, Welfare Economics and British Socialism, 1931–48'. *History of Political Thought*, 25.3 (2004): 508–35.

Jackson, Ben. *Equality and the British Left: A Study in Progressive Political Thought, 1900–64* (Manchester: Manchester University Press, 2007).

Jahanbegloo, Ramin, ed. *Conversations with Isaiah Berlin* (London: Peter Halban, 1992).

Johnson, Francis. *Keir Hardie's Socialism* (London: Independent Labour Party, 1922).

Jordison, Sam. 'Do You Really Know What "Orwellian" Means?' *The Guardian*, 11 November 2014.

Judt, Tony. *Postwar: A History of Europe since 1945* (London: Pimlico, 2007).

Kant, Immanuel. *The Critique of Practical Reason*. In *Practical Philosophy*, translated by Mary J. Gregor (Cambridge: Cambridge University Press, 1996), 133–272.

Kant, Immanuel. *Groundwork of the Metaphysics of Morals*. Edited by Mary J. Gregor (Cambridge: Cambridge University Press, 1997).

Kelvin, Norman, ed. *William Morris on Art and Socialism* (Mineola, NY: Dover Publications, Inc., 1999).

Kermode, Frank. 'The Essential Orwell'. *London Review of Books*, 3.1 (22 January 1981): 5–6.

Kerr, Douglas. 'Orwell's BBC Broadcasts: Colonial Discourse and the Rhetoric of Propaganda'. *Textual Practice*, 16.3 (2002): 473–90.

Kirschner, Paul. 'The Dual Purpose of *Animal Farm*'. *The Review of English Studies*, 55.222 (2004): 759–86.

Koestler, Arthur. *Darkness at Noon*. Translated by Daphne Hardy (London: Jonathan Cape, 1940).

Koestler, Arthur. 'A Rebel's Progress'. *The Observer* (London), 29 January 1950.

Kolakowski, Leszek. *Toward a Marxist Humanism: Essays on the Left Today*. Translated by Jane Zielonko Peel (New York: Grove Press, 1968).

Kropotkin, Peter. *The Conquest of Bread and Other Writings*. Edited by Marshall S. Shatz (Cambridge: Cambridge University Press, 1995).

Laski, Harold. *Authority in the Modern State* (New Haven, CT: Yale University Press, 1919).

Laski, Harold. *The Foundations of Sovereignty and Other Essays* (London: Allen & Unwin, 1921).

Laski, Harold. *A Grammar of Politics* (London:Yale University Press; Allen & Unwin, 1925).

Laski, Harold. *Socialism and Freedom*. Fabian Tract; 216 (London: Fabian Society, 1925).

Laski, Harold. *Communism* (London:Williams & Norgate, 1927).

Laski, Harold. *Liberty and the Modern State* (London: Faber, 1930).

Laski, Harold. 'A Plea for Equality'. In *The Dangers of Obedience and Other Essays* (NewYork and London: Harper & Bros., 1930), 207–37.

Laski, Harold. *Democracy in Crisis*.Weil Lectures on American Citizenship (London: George Allen & Unwin, 1933).

Laski, Harold.'The Road to Wigan Pier'. *The Left News*, 11 (1937): 275–6.

Laski, Harold. 'Democracy in War Time'. In *Victory or Vested Interest?*, edited by G. D. H. Cole (London: G. Routledge, 1942), 38–56.

Laski, Harold. *Reflections on the Revolution of Our Time* (London: Allen & Unwin, 1943).

Laski, Harold. *The Webbs and Soviet Communism* (London: Fabian Publications, 1943).

Laski, Harold. *Faith, Reason, and Civilisation:An Essay in Historical Analysis* (London: V. Gollancz, 1944).

Laski, Harold. *Will Planning Restrict Freedom?* (Cheam:The Architectural Press, 1944).

Laski, Harold. *Reflections on the Constitution:The House of Commons, the Cabinet, the Civil Service* (Manchester: Manchester University Press, 1951).

Leavis, F. R. 'Retrospect of a Decade'. *Scrutiny*, 9.1 (1940): 70–2.

Lenin,V. I. *Collected Works*, 45 vols. (Moscow: Progress Publishers, 1960–70).

Letemendia,V. C. 'Revolution on Animal Farm: Orwell's Neglected Commentary'. *Journal of Modern Literature*, 18.1 (1992): 127–37.

Leventhal, F. M. 'A Tonic to the Nation:The Festival of Britain, 1951'. *Albion*, 27.3 (1995): 445–53.

Lewis, C. Day. *A Time to Dance: And Other Poems* (London: Leonard and Virginia Woolf at the Hogarth Press, 1935).

Lewis, John. *Marxism and Modern Idealism* (New York: International Publishers, 1945).

Locke, John. *Two Treatises of Government*. Edited by Peter Laslett (Cambridge: Cambridge University Press, 1988).

Long, Robert T. 'Mill's Higher Pleasures and the Choice of Character'. *Utilitas*, 4.2 (1992): 279–97.

Lucas, Scott. *Orwell* (London: Haus, 2003).

Lukács, Georg. *History and Class Consciousness*. Translated by Rodney Livingstone (London: Merlin, 1971).

Lukács, György. *Lenin:A Study on the Unity of His Thought*. Translated by Nicholas Jacobs (London:Verso, 2009).

Lukes, Steven. *Marxism and Morality* (Oxford: Clarendon Press, 1985).

Luxemburg, Rosa. *The Russian Revolution*. Translated by Bertram D. Wolfe (New York:Workers Age Publishers, 1940).

Lyons, Eugene. *Assignment in Utopia* (New York: Harcourt, Brace, & Co., 1937).

McCrea, Barry. *In the Company of Strangers: Family and Narrative in Dickens, Conan Doyle, Joyce, and Proust* (New York: Columbia University Press, 2011).

Macdonald, Dwight. 'The British Genius'. *Partisan Review*, 9.2 (1942): 166–8.

McDowell, John. *Mind and World* (Cambridge, MA: Cambridge University Press, 1996).

MacFarlane, Robert. *The Wild Places* (London: Granta, 2007).

Machiavelli. *The Prince*. Edited by Quentin Skinner and Russell Price (Cambridge: Cambridge University Press, 1988).

McLellan, David. *Karl Marx: His Life and Thought* (London: Harper & Row, 1973).

Macmurray, John. *The Philosophy of Communism* (London: Faber & Faber, 1933).

MacNeice, Louis. 'Poetry To-day'. In *The Arts To-day*, edited by Geoffrey Grigson (London: John Lane, 1935), 25–67.

MacNeice, Louis. *The Strings are False: An Unfinished Autobiography* (London: Faber & Faber, 1965).

Mandeville, Bernard. *The Fable of the Bees: or, Private Vices Publick Benefits*. 6th ed., 2 vols. (London: J. Tonson, 1729).

Marcuse, Herbert. *Negations*. Translated by Jeremy J. Shapiro (London: Free Association Books, 1988).

Martin, Kingsley. *Father Figures: A First Volume of Autobiography, 1897–1931* (London: Hutchinson, 1966).

Marx, Karl, and Friedrich Engels. *Collected Works*, 50 Vols. (London: Lawrence and Wishart, 1975–2000).

Massingham, H. J., ed. *The Natural Order: Essays in the Return to Husbandry* (London: J. M. Dent, 1945).

Matthew. In *The King James Study Bible: King James Version* (Nashville, TN: Thomas Nelson Publishers, 2008).

Mayne, Richard. 'The Gentleman Beneath'. *Times Literary Supplement*, 26 November 1982, 1292.

Medvedev, Roy. *Let History Judge: The Origins and Consequences of Stalinism* (New York: Columbia University Press, 1989).

Meinecke, Friedrich. *Machiavellism: The Doctrine of Raison d'État and its Place in Modern History*. Translated by Douglas Scott (London: Transaction Publishers, 1988).

Meyers, Jeffrey. *Orwell: Life and Art* (Urbana, IL: University of Illinois, 2010).

Mill, J. S. *The Collected Works of John Stuart Mill*, edited by J. M. Robson, 33 vols. Vol. 10 (London and Toronto: University of Toronto Press, 1963–9).

Miller, William Ian. *The Anatomy of Disgust* (Cambridge, MA: Harvard University Press, 1997).

Milton, John. *Complete Poems and Major Prose*. Edited by Merritt Y. Hughes (Indianapolis, IN: Hackett, 1957).

Milton, John. *The Complete Works of John Milton*. Edited by Barbara Kiefer Lewalski and Estelle Haan. Vol. III: *The Shorter Poems* (Oxford: Oxford University Press, 2012).

Morgan, Kenneth O. *Keir Hardie: Radical and Socialist* (London: Weidenfeld and Nicolson, 1975).

Morgan, Kevin. *Harry Pollitt* (London: Lawrence and Wishart, 1985).

Morris, William. 'The Socialist Ideal'. In *The Collected Works of William Morris*, edited by May Morris. Vol. 23 (London: Longman's, 1915), 255–63.

Morris, William. 'The Society of the Future'. In *William Morris: Artist, Writer, Socialist*, edited by May Morris. Vol. 2 (Oxford: Blackwell, 1936), 443–68.

Morris, William. 'Art and Labour'. In *The Unpublished Lectures of William Morris*, edited by Eugene D. LeMire (Detroit, MI: Wayne State University, 1969), 94–118.

Morris, William. *The Unpublished Lectures of William Morris*. Edited by Eugene D. LeMire (Detroit, MI: Wayne State University Press, 1969).

Muggeridge, Malcolm. *The Thirties: 1930–1940 in Great Britain* (London: Hamish Hamilton, 1940).

Muggeridge, Malcolm. *Chronicles of Wasted Time*, 2 vols. (London: Collins, 1972–3).

Murray, Gilbert. 'A Plea for Reason'. In *The Rationalist Annual* (London: The Rationalist Press Association, 1932), 3–6.

Murry, John Middleton. *The Necessity of Communism* (London: J. Cape, 1932).

Murry, John Middleton. *Adam and Eve: An Essay Towards a New and Better Society* (London: Dakers, 1944).

Murry, John Middleton, John Macmurray, Neville Aldridge Holdaway, and G. D. H. Cole. *Marxism* (London: Chapman & Hall, 1935).

Nagel, Thomas. *Equality and Partiality* (Oxford: Oxford University Press, 1991).

Needham, John. 'Biology and Mr. Huxley'. *Scrutiny*, 1.18 (May 1932): 76–8.

Newsinger, John. 'The American Connection: George Orwell, Literary Trotskyism and the New York Intellectuals'. *Labour History Review*, 64.1 (1999): 23–43.

Newsinger, John. *Orwell's Politics* (London: Macmillan, 1999).

Nussbaum, Martha C. *Love's Knowledge: Essays on Philosophy and Literature* (Oxford: Oxford University Press, 1990).

Nussbaum, Martha C. 'Perception and Revolution: *The Princess Casamassima* and the Political Imagination'. In *Love's Knowledge: Essays on Philosophy and Literature* (Oxford: Oxford University Press, 1990), 195–219.

Nussbaum, Martha C. 'Compassion: The Basic Social Emotion'. *Social Philosophy and Policy*, 13 (1996): 27–58.

Nussbaum, Martha C. *Poetic Justice: The Literary Imagination and Public Life* (Boston, MA: Beacon Press, 1996).

Nussbaum, Martha C. *Political Emotions: Why Love Matters for Justice* (Cambridge, MA: The Belknap Press of Harvard University Press, 2013).

Oakeshott, Michael. 'The Claims of Politics'. *Scrutiny*, 8.2 (September 1939): 146–51.

Oakeshott, Michael. 'Review of *The State and the Citizen*, by J. D. Mabbott'. *Mind*, 58 (1949): 378–89.

Oakeshott, Michael. 'Rationalism'. In *Politics and Other Essays* (Indianapolis, IN: Liberty Fund, 1991).

O'Casey, Sean. 'Rebel Orwell'. In *Sunset and Evening Star* (London: Macmillan, 1954), 124–42.

Orr, Linda. 'French Romantic Histories of the Revolution: Michelet, Blanc, Tocqueville – A Narrative'. *The Eighteenth Century*, 30.2 (1989): 123–42.

Orwell, George. *The Complete Works of George Orwell.* Edited by Peter Davison (London: Secker & Warburg, 1998).

Overy, Richard J. *The Morbid Age: Britain and the Crisis of Civilization* (London: Allen Lane, 2009).

Ozouf, Monica. *Festivals and the French Revolution* (Cambridge, MA: Harvard University Press, 1988).

Ozouf, Monica. 'Fraternity'. In *A Critical Dictionary of the French Revolution*, edited by François Furet, translated by Arthur Goldhammer (Cambridge, MA: Harvard University Press, 1989), 697–703.

Paine, Thomas. 'Rights of Man'. In *Political Writings*, edited by Paul Kuklick (Cambridge: Cambridge University Press, 2000), 155–263.

Patai, Daphne. *The Orwell Mystique: A Study in Male Ideology* (Amherst, MA: University of Massachusetts Press, 1984).

Payne, Stanley G. *The Franco Regime, 1936–1975* (Madison, WI: University of Wisconsin Press, 1987).

Payne, Stanley G. *The Spanish Civil War, the Soviet Union, and Communism* (New Haven, CT; London: Yale University Press, 2004).

Peffer, Rodney G. *Marxism, Morality and Social Justice* (Princeton, NJ: Princeton University Press, 1990).

Plato. *Laws.* Translated and edited by Trevor J. Saunders (London: Penguin Books, 1970).

Plato. *Gorgias.* Translated by Robin Waterfield (Oxford: Oxford University Press, 1994).

Plato. *The Republic.* Edited by G. R. F. Ferrari, translated by Tom Griffith (Cambridge: Cambridge University Press, 2000).

Plato. *Gorgias.* Translated by Walter Hamilton, edited by Chris Emlyn-Jones (London: Penguin Books, 2004).

Plato. *The Laws.* Translated by Tom Griffith, edited by Malcolm Schofield (Cambridge: Cambridge University Press, 2016).

Plekhanov, G. V. *Fundamental Problems of Marxism.* Translated by Julius Katzer (Moscow: Progress Publishers, 1962).

Popper, Karl. *The Open Society and its Enemies*, 2 vols. (London and New York: Routledge, 2002).

Powell, Anthony. *To Keep the Ball Rolling: The Memoirs of Anthony Powell.* Volume 1: *Infants of the Spring* (London: Heinemann, 1976).

Preston, Paul. 'Lights and Shadows in George Orwell's *Homage to Catalonia*'. *Bulletin of Spanish Studies*, published online 23 October 2017.

Putnam, Hilary. 'Literature, Science and Reflection'. In *Meaning and the Moral Sciences* (London: Routledge, 1978), 83–94.

Rae, Douglas W. *Equalities* (Cambridge, MA: Harvard University Press, 1981).

Rae, Patricia. 'Mr. Charrington's Junk Shop: T. S. Eliot and Modernist Poetics in *Nineteen Eighty-Four*'. *Twentieth Century Literature*, 43.2 (Summer 1997): 196–220.

Rae, Patricia. 'There'll be No More Fishing this Side of the Grave: Radical Nostalgia in George Orwell's *Coming Up for Air*'. In *Modernism and Nostalgia: Bodies,*

Locations, Aesthetics, edited by Tammy Clewell (Houndmills, Basingstoke: Palgrave, 2013), 149–65.

Rai, Alok. *Orwell and the Politics of Despair: A Critical Study of the Writings of George Orwell* (Cambridge: Cambridge University Press, 1988).

Rauschning, Hermann. *Hitler Speaks: A Series of Political Conversations with Adolf Hitler on his Real Aims* (London: Thornton Butterworth, 1939).

Read, Herbert et al. 'Sixteen Comments on Auden'. *New Verse*, 26–7 (November 1937): 23–9, 28.

Reaves, R. B. 'Orwell's "Second Thoughts on James Burnham" and *1984*'. *College Literature*, 11.1 (1984): 13–21.

Rees, Richard. *Fugitive from the Camp of Victory* (London: Secker & Warburg, 1961).

Reichal, Peter. 'Festival and Cult: Masculine and Militaristic Mechanisms of National Socialism'. In *Shaping the Superman: Fascist Body as Political Icon*, edited by J. A. Mangan (London: Frank Cass, 1999), 153–68.

Riley, Jonathan. 'Interpreting Mill's Qualitative Hedonism'. *Philosophical Quarterly*, 53.212 (2003): 410–18.

Roazen, Paul. 'Orwell, Freud, and *1984*'. *Virginia Quarterly Review*, 54 (1978): 675–95.

Roazen, Paul. *Encountering Freud: The Politics and Histories of Psychoanalysis* (New York: Transaction Publishers, 1990).

Roberts, Michael. 'Preface'. In *New Signatures* (London: Hogarth, 1932): 7–20.

Robinson, Emma. 'George Orwell, Internment and the Illusion of Liberty'. *Literature and History* 23.2 (2014): 35–50.

Rodden, John. 'Orwell on Religion: The Catholic and Jewish Questions'. *College Literature*, 11 (1984): 44–58.

Rodden, John. 'George Orwell and British Catholicism'. *Renascence*, 41 (1989): 143–68.

Rodden, John. *Politics of Literary Reputation: The Making and Claiming of St. George Orwell* (New York: Oxford University Press, 1990).

Rodden, John. *George Orwell: The Politics of Literary Reputation* (New Brunswick, NJ: Transaction Publishers, 2002).

Rodden, John. 'Orwell, Marx, and the Marxists'. In *Scenes from an Afterlife: The Legacy of George Orwell* (Wilmington, DE: ISI Books, 2003), 177–94.

Rodden, John. 'On the Ethics of Admiration and Detraction'. *Midwest Quarterly*, 46.3 (2005): 284–98.

Rodden, John. *The Unexamined Orwell* (Austin, TX: University of Texas Press, 2011).

Rolf, Malte. *Soviet Mass Festivals, 1917–1991* (Pittsburgh, PA: University of Pittsburgh Press, 2013).

Rorty, Richard. 'The Last Intellectual in Europe: George Orwell'. In *Contingency, Irony, and Solidarity* (Cambridge: Cambridge University Press), 169–88.

Rousseau, Jean-Jacques. *Oeuvres Complètes De J. J. Rousseau*, 4 vols. (Paris: A. Houssiaux, 1852).

Rousseau, Jean-Jacques. *Politics and the Arts: Letter to M. D'Alembert*. Translated by Allan Bloom (Ithaca, NY: Cornell University Press, 1968).

Rousseau, Jean-Jacques. *Émile*. Translated by Allan Bloom (London: Penguin Books, 1991).

Rousseau, Jean-Jacques. *The Social Contract and Other Later Political Writings*. Edited and translated by Victor Gourevitch (Cambridge: Cambridge University Press, 1997).

Rousseau, Jean-Jacques. *Reveries of a Solitary Walker*. Translated by Russell Goulbourne (Oxford: Oxford University Press, 2011).

Runciman, David. *Political Hypocrisy: The Mask of Power, from Hobbes to Orwell and Beyond* (Oxford: Princeton University Press, 2008).

Ruskin, John. *The Stones of Venice*. Edited by William Morris (Hammersmith: Kelmscott Press, 1892).

Russell, Bertrand. *Roads to Freedom: Socialism, Anarchism and Syndicalism* (London: Allen & Unwin, 1918).

Russell, Bertrand. *The Practice and Theory of Bolshevism* (London: Allen & Unwin, 1920).

Russell, Bertrand. *In Praise of Idleness and Other Essays* (London: Allen & Unwin, 1935).

Russell, Bertrand. *Power: A New Social Analysis* (London: G. Allen & Unwin, 1938).

Russell, Bertrand. 'What is Democracy?' In *What is Democracy?* (London: National Peace Council, 1946), 14–16.

Russell, Bertrand. *Philosophy and Politics* (London: Cambridge University Press, 1947).

Russell, Bertrand. 'The Road to Happiness'. In *Portraits from Memory and Other Essays* (London: Allen & Unwin, 1956), 198–202.

Russell, Bertrand. 'Symptoms of Orwell's 1984'. In *Portraits from Memory* (London: Allen & Unwin, 1956), 203–10.

Russell, Bertrand. *Principles of Social Reconstruction*, 15th ed. (London: Unwin, 1971).

Russell, Bertrand. *Authority and the Individual* (London: Routledge, 2010).

Russell, Bertrand. *Autobiographies* (London: Routledge, 2010).

Russell, Bertrand. *The Conquest of Happiness* (London: Routledge, 2012).

Saunders, Frances Stonor. *The Cultural Cold War: The CIA and the World of Arts and Letters* (New York: The New Press, 1999).

Saunders, Loraine. *The Unsung Artistry of George Orwell: The Novels from Burmese Days to Nineteen Eighty-Four* (Aldershot: Ashgate, 2008).

Schmitt, Carl. *The Crisis of Parliamentary Democracy*. Translated by Ellen Kennedy (Cambridge, MA: MIT Press, 1988).

Schmitt, Carl. *The Concept of the Political*. Translated by George Schwab (Chicago, IL: University of Chicago Press, 1996).

Schmitt, Carl. *Political Theology: Four Chapters on the Concept of Sovereignty*. Translated by George Schwab (Chicago, IL; London: University of Chicago Press, 2005).

Schmitt, Carl. *The Leviathan in the State Theory of Thomas Hobbes*. Translated by George Schwab and Erna Hilfstein (Chicago, IL: University of Chicago Press, 2008).

Schumpeter, Joseph A. *Capitalism, Socialism, and Democracy* (London: Routledge, 1992).

Sedley, Stephen. 'An Immodest Proposal'. In *Inside the Myth. Orwell: Views from the Left*, edited by Christopher Norris (London: Lawrence & Wishart, 1984), 155–62.

Shaw, G. B. *The Intelligent Woman's Guide to Socialism and Capitalism* (London: Constable and Company, 1928).

Shaw, G. B. *Look, You Boob! What Bernard Shaw Told the Americans About Russia! His Famous Broadcast* (London: Friends of the Soviet Union, 1932).

Shaw, G. B. 'Preface' to *On the Rocks*. In *The Works of Bernard Shaw*. Vol. 31 (London: Constable, 1934), 145–91.

Shaw, G. B. *Collected Letters*. Edited by Dan H. Laurence. Vol. 1 (London: Max Reinhardt Ltd, 1965).

Shaw, G. B. *The Road to Equality: Ten Unpublished Lectures and Essays, 1884–1918*. Edited by Louis Crompton (Boston, MA: Beacon Press, 1971).

Shaw, G. B., H. G. Wells, J. M. Keynes, Ernst Toller, and others. *The Stalin-Wells Talk: The Verbatim Report and Discussion* (London: New Statesman and Nation, 1934).

Sherry, Vincent. 'George Orwell and T. S. Eliot: The Sense of the Past'. *College Literature*, 14.2 (1987): 85–100.

Shklar, Judith. *Ordinary Vices* (Cambridge, MA: The Belknap Press of Harvard University Press, 1984).

Shklar, Judith. '*Nineteen Eighty-Four*: Should Political Theory Care?'. *Political Theory*, 13.1 (1985): 5–18.

Sidgwick, Henry. *The Methods of Ethics*. Repr. 7th ed. (Indianapolis, IN: Hackett, 1981).

Silone, Ignazio. *The School for Dictators*. Translated by Gwenda David and Eric Mosbacher (London: Jonathan Cape, 1939).

Singer, Peter. 'All Animals are Equal'. *Philosophical Exchange*, 1.5 (1974): 243–57.

Skinner, Quentin. 'A Third Concept of Liberty.' *London Review of Books*, 24.7 (April 2002): 16–18.

Slaughter, Joseph R. *Human Rights, Inc.: The World Novel, Narrative Form, and International Law* (New York: Oxford University Press, 2007).

Smith, Adam. *An Inquiry into the Nature and Causes of the Wealth of Nations*. Edited by R. H. Campbell, A. S. Kinner, and W. B. Todd, 2 vols. (Oxford: Oxford University Press, 2002).

Smith, Adam. *The Theory of Moral Sentiments*. Edited by Knud Haakonssen (Cambridge: Cambridge University Press, 2002).

Smith, James. *British Writers and MI5 Surveillance 1930–1960* (Cambridge: Cambridge University Press, 2012).

Spears, Monroe K. *The Poetry of W. H. Auden* (New York: Oxford University Press, 1963).

Spender, Stephen. *Forward from Liberalism* (London: Victor Gollancz, 1937).

Spender, Stephen. 'A Look at the Worst'. *Horizon*, 2.9 (September 1940): 103–17.

Spender, Stephen. 'Preface'. In *The Temple* (London: Faber, 1988), ix–xiii.

Spiller, Leroy. 'George Orwell and British Catholicism'. *Logos*, 6 (2003): 150–63.

'Socialism and Ethics (III) – by a Marxist'. *The Left News*, 58 (April 1941): 1698.

Stalin, J. V. *The New Democracy: Stalin's Speech on the New Constitution* (London: Lawrence & Wishart, 1936).

Stalin, J. V. *Collected Works*, 13 vols. (Moscow: Foreign Languages Publishing House, 1952–5).

Stephens, James Fitzjames. *Liberty, Equality, Fraternity*, 2nd ed. (London: Smith, Elder & Co., 1874).

Stewart, Anthony. *Orwell, Doubleness and Decency* (London: Routledge, 2003).

Stjernø, Steinar. *Solidarity in Europe: The History of an Idea* (Cambridge: Cambridge University Press, 2004).

Stone, Dan. *Breeding Superman: Nietzsche, Race and Eugenics in Edwardian and Interwar Britain* (Liverpool: Liverpool University Press, 2002).

Stone, John. 'George Orwell on Politics and War'. *Review of International Studies*, 43.2 (2017): 221–39.

Strachey, John. *The Theory and Practice of Socialism* (London: Victor Gollancz, 1936).

Strachey, John. *A Faith to Fight For* (London: V. Gollancz, 1941).

Strachey, John. 'Totalitarianism'. *The Left News*, 55 (January 1941): 1603–8.

Strauss, Leo. *What is Political Philosophy?* (Chicago, IL: The University of Chicago Press, 1959).

Taunton, Matthew. '2 + 2 = 5: The Politics of Number in Writing about the Soviet Union'. *Textual Practice*, 29.5 (2015): 993–1016.

Tawney, R. H. *The Acquisitive Society* (London: G. Bell & Sons, 1921).

Tawney, R. H. *Equality* (London: Allen & Unwin, 1931).

Tawney, R. H. *The Attack and Other Papers* (London: Allen & Unwin, 1953).

Tawney, R. H. *R.H. Tawney's Commonplace Book*. Edited by J. M. Winter and D. M. Joslin (Cambridge: Cambridge University Press, 1972).

Taylor, Charles. 'What's Wrong with Negative Liberty'. In *The Idea of Freedom*, edited by A. Ryan (Oxford: Oxford University Press, 1979), 175–93.

Taylor, D. H. *Orwell: The Life* (London: Chatto & Windus, 2003).

The U.S. Congress. *A Declaration by the Representatives of the United States of America* (Boston, MA: John Gill, Powars, and Willis, 1776).

Thucydides. *The Peloponnesian War*. Translated by Martin Hammond (Oxford: Oxford University Press, 2009).

de Tocqueville, Alexis. *Democracy in America* (London: Everyman, 1994).

Toye, Richard. *The Labour Party and the Planned Economy, 1931–1951* (Woodbridge: Royal Historical Society/Boydell Press, 2003).

Trilling, Lionel. 'George Orwell and the Politics of Truth'. In *The Opposing Self: Nine Essays in Criticism* (London: Secker & Warburg, 1955), 151–72.

Trotsky, Leon. *The Defence of Terrorism: A Reply to Karl Kautsky* (London: Allen & Unwin, 1921).

Trotsky, Leon. *The History of the Russian Revolution*. Edited by Max Eastman (London: Victor Gollancz, 1936).

Trotsky, Leon. 'I Stake My Life!'. In *Dewey Reports on the Moscow Trials* (London: Workers International League, 1937).

Trotsky, Leon. *The Revolution Betrayed: What is the Soviet Union and Where is it Going?* Translated by Max Eastman (London: Faber & Faber, 1937).

Trotsky, Leon. *The Stalin School of Falsification*. Translated by Max Shachtman (New York: Pioneer Publishers, 1937).

Trotsky, Leon. 'Art and Politics'. *Partisan Review*, 5.3 (June 1938): 3–11.

Trotsky, Leon. 'The Priests of Half-Truth'. *Socialist Appeal*, 2.16 (16 April 1938): 1–4.

Trotsky, Leon. 'Their Morals and Ours'. *The New International*, 4.6 (1938): 163–73.

Turgenev, Ivan. 'Prayer'. In *Dream Tales and Prose Poems*. Translated by Constance Garnett (London: William Heinemann, 1897), 323–4.

Upward, Edward. 'A Marxist Interpretation of Literature'. In *The Mind in Chains*, edited by C. Day Lewis (London: Frederick Muller, 1937), 39–56.

Vaninskaya, Anna. 'The Orwell Century and After: Rethinking Reception and Reputation'. *Modern Intellectual History*, 5.03 (2008): 597–617.

Vaninskaya, Anna. *William Morris and the Idea of Community: Romance, History and Propaganda, 1880–1914* (Edinburgh: Edinburgh University Press, 2010).

Viroli, Maurizio. *For Love of Country: An Essay on Patriotism and Nationalism* (Oxford: Clarendon Press, 1995).

Voltaire. *Candide, or Optimism*. Translated by Theo Cuffe, edited by Michael Wood (London: Penguin Books, 2005).

Voorhees, Richard J. *The Paradox of George Orwell* (West Lafayette, IN: Purdue University Press, 1960).

Walker, Roy, ed. *The Wisdom of Gandhi in His Own Words* (London: A. Dakers, 1943).

Wallas, Graham. *The Great Society* (London: Macmillan, 1914).

Walzer, Michael. 'George Orwell's England'. In *The Company of Critics: Social Criticism and Political Commitment in the Twentieth Century* (New York: Basic Books, 1988), 117–35.

Warner, Rex. 'Dostoievsky and the Collapse of Liberalism'. In *The Cult of Power* (London: John Lane, 1946), 39–88.

Watson, George. 'Orwell's Nazi Renegade'. *The Sewanee Review*, 94.3 (1986): 486–95.

Webb, Sidney. *Socialism in England* (London: Swan Sonnenschein, 1890).

Webb, Sidney, and Beatrice Webb. *The Decay of Capitalist Civilisation*, 3rd ed. (London: Allen & Unwin, 1923).

Webb, Sidney, and Beatrice Webb. *Soviet Communism: A New Civilisation?*, 2 vols. (London: Longman, 1935).

Weber, Max. 'Science as a Vocation'. In *From Max Weber: Essays in Sociology*, edited and translated by H. H. Gerth (London: Routledge, 1991), 129–56.

Weber, Max. *The Protestant Ethic and the 'Spirit' of Capitalism and Other Writings*. Edited by Peter R. Baehr and Gordon C. Wells (New York: Penguin Books, 2002).

Wells, H. G. *Anticipations of the Reaction of Mechanical and Scientific Progress upon Human Life and Thought*, 2nd ed. (London: Chapman, 1902).

Wells, H. G. *The Open Conspiracy and Other Writings* (London: Waterlow and Sons, 1933).

Wells, H. G. *A Modern Utopia*. Edited by Gregory Claeys (London: Penguin, 2005).

Wells, H. G. *The Time Machine*. Edited by Patrick Parrinder (London: Penguin Books, 2005).

West, Alick. *Crisis and Criticism* (London: Lawrence & Wishart, 1937).

Westen, Peter. *Speaking of Equality: An Analysis of the Rhetorical Force of 'Equality' in Moral and Legal Discourse* (Princeton, NJ: Princeton University Press, 1990).

'W. H. Auden on George Orwell'. *The Spectator*, 7438 (16 January 1971): 18–19.

White, Stewart. *Equality* (Oxford: Blackwell, 2006).

Wilde, Oscar. 'The Soul of Man under Socialism'. In *The Complete Works of Oscar Wilde* (Glasgow: HarperCollins, 1999), 1174–97.

Williams, Bernard. 'The Idea of Equality'. In *Problems of the Self* (Cambridge: Cambridge University Press, 1973), 230–49.

Williams, Bernard. *Truth and Truthfulness: An Essay in Genealogy* (Princeton, NJ: Princeton University Press, 2002).

Williams, Raymond. *Orwell* (London: Fontana, 1971).

Wittgenstein, Ludwig. *Tractatus Logico-Philosophicus* (London and New York: Routledge, 2001).

Wittgenstein, Ludwig. *Philosophical Investigations: The German Text with a Revised English Translation*. Translated by G. E. M. Anscombe (Oxford: Blackwell, 2002).

Woloch, Alex. *Or Orwell: Writing and Democratic Socialism* (Cambridge, MA: Harvard University Press, 2016).

Wood, Alan. 'Marx and Equality'. In *Analytical Marxism*, edited by John E. Roemer (Cambridge: Cambridge University Press, 1986).

Wood, Allen. W. *Karl Marx* (London: Routledge, 1981).

Wood, Allen. W. *Kant's Ethical Thought* (Cambridge: Cambridge University Press, 1999).

Wood, Charles. *Successful Living in this Machine Age* (London: J. Cape, 1932).

Woolf, Leonard. *The Modern State* (London: George Allen, 1933).

Woolf, Leonard. *Barbarians at the Gate*. Left Book Club (London: Victor Gollancz, 1939).

Woolf, Leonard. *An Autobiography of the Years 1919–39* (London: Hogarth Press, 1968).

Woolf, Virginia. *The Years* (Oxford: Oxford University Press, 2009).

Yack, Bernard. 'Community and Conflict in Aristotle's Political Philosophy'. *The Review of Politics*, 47.1 (1985): 92–112.

Yack, Bernard. 'The Myth of the Civic Nation'. In *Theorizing Nationalism*, edited by Ronald Beiner (Albany, NY: SUNY Press, 1999), 103–18.

Zamyatin, Yevgeny. *We*. Translated by Clarence Brown (London: Penguin Books, 1993).

Zwerdling, Alex. *Orwell and the Left* (New Haven, CT: Yale University Press, 1974).

Index